Renewal Journals
Volume 1 (1-5)

Revival
Church Growth
Community
Healing
Signs & Wonders

Geoff Waugh (Editor)

Renewal Journals

ISBN-13: 978-1466326996
ISBN-10: 1466326999

Printed by CreateSpace, Charleston, SC, USA, 2011

Renewal Journal Publications
www.renewaljournal.com
Citipointe Ministry College
School of Ministries
Christian Heritage College
PO Box 2111, Mansfield, Brisbane, Qld, 4122
Australia

 Renewal Journal

Contents

5 *Signs and Wonders*   417

Cover Photo

On the last and greatest day of the festival, Jesus stood and said in a loud voice, "Let anyone who is thirsty come to me and drink. Whoever believes in me, as Scripture has said, rivers of living water will flow from within them (John 7:37-38).

Renewal Journal Logo

Ancient lamp and parchment scroll; also basin and towel – anointed ministry, in the context of the cross and the Light of the World.

Renewal Journal
1 Revival

Geoff Waugh (Editor)

Renewal Journal
1 Revival

Contents

Renewal Journal 1: Revival

Cover photo: 1 Revival
Jerusalem – Temple Mount with Calvary beyond to the
west.

Editorial

Revive us again
Psalm 85:6

Welcome to the first issue of the Renewal Journal. It is a resource in renewal ministries for the whole church, the body of Christ.

This issue describes a little of the amazing move of God's Spirit in the world today. Future issues will give more details, especially on how renewal and revival affect us. We can be involved. We need to be. We can pray for revival and believe God's promises. We can humble ourselves, pray, seek God, and repent (2 Chronicles 7:14). We need to repent of our disobedience, for we have not loved God wholeheartedly and we have not always loved one another.

Thousands of praying groups now meet in unity across the land like showers of glowing sparks blown by God's wind. Prayer cells, home groups, church prayer meetings, vocational groups, student groups and informal clusters of friends gather regularly in ever increasing numbers. Your praying groups are part of that vast movement raised up by God.

We are learning to pray and minister as Jesus did, as he taught his disciples to do, and as he told them to teach others to do (Matthew 28:18-20). It's a massive revolution in prayer and ministry in homes, farms, schools, colleges, universities, and work places, as well as in many churches.

This journal encourages you to pray in faith for renewal and revival. You can make a difference - a big difference. Pray in unity with others. It only takes two or three, as Jesus told us (Matthew 18:20).

The articles in this issue by Stuart Robinson and Edwin Orr show the vital link between earnest prayer and revival. Djiniyini Gondarra describes recent touches of God's Spirit which have affected Aboriginal communities. John Greenfield's writings recall the impact of the Moravian revival, and I give an overview of revival movements including some current examples.

Pray without ceasing

All across the land thousands of small groups are praying. Many are spontaneous, brought together by God. Some congregations have dozens or scores of praying groups now. Every revival began this way. Your part in this is vital.

We urge you to pray on Saturday nights and Sunday mornings for your leaders as they prepare, pray and preach. We also urge you to join with us and others praying on Mondays every week (in groups or alone) for renewal and revival, for God's glory. Be encouraged as you join with thousands of others in earnest prayer for revival in the land.

If you have 31 people willing to set aside one day a month to fast and pray for revival and for your ministry, you would have someone in your church or fellowship doing so every day of the year. That is now happening in some churches.

If you have 168 people willing to set aside one hour a week to pray for revival and for your ministry, you could have continuous prayer around the clock, in hourly shifts, day and night all year long. The Moravians did that for 100 years. We can now, in this day of God's power.

It is well said that revival is just the church returning to New Testament Christianity and impacting the community as it did then.

May revival fire burn brightly within us all so that thousands believe, the church comes alive, and communities are radically transformed by God.

To God be the glory.

1 Praying the Price

Stuart Robinson

Rev Dr Stuart Robinson is the Senior Pastor at the Blackburn Baptist Church, Victoria, Australia.

Luke 11:1 - 'Lord teach us to pray.'

Introduction

In 1952 Albert Einstein was asked by a Princeton doctoral student what was left in the world for original dissertation research? Einstein replied, 'Find out about prayer'.

English preacher Sidlow Baxter, when he was eighty-five years of age, said, 'I have pastored only three churches in my more than sixty years of ministry. We had revival in every one. And not one of them came as a result of my preaching. They came as a result of the membership entering into a covenant to pray until revival came. And it did come, every time' (Willhite 1988:111).

Chaplain of the United States Senate, Richard Halverson, advised that we really don't have any alternatives to prayer. He says, 'You can organise until you are exhausted. You can plan, program and subsidise all your plans. But if you fail to pray, it is a waste of time. Prayer is not optional. It is mandatory. Not to pray is to disobey God' (Bryant 1984:39).

Roy Pointer, after extensive research in Baptist churches in the United Kingdom, arrived at the conclusion that wherever there was positive growth, there was one recurring factor: they were all praying churches.

In the United States of America, at Larry Lea's Church on the Rock in Rockwall, Texas, numerical growth was from 13 people in 1980 to 11,000 people by 1988. When he was asked about such amazing growth, he said 'I didn't start a church - I started a prayer meeting'. When David Shibley, the minister responsible for prayer in that church was asked the secret of the church, he said, 'The evangelistic program of our church is the daily prayer meeting. Every morning, Monday through Friday, we meet at 5.00 a.m. to pray. If we see the harvest of conversions fall off for more than a week, we see that as a spiritual red alert and seek the Lord' (Shibley 1985:7).

In Korea, where the church has grown from almost zero to a projected 50% of the entire population in this century alone, Pastor Paul Yonggi Cho attributes his church's conversion rate of 12,000 people per month as primarily due to ceaseless prayer.

In Korea it is normal for church members to go to bed early so they can arise at 4.00 a.m. to participate in united prayer. It is normal for them to pray all through Friday nights. It is normal to go out to prayer retreats.

Cho says that any church might see this sort of phenomenal growth if they are prepared to 'pray the price,' to 'pray and obey.'

Cho was once asked by a local pastor why was it that Cho's church membership was 750,000 and his was only 3,000 when he was better educated, preached better sermons and even had a foreign wife? Cho enquired, 'How much do you pray?' The pastor said, 'Thirty minutes a day.' To which Cho replied, 'There is your answer. I pray from three to five hours per day.'

In America one survey has shown that pastors on average pray 22

Stuart Robinson

minutes per day. In mainline churches, it is less than that. In Japan they pray 44 minutes a day, Korea 90 minutes a day, and China 120 minutes a day. It's not surprising that the growth rate of churches in those countries is directly proportional to the amount of time pastors are spending in prayer.

Growth - a Supernatural Process

The church is a living organism. It is God's creation with Jesus Christ as its head (Colossians 1:18). From Him life flows (John 14:6). We have a responsibility to cooperate with God (1 Corinthians 3:6). We know that unless the Lord builds the house we labour in vain (Psalm 127:1).

The transfer of a soul from the kingdom of darkness to that of light is a spiritual, supernatural process (Colossians 1:14). It is the Father who draws (John 6:44).

It is the Holy Spirit who convicts (John 16:8-11). He causes confession to be made (1 Corinthians 12:3). He completes conversion (Titus 3:5). It is the Holy Spirit who also strengthens and empowers (Ephesians 3:16). He guides into truth (John 16:16). He gives spiritual gifts which promote unity (1 Corinthians 12:25), building up the church (1 Corinthians 14:12), thus avoiding disunity and strife which stunt growth.

This is fundamental spiritual truth accepted and believed by all Christians. However, the degree to which we are convinced that all real growth is ultimately a supernatural process and are prepared to act upon that belief, will be directly reflected in the priority that we give to corporate and personal prayer in the life of the church.

It is only when we begin to see that nothing that matters will occur except in answer to prayer that prayer will become more than an optional program for the faithful few, and instead it will become the driving force of our churches.

Obviously God wants our pastors, other leaders and His people to recognise that only He can do extra-ordinary things. When we accept that simple premise, we may begin to pray.

13

In the Bible

The battle which Joshua won, as recorded in Exodus 17:8-13, was not so dependent upon what he and his troops were doing down on the plain. It was directly dependent upon Moses' prayerful intercession from on top of a nearby hill, with the support of Aaron and Hur.

In the Old Testament, not counting the Psalms, there are 77 explicit references to prayer.

The pace quickens in the New Testament. There are 94 references alone which relate directly to Jesus and prayer. The apostles picked up this theme and practice.

So Paul says, 'Pray continually, for this is God's will for you' (1 Thessalonians 5:16).

Peter urges believers to be 'clear minded and self controlled' so that they can pray (1 Peter 4:7).

James declares that prayer is 'powerful and effective' (James 5:16).

John assures us that 'God hears and answers' (1 John 5:15).

In the book of Acts there are 36 references to the church growing. Fifty-eight percent (i.e. 21 of those instances) are within the context of prayer.

We would all love to see growth in every church in the world like it was at Pentecost and immediately thereafter. The key to what happened there is found in Acts 1:14 when it says: 'They were all joined together constantly in prayer.'

They were all joined together - one mind, one purpose, one accord. That is the prerequisite for effectiveness. Then, they were all joined together constantly in prayer. The word used there means to be 'busily engaged in, to be devoted to, to persist in adhering to a thing, to intently attend to it.' And it is in the form of a present participle. It means that the practice was continued ceaselessly. The same word and part of speech is used in Acts 2:42: 'They devoted themselves... to prayer.' Over in Colossians 4:2, Paul uses the same word again in the imperative form: 'Devote yourselves to prayer.'

Most significant expansion movements of the church through its history took up that imperative.

In history

When we read the biographies of William Carey, Adoniram Judson, David Livingstone, Hudson Taylor, or whomever, the initiating thrust of the work of their lives began in prayer encounters.

About a century ago, John R. Mott led an extraordinary movement which became known as the Student Christian Movement. It was based amongst college and university students. It supplied 20,000 career missionaries in the space of thirty years. John Mott said that the source of this amazing awakening lay in united intercessory prayer. It wasn't just that these missionaries were recruited and sent out in prayer; their work was also sustained through prayer.

Hudson Taylor told a story of a missionary couple who were in charge of ten stations. They wrote to their home secretary confessing their absolute lack of progress, and they urged the secretary to find intercessors for each station. After a while, in seven of those stations, opposition melted, spiritual revival broke out and the churches grew strongly. But in three there was no change. When they returned home on their next furlough, the secretary cleared up the mystery. He had succeeded in getting intercessors for only seven of the ten stations. S. D. Gordon (1983:40) concludes, 'The greatest thing anyone can do for God and man is to pray.'

Luther, Calvin, Knox, Latimer, Finney, Moody, all the 'greats of God' practised prayer and fasting to enhance ministry effectiveness.

John Wesley was so impressed by such precedents that he would not even ordain a person to ministry unless he agreed to fast at least until 4.00 p.m. each Wednesday and Friday.

Yonggi Cho (1984:103) says, 'Normally I teach new believers to fast for three days. Once they have become accustomed to three-day fasts, they will be able to fast for a period of seven days. Then they will move to ten-day fasts. Some have even gone for forty days.'

These people seem to have latched onto something which we here in Australia hardly know anything about. We are so busy, so active. We try so hard to get something good up and running. But it doesn't seem to grow much, or permanently change many lives. Why? Is it that the ground in Australia is too hard? Compared with other times and places, this could hardly be so. For example, back in the 18th century things didn't look good.

Eighteenth century

France was working through its bloody revolution, as terroristic as any of our modern era. America had declared its Rights of Man in 1776. Voltaire was preaching that the church was only a system of oppression for the human spirit. Karl Marx would later agree. A new morality had arisen. Amongst both sexes in all ranks of society, Christianity was held in almost universal contempt. Demonic forces seemed to have been unleashed to drive the church out of existence. In many places it was almost down and out. Preachers and people would be pelted with stones and coal in places in England if they dared to testify to Jesus Christ in public.

But even before those satanic forces collaborated to confound and confuse, it appears that the Holy Spirit had prepared His defence, like a plot out of some Peretti novel.

In the 1740s, John Erskine of Edinburgh published a pamphlet encouraging people to pray for Scotland and elsewhere. Over in America, the challenge was picked up by Jonathan Edwards, who wrote a treatise called, 'A Humble Attempt to Promote Explicit Agreement and Visible Union of God's People in Extra-ordinary Prayer for the Revival of Religion and the Advancement of Christ's Kingdom.'

For forty years, John Erskine orchestrated what became a Concert of Prayer through voluminous correspondence around the world. In the face of apparent social, political and moral deterioration, he persisted.

And then the Lord of the universe stepped in and took over. On Christmas day 1781, at St. Just Church in Cornwall, at 3.00 a.m., intercessors met to sing and pray. The heavens opened at last and they knew it. They prayed through until 9.00 a.m. and regathered on Christmas evening. Throughout January and February, the movement continued. By March 1782 they were praying until midnight. No significant preachers were involved - just people praying and the Holy Spirit responding.

Two years later in 1784, when 83-year old John Wesley visited that area, he wrote, 'This country is all on fire and the flame is spreading from village to village.'

And spread it did. The chapel which George Whitefield had built decades previously in Tottenham Court Road had to be enlarged to seat 5,000 people - the largest in the world at that time. Baptist churches in North Hampton, Leicester, and the Midlands, set aside regular nights devoted to the drumbeat of prayer for revival. Methodists and Anglicans joined in.

Matthew Henry wrote, 'When God intends great mercy for His people, He first sets them praying.'

Across the country prayer meetings were networking for revival. A passion for evangelism arose. Converts were being won - not through the regular services of the churches, but at the prayer meetings! Some were held at 5.00 a.m., some at midnight. Some pre-Christians were drawn by dreams and visions. Some came to scoff but were thrown to the ground under the power of the Holy Spirit. Sometimes there was noise and confusion; sometimes stillness and solemnity. But always there was that ceaseless outpouring of the Holy Spirit. Whole denominations doubled, tripled and quadrupled in the next few years. It swept out from England to Wales, Scotland, United States, Canada and to some Third World countries.

Social Impact

The social impact of reformed lives was incredible. William Wilberforce, William Pitt, Edmund Bourke, and Charles Fox, all touched by this movement, worked ceaselessly for the abolition of the slave trade in 1807.

William Buxton worked on for the emancipation of all slaves in the British Empire and saw it happen in 1834.

John Howard and Elizabeth Fry gave their lives to radically reform the prison system.

Florence Nightingale founded modern nursing.

Ashley Cooper, the seventh Earl of Shaftesbury, came to the rescue of the working poor to end their sixteen-hour, seven-day-a-week work grind. He worked to stop exploitation of women and children in coal mines, the suffocation of boys as sweeps in chimneys. He established public parks and gymnasia, gardens, public libraries, night schools and choral societies.

The Christian Socialist Movement, which became the British Trade Union movement, was birthed.

The Royal Society for the Prevention of Cruelty to Animals was formed to protect animals.

There was amazing growth in churches, and an astounding change in society came about because for forty years a man prayed and worked, seeing the establishment of thousands of similar prayer meetings, all united in calling on God for revival.

Missionary societies were established. William Carey was one who got swept up in that movement. We speak of him as the 'father of modern missions'. The environment of his situation was that he was a member of a ministers' revival prayer group which had been meeting for two years in Northampton in 1784-86. It was in 1786 he shared his vision of God's desire to see the heathen won for the Lord.

He went on to establish what later became known as the Baptist Missionary Society. In 1795 the London Missionary Society was formed. In 1796 the Scottish Missionary Society was established, and later still the Church Missionary Society of the Anglicans was commenced.

Nineteenth Century

The prayer movement had a tremendous impact, but waned until the middle of the 19th century. Then God started something up in Canada, and the necessity to pray was picked up in New York.

A quiet man called Jeremiah Lanphier had been appointed by the Dutch Reformed Church as a missionary to the central business district. Because the church was in decline and the life of the city was somewhat similar, he didn't know what to do. He was a layman. He called a prayer meeting in the city to be held at noon each Wednesday. Its first meeting was on the 23rd September 1857. Eventually, five other men turned up. Two weeks later, they decided to move to a daily schedule of prayer. Within six months, 10,000 men were gathering to pray and that movement spread across America.

Surprise, surprise! Within two years there were one million new believers added to the church. The movement swept out to touch England, Scotland, Wales and Ulster.

Ireland was as tough a nut to crack as any. But when news reached Ireland of what was happening in America, James McQuilkan gathered three young men to meet for prayer in the Kells schoolhouse on March 14, 1859. They prayed and prayed for revival. Within a couple of months a similar prayer meeting was launched in Belfast. By September 21, 20,000 people assembled to pray for the whole of Ireland.

It was later estimated that 100,000 converts resulted directly from these prayer movements in Ireland. It has also been estimated that in the years 1859-60, some 1,150,000 people were added to the church, wherever concerts of prayer were in operation.

Twentieth century

Many would be aware of the Welsh Revival this century. It commenced in October 1904. It was spontaneous and was characterised by simultaneous, lengthy prayer meetings. In the first two months, 70,000 people came to the Lord. In 1905 in London alone, the Wesleyan Methodists increased from their base membership of 54,785 by an additional 50,021 people.

Coming closer in time and nearer to Australia, in the Enga churches in Papua New Guinea there was a desperate spiritual state 20 years ago. To redress the situation, people there committed themselves to pray.

Prayer meetings began amongst pastors, missionaries and Bible College students. It spread out to the villages. In some villages, groups of people agreed to pray together every day until God sent new life to the church.

On 15 September 1973, without any prior indication, simultaneously, spontaneously, in village after village as pastors stood to deliver their normal Sunday morning messages, the Holy Spirit descended bringing conviction, confession, repentance and revival.

Normal work stopped as people in their thousands hurried to special meetings. Prayer groups met daily, morning and evening. Thousands of Christians were restored and thousands of pagans were converted. Whole villages became Christian, and the church grew not only in size but in maturity.

In the Philippines in the 1980s, as a result of some people attending an international prayer conference in Korea, 200 missionaries of the Philippine Missionary Fellowship each organised prayer group meetings daily at 7.00 p.m. to pray for the growth of the church. They report that within a couple of years this directly resulted in the formation of 310 new churches.

Spectacular growth is occurring in Argentina. Jose Luis Vasquez saw his church explode from 600 to 4,500 with a constituency of 10,000 members in five years following a visit from Carlos Annacondia. Hector Gimenez started his church from zero in 1983. His congregation now numbers 70,000. Omar Cabrera started his church in 1972 with 15 members. There is now a combined membership of 90,000 members.

Peter Wagner, who is intensely investigating what lies behind such effective ministry, has arrived at the conclusion that powerful intercessory prayer is the chief weapon. Much of it is happening in a Pentecostal, charismatic environment. But the structure or doctrine is not the essential thing.

Walter Hollenweger, a prolific researcher into Pentecostalism said that for them, from the earliest Pentecostals onwards, it was more important to pray than to organise (1972:29).

Wherever that principle is invoked, amazing things happen. In 1982 Christians in East Germany started to form small groups of ten to twelve persons, committed to meet to pray for peace. By October 1989, 50,000 people were involved in Monday night prayer meetings. In 1990, when those praying people moved quietly into the streets, their numbers quickly swelled to 300,000 and 'the wall came tumbling down.'

In Cuba in 1990, an Assemblies of God pastor whose congregation never exceeded 100 people meeting once a week suddenly found himself conducting 12 services per day for 7,000 people. They started queuing at 2.00 a.m. and even broke down the doors just to get into the prayer meetings.

Asked to explain these phenomena, Cuban Christians say 'it has come because we have paid the price. We have suffered for the Gospel and we have prayed for many, many years' (O'Connor 1990:7-9).

When a group known as the Overseas Missionary Society saw that after 25 years of work in India all they could report was 2,000 believers in 25 churches, they adopted a new strategy. In their homelands they recruited 1,000 people committed to pray for the work in India for just 15 minutes per day. Within a few years the church exploded
to 73,000 members in 550 churches.

Will we 'pray the price'?

Today there is great pressure from many directions in our society to work harder, to become smarter, to produce results, or to be moved aside. The church in many western countries is in danger of absorbing this mentality into its own attitudes and practices, forgetting that in the divine-human endeavour, success comes not by might nor by power but by a gracious release of God's Holy Spirit (Zechariah 4:6).

Years ago, R. A. Torrey (1974:190) said, 'We live in a day characterised by the multiplication of man's machinery and the diminution of God's power. The great cry of our day is work, work, work! Organise,

organise, organise! Give us some new society! Tell us some new methods! Devise some new machinery! But the great need of our day is prayer, more prayer and better prayer.'

Friends, in the church in the west we now have the most up to date, state of the art technology available to communicate the Gospel. Yet comparatively little seems to be happening in so many countries.

In terms of the growth and mission of our churches, could it be that whilst the world has learned to communicate with robots on Mars, in sections of the church we have forgotten to communicate with the Lord of the earth?

If that is so, then our best course of action is to stand again with the company of the first disciples and, like them, return to the Head of the church - Jesus Christ - and say 'Lord, teach us to pray' (Luke 11:1).

References

David Bryant (1984) *Concerts of Prayer*. Ventura, California: Ventura.
Paul Y Cho (1984) *Prayer: Key to Revival.* Waco, Texas: Word.
S D Gordon (1983) 'Prayer, the greatest thing,' *Australia's New Day*, April, 40.
Walter J Hollenwager (1972) *The Pentecostals.* Minneapolis, Minnesota: Augsburg.
Greg O'Connor (1990) 'Miracles in Cuba,' *New Day*, May.
David Shibley (1985) *Let's Pray in the Harvest.* Rockwall, Texas: Church on the Rock.
R A Torrey (1974) *The Power of Prayer.* Grand Rapids, Michigan: Zondervan.
Bob J Whillhite (1988) *Why Pray?* Altamonte Springs, Florida: Creation House.

2 Prayer and Revival

J Edwin Orr

Dr J. Edwin Orr was a leading scholar of revivals who published detailed books about evangelical awakenings. His research discovered major spiritual awakenings about every fifty years following the great awakening from the mid-eighteenth century in which John and Charles Wesley, George Whitefield and Jonathan Edwards featured prominently. This article, based on one of Edwin Orr's messages, is adapted from articles reproduced in the National Fellowship for Revival newsletters in New Zealand and Australia.

Dr A. T. Pierson once said, 'There has never been a spiritual awakening in any country or locality that did not begin in united prayer.' Let me recount what God has done through concerted, united, sustained prayer.

Not many people realize that in the wake of the American Revolution (following 1776-1781) there was a moral slump. Drunkenness became epidemic. Out of a population of five million, 300,000 were confirmed drunkards; they were burying fifteen thousand of them each year. Profanity was of the most shocking kind. For the first time in the history of the American settlement, women were afraid to go out at night for fear of assault. Bank robberies were a daily occurrence.

What about the churches? The Methodists were losing more members than they were gaining. The Baptists said that they had their most wintery season. The Presbyterians in general assembly deplored the nation's ungodliness. In a typical Congregational church, the Rev. Samuel Shepherd of Lennos, Massachusetts, in sixteen years had not taken one young person into fellowship. The Lutherans were so languishing that they discussed uniting with Episcopalians who were even worse off. The Protestant Episcopal Bishop of New York, Bishop Samuel Provost, quit functioning; he had confirmed no one for so long that he decided he was out of work, so he took up other employment.

The Chief Justice of the United States, John Marshall, wrote to the Bishop of Virginia, James Madison, that the Church 'was too far gone ever to be redeemed.' Voltaire averred and Tom Paine echoed, 'Christianity will be forgotten in thirty years.

Take the liberal arts colleges at that time. A poll taken at Harvard had discovered not one believer in the whole student body. They took a poll at Princeton, a much more evangelical place, where they discovered only two believers in the student body, and only five that did not belong to the filthy speech movement of that day. Sudents rioted. They held a mock communion at Williams College, and they put on anti-Christian plays at Dartmouth. They burned down the Nassau Hall at Princeton. They forced the resignation of the president of Harvard. They took a Bible out of a local Presbyterian church in New Jersey, and they burnt it in a public bonfire. Christians were so few on campus in the 1790's that they met in secret, like a communist cell, and kept their minutes in code so that no one would know.

How did the situation change? It came through a concert of prayer.

There was a Scottish Presbyterian minister in Edinburgh named John Erskine, who published a Memorial (as he called it) pleading with the people of Scotland and elsewhere to unite in prayer for the revival of religion. He sent one copy of this little book to Jonathan Edwards in New England. The great theologian was so moved he wrote a response which grew longer than a letter, so that finally he published it is a book entitled 'A Humble Attempt to Promote Explicit Agreement and Visible Union of all God's People in Extraordinary Prayer for the Revival of Religion and the Advancement of Christ's Kingdom on Earth, pursuant to Scripture

Promises and Prophecies...'

Is not this what is missing so much from all our evangelistic efforts: explicit agreement, visible unity, unusual prayer?

1792-1800

This movement had started in Britain through William Carey, Andrew Fuller and John Sutcliffe and other leaders who began what the British called the Union of Prayer. Hence, the year after John Wesley died (he died in 1791), the second great awakening began and swept Great Britain.

In New England, there was a man of prayer named Isaac Backus, a Baptist pastor, who in 1794, when conditions were at their worst, addressed an urgent plea for prayer for revival to pastors of every Christian denomination in the United States.

Churches knew that their backs were to the wall. All the churches adopted the plan until America, like Britain was interlaced with a network of prayer meetings, which set aside the first Monday of each month to pray. It was not long before revival came.

When the revival reached the frontier in Kentucky, it encountered a people really wild and irreligious. Congress had discovered that in Kentucky there had not been more than one court of justice held in five years. Peter Cartwright, Methodist evangelist, wrote that when his father had settled in Logan County, it was known as Rogue's Harbour. The decent people in Kentucky formed regiments of vigilantes to fight for law and order, then fought a pitched battle with outlaws and lost.

There was a Scotch-Irish Presbyterian minister named James McGready whose chief claim to fame was that he was so ugly that he attracted attention. McGready settled in Logan County, pastor of three little churches. He wrote in his diary that the winter of 1799 for the most part was 'weeping and mourning with the people of God.' Lawlessness prevailed everywhere.

McGready was such a man of prayer that not only did he promote the concert of prayer every first Monday of the month, but he got his people to pray for him at sunset on Saturday evening and sunrise Sunday morning.

Then in the summer of 1800 come the great Kentucky revival. Eleven thousand people came to a communion service. McGready hollered for help, regardless of denomination.

Out of that second great awakening, came the whole modern missionary movement and it's societies. Out of it came the abolition of slavery, popular education, Bible Societies, Sunday Schools, and many social benefits accompanying the evangelistic drive.

1858-1860

Following the second great awakening, which began in 1792 just after the death of John Wesley and continued into the turn of the century, conditions again deteriorated. This is illustrated from the United States.

The country was seriously divided over the issue of slavery, and second, people were making money lavishly.

In September 1857, a man of prayer, Jeremiah Lanphier, started a businessmen's prayer meeting in the upper room of the Dutch Reformed Church Consistory Building in Manhattan. In response to his advertisement, only six people out of a population of a million showed up. But the following week there were fourteen, and then twenty-three when it was decided to meet everyday for prayer. By late winter they were filling the Dutch Reformed Church, then the Methodist Church on John Street, then Trinity Episcopal Church on Broadway at Wall Street. In February and March of 1858, every church and public hall in down town New York was filled.

Horace Greeley, the famous editor, sent a reporter with horse and buggy racing round the prayer meetings to see how many men were praying. In one hour he could get to only twelve meetings, but he counted 6,100 men attending.

Then a landslide of prayer began, which overflowed to the churches in the evenings. People began to be converted, ten thousand a week in New York City alone. The movement spread throughout New England, the church bells bringing people to prayer at eight in the morning, twelve noon, and six in the evening. The revival raced up the Hudson and down the Mohawk, where the Baptists, for example, had so many people to baptise that they went down to the river, cut a big hole in the ice, and baptised them in the cold water. When Baptists do that they are really on fire!

When the revival reached Chicago, a young shoe salesman went to the superintendent of the Plymouth Congregational Church, and asked if he might teach Sunday School. The superintendent said, 'I am sorry, young fellow. I have sixteen teachers too many, but I will put you on the waiting list.'

The young man insisted, 'I want to do something just now.'

'Well, start a class.'

'How do I start a class?'

'Get some boys off the street but don't bring them here. Take them out into the country and after a month you will have control of them, so bring them in. They will be your class.'

He took them to a beach on Lake Michigan and he taught them Bible verses and Bible games. Then he took them to the Plymouth Congregational Church. The name of that young man was Dwight Lyman Moody, and that was the beginning of a ministry that lasted forty years.

Trinity Episcopal Church in Chicago had a hundred and twenty-one members in 1857; fourteen hundred in 1860. That was typical of the churches. More than a million people were converted to God in one year out of a population of thirty million.

Then that same revival jumped the Atlantic, appeared in Ulster, Scotland and Wales, then England, parts of Europe, South Africa and South India - anywhere there was an evangelical cause. It sent mission pioneers to many countries. Effects were felt for forty years. Having begun in a movement of prayer, it was sustained by a movement of prayer.

1904-1905

That movement lasted for a generation, but at the turn of the century there was need of awakening again. A general movement of prayer began, with special prayer meetings at Moody Bible Institute, at Keswick Conventions in England, and places as far apart as Melbourne, Wonsan in Korea, and the Nilgiri Hills of India. So all around the world believers were praying that there might be another great awakening in the twentieth century.

* * *

In the revival of 1905, I read of a young man who became a famous professor, Kenneth Scott Latourette. He reported that, at Yale in 1905, 25% of the student body were enrolled in prayer meetings and in Bible study.

As far as churches were concerned, the ministers of Atlantic City reported that of a population of fifty thousand there were only fifty adults left unconverted.

Take Portland in Oregon: two hundred and forty major stores closed from 11 to 2 each day to enable people to attend prayer meetings, signing an agreement so that no one would cheat and stay open.

Take First Baptist Church of Paducah in Kentucky: the pastor, an old man, Dr J. J. Cheek, took a thousand members in two months and died of overwork, the Southern Baptists saying, 'a glorious ending to a devoted ministry.'

That is what was happening in the United States in 1905. But how did it begin?

* * *

Most people have heard of the Welsh Revival which started in 1904. It began as a movement of prayer.

Seth Joshua, the Presbyterian evangelist, came to Newcastle Emlyn College where a former coal miner, Evan Roberts aged 26, was studying for the ministry. The students were so moved that they asked if they could attend Joshua's next campaign nearby. So they cancelled classes to go to Blaenanerch where Seth Joshua prayed publicly, 'O God, bend us.'

Evan Roberts went forward where he prayed with great agony, 'O God, bend me.'

Upon his return he could not concentrate on his studies. He went to the principal of his college and explained, 'I keep hearing a voice that tells me I must go home and speak to our young people in my home church. Principal Phillips, is that the voice of the devil or the voice of the Spirit?'

Principal Phillips answered wisely, 'The devil never gives orders like that. You can have a week off.'

So he went back home to Loughor and announced to the pastor, 'I've come to preach.'

The pastor was not at all convinced, but asked, 'How about speaking at the prayer meeting on Monday?'

He did not even let him speak to the prayer meeting, but told the praying people, 'Our young brother, Evan Roberts, feels he has a message for you if you care to wait.'

Seventeen people waited behind, and were impressed with the directness of the young man's words. Evan Roberts told his fellow members, 'I have a message for you from God. You must confess any known sin to God and put any wrong done to others right. Second, you must put away any doubtful habit. Third, you must obey the Spirit promptly. Finally, you must confess your faith in Christ publicly.'

By ten o'clock all seventeen had responded. The pastor was so pleased that he asked, 'How about your speaking at the mission service tomorrow night? Midweek service Wednesday night?'

He preached all week, and was asked to stay another week. Then the break came.

Suddenly the dull ecclesiastical columns in the Welsh papers changed:

'Great crowds of people drawn to Loughor.'

The main road between Llanelly and Swansea on which the church was situated was packed with people trying to get into the church. Shopkeepers closed early to find a place in the big church.

Now the news was out. A reporter was sent down and he described vividly what he saw: a strange meeting which closed at 4.25 in the morning, and even then people did not seem willing to go home. There was a very British summary: 'I felt that this was no ordinary gathering.'

Next day, every grocery shop in that industrial valley was emptied of groceries by people attending the meetings, and on Sunday every church was filled.

The movement went like a tidal wave over Wales, in five months there being a hundred thousand people converted throughout the country. Five years later, Dr J. V. Morgan wrote a book to debunk the revival, his main criticism being that, of a hundred thousand joining the churches in five months of excitement, after five years only seventy-five thousand still stood in the membership of those churches!

The social impact was astounding. For example, judges were presented with white gloves, not a case to try; no robberies, no burglaries, no rapes, no murders, and no embezzlements, nothing. District councils held emergency meetings to discuss what to do with the police now that they were unemployed.

In one place the sergeant of police was sent for and asked, 'What do you do with your time?'

He replied, 'Before the revival, we had two main jobs, to prevent crime and to control crowds, as at football games. Since the revival started there is practically no crime. So we just go with the crowds.'

A councillor asked, 'What does that mean?'

The sergeant replied, 'You know where the crowds are. They are packing out the churches.'

'But how does that affect the police?'

He was told, 'We have seventeen police in our station, but we have three quartets, and if any church wants a quartet to sing, they simply call the police station.'

As the revival swept Wales, drunkenness was cut in half. There was a wave of bankruptcies, but nearly all taverns. There was even a slowdown in the mines, for so many Welsh coal miners were converted and stopped using bad language that the horses that dragged the coal trucks in the mines could not understand what was being said to them.

That revival also affected sexual moral standards. I had discovered through the figures given by British government experts that in Radnorshire and Merionethshire the illegitimate birth rate had dropped 44% within a year of the beginning of the revival.

The revival swept Britain, Scandinavia, Germany, North America, Australasia, Africa, Brazil, Mexico, Chile.

As always, it began through a movement of prayer.

What do we mean by extraordinary prayer? We share ordinary prayer in regular worship services, before meals, and the like. But when people are found getting up at six in the morning to pray, or having a half night of prayer until midnight, or giving up their lunch time to pray at noonday prayer meetings, that is extraordinary prayer. It must be united and concerted.

J Edwin Orr described revival this way:

An Evangelical Awakening is a movement of the Holy Spirit bringing about a revival of New Testament Christianity in the Church of Christ and in its related community. … The outpouring of the Spirit accomplishes the reviving of the Church, the awakening of the masses and the movements of uninstructed people toward the Christian faith; the revived Church, by many or by few, is moved to engage in evangelism, in teaching and in social action.

Such an awakening may run its course briefly, or it may last a lifetime. It may come about in various ways, though there seems to be a pattern common to all such movements throughout history.

The major marks of an Evangelical Awakening are always some repetition of the phenomena of the Acts of the Apostles, followed by the revitalization of nominal Christians and by bringing outsiders into vital touch with the Divine Dynamic causing all such Awakenings – the Spirit of God.

J Edwin Orr, 1973, *The Eager Feet,* Moody, p. vii.

3 Pentecost for Australian Aborigines

Djiniyini Gondarra

The Revd Dr Djiniyini Gondarra is a Uniting Church minister and former Moderator of the Northern Synod of the Uniting Church in Australia.

This is a very brief outline of the revival which took place in Arnhem Land in the Uniting Church parishes, beginning in Galiwin'ku, a community with a population of 1500 to 1600 on Elcho Island, 400 miles east of Darwin in Northern Australia.

In the early years, Galiwin'ku Community was the mission station established by the Methodist Overseas Mission back in 1942 under the leadership of Rev. Harold Shepherdson. He was accepted by the Methodist Mission Board in 1927 as a lay missionary, engineer and saw miller. Because of his long outstanding Christian leadership and humility he was ordained at Galiwin'ku, Elcho Island, on 19th October, 1954. He and his wife Ella Shepherdson would have been the last pioneer missionaries to leave their beloved home and people in Arnhem Land.

The missionary movement in Arnhem Land has taken as its mandate the great commission in Matthew 28:19-20 which says: "Go, then, to all peoples everywhere and make them my disciples, baptise them in the name of the Father, the Son and the Holy Spirit, and teach them to obey everything I have commanded you. And I will be with you always, to the end of the age."

I understand that mission is to include every aspect of the work which the church is sent into the world to do, and I understand evangelism in a different sense which is called holistic evangelism. It is a means of communication of the good news about Jesus Christ as it affects the whole of life.

You will remember very well the story in Acts 1:6-8 when Jesus and his disciples met together before the ascension took place. The disciples asked whether God's reign was now come in full. Jesus told them it was not their business to worry about that, but they would receive power when the Holy Spirit came upon them and they would be his witnesses beginning in Jerusalem and going outwards into Judea, Samaria and on to the ends of the earth.

There is something quite unpredictable, unexpected and mysterious about the way that God's rule is realised in communities and in the lives of individuals. So the disciples were told to wait for the Holy Spirit and then they would be witnesses when Pentecost came. Something quite unplanned and unexpected happened. They began to babble in other strange languages and people asked what is this that is happening? What is going on?

Difficult times

Galiwin'ku, Elcho Island, experienced the revival on 14th March, 1979. That year was a very hard year because the churches in Arnhem Land were going through very difficult times. There was suffering, hardship and even persecution.

Many people left the church and the Christian gospel no longer had interest and value in their lives. Many began to speak against Christianity or even wanted to get rid of the church.

This attitude was affected by the changes that were happening. Money and other things were coming into the community from the government. The people became more rich and were handling lots of things such as motor cars, T.V., motor boats, and good houses. The responsibilities were in the hands of the Aboriginal people and no longer in the missionaries= hands.

The earthly values became the centre of Aboriginal life. There was more liquor coming into the communities every day, and more fighting was going on. There were more families hurt, and more deaths and incidents happening which were caused by drinking.

Whole communities in Arnhem Land were in great chaos. The people were in confusion and without direction. The Aboriginal people were listening to many voices. The government was saying you are free people and you must have everything you want, just like the other Australians. And there were promises from one to another.

To me, the Aboriginal people in Arnhem Land were like the Israelites in Egypt being slaves in bondage because of all the changes that were brought into the community. They were like the vacuum suction which was sucking in everything that comes without knowing that many of the things that came into communities were really unpleasant and only destroyed the harmony and the good relationship with the people and the communities.

I thank God that I was being called back to serve my own people in Arnhem Land, especially to Galiwin'ku. In 1975 I had just completed my theological training in Papua New Guinea in Raronga Theological College and was appointed to Galiwin'ku parish. My ordination took place in 1976 in Galiwin'ku parish, and I was ordained by the Arnhem Land Presbytery. I was appointed then to Galiwin'ku parish as parish minister.

This celebration took place when there were lots of changes happening and when the church was challenged by the power of evil which clothes itself in greed, selfishness, drunkenness, and in wealth. As I went on my daily pastoral visitation around the camp I would hear the drunks swearing and bashing up their wives and throwing stones on the houses, and glass being broken in the houses. And sometimes the drunks would go into the church and smoke cigarettes in the holy house of God. This was really terrible. The whole of Arnhem Land was being held by the hands of satan.

I remember one day I woke up early in the morning and went for a walk down the beach and started talking to myself. I said, "Lord, why have you called me to the ministry? Why have you called me back to my own people? Why not to somewhere else, because there is so much suffering and hardship?"

35

I then returned to the manse where Gelung, my wife, and the children were. This was our last day before we left for our holidays to the south, visiting old missionary friends and also taking part in the lovely wedding held in Sydney for Barry and Barbara Bullick, one of our missionary workers still remaining in Galiwin'ku Community.

It was almost 6.30 a.m. and it was my turn to lead the morning devotions. The bell had already rung and I had rushed into the church. When I got there, there were only four people inside the church. We used to have our morning devotions every day early in the morning because this system had been formed by the missionaries in the early years.

God had given me the Word to read and share with those four people who were present in the church with me. The reading I selected was from the Old Testament, Ezekiel 37:1-14, the valley of dry bones. Most of you know the story very well, how God Yahweh commanded the prophet Ezekiel to prophecy to the dry bones, and how that the dry bones represent the whole house of Israel, how they were just like bones dried up and their hope had perished. They were completely cut off.

After the morning prayers, Gelung, the children and I were ready to leave for Gove and then go on to Cairns in North Queensland. We were away for four weeks and returned on 14th March, 1979.

20th century Pentecost

To me and all the Galiwin'ku Community, both the Aboriginal Christians and the white Christians, these dates and the month were very important because this is the mark of the birth of the Pentecost experience in the Arnhem Land churches or the birth of the Arnhem Land churches. To us it was like Pentecost in this 20th Century.

It happened when Gelung, the children and I arrived very late in the afternoon from our holidays through Gove on the late Missionary Aviation Fellowship aircraft to Galiwin'ku. When we landed at Galiwin=ku airport we were welcomed and met by many crowds of people.
They all seemed to be saying to us, "We would like you to start the Bible Class fellowship once again." It seemed to me that God, after our leaving, had been walking on and preparing many people's lives to wait upon the outpouring of his Holy Spirit that would soon come upon them.

Gelung and I were so tired from the long trip from Cairns to Gove and then from Gove to Galiwin'ku that we expected to rest and sort out some of the things and unpack. But we just committed ourselves to the needs of our brothers and sisters who had welcomed and met us at the airport that afternoon.

After the evening dinner, we called our friends to come and join us in the Bible Class meeting. We just sang some hymns and choruses translated into Gupapuynu and into Djambarrpuynu. There were only seven or eight people who were involved or came to the Bible Class meeting, and many of our friends didn't turn up. We didn't get worried about it.

I began to talk to them that this was God's will for us to get together this evening because God had planned this meeting through them so that we will see something of his great love which will be poured out on each one of them. I said a word of thanks to those few faithful Christians who had been praying for renewal in our church, and I shared with them that I too had been praying for the revival or the renewal for this church and for the whole of Arnhem Land churches, because to our heavenly Father everything is possible. He can do mighty things in our churches throughout our great land.

These were some of the words of challenge I gave to those of my beloved brothers and sisters. Gelung, my wife, also shared something of her experience of the power and miracles that she felt deep down in her heart when she was about to die in Darwin Hospital delivering our fourth child. It was God's power that brought the healing and the wholeness in her body

I then asked the group to hold each other's hands and I began to pray for the people and for the church, that God would pour out his Holy Spirit to bring healing and renewal to the hearts of men and women, and to the children.

Suddenly we began to feel God's Spirit moving in our hearts and the whole form of our prayer suddenly changed and everybody began to pray in the Spirit and in harmony. And there was a great noise going on in the room and we began to ask one another what was going on.

Some of us said that God had now visited us and once again established his kingdom among his people who have been bound for so long by the power of evil. Now the Lord is setting his church free and bringing us into the freedom of happiness and into reconciliation and to restoration.

In that same evening the word just spread like the flames of fire and reached the whole community in Galiwin'ku. Gelung and I couldn't sleep at all that night because people were just coming for the ministry, bringing the sick to be prayed for, for healing. Others came to bring their problems. Even a husband and wife came to bring their marriage problem, so the Lord touched them and healed their marriage.

Next morning the Galiwin'ku Community once again became the new community. The love of Jesus was being shared and many expressions of forgiveness were taking place in the families and in the tribes. Wherever I went I could hear people singing and humming Christian choruses and hymns! Before then I would have expected to hear only fighting and swearing and many other troublesome things that would hurt your feelings and make you feel sad.

Many unplanned and unexpected things happened every time we went from camp to camp to meet with the people. The fellowship was held every night and more and more people gave their lives to Christ, and it went on and on until sometimes the fellowship meeting would end around about midnight. There was more singing, testimony, and ministry going on. People did not feel tired in the morning, but still went to work.

Many Christians were beginning to discover what their ministry was, and a few others had a strong sense of call to be trained to become Ministers of the Word. Now today these ministers who have done their training through Nungilinya College have been ordained. These are some of the results of the revival in Arnhem Land. Many others have been trained to take up a special ministry in the parish.

The spirit of revival has not only affected the Uniting Church communities and the parishes, but Anglican churches in Arnhem Land as well, such as in Angurugu, Umbakumba, Roper River, Numbulwar and Oenpelli. These all have experienced the revival, and have been touched by the joy and the happiness and the love of Christ.

The outpouring of the Holy Spirit in Arnhem Land has swept further to the Centre in Pitjantjatjara and across the west into many Aboriginal settlements and communities. I remember when Rev. Rronang Garrawurra, Gelung and I were invited by the Warburton Ranges people and how we saw God's Spirit move in the lives of many people. Five hundred people came to the Lord and were baptised in the name of the Father, the Son, and the Holy Spirit.

There was a great revival that swept further west. I would describe these experiences like a wild bush fire burning from one side of Australia to the other side of our great land. The experience of revival in Arnhem Land is still active in many of our Aboriginal parishes and the churches.

We would like to share these experiences in many white churches where doors are closed to the power of the Holy Spirit. It has always been my humble prayer that the whole of Australian Christians, both black and white, will one day be touched by this great and mighty power of the living God.

This article is reproduced from Church on Fire, *edited by G. Waugh and is adapted with permission from Djiniyini Gondarra's book* Let my people go *published by Bethel Presbytery of the Northern Synod of the Uniting Church in Australia.*

Dr Martyn Lloyd-Jones described revival this way:

It is an experience in the life of the Church when the Holy Spirit does an unusual work. He does that work, primarily, amongst the members of the Church; it is a reviving of the believers. You cannot revive something that has never had life, so revival, by definition, is first of all an enlivening and quickening and awakening of lethargic, sleeping, almost moribund Church members. Suddenly the power of the Spirit comes upon them and they are brought into a new and more profound awareness of the truths that they previously held intellectually, and perhaps at a deeper level too. They are humbled, they are convicted of sin, they are terrified at themselves. Many of them feel they had never been Christians. And they come to see the great salvation of God in all its glory and to feel its power. Then, as the result of their quickening and enlivening, they begin to pray. New power comes into the preaching of ministers, and the result of this is that large numbers who were previously outside the Church are converted and brought in.

Martyn Lloyd-Jones, 1959, "Revival: An Historical and Theological Survey" in *How Shall they Hear?* the compiled papers from the Puritan and Reformed Studies Conference of 1959 in London. Reproduced in R E Davies, 1992, *I will Pour out My Spirit,* Monarch, p. 17

4 Power from on High

John Greenfield

The Rev John Greenfield, an American Moravian evangelist, published his book Power from on High in 1927 on the 200th anniversary of the Moravian revival. The information in this article is from that book, now out of print. The Moravians, a refugee colony from Bohemia, settled on the estates of Count Nicholas Zinzendorf (painted) in Herrnhut, Germany, where a powerful revival began in 1727. It launched 100 years of continuous prayer and within 25 years 100 Moravians were missionaries, more than the rest of the Protestant church had sent out in two centuries.

A modern Pentecost

A Moravian historian wrote that Church history

> abounds in records of special outpourings of the Holy Ghost, and verily the thirteenth of August, 1727, was a day of the outpouring of the Holy Spirit. We saw the hand of God and His wonders, and we were all under the cloud of our fathers baptized with their Spirit. The Holy Ghost came upon us and in those days great signs and wonders took place in our midst.

> From that time scarcely a day passed but what we beheld His almighty workings amongst us. A great hunger after the Word of God took possession of us so that we had to have three services

every day, viz. 5.0 and 7.30 a.m. and 9.0 p.m. Every one desired above everything else that the Holy Spirit might have full control. Self-love and self-will, as well as all disobedience, disappeared and an overwhelming flood of grace swept us all out into the great ocean of Divine Love (1927:14).

No one present could tell exactly what happened on that Wednesday morning, 13 August 1727 at the specially called Communion service. They hardly knew if they had been on earth or in heaven. Count Nicholas Zinzendorf, the young leader of that community, gave this account many years later:

We needed to come to the Communion with a sense of the loving nearness of the Saviour. This was the great comfort which has made this day a generation ago to be a festival, because on this day twenty-seven years ago the Congregation of Herrnhut, assembled for communion (at the Berthelsdorf church) were all dissatisfied with themselves. They had quit judging each other because they had become convinced, each one, of his lack of worth in the sight of God and each felt himself at this Communion to be in view of the noble countenance of the Saviour.

> O head so full of bruises,
> So full of pain and scorn.

In this view of the man of sorrows and acquainted with grief, their hearts told them that He would be their patron and their priest who was at once changing their tears into oil of gladness and their misery into happiness. This firm confidence changed them in a single moment into a happy people which they are to this day, and into their happiness they have since led many thousands of others through the memory and help which the heavenly grace once given to themselves, so many thousand times confirmed to them since then (1927:15).

Zinzendorf described it as 'a sense of the nearness of Christ' given to everyone present, and also to others of their community who were working elsewhere at the time.

The congregation was young. Zinzendorf, the human leader, was 27, which was about the average age of the group.

The Moravian brethren had sprung from the labours and martyrdom of the Bohemian Reformer, John Hus. They had experienced centuries of persecution. Many had been killed, imprisoned, tortured or banished from their homeland. This group had fled for refuge to Germany where the young Christian nobleman, Count Zinzendorf, offered them asylum on his estates in Saxony. They named their new home Herrnhut, 'the Lord's Watch'. From there, after their baptism in the Holy Spirit, they became evangelists and missionaries.

Fifty years before the beginning of modern Foreign Missions by William Carey, the Moravian Church had sent out over 100 missionaries. Their English missionary magazine, Periodical Accounts, inspired William Carey. He threw a copy of the paper on a table at a Baptist meeting, saying, 'See what the Moravians have done! Cannot we follow their example and in obedience to our Heavenly Master go out into the world, and preach the Gospel to the heathen?' (1927:19).

That missionary zeal began with the outpouring of the Holy Spirit. Count Zinzendorf observed: 'The Saviour permitted to come upon us a Spirit of whom we had hitherto not had any experience or knowledge. ... Hitherto we had been the leaders and helpers. Now the Holy Spirit Himself took full control of everything and everybody' (1927:21).

When the Spirit came

Prayer precedes Pentecost. The disgruntled community at Herrnhut early in 1727 was deeply divided and critical of one another. Heated controversies threatened to disrupt the community. The majority were from the ancient Moravian Church of the Brethren. Other believers attracted to Herrnhut included Lutherans, Reformed, and Baptists. They argued about predestination, holiness, and baptism.

The young German nobleman, Count Zinzendorf, pleaded for unity, love and repentance. Converted in early childhood, at four years of age he composed and signed a covenant: 'Dear Saviour, do Thou be mine, and I will be Thine.' His life motto was, 'I have one passion: it is Jesus, Jesus only.'
Count Zinzendorf learned the secret of prevailing prayer. He actively established prayer groups as a teenager, and on leaving the college at Halle at sixteen he gave the famous Professor Francke a list of seven praying

societies he had established.

After he finished university his education was furthered by travel to foreign countries. Everywhere he went, his passion for Jesus controlled him. In the Dusseldorf Gallery of paintings he was deeply moved by a painting of the crucifixion over which were the words:

> Hoc feci pro te;
> Quid facis pro me?

> This have I done for thee;
> What have you done for me?

At Herrnhut, Zinzendorf visited all the adult members of the deeply divided community. He drew up a covenant calling upon them 'to seek out and emphasize the points in which they agreed' rather than stressing their differences. On 12 May 1727 they all signed an agreement to dedicate their lives, as he dedicated his, to the service of the Lord Jesus Christ.

The Moravian revival of 1727 was thus preceded and then sustained by extraordinary praying. A spirit of grace, unity and supplications grew among them.

On 16 July the Count poured out his soul in a prayer accompanied with a flood of tears. This prayer produced an extraordinary effect. The whole community began praying as never before.

On 22 July many of the community covenanted together on their own accord to meet often to pour out their hearts in prayer and hymns.

On 5 August the Count spent the whole night in prayer with about twelve or fourteen others following a large meeting for prayer at midnight where great emotion prevailed.

On Sunday, 10 August, Pastor Rothe, while leading the service at Herrnhut, was overwhelmed by the power of the Lord about noon. He sank down into the dust before God. So did the whole congregation. They continued till midnight in prayer and singing, weeping and praying.

On Wednesday, 13 August, the Holy Spirit was poured out on them all.

Their prayers were answered in ways far beyond anyone's expectations. Many of them decided to set aside certain times for continued earnest prayer.

On 26 August, twenty-four men and twenty-four women covenanted together to continue praying in intervals of one hour each, day and night, each hour allocated by lots to different people.

On 27 August, this new regulation began. Others joined the intercessors and the number involved increased to seventy-seven. They all carefully observed the hour which had been appointed for them. The intercessors had a weekly meeting where prayer needs were given to them.

The children, also touched powerfully by God, began a similar plan among themselves. Those who heard their infant supplications were deeply moved. The children's prayers and supplications had a powerful effect on the whole community.

That astonishing prayer meeting beginning in 1727 went on for one hundred years. It was unique. Known as the Hourly Intercession, it involved relays of men and women in prayer without ceasing made to God. That prayer also led to action, especially evangelism. More than one hundred missionaries left that village community in the next twenty-five years, all constantly supported in prayer.

The Spirit's witness

One result of their baptism in the Holy Spirit was a joyful assurance of their pardon and salvation. This made a strong impact on people in many countries, including the Wesleys.

In 1736 John and Charles Wesley sailed to America as Anglican missionaries. A company of Moravian immigrants were also on the vessel. During a terrible storm they all faced the danger of shipwreck. John Wesley wrote in his journal:

> At seven I went to the Germans. I had long before observed the great seriousness of their behaviour. Of their humility they had given a continual proof by performing those servile offices for the other passengers which none of the English would undertake; for which they desired and would receive no pay, saying, 'It was good

for their proud hearts,' and 'their loving Saviour had done more for them.' And every day had given them occasion of showing a meekness, which no injury could move. If they were pushed, struck or thrown down, they rose again and went away; but no complaint was found in their mouth. Here was now an opportunity of trying whether they were delivered from the spirit of fear, as well as from that of pride, anger and revenge. In the midst of the Psalm wherewith their service began, the sea broke over, split the main-sail in pieces, covered the ship and poured in between the decks, as if the great deep had already swallowed us up. A terrible screaming began among the English. The Germans calmly sung on. I asked one of them afterwards: 'Were you not afraid?' He answered, 'I thank God, no.' I asked: 'But were not your women and children afraid?' He replied mildly: 'No, our women and children are not afraid to die' (1927:35-36).

In Georgia, John Wesley sought spiritual counsel from the Moravian Bishop, A. G. Spangenberg. Back in England in 1738 the Wesley brothers became intimately acquainted with the Moravians, especially Peter Boehler who later became a leading Moravian bishop.

On 4 March, 1738, Wesley wrote in his diary:

I found my brother at Oxford recovering from his pleurisy; and with him Peter Boehler: by whom (in the hand of the great God) I was, on Sunday, the 5th, clearly convinced of unbelief; of the want of that faith whereby alone we are saved. Immediately it struck into my mind, 'Leave off preaching. How can you preach to others who have not faith yourself?' I asked Boehler whether he thought I should leave it off, or not. He answered, 'By no means.' I asked: 'But what can I preach? He said: 'Preach faith till you have faith.' Accordingly, Monday, 6, I began preaching this new doctrine, though my soul started back from the work. The first person to whom I offered salvation by faith alone, was a prisoner under sentence of death (1927:37).

Eventually John Wesley came to assurance of salvation. His own testimony reads:

Wednesday, May 3, 1738. My brother had a long and particular conversation with Peter Boehler. And it now pleased God to open his eyes; so that he also saw clearly, what was the nature of that one true living faith, whereby alone 'through grace' we are saved.

Wednesday, May 24. In the evening I went very unwillingly to a society in Aldersgate Street, where one was reading Luther's preface to the Epistle to the Romans. About a quarter before nine, while he was describing the change which God works in the heart through faith in Christ, I felt my heart strangely warmed. I felt I did trust in Christ, Christ alone, for salvation; and an assurance was given me, that He had taken away my sins, even mine, and saved me from the law of sin and death.

Friday, May 26. My soul continued in peace, but yet in heaviness, because of manifold temptations. I asked Mr. Telchig, the Moravian, what to do. He said: 'You must not fight with them as you did before, but flee from them the moment they appear, and take shelter in the wounds of Jesus (1927:38).

The Methodists and Moravians often met together then for Bible study and prayer. George Whitefield's biographer wrote:

Whitefield began the New Year (1739) as gloriously as he ended that which had just expired. He received Sacrament, preached twice, expounded twice, attended a Moravian love feast in Fetter Lane, where he spent the whole night in prayer to God, psalms and thanksgivings; and then pronounced 'this to the happiest New Year's Day he had ever seen.'

This love feast at Fetter Lane was a memorable one. Besides about sixty Moravians, there were present not fewer than seven of the Oxford Methodists, namely John and Charles Wesley, George Whitefield, Wesley Hall, Benjamin Ingham, Charles Kinchin and Richards Hitchins, all of them ordained clergymen of the Church of England. Wesley writes: 'About three in the morning, as we were continuing instant in prayer, the power of God came mightily upon us, insomuch that many cried for exceeding joy, and many fell to the ground. As soon as we were recovered a little from that awe and amazement at the presence of His Majesty, we broke out with one voice - 'We praise Thee, O God; we acknowledge Thee to be the

Lord!' (1927:38-39).

What the Moravians imparted to John Wesley is summarised by one of his biographers, W. H. Fitchett:

> In substance it was three things which lie in the very alphabet of Christianity, but which somehow the teachings of a godly home, of a great University, and of an ancient Church, and of famous books, had not taught Wesley. These are that salvation is through Christ's Atonement alone, and not through our own works; that its sole condition is faith; and that it is attested to the spiritual consciousness by the Holy Spirit. These truths to-day are platitudes; to Wesley they were, at this stage of his life, discoveries (1927:40).

Wesley's estimate of the Moravian revival which resulted in his own conversion was prophetic. When Peter Boehler, nine years his junior, left England for America after several months, Wesley recorded in his journal:

> Peter Boehler left London to embark for Carolina. Oh what a work hath God begun since his coming into England! Such an one as shall never come to an end, till Heaven and earth pass away! (1927:40).

Peter Boehler wrote to Count Zinzendorf, saying 'The English people made a wonderful to do about me; and though I could not speak much English they were always wanting me to tell them about the Saviour, His blood and wounds, and the forgiveness of sins' (1927:40-41).

Witnesses unto Me

Zinzendorf's speaking, preaching and letters were full of Christ. Everywhere the Moravians went they spoke of their Lord, sang of him, and witnessed naturally. The Holy Spirit had filled them, as in the early church, with great love for their Lord.

Their Bishop Spangenberg, for example, told how Johannes, an Indian chief who had been a very wicked man, was converted. The chief said that once a preacher came to their tribe and proved to them that there was a God. They informed him that they were not ignorant of that and told him to go away. Another preacher came and told them not to steal, drink too much, or lie.

They regarded him as a fool because they already knew that, and they sent him off to preach to his own people who were worse than the Indians in those vices.

Then Christian Henry Rauch, one of the Moravian Brethren, came to his hut, sat with him and told him about Jesus. Then fatigued from his journey, Christian Henry lay down and slept, unafraid of the chief. Johannes could not get the Moravian's words out of his mind. He dreamt of the cross. He told his tribe about Jesus and they repented as the Holy Spirit moved their hearts. Johannes said to the bishop, 'Thus, through the grace of God, the awakening among us took place. I tell you therefore, brethren, preach to the heathen Christ and His blood and death, if you would wish to produce a blessing among them.' (1927:53).

In Europe, a Countess with close friends among kings, emperors and princes, famous for her brilliant gifts and witty conversation, found that none of her amusements and recreations satisfied her any longer. A humble Moravian shoemaker came into her presence and she was struck with his remarkable cheerfulness. She asked him why he was so happy and he replied that 'Jesus has forgiven my sins. He forgives me every day and He loves me and that makes me happy through all the hours.' The Countess thought about that and began to pray. Conviction led her into the same joyful faith and she became a great witness for Christ among titled people, especially in the court of the Emperor of Russia, Alexander I, her close friend.

A new song

Then, as now, the baptism in the Holy Spirit upon the Moravians and then the Methodists, produced a flood sacred song. Many of the best hyumns may be traced to this outpouring of the Holy Spirit. Moravian hymns were filled with praise to Christ, adoration of him as God, and proclamation of His virtues and work.

Moravian hymns were generally prayers to Christ. It was a Moravian characteristic that their prayers were generally addressed to their Saviour. Honouring the Son they honoured the Father who had sent him as well as the Holy Spirit who glorified Christ.

A truly converted Catholic or Protestant, Calvanist or Lutheran, Moravian or Arminian, Baptist or Quaker, when baptised in the Holy Spirit and with fire often breaks out into sacred song that is prayer or praise addressed to Jesus.

This was so in Herrnhut. The chief singer then was the godly young nobleman Count Zinzendorf. He became the prince of German hymn writers.

England saw similar developments. One of the many spiritual children of Peter Boehler was John Gambold, a young clergyman of the Church of England, an Oxford graduate and a friend of the Wesleys. He joined the Moravian Church and became its first English Bishop. Some of his hymns and sacred songs became well known.

Another of Peter Boehler's English converts was James Hutton, a famous book seller. He also wrote some precious hymns.

The best known English Moravian hymn writer during the Great Revival was John Cennick. At one of Cennick's famous open air meetings a young Scottish labourer, John Montgomery, was converted. He joined the Moravian Church and John and Mary Montgomery become Moravian missionaries in the West Indies where they died and were buried. Their son James was educated in the Moravian school at Fulneck. James Montgomery ranks with great hymn writers of that era.

Charles Wesley had more than 6,000 hymns published after his conversion in 1738 through the witness and prayers of Peter Boehler.

> The majority of his hymns testify to his great experience of salvation. Peter Boehler had told him: 'If I had a thousand tongues I would praise Jesus with every one of them.' This prompted Wesley shortly after his conversion to write the immortal lines:

> Oh for a thousand tongues to sing
> My dear Redeemer's praise
> The glories of my God and King
> The triumphs of His grace.
> He breaks the power of cancelled sin,
> He sets the prisoner free;
> His blood can make the foulest clean,
> His blood availed for me (1927:84).

Fruit that abides

A traveller of that period wrote this striking testimony, 'In all my journeys I have found only three objects that exceeded my expectations, viz.: the ocean, Count Zinzendorf and the Herrnhut congregation' (1927:67). Herrnhut had become a spiritual centre visited by people from all parts of Europe seeking to be saved or to be baptised in the Holy Spirit and with fire.

John Wesley's visit to Herrnhut was typical of thousands of others. 'God has given me at length,' he wrote to his brother Samuel, 'the desire of my heart. I am with a Church whose conversation is in Heaven; in whom is the mind that was in Christ, and who so walk as He walked'. In his journal he wrote, 'I would gladly have spent my life here; but my Master called me to labour in another part of His vineyard. O when shall this Christianity cover the earth, as the waters cover the sea?' (1927:67).

At the end of his life Count Zinzendorf could triumphantly say:

> I am going to my Saviour. I am ready. There is nothing to hinder me now. I cannot say how much I love you all. Who would have believed that the prayer of Christ, 'that they all may be one,' could have been so strikingly fulfilled among us! I only asked for first-fruits among the heathen, and thousands have been given me. Are we not as in Heaven! Do we not live together like the angels! The Lord and His servants understand each other. I am ready (1927:68).

Over four thousand people followed his body to its resting place on the Hutberg, including Moravian ministers from Holland, England, Ireland, North America and Greenland. His tombstone bore this inscription:

> Here lie the remains of the immortal man of God, Nicholas Lewis, Count and Lord of Zinzendorf and Pattendorf; who through the grace of God and his own unwearied service, became the ordinary of the Brethren's Church, renewed in this eighteenth century. He was born in Dresden on May 26, 1700, and entered into the joy of his Lord at Herrnhut on May 9, 1760. He was appointed to bring forth fruit, and that his fruit should abide (1927:69).

Renew our days

The renewal of the Moravian Church can stir our hearts to pray, 'Renew our days as of old.'

In 1927, 200 years after the revival in of the Moravian Church, the editor of The Biblical Review, New York, wrote:

> No matter whether one is sympathetic toward the idea of revivals or not, if he wants to study the question thoroughly, he cannot afford to overlook the history and teachings of the Moravians. Theirs has been from the beginning a great Revival Church, and its service to the general cause of Christianity, and to foreign missions in particular, is deserving of wide recognition. The story of their spiritual development and its influence is one of the most inspiring in the annals of Christianity (1927:80).

Their first great experience which gave the Moravians such spiritual power was a personal experience of salvation.

The second great experience which gave them such spiritual power and leadership was the baptism in the Holy Spirit.

Dr. J. Kenneth Pfohl, a Moravian pastor, wrote in *The Moravian* in 1927:

> The great Moravian Pentecost was not a shower of blessing out of a cloudless sky. It did come suddenly, as suddenly as the blessing of its great predecessor in Jerusalem, when the Christian Church was born. Yet, for long there had been signs of abundance of rain, though many recognized them not.
> In short the blessing of the 13th of August, 1727, was diligently and earnestly prepared for. We know of no annals of Church history which evidence greater desire for an outpouring of the Holy Spirit and more patient and persistent effort in that direction than those of our own Church between the years 1725 and 1727. Two distinct lines of preparation and spiritual effort for the blessing are evident. One was prayer; the other was individual work with individuals. We are told that 'men and women met for prayer and praise at one another's homes and the Church of Berthelsdorf was crowded out.' Then the Spirit came in great power. Then the entire company

John Greenfield

experienced the blessing at one and the same time (1927:86).

In another article in *The Moravian*, Dr E. S. Hagen declared:

The great revival in 1727 in Herrnhut was the normal and logical result of prayer and the preaching of the Word of the Cross. 'Christ and Him Crucified' was our brethren's confession of faith, and 'the inward witness of remission of sins through faith in His blood' their blessed and quickening experience. Lecky in his History of Morals says of John Wesley's conversion, May 24, 1738, in the prayer meeting of Moravian Brethren in Aldersgate Street: 'What happened in that little room was of more importance to England than all the victories of Pitt by land or sea.' ...

A renewal of our days as of old involves a return to fervent prayer and to the earnest and effectual preaching of the remission of sins through the vicarious sacrifice and the shedding of the blood of Jesus Christ the Son of God. Revival time is coming. We cherish a high expectancy of it. Sooner than we dream of, to God's people, who give themselves to earnest, persevering prayer, and the Scriptural testimony concerning the Gospel of our Lord Jesus Christ, the windows of Heaven will be opened (1927:90-91).

The day of revivals is not past. The Holy Spirit still waits to fill believers with power from on high.

Adapted from John Greenfield (1927) *Power from on High*. Edingburgh: Marshall, Morgan and Scott.

53

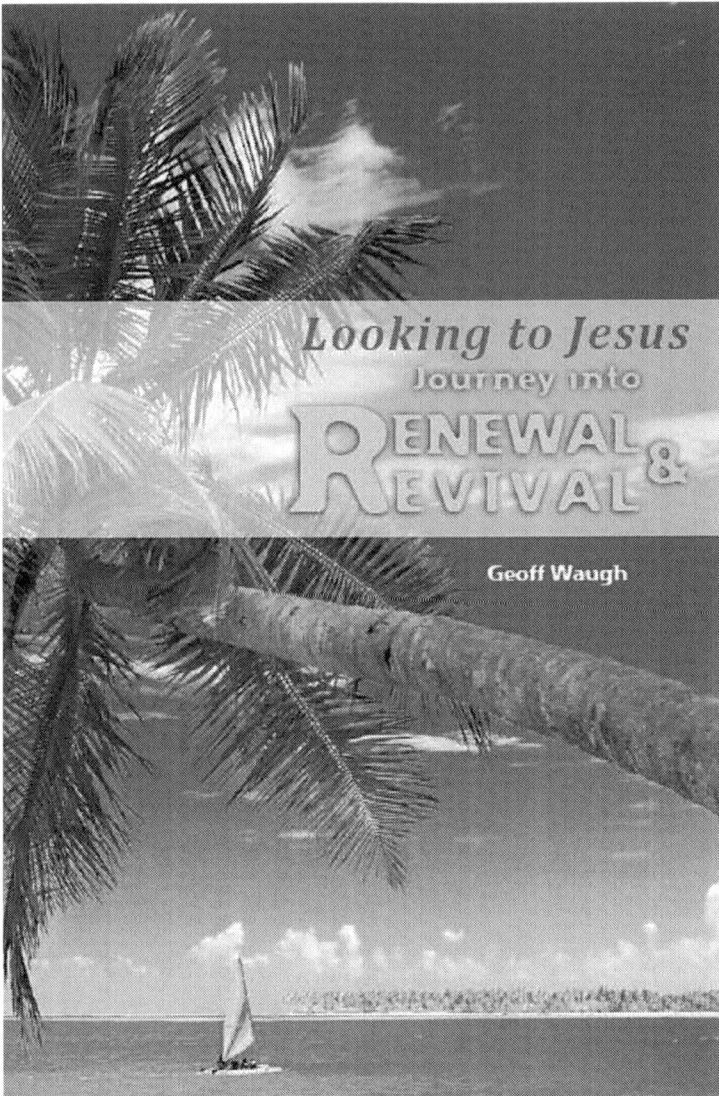

Looking to Jesus
Journey into Renewal and Revival

5 *Revival Fire*

Geoff Waugh

Rev Dr Geoff Waugh (Baptist), initial editor of the Renewal Journal, taught on renewal and revival at Alcorn College (Methodist), Trinity Theological College (Uniting) and Christian Heritage College (charismatic) in Brisbane as well as teaching in Bible Schools and with church leaders in many nations, especially in the South Pacific. His research on revivals is available on www.renewaljournal.com

God moves in awesome power at times. Signs everywhere point to that again now. Many people report a burden for and expectation of revival. We can believe for it, pray for it, and prepare for it.

Selwyn Hughes, author of the popular *Every Day with Jesus* writes,

> In all the years that I have been a Christian I have never witnessed such a burden and expectancy for revival as I do at this moment among the true people of God. Wherever I go I meet prayerful Christians whose spirit witnesses with my own that a mighty Holy Spirit revival is on the way. The 1960's and 1070's were characterised by the word 'renewal'. Then in the eighties, the word began slowly losing currency, and another appeared to take its place - revival. And why? Because great and wonderful though renewal is, many are beginning to see that there are greater things in our

Father's storehouse, and slowly but surely their faith is rising to a flash point (Hughes 1990:7).

Revival may not be wanted because it involves humility, awareness of our unworthiness, confession of sin, repentance, restitution, seeking and offering forgiveness, and following Christ wholeheartedly. It then impacts society with conviction, godliness, justice, peace and righteousness. This is not always welcome.

What is revival?

As individuals and churches are renewed they prepare the way for revival in the land. A spiritual awakening touches the community when God's Spirit moves in power. Often this awakening begins in people earnestly praying for and expecting revival.

Arthur Wallis (1956:20-23) observes:

Numerous writings ... confirm that revival is Divine intervention in the normal course of spiritual things. It is God revealing Himself to man in awesome holiness and irresistible power. It is such a manifest working of God that human personalities are overshadowed and human programs abandoned. It is man retiring into the background because God has taken the field. It is the Lord ... working in extraordinary power on saint and sinner. ... Revival must of necessity make an impact on the community and this is one means by which we may distinguish it from the more usual operations of the Holy Spirit.

Edwin Orr`s research indicated that

A spiritual awakening is a movement of the Holy Spirit bringing about a revival of New Testament Christianity in the Church of Christ and its related community. ... It accomplishes the reviving of the Church, the awakening of the masses and the movements of uninstructed people toward the Christian faith; the revived church by many or few is moved to engage in evangelism, teaching and social action (1975: vii-viii).

Roy Hession (1973:11-23) observed that

the outward forms of revivals do, of course, differ considerably, but the inward and permanent content of them is always the same: a new experience of conviction of sin among the saints; a new vision of the Cross and of Jesus and of redemption; a new willingness on man's part for brokenness, repentance, confession, and restitution; a joyful experience of the power of the blood of Jesus to cleanse fully from sin and restore and heal all that sin has lost and broken; a new entering into the fullness of the Holy Spirit and of His power to do His own work through His people; and a new gathering in of the lost ones to Jesus. ... Revival is just the life of the Lord Jesus poured into human hearts.

Bible Revivals

Scripture gives a constant call for individual and communal repentance issuing in righteousness and justice.

Wilbur Smith notes seven revivals in the Old Testament in addition to the one with Jonah. These revivals involved:
1. Jacob's household (Genesis 35:1-15),
2. Asa (2 Chronicles 15:1-15),
3. Joash (2 Kings 11-12; 2 Chronicles 23-24),
4. Hezekiah (2 Kings 18:1-8; 2 Chronicles 29-31),
5. Josiah (2 Kings 22-23; 2 Chronicles 34-35),
6. Haggai and Zechariah with Zerubbabel (Ezra 5-6)
7. Ezra with Nehemiah (Nehemiah 9:1-6; 12:44-47).

He noted nine characteristics of these revivals:
1. They occurred in times of moral darkness and national depression;
2. Each began in the heart of a consecrated servant of God who became the energizing power behind it;
3. Each revival rested on the Word of God, and most were the result of proclaiming God's Word with power;
4. All resulted in a return to the worship of God;
5. Each witnessed the destruction of idols where they existed;
6. In each revival, there was a recorded separation from sin;
7. In every revival the people returned to obeying God's laws;
8. There was a restoration of great joy and gladness;
9. Each revival was followed by a period of national prosperity.

The early church lived in continuous revival. It saw rapid growth in the power of the Holy Spirit from the initial outburst at Pentecost. Multitudes joined the church. At Pentecost 3,000 were won in one day (2:41). Soon after that there were 5,000 involved (4:4). Then great multitudes (5:14; 6:7; 9:31; 11:21, 24; 12:24 and 16:5).

Those Christians were dynamic. Not faultless, as the epistles indicate, but on fire. They were accused before the civil authorities as 'these people who have been turning the world upside down' (Acts 17:6).

Revival makes that kind of an impact in the community.

Various renewal and revival movements stirred the church and the community throughout history. The eighteenth century saw the first great awakening, and powerful revivals have spread world wide since then until the astounding developments now.

Eighteenth century

The Moravians

The Moravians, a refugee colony from Amenia on the estates of Count Nicholas von Zinzendorf at the village of Herrnhut in Germany, experienced a visitation of God in 1727 which launched revival with 100 years of continuous prayer and 100 missionaries sent out within 25 years.

On May 12th, 1727, they entered into a covenant together 'to dedicate their lives to the service of the Lord Jesus.' ... A period of extraordinary prayer followed, which both preceded and followed the outpouring. It started in early July of that year, but already, for the best part of two years, there had been prayer and praise gatherings in the homes of the people. In July they started to meet together more frequently... Some spent whole nights in prayer. ...

At about noon on Sunday August 10th, 1727, the preacher at the morning service felt himself overwhelmed by a wonderful and irresistible power of the Lord. He sank down in the dust before God, and the whole congregation joined him 'in an ecstasy of feeling'. They continued until midnight engaged in prayer, singing, weeping and supplication.

On Wednesday August 13th the church came together for a specially called communion service. They were all dissatisfied with themselves. 'They had quit judging each other because they had become convinced, each one, of his lack of worth in the sight of God and each felt himself at this communion to be in view of the Saviour.'

> They left that communion at noon, hardly knowing whether they belonged to earth or had already gone to heaven. It was a day of outpouring of the Holy Spirit. 'We saw the hand of God and were all baptized with his Holy Spirit ... The Holy Ghost came upon us and in those days great signs and wonders took place in our midst. Scarcely a day passed from then on when they did not witness God's almighty workings among them. A great hunger for God's word took hold of them. They started meeting three times daily – at 5 am, 7.30 am, and 9 pm. Self-love and self-will and all disobedience disappeared, as everyone sought to let the Holy Spirit have full control.

> Two weeks later, they entered into the twenty-four-hour prayer covenant which was to become such a feature of their life for over 100 years... 'The spirit of prayer and supplication at that time poured out upon the children was so powerful and efficacious that it is impossible to give an adequate description of it.'

> Supernatural knowledge and power was given to them. Previously timid people became flaming evangelists (Mills 1990:204-5).

The Great Awakening

Jonathan Edwards (1703-1764), the preacher and scholar who later became a President of Princeton University, was a prominent leader in a revival movement which came to be called the Great Awakening as it spread through the communities of New England and the pioneering settlements in America. Converts to Christianity reached 50,000 out of a total of 250,000 colonists. The years of 1734-35 saw an unusually powerful move of God's Spirit in thousands of people. Edwards described the characteristics of the revival as, first, an extraordinary sense of the awful majesty, greatness and holiness of God, and second, a great longing for humility before God and adoration of God.

Edwards published the journal of David Brainerd, a missionary to the North American Indians from 1743 to his death at 29 in 1747. Brainerd tells of revival breaking out among Indians in October 1745 when the power of God seemed to come like a rushing mighty wind. The Indians were overwhelmed by God. The revival had greatest impact when Brainerd emphasised the compassion of the Saviour, the provisions of the gospel, and the free offer of divine grace. Idolatry was abandoned, marriages repaired, drunkenness practically disappeared, honesty and repayments of debts prevailed. Money once wasted on excessive drinking was used for family and communal needs. Their communities were filled with love.

The power of God seemed to descend on the assembly 'like a rushing mighty wind' and with an astonishing energy bore all down before it. I stood amazed at the influence that seized the audience almost universally and could compare it to nothing more aptly than the irresistible force of a mighty torrent... Almost all persons of all ages were bowed down with concern together and scarce was able to withstand the shock of astonishing operation (Pratney 1984: 15).

On November 20, he described the revival at Crossweeksung in his general comments about that year, which had involved horse riding over 3,000 miles to reach Indian tribes in New England:

He notes that revivals have been criticised as scaring people with hell and damnation, but

> this great awakening, this surprising concern, was never excited by any harangues of terror, but always appeared most remarkable when I insisted upon the compassions of a dying Saviour, the plentiful provisions of the gospel, and the free offers of divine grace to needy distressed sinners.

> The effects of this work have likewise been very remarkable. ... Their pagan notions and idolatrous practices seem to be entirely abandoned in these parts. They are regulated and appear regularly disposed in the affairs of marriage. They seem generally divorced from drunkeness ... although before it was common for some or other of them to be drunk almost every day... A principle of honesty and justice appears in many of them, and they seem concerned to discharge their old debts... Their manner of living is much more

decent and comfortable than formerly, having now the benefit of that money which they used to consume upon strong drink. Love seems to reign among them, especially those who have given evidence of a saving change (Howard 1949, 239-251).

In 1735, when the New England revival was strongest, George Whitefield in England and Howell Harris in Wales were converted. Both were 21 and both ignited revival fires, seeing thousands converted and communities changed. By 1736 Harris began forming his converts into societies and by 1739 there were nearly thirty such societies. Whitefield travelled extensively, visiting John Wesley in Georgia in 1738, then ministering powerfully with Howell Harris in Wales 1739 and with Jonathan Edwards in New England in 1740, all in his early twenties.

Also in 1735, John Wesley went to Georgia. Whitefield sailed to Georgia at Wesley's invitation early in 1738, but they returned to England because Wesley was frustrated in his work. Then in May that year both John and Charles Wesley were converted, Charles first, and three days later on 24th May John found his heart strangely warmed in the meeting in Aldersgate Street when he listened to a reading of the preface to Luther's commenatry on Romans.

1739 saw astonishing expansion of revival in England. On 1st January the Wesleys and Whitefield and four others from their former Holy Club at Oxford in their students days, along with 60 others of whom many were Moravians, met at Fetter Lane in London for prayer and a love feast. The Spirit of God moved powerfully on them all. Many fell to the ground, resting in the Spirit. The meeting went all night and they realised they had been empowered in a fresh visitation from God.

> On 1 January 1739 a remarkable love feast was held at Fetter Lane in London. There the leaders of the Revival were welded into a fellowship of the Spirit in a way similar to what had happened at Herrnhut in 1727. The Wesleys were present, along with Whitefield and Benjamin Ingham, who was to become an outstanding evangelist among the Moravians. 'About three in the morning, as we were continuing instant in prayer,' John Wesley recorded in his Journal, 'the power of God came mightily upon us insomuch that many cried out for exceeding joy and many fell to the ground. As soon as we were recovered a little from that awe and amazement at the presence

of His majesty, we broke out with one voice, 'We praise Thee, O God, we acknowledge Thee to be the Lord.' This Pentecost on New Year's Day confirmed that the Awakening had come and launched the campaign of extensive evangelization which sprang from it (Wood 1990:449).

Revival fire spread rapidly. In February 1739 Whitefield started preaching to the Kingswood coal miners in the open fields with about 200 attending in the south west of Engalnd near the Welsh border. By March 20,000 attended. Whitefield invited Wesley to take over then and so in April Wesley began his famous open air preaching (which continued for 50 years) with those crowds at Kingswood. He returned to London in June reporting on the amazing move of God's Spirit with many conversions and many people falling prostrate under God's power - a phenonemon which he never encouraged! Features of this revival were enthusiastic singing, powerful preaching, and the gathering of converts into small societies called weekly Class Meetings.

Revival caught fire in Scotland also. After returning from America in 1741, Whitefield visited Glasgow. Two ministers in villages nearby invited him to return in 1742 because revival had already begun in their area. Conversions and prayer groups multiplied. Whitefield preached there at Cambuslang about four miles from Glasgow.

The opening meetings on a Sunday saw the great crowds on the hill side gripped with conviction, repentance and weeping more than he had seen elsewhere. The next weekend 20,000 gathered on the Saturday and up to 50,000 on the Sunday for the quarterly communion. The visit was charged with Pentecostal power which even amazed Whitefield.

That Great Awakening in Great Britain and America, established the Methodists with 140,000 members by the end of the century, and other churches and Christians were renewed and empowered. It impacted the nation with social change and created the climate for political reform.

Toward the end of the century revival fires burst again in England through prayer groups spreading everywhere. On Christmas day 1781 in Cornwall intercessors met to sing and pray from 3 a.m. and God's Spirit moved on them. They prayed until 9 a.m. and regathered that Christmas evening. Throughout January and February, the movement continued. By March

1782 they were praying until midnight. The movement spread. Churches filled and denominations doubled, tripled and quadrupled (Robinson 1992:9). By 1792, the year after John Wesley died, this second great awakening swept Great Britain and was stirring America and other countries.

In New England, Isaac Backus, a Baptist pastor, addressed an urgent plea for prayer for revival to pastors of every Christian denomination in the United States in 1794. The churches adopted the plan until America, like Britain, was interlaced with a network of prayer meetings. They met on the first Monday of each month to pray. It was not long before revival came.

James McGready, a Presbyterian minister in Kentucky, promoted the concert of prayer every first Monday of the month, and urged his people to pray for him at sunset on Saturday evening and sunrise Sunday morning. Revival swept Kentucky in the summer of 1800. Eleven thousand people came to a communion service.

That second great awakening produced the modern missionary movement and it's societies, engendered support for Bible societies, saw the abolition of slavery, and resulted in many social reforms.

Nineteenth Century

Various revival movements influenced society in the 1800s, but 1858 in America and 1859 in Britain were outstanding.

Typically, it followed a low ebb of spiritual life. Concerned Christians began praying earnestly and anticipating a new move of God's Spirit.

Revival broke out at evangelistic meetings in Hamilton, Ontario in Canada during October 1857 with attendances at meetings reaching 6,000, and three or four hundred converted including many civic leaders. It was widely reported.

Jeremiah Lanphier, a city missioner, began a weekly noon prayer meeting in New York in September that year. By October it grew into a daily prayer meeting attended by many businessmen. Anticipation of revival grew, especially with the financial collapse that October after a year of depression. Materialism was shaken.

At the beginning of 1858 that Fulton Street prayer meeting had grown so much they were holding three simultaneous prayer meetings in the building and other prayer groups were starting in the city. By March newspapers carried front page reports of over 6,000 attending daily prayer meetings in New York, 6,000 attending them in Pittsburgh, and daily prayer meetings were held in Washington at five different times to accommodate the crowds.

Other cities followed the pattern. Soon a common mid-day sign on businesses read, 'Will re-open at the close of the prayer meeting.'

By May, 50,000 of New York's 800,000 people were new converts. A newspaper reported that New England was profoundly changed by the revival and in several towns no unconverted adults could be found!

In 1858 a leading Methodist paper reported these features of the revival: few sermons were needed, lay people witnessed, seekers flocked to the altar, nearly all seekers were blessed, experiences remained clear, converts had holy boldness, religion became a social topic, family altars were strengthened, testimony given nightly was abundant, and conversations were marked with seriousness.

Edwin Orr's research revealed that in 1858-59 a million Americans were converted in a population of thirty million and at least a million Christians were renewed, with lasting results in church attendances and moral reform in society.

Charles Finney (1792-1875) became one of the most famous preachers of that era. A keen sportsman and young lawyer, he had a mighty empowering by God's Spirit on the night of his conversion including a vision of Jesus. During the height of the revival he often saw the awesome holiness of God come upon people, not only in meetings but also in the community, bringing multitudes to repentance and conversion.

Wherever he travelled, instead of bringing a song leader Finney brought a someone to pray, especially Daniel Nash, known as Father Nash. Finney taught theology at Oberlin College which pioneered co-education and enrolled both blacks and whites. His 'Lectures on Revival' were widely read and helped to fan revival fire in America and England.

Revival swept Great Britain also. During September 1857, the same month the Fulton Street meetings began, four young Irishmen commenced a weekly prayer meeting in a village school near Kells. That is generally seen as the start of the Ulster revival of 1859 which brought 100,000 converts into the churches of Ireland.

Through 1858 innumerable prayer meetings started, and revival was a common theme of preachers. God's Spirit moved powerfully in small and large gatherings bringing great conviction of sin, deep repentance, and lasting moral change. Prostrations were common - people lying prostrate in conviction and repentance, unable to rise for some time. By 1860 crime was reduced, judges in Ulster several times had no cases to try. At one time in County Antrim no crime was reported to the police and no prisoners were held in police custody.

Edwin Orr noted that this revival made a greater impact on Ireland than anything known since Patrick brought Christianity there. By the end of 1860 the effects of the Ulster revival were listed as thronged services, unprecedented numbers of communicants, abundant prayer meetings, increased family prayers, unmatched scripture reading, prosperous Sunday Schools, converts remaining steadfast, increased giving, vice abated, and crime reduced.

Revival fire ignites fire. Throughout 1859 the same deep conviction and lasting conversions revived thousands of people in Wales, Scotland and England.

Revival in Wales found expression in glorious praise including harmonies unique to the Welsh which involved preacher and people in turn. There too, 100,000 converts (one tenth of the total population) were added to the church and crime was greatly reduced.

Scotland and England were similarly visited with revival. Again, prayer increased enormously and preaching caught fire with many anointed evangelists seeing thousands converted. Charles Haddon Spurgeon, that prince of preachers, saw 1859 as the high water mark although he had already been preaching in London for five years with great blessing and huge crowds.

Twentieth Century

The early twentieth century revival was worldwide. It did not begin with the phenomenal Welsh revival of 1904-05 but began with prayer meetings which seemed to arise spontaneously all over the world.

Wales

The Welsh Revival was the farthest-reaching of the movements of the general Awakening, for it affected the whole of the Evangelical cause in India, Korea and China, renewed revival in Japan and South Africa, and sent a wave of awakening over Africa, Latin America, and the South Seas.

The story of the Welsh Revival is astounding. Begun with prayer meetings of less than a score of intercessors, when it burst its bounds the churches of Wales were crowded for more than two years. A hundred thousand outsiders were converted and added to the churches, the vast majority remaining true to the end. Drunkenness was immediately cut in half, and many taverns went bankrupt.

Crime was so diminished that judges were presented with white gloves signifying that there were no cases of murder, assault, rape or robbery or the like to consider. The police became 'unemployed' in many districts. Stoppages occurred in coal mines, not due to unpleasantness between management and workers, but because so many foul-mouthed miners became converted and stopped using foul language that the horses which hauled the coal trucks in the mines could no longer understand what was being said to them, and transportation ground to a halt (Orr 1975:193).

Touches of revival had stirred New Quay, Cardiganshire, where Joseph Jenkins was minister of a church in which he led teams of revived young people in conducting testimony meetings throughout the area. The Presbyterian evangelist, Seth Joshua, arrived there in September 1904 to find remarkable moves of the Spirit in his meetings.

On Sunday 18th, he reported that he had 'never seen the power of the Holy Spirit so powerfully manifested among the people as at this place just now.' His meetings lasted far into the night.

> 19th. Revival is breaking out here in greater power ... the young people receiving the greatest measure of blessing. They break out into prayer, praise, testimony and exhortation.
>
> 20th ... I cannot leave the building until 12 and even 1 o'clock in the morning - I closed the service several times and yet it would break out again quite beyond control of human power.
>
> 21st. Yes, several souls ... they are not drunkards or open sinners, but are members of the visible church not grafted into the true Vine ... the joy is intense.
>
> 22nd. We held another remarkable meeting tonight. Group after group came out to the front, seeking the 'full assurance of faith.'
>
> 23rd. I am of the opinion that forty conversions took place this week. I also think that those seeking assurance may be fairly counted as converts, for they had never received Jesus as personal Saviour before (Orr 1975c:3).

Seth Joshua then held meetings at Newcastle Emlyn at which students fromthe Methodist Academy attended, among them was Sidney Evans a room mate of Evan Roberts. The students, including Evan Roberts, attended the next Joshua meetings in Blaenannerch. There Seth Joshua closed his ministry on the Thursday morning crying out in Welsh, 'Lord ... bend us' Evan Robertswent to the front, kneeling and fervently praying 'Lord, bend me.'

Evan Roberts in his twenties was one of God's agents in that national and worldwide revival.

'For ten or eleven years I have prayed for revival,' he wrote to a friend. 'I could sit up all night to read or talk about revivals... It was the Spirit that moved me to think about a revival' (Orr 1975:4).

This young miner who then became a blacksmith had attended church as a teenager on Sunday, prayer meeting Monday, youth meeting Tuesday, congregational meeting Wednesday, temperance meeting Thursday, and class meeting Friday. Saturday night was free, probably as bath night in preparation for Sunday!

He offered for the ministry in 1903. Before entering the Academy he had a deep encounter with God and had a vision of all Wales being lifted up to heaven. After this he regularly slept lightly till 1 a.m., woke for hours of communion with God, and then returned to sleep. He was convinced revival would touch all Wales and eventually led a small band all over the country praying and preaching.

In October 1904 in his first year at the Academy, after the impact of the Spirit on him at Seth Joshua's meetings, he took leave to return home to challenge his friends, especially the young people.

The Spirit of God convicted people as Evan Roberts insisted:
1. You must put away any unconfessed sin.
2. You must put away any doubtful habit.
3. You must obey the Spirit promptly.
4. You must confess Christ publicly.

He believed that a baptism in the Spirit was the essence of revival and that the primary condition of revival is that individuals should experience such a baptism in the Spirit.

Evan Roberts travelled the Welsh valleys, often never preaching but sitting head-in-hands earnestly praying. In Neath he spent a week in prayer without leaving his rooms. The revival packed the churches out, but no one saw him all that week. He paid a price in prayer and tears.

Churches filled. The revival spread. Meetings continued all day as well as each night, often late into the night or through to morning. Crowds were getting right with God and with one another in confession, repentance and restitution of wrongs done. People prayed fervently and worshipped God with great joy.

Police had so little to do they joined the crowds in the churches, sometimes forming singing groups. Cursing and profanity diminished so much it caused slowdowns in the mines because the pit ponies could no longer understand their instructions and stood still, confused.

Oswald Smith described it this way:

It was 1904. All Wales was aflame. The nation had drifted far from God. The spiritual conditions were low indeed. Church attendance was poor and sin abounded on every side.

Suddenly, like an unexpected tornado, the Spirit of God swept over the land. The churches were crowded so that multitudes were unable to get in. Meetings lasted from ten in the morning until twelve at night. Three definite services were held each day.

Evan Roberts was the human instrument, but there was very little preaching. Singing, testimony and prayer were the chief features. There were no hymn books, they had learned the hymns in childhood; no choir, for everybody sang; no collection, and no advertising.

Nothing had ever come over Wales with such far-reaching results. Infidels were converted; drunkards, thieves and gamblers saved; and thousands reclaimed to respectability. Confessions of awful sins were heard on every side. Old debts were paid. The theatre had to leave for want of patronage. Mules in coal mines refused to work, being unused to kindness! In five weeks, twenty thousand people joined the churches (Olford 1968:67).

News of that revival, and many people who had been involved, soon spread around the world. 'The Welsh Revival was the farthest-reaching of the movements of the general Awakening, for it affected the whole of the Evangelical cause in India, Korea and China, renewed revival in Japan and South Africa, and sent a wave of awakening over Africa, Latin America, and the South Seas' (Orr 1975:193).

Half a century later a similar move of God, but on a smaller scale, was stirring the Hebrides.

Hebrides

Following the trauma of World War II, spiritual life was at a low ebb in the Scottish Hebrides. By 1949 Peggy and Christine Smith (84 and 82) had prayed constantly for revival in their cottage near Barvas village on the Isle of Lewis, the largest of the Hebrides Islands in the bleak north west of Scotland. God showed Peggy in a dream that revival was coming. Months later, early one winter's morning as the sisters were praying, God give them an unshakeable conviction that revival was near.

Peggy asked her minister James Murray Mackay to call the church leaders to prayer. Three nights a week the leaders prayed together for months. One night, having begun to pray at 10 p.m., a young deacon from the Free Church read Psalm 24 and challenged everyone to be clean before God. As they waited on God his awesome presence swept over them in the barn at 4 a.m.

Mackay invited Duncan Campbell to come and lead meetings. Within two weeks he came. God had intervened and changed Duncan's plans and commitments. At the close of his first meeting in the Presbyterian church in Barvas the travel weary preacher was invited to join an all night prayer meeting! Thirty people gathered for prayer in a nearby cottage. Duncan Campbell described it:

> God was beginning to move, the heavens were opening, we were there on our faces before God. Three o'clock in the morning came, and GOD SWEPT IN. About a dozen men and women lay prostrate on the floor, speechless. Something had happened; we knew that the forces of darkness were going to be driven back, and men were going to be delivered. We left the cottage at 3 a.m. to discover men and women seeking God. I walked along a country road, and found three men on their faces, crying to God for mercy. There was a light in every home, no one seemed to think of sleep (Whittaker 1984:159).

When Duncan and his friends arrived at the church that morning it was already crowded. People had gathered from all over the island, some coming in buses and vans. No one discovered who told them to come. God led them. Large numbers were converted as God's Spirit convicted multitudes of sin, many lying prostrate, many weeping. After that amazing day in the church, Duncan pronounced the benediction, but then a young man began to pray aloud. He prayed for 45 minutes. Again the church filled with people repenting and the service continued till 4 a.m. the next morning before Duncan could pronounce the benediction again.

Even then he was unable to go home to bed. As he was leaving the church a messenger told him, 'Mr. Campbell, people are gathered at the police station, from the other end of the parish; they are in great spiritual distress. Can anyone here come along and pray with them?' Campbell went and what a sight met him. Under the still starlit sky he found men and women on the road, others by the side of a cottage, and some behind a peat stack - all crying to God for mercy. The revival had come.

That went on for five weeks with services from early morning until late at night - or into the early hours of the morning. Then it spread to the neighbouring parishes. What had happened in Barvas was repeated over and over again. Duncan Campbell said that a feature of the revival was the overwhelming sense of the presence of God. His sacred presence was everywhere (Whittaker 1984:160).

That move of God in answer to prevailing prayer continued in the area into the fifties and peaked again on the previously resistant island of North Uist in 1957. Meetings were again crowded and night after night people cried out to God for salvation.

Similar revivals have catapulted the church into amazing growth throughout this century. The story is too vast to tell. A few highlights indicate something of this miraculous work of God.

North America

Many visitations of God have touched North America this century. Some, such as the following, have been widely reported.

Azusa Street, Los Angeles 1906-1913

William J. Seymour, a negro, studied in Charles Parham's Bible School in Topeka, Kansas where on 1 January 1901 Agnes Ozman had spoken in tongues as did half of the 34 students. Those events have been seen as the beginning of Pentecostalism in America.

Elder William Seymour began The Apostolic Faith Mission located at 312 Azusa Street in Los Angeles on Easter Saturday, 14 April 1906 with about 100 attending including blacks and whites. It grew out of a cottage prayer meeting.

At Azusa, services were long, and on the whole they were spontaneous. In its early days music was a cappella, although one or two instruments were included at times. There were songs, testimonies given by visitors or read from those who wrote in, prayer, altar calls for salvation or sanctification or for baptism in the Holy Spirit. And there was preaching. Sermons were generally not prepared in advance but were typically spontaneous J. Seymour was clearly in charge, but much freedom was given to visiting preachers. There was also prayer for the sick. Many shouted. Others were 'slain in the Spirit' or fell under the power. There were periods of extended silence and of singing in tongues. No offerings were collected, but there was a receptacle near the door for gifts...

Growth was quick and substantial. Most sources indicate the presence of about 300-350 worshippers inside the forty-by-sixty-foot white-washed wood-frame structure, with others mingling outside... At times it may have been double that.

The significance of Azusa was centrifugal as those who were touched by it took their experiences elsewhere and touched the lives of others. Coupled with the theological threads of personal salvation, holiness, divine healing, baptism in the Spirit with power for ministry, and an anticipation of the imminent return of Jesus Christ, ample motivation was provided to assure the revival a long-term impact' (Burgess & McGee 1988:31-36).

Asbury College, February 1970

A revival broke out in Asbury College in Wilmore, Kentucky, on Tuesday 3 February 1970. The regular morning chapel commencing at 10 o'clock saw God move on the students in such a way that many came weeping to the front to kneel in repentance, others gave testimonies including confession of sin, and all this was mixed with spontaneous singing. Lectures were cancelled for the day as the auditorium filled with over 1,000 people. Few left for meals. By midnight over 500 still remained praying and worshipping. Several hundred committed their lives to Christ that day. By 6 a.m. next morning 75 students were still praying in the hall, and through the Wednesday it filled again as all lectures were again cancelled for the day. The time was filled with praying, singing, confessions and testimonies.

As they continued in prayer that week many students felt called to share what was happening with other colleges and churches. Invitations were coming from around the country as news of the revival spread. So teams went out from the next weekend to tell the story and give their testimonies.
 Almost half the student body of 1000 was involved in the teams witnessing about the revival.

In the first week after the revival began teams of students visited 16 states by invitation and saw several thousand conversions through their witnessing. After six weeks over 1,000 teams had gone from the college to witness, some of these into Latin America with finance provided by the home churches of the students. In addition, the neighbouring Theological Seminary sent out several hundred teams of their students who had also been caught up in this revival.

Those remaining at the college prayed for the teams and heard their reports on their return. Wherever teams went the revival spread. The college remained a centre of the revival with meetings continuing at night and weekends there along with spontaneous prayer groups meeting every day. Hundreds of people kept coming to the college to see this revival and participate in it. They took reports and their own testimonies of changed lives back to their churches or colleges. So the revival spread.

The Jesus People, 1971

By June 1971 revival movements had spilled over into the society with thousands of young people gathering in halls and theatres to sing, witness and repent, quitting drugs and immorality. The pendulum had swung from the permissive hippie drop-outs of the sixties to a new wave of conversion and cleansing in the seventies. Time magazine carried a cover article on the Jesus Movement.

Such national attention also attracted cultic followers of the movement, but amid the extremes a powerful revival movement kept spreading. Mass baptisms were held in the ocean with outdoor meetings and teams witnessing on the beaches and in the city streets. New church groups such as Calvary Chapel and its many offshoots emerged which did not fit traditional denominations. People turned up to these churches in bare feet and old clothes as well as more traditional attire. Witnessing and evangelism burst spontaneously from lives changed by the love and power of God.

Canada, October 1971

Wilbert (Bill) McLeod, a Baptist minister in his mid-fifties, had seen many people healed in answer to prayer, often praying with a group of deacons. Bill invited the twin evangelists Ralph and Lou Sutera to speak at his church in Saskatoon. Revival broke out with their visit which began on Wednesday 13 October 1971. By the weekend an amazing spirit gripped the people. Many confessed their sins publicly. The first to do so were the twelve counsellors chosen to pray with enquirers. Numbers grew rapidly till the meetings had to be moved to a larger church building and then to the Civic Auditorium seating 2000. The movement spread to other churches.

The meetings lasted many hours. People did not want to leave. Some stayed on for a later meeting called the Afterglow. Here people received prayer and counsel from the group as they continued to worship God and pray together. Humble confession of sin and reconciliations were common. Many were converted.

Taxi drivers became amazed that people were getting cabs home from church late into the night or early into the morning. Others were calling for taxis to take them to church late into the night as they were convicted by the Lord.

Young people featured prominently. Almost half those converted were young. They gave testimonies of lives that had been cleaned up by God and how relationships with their families were restored. The atmosphere in schools and colleges changed from rebellion and cheating to co-operation with many Bible study and prayer groups forming in the schools and universities.

Criminals were also confessing their sins and giving themselves up to the police. Restitution was common. People prayed long overdue bills. Some businesses opened new accounts to account for the conscience money being paid to them. Those who cheated at restaurants or hotels returned to pay their full bill. Stolen goods were returned.

In November a team went to Winnipeg and told of the revival at a meeting for ministers. The Holy Spirit moved powerfully and many broke down confessing their sins. Rivalries and jealousies were confessed and forgiven. Many went home to put things right with their families. The ministers took this fire back into their churches and the revival spread there also with meetings going late into the night as numbers grew and hundreds were converted or restored.

Sherwood Wirt (1975:46) reported on Bill McLeod preaching at Winnipeg on 15 December 1971:

> I confess that what I saw amazed me. This man preached for only fifteen minutes, and he didn't even give an invitation! He announced the closing hymn, whereupon a hundred people came out of their seats and knelt at the front of the church. All he said was, That's right, keep coming!

> Many were young. Many were in tears. All were from the Canadian Midwest, which is not known for its euphoria.

> It could be said that what I was witnessing was revival. I believe it was.

Bill McLeod and a team of six brought the revival to the eastern Canada when they were invited to speak at the Central Baptist Seminary in Toronto. The meeting there began at 10 a.m. and went through till 1.15 a.m. next morning. Dinner was cancelled as no one wanted to leave. They did stop for supper, then went on again.

When the Sutera brothers commenced meetings in Vancouver on the West Coast on Sunday 5 May 1972 revival broke out there also in the Ebenezer Baptist Church with 2,000 attending that first Sunday. The next Sunday 3,000 people attended in two churches. After a few weeks five churches were filled.

The revival spread in many churches across Canada and into northern U S A especially in Oregon. Everywhere the marks of the revival included honesty before God and others, with confession of sin and an outpouring of the love of God in those who repented.

The German speaking churches were also touched by the revival and by May 1972 they chartered a flight to Germany for teams to minister there.

The Afterglow meetings were common everywhere in the revival. After a meeting had finished those who wanted to stay on for prayer did so. Usually each person desiring prayer knelt at a chair and others laid hands on them and prayed for them. Many repented and were filled with the Spirit in the Afterglow meetings which often went to midnight or later.

Vineyard Fellowships

In 1977 John Wimber began pastoring the fellowship of about 40 people which had been commenced by his wife, Carol. It later became the headquarters of the Vineyard Christian Fellowships. John preached from Luke's gospel and began to pray for healings with no visible results for nine months although the worship and evangelism attracted many people. Then healings began to happen and became a regular part of Vineyard ministry.

> In [1980] the congregation had an experience of corporate renewal. On the evening of Mothers' Day a young man who had been attending the church gave a testimony and asked those under twenty-five to come forward. He then invoked the Holy Spirit and the young people - about 400 of them - fell to the floor, weeping, wailing and speaking in tongues. Wimber and the rest of the congregation had never experienced anything like that before (Gunstone 1989:11).

A revival had begun. In the next four months they baptised 700 new converts. They began ministering in the Spirit's power in new ways and healings became a regular part of their church's life and their international teaching ministry. The church grew to 6,000 in a decade and commenced many other Vineyard fellowships.

Latin America

Peter Wagner's research describes Latin American Protestants growing from 50,000 in 1900 to over 5 million in the 1950s, over 10 million in the 1960s, over 20 million in the 1970s, around 50 million by the end of the eighties and over 137 million by 2000. Over 100 new churches begin every week.

Pentecostals are the biggest proportion of this growth. One quarter of the Protestants were Pentecostal by the 1950s; three quarters by the 1980s. By then 90% of Protestants in Chile were Pentecostal (Wagner 1986:27).

Edward Miller tells of revival breaking out in Argentina from 1948. After he prayed earnestly for months, God told him to call his little church of 8 people to prayer every night from 8 p.m. to midnight. On the fourth night as they obeyed God the Holy Spirit fell on them. They heard the sound of strong wind. The church soon filled. There was much weeping, confessing and praying. By Saturday teams were going out and ministering in the Spirit's power.
* Two teenage girls wept as they walked down the street and met two doctors who mocked, but listened to their testimonies, were convicted, and knelt asking for prayer.
* Two young people visited a lady whose mother was paralysed and had been in bed for 5 years. They prayed for her, and she got up and drank tea with them.
* Two elderly people visited man in coma, a cripple with his liver damaged from drink. They prayed for him and he was healed.

A young rebel, Alexander and his band came to mock at one of the services aiming to disrupt it. God convicted him and he repented, so the other rebels rose to leave but fell under the Spirit's power on the way out. All were converted. Two went to the Bible Training Institute.

Later, when Edward Miller was teaching at the Bible Training Institute in the small town of City Bell near Buenos Aires, he was led to cancel teaching there and call the school to prayer.

The move of God in that Institute began in an unusual way on 4 June 1951. Alexander, now in Bible School, was still in prayer outside in fields long after midnight when he sensed a strange feeling of something pressing down upon him, an great light surrounding him and a heavenly being enfolding him. The boy was terrified and fled back to the Institute.

The heavenly visitor entered the Institute with him, and in a few moments all the students were awake with the fear of God upon them. They began to cry out in repentance as God by his Spirit dealt with them. The next day the Spirit of God came again upon Alexander as he was given prophecies of God's moving in far off countries. The following day Alexander again saw the Lord in the Spirit, but this time he began to speak slowly and distinctly the words he heard from the angel of God. No one could understand what he was saying, however, until another lad named Celsio (with even less education than Alexander), overcome with the Spirit of God markedly upon him, began to interpret. These communications (written because he choked up when he tried to talk) were a challenge from God to pray and indeed the Institute became a centre of prayer till the vacation time, when teams went out to preach the kingdom. It was the beginning of new stirrings of the Spirit across the land (Pytches 1989:49-51).

The Bible Institute continued in prayer for 4 months, 8-10 hours a day, weeping. Bricks became saturated; one young man prayed against the wall daily, weeping. After 6 hours the tear stains reached the floor, and after 8 hours had formed a puddle on floor. The Lord gave them prophecies of revival in Argentina and around the world. They were told the largest auditoriums would be filled, and this happened with the visit of Tommy Hicks to Argentina.

Tommy Hicks was involved in revival in Latin America. In 1952 he was conducting a series of meetings in California when God showed him a vision. While he was praying he saw a map of South America covered with a vast field of golden wheat ripe for harvesting. The wheat turned into human beings calling him to come and help them.

He wrote in his Bible a prophecy he received about going by air to that land before two summers passed. Three months later, after an evangelistic crusade, a pastor's wife in California gave that same prophecy to him that he had written down. Cash began to arrive till he had enough to buy a one way air ticket to Buenos Aires. On his way there after meetings in Chile, the word Peron came to his mind. He asked the air stewardess if she knew what it meant. She told him Peron was the President of Argentina. After he made an appointment with the Minister of Religion, wanting to see the President, he prayed for the Minister's secretary who was limping. He was healed. So the Minister made an appointment for Hicks to see the President. Through prayer the President was healed of an ugly eczema and gave Hicks the use of a stadium and free access to the state radio and press. The crusade was a spiritual breakthrough.

Brazil also had revival. Edwin Orr visited each of the 25 states and territories in Brazil in 1952 seeing powerful moves of the spirit in his meetings which were supported by all denominations. The evangelical church council declared that the year of 1952 saw the first of such a general spiritual awakening in the country's history. Many meetings had to be moved into soccer stadiums, some churches increased in numbers by 50% in one week, and the revival movement continued in local churches in Brazil.

Many congregations in Latin America now are huge. By the eighties the Brazil for Christ Church in Sao Paulo seated 25,000 on a mile and a half of benches. The Jotabeche Methodist Pentecostal Church of Santiago in Chile has over 90,000 members. One of the largest fellowships in Argentina is the Vision of the Future church pastored by Omar and Marfa Cabrera and a committed team of leaders. They had 30,000 in 1979. That grew to over 145,000 by 1988. The Cabreras have a powerful personal and mass deliverance ministry, taking authority over demons in areas and in people.

Small rural churches spring up across the continent far outstripping the provision of trained leadership. By the 1960s the Presbyterians of Guatemala had initiated Theological Education by Extension, including weekly local seminars for on-the-job leadership development. This pattern is spreading worldwide in distance education programs.

1988 saw astounding revival in Cuba. The Pentecostals, Baptists, independent evangelical churches and some Methodist and Nazarene churches experienced powerful revival. One Assemblies of God church had around 100,000 visit it in six months, many coming in bus loads. One weekend they had 8,000 visitors, and on one day the four pastors (including two youth pastors) prayed with over 300 people.

In central Cuba, a miraculous healing took place at a 150-seat chapel at the beginning of a nine-day mission. The repercussions were so astounding that at one time 5,000 people crowded into the chapel. During those nine days, 1,200 people became Christians, and there were further healings. The two pastors were put in prison, but Cuban believers commented, 'Although the authorities stopped this crusade, they cannot stop the Holy Spirit.' Revival spread to the rest of Cuba (Mills 1990:18).

In many Pentecostal churches the lame walked, the blind saw, the deaf heard, and people's teeth were filled. Often 2,000 to 3,000 attended meetings. In one evangelical church over 15,000 people accepted Christ in three months. A Baptist pastor reported signs and wonders occurring continuously with many former atheists and communists testifying to God's power. So many have been converted that churches cannot hold them so they must met in house churches.

In Cuba in 1990, an Assemblies of God pastor whose congregation never exceeded 100 people meeting once a week suddenly found himself conducting 12 services per day for 7,000 people. They started queuing at 2.00 a.m. and even broke down doors just to get into the prayer meetings (Robinson 1992:14).

Africa

The church in Africa has grown from around 10 million in 1900 to over 200 million in the 1980s and over 300 million in the nineties. By 2000 that number passed 400 million, half the population. In the early 1900s one out of every 13,000 were Christians; now one out of three are reported as being Christians.

Africa has seen many powerful revivals, such as the Belgian Congo outpouring with C T Studd in 1914. 'The whole place was charged as if with an electric current. Men were falling, jumping, laughing, crying, singing, confessing and some shaking terribly,' he reported. 'As I led in prayer the Spirit came down in mighty power sweeping the congregation. My whole body trembled with the power. We saw a marvellous sight, people literally filled and drunk with the Spirit.'

Between 1946 and 1949 the Belgian Congo experienced a further visitation of God. It followed much prayer and fasting. Visions were common. Multitudes repented. Witch doctors burned their charms and became Christian.

Following independence in 1960 that country, then called Zaire, experienced a blood bath at the hands of rebels. Over 30 missionaries were martyred in Zaire in 1960-1965 as were hundreds of pastors and thousands of their members. Whole congregations were wiped out. In one place the Christians were driven into a church building and all burned alive. Yet the persecuted church of Zaire saw a remarkable revival. Born in agonising prayer and fanned by supernatural visitations of God, it grew in a powerful underground movement. The people, appalled at the killings, turned to God in thousands.

As the troubles subsided there was an extraordinary revival. More than one rebel said, 'The more we kill these Christians the more they multiply. They have got a power we haven't got.' Disillusioned with politics, there was a sudden wholesale turning to God among the people. A Congolese pastor revealed, 'During the long period when we were cut off from the missionaries we had a remarkable visitation of the Spirit of God. The pastors of our district had been fasting and praying because of the bloodshed and persecutions. As we were praying the Spirit descended on us in a wonderful way and His gifts operated among us. He told us many things in prophecy which have all come true. The Holy Spirit began to convict of sin as we went back to our churches to preach, and streams of men and women believed on the Lord Jesus and confessed their sins exactly as in Acts 19:17-20, bringing their heathen charms. This revival lasted eight months.' This was repeated throughout the great area of the Zaire Evangelical Mission; revival broke out everywhere and thousands upon thousands were converted and added to the churches (Whittaker 1984:117).

Similarly, persecution in Uganda for eight terrible years following Idi Amin's coup in 1971, saw the church refined and aflame. In those years the Christians increased from 52% to around 70% of the twelve million population.

Many African revivals experience supernatural manifestations, visions, prophecies, and healings. For 40 years there has been continuous revival in East Africa. Revivals include a powerful move of God in Ethiopia in 1978. Revived Christians survived the Mau Mau massacres in Kenya and the church continued to grow. For example, 700 new churches began in Kenya in 1980 alone, a rate of about two a day. Nigeria experienced revivals in 1983-1984, accelerating church growth there (Pratney 1984:267-8).

Outstanding leaders have emerged including men such as the Zulu Nicholas Bhengu. Fluent in Zulu, Xhosa, English and Afrikaans, this dynamic leader of the Back to God Crusade moved across southern Africa for 40 years and started over 1,000 churches through the mighty outpourings of the Holy Spirit.

Reinhard Bonnke, a German evangelist called to Africa, has led amazing crusades filled with the power of God in which thousands are converted, healed and delivered of evil spirits. His multi-racial team in Christ For All Nations crusades ministered in a 10,000-seater tent which was often too small. In 1980 alone 100,000 people made commitments to Christ in his crusades, and those huge numbers have continued and increased each year since. In 1983 he erected tent which seats 30,000 with which he plans to lead missions from Cape Town to Cairo.

The New Life for All movement challenges Christians to pray daily for ten people until each becomes a Christian. They tell those people of their daily prayers for them. As each is converted a new name is added to the list to keep it at ten. The new convert does the same, praying daily for ten others. That simple commitment has fuelled revival in Africa.

India

The turn of the century prepared the way for revival movements in India. From 1895 the first Saturday of each month was set aside in Bombay for prayer for revival, and other centres followed this pattern. Revival came in 1905, again linked with world wide outpourings as in Wales.

Distress caused by famine in 1904 also caused Christians to pray all over India. As news of revival in Wales reached India, and returning missionaries told of God's move there, expectation and prayer grew across India.

Revival moved in groups across Eastern India especially among the tribal people. Revival swept through the Khasi hills and among the Garos to their west and into the Naga Hills. It turned the hills people from head hunters into predominantly Christian within a generation. Bengal was also touched by the revival as news from the north motivated Christians to pray, repent and believe.

Any Carmichael wrote of revival in Dohnavur, especially among the young people. They experienced deep repentance and conversion in large numbers.

The awakening in Kerala among Anglicans and Mar Thoma Christians produced simultaneous audible prayer, alien to their normal traditions. At one convention 17,000 broke into simultaneous audible prayer.

Pandita Ramabai heard of revivals and commenced special prayer circles with hundreds of her helpers and friends at Mukti from the beginning of 1905. This movement spread first among the girls and women, touching thousands. It spilled over into the community. It spread with teams visiting Poona 40 miles away. Churches in Bombay were revived and filled with new vigour.

Revival affected India most strongly in the South and East, but North India also saw God's power change lives. John Hyde, known as Praying Hyde, spent days and nights in prayer with friends for revival in India. In schools, a seminary and then in conventions among the resistant Muslims, Sikhs and Hindus of North East India the revival spread. The Sialkot annual conventions grew in numbers and impact. A young Sikh named Sundar Singh had a vision of Jesus on 18 December 1904 and was converted. He became a Christian Sadhu mystic and evangelist in India and Tibet.

Orr (1975:156) notes that 'in the 1905 Revival, independence of the national Church was stressed, for, in the aftermath of revival, new men were ready for new work in new fields, men who had formerly been agents and employees of the Missions now were carrying revival and evangelism to the villages.'

Korea

The first Protestant missionaries went to Korea in the 1880s. By the 1980s one quarter of South Koreans were Christian. In 1980 Here's Life Korea crusade drew 2,700,000, the largest single Christian meetings in history.

Revival in Korea broke out in the nation in 1907. Presbyterian missionaries, hearing of revival in Wales, and of a similar revival among Welsh Presbyterian work in Assam, prayed earnestly for the same in Korea. 1500 representatives gathered for the annual New Year Bible studies in which a spirit of prayer broke out. The leaders allowed everyone to pray aloud simultaneously as so many were wanting to pray, and that became a characteristic of Korean prayer meetings.

The meetings carried on day after day, with confessions of sins, weeping and trembling. The heathen were astounded. The delegates of the New Year gathering returned to their churches taking with them this spirit of prayer which strongly impacted the churches of the nation with revival. Everywhere conviction of sin, confession and restitution were common.

Brutal persecution at the hands of the Japanese and then the Russian and Chinese communists saw thousands killed, but still the church grew in fervent prayer. Prior to the Russian invasion thousands of North Koreans gathered every morning at 5 a.m. Sometimes 10,000 were gathered in one place for prayer each morning.

Early morning daily prayer meetings became common, as did nights of prayer especially on Friday nights, and this emphasis on prayer has continued as a feature of church life in Korea. Over a million gather every morning around 5 a.m. for prayer in the churches. Prayer and fasting is normal. Churches have over 100 prayer retreats in the hills called Prayer Mountains to which thousands go to pray, often with fasting. Healings and supernatural manifestations continue.

Now the city of Seoul has 6,000 churches, many huge. Koreans have sent over 10,000 missionaries into other Asian countries.

Paul Yonggi Cho has amazing growth in Seoul where he is senior pastor of a Full Gospel church of 800,000 with over 25,000 home cell groups, and 12,000 conversions reported every month. During the week over 3,000 a day and over 5,000 at weekends pray at their prayer mountain.

China

In 1950, missionaries expelled from China left behind one million evangelical Christians, and three million Catholics. Conservative figures run from 50 to 80 million Christians in China now and some Asian researchers report 100 million Christians estimated out of 960 million population. This underground revival spread through thousands of house churches. Miracles, healings, visions and supernatural interventions of God marked this outpouring of the Spirit.

Many suffered and died in persecution. David Wong tells of a pastor imprisoned for over 22 years who left behind a church of 150 people scattered through the hill villages in northern China. On his release in the 1980s he discovered the church in that area had grown to 5,000. Three years later it had trebled to 15,000.

Mama Kwong, exiled in Japan because of her virile Christian leadership, tells how over 30 years she helped to lead one million to the Lord through preaching and home cell meetings. She was imprisoned three times. Such leaders often faced long imprisonment or martyrdom, and her own son and others were nailed alive to church walls. The blood of the martyrs is still the seed of the church in China.

> Mama Kwong says that during those days [1960s], God chose 300 dedicated Christians to start a new church. As they gathered at 3 a.m. one morning, they saw a vision of the Lord and clearly heard His voice saying, 'Although Communism is evil, I will open the door and no-one will shut it.' As the 300 went out and shared the gospel, tremendous miracles began to happen. Whole towns and villages turned to Christ' (Whittaker 1984:153).

A Hong Kong and China Report of March 1991 produced by the Revival Christian Church tells of continuing opposition and imprisonment, but also of astounding church growth.

In 1989 preachers from Henan province visited North Anhul province and found several thousand believers in care of an older pastor from Shanghai. On the first night of their meetings that winter with 1,000 present 30 people were baptised. First was a lady who had convulsions if she went into cold water. She was healed of that and other ills and found the water warm. A twelve year old boy, deaf and dumb, was baptised and spoke, 'Mother, Father, the water is not cold - the water is not cold.' A lady nearly 90, disabled after an accident in her twenties, was completely healed in the water. By the third and fourth night over 1,000 were baptised.

A young man who has been leading teams since he was 17, reported in 1990 at the age of 20: 'When the church first sent us out to preach the

Gospel, after two to three months of ministering we usually saw 20-30 converts. But now it is not 20. It is 200, 300, and often 600 or more will be converted.'

In 12 March 1991, the South China Morning Post, acknowledged there were one million Christians in central Henan province, many having made the previously unheard of decision to voluntarily withdraw from the party. 'While political activities are cold-shouldered, religious ones are drawing large crowds.'

Asia Outreach reported that Outer Mongolia had four known Christians by the beginning of 1991. That grew to over 70 by August, and many churches and a Bible school have been established since then.

Russia

In 1990, the Soviet Union acknowledged before its demise that 90 million of its 290 million inhabitants confess allegiance to a church or religious community. Christians have estimated over 97 million were Christian (Pratney 1984:273).

Sergie Kordakov, a teenage thug leader of tough marines, worked for the KGB including breaking up house churches or Christian home groups, arresting the pastors and beating the Christians, especially any young people found there. He was eventually converted through the witness of a young girl Natasha who kept coming to home groups inspite of being bashed. He noted how a secret revival was sweeping Russia involving many young people as well as older Christians.

Another young man, Vanya saw God's miraculous protection and intervention in his military service where he unashamedly witnessed to his faith in God, before his mysterious death..

The earnest prayers of suffering Christians through most of this century has been a significant part in more recent freedom to worship God experienced in Russia and its neighbours. Reports from Russia have included huge numbers turning to Christ recently. In 1991, for example, 70,000 out of 90,000 made commitments to Christ in an evangelism rally in Leningrad. Churches are packed. All available Bibles were sold. In 1992 David

Yonggi Cho preached in eastern Russia with 35,000 making commitments to Christ (see D Y Cho, "Speaking God's Word" in Issue 8: Awakening).

Nepal (Himalayas)

Nepal has been traditionally resistant to Christianity. That is changing. David Wang (Asian Report, May/June 1991) tells of a former Lama priest, illiterate, who has been a pastor for 13 years and pastors 43 fellowships with total of 32,000 people. Another pastor oversees 40,000 people. Most conversions in Nepal involve casting out demons.

Burma

Missionaries were expelled from Burma in the 1960s but the church continues to grow. The largest known baptismal service in the world happened there at the Kachin Baptist Centenial Convention in 1977 with 6,000 baptised in one day.

Cambodia

In September 1973 Todd Burke arrived in Cambodia on a one week visitor's visa. Just 23 years old, he felt a strong call from God to minister there, the only charismatic missionary in the country. Beginning with two English classes a day, conducted through an interpreter, he taught from the Good News Bible. Those interested in knowing more about Jesus stayed after class and he saw daily conversions and people filled with the Spirit and healed. Revival broke out in the war torn capital of Phnom Penh and rapidly spread to surrounding areas.

During that September Todd's wife DeAnn joined him, they received permission to stay in the country, and mounted a three day crusade in a stadium where thousands attended and hundreds were saved and healed supernaturally. A powerful church spread through a network of small house churches. Todd met with the leaders of these groups at early morning prayer meetings every day at 6 a.m. Most pastors were voluntary workers holding normal jobs. Some cycled in from the country and returned for work each morning. Healings, miracles and deliverance from demonic powers were regular events, attracting new converts who in turn were filled with the power of the Spirit and soon began witnessing and praying for others.

87

When the country fell to the communists in 1975 the Burkes had to leave. They left behind an amazing church anointed by the power of God before it was buried by going underground to survive. They recorded their story of those two years of revival in Anointed for Burial (1977).

Indonesia

The Spirit of God brought revival to Indonesia during the troubled and politically uncertain times there in the sixties. Much of it happened outside the established church, with a later acceptance of it in some churches. Thousands of Moslems were converted, the biggest Christian impact on Islam in history.

A Bible School in East Java experienced revival with deep repentance, confession, renunciation of occult practices, burnings of fetishes and amulets and a new humility and unity among staff and students. The Lord led individual students and teams in powerful evangelism in many islands.

A team visited Timor and saw evidences of revival beginning which burst into unprecedented power in September 1965. This revival spread in the uncertain days following the attempted army coup on 30 September, 1965 in Indonesia. Four days previously a visitation from God had begun in Timor.

A rebellious young man had received a vision of the Lord who commanded him to repent, burn his fetishes, and confess his sins in church. He did. He attended the Reformed Church in Soe, a mountain town of about 5,000 people, where the revival broke out at that service on Sunday 26 September 1965. People heard the sound of a tornado wind. Flames on the church building prompted police to set off the fire alarm to summon the volunteer fire fighters. Many people were converted that night. Many were filled with the Spirit including speaking in tongues, some in English. By midnight teams of lay people had been organised to begin spreading the gospel the next day. They gave themselves full time to visiting churches and villages and saw thousands converted with multitudes healed and delivered. In one town alone they saw 9,000 people converted in two weeks.

Another young man, Mel Tari witnessed this visitation of God and later became part of Team 42. Eventually, about 90 evangelistic teams were formed which functioned powerfully with spiritual gifts. Healings and evangelism increased dramatically. Specific directions from the Lord led the teams into powerful ministry with thousands becoming Christians. They saw many healings, miracles such as water being turned to non-alcoholic wine for communion, some instantaneous healings, deliverance from witchcraft and demonic powers, and some people raised from death through prayer.

The teams were often guided supernaturally including provision of light at night on jungle trails, angelic guides and protection, meagre supplies of food multiplied in pastors' homes when a team ate together there during famines, and witch doctors being converted after they saw power encounters when the teams' prayers banished demons rendering the witch doctors powerless.

The teams learned to listen to the Lord and obey him. His leadings came in many biblical ways:
1. God spoke audibly as with Samuel or Saul of Tarsus,
2. many had visions as did Mary or Cornelius,
3. there were inspired dreams such as Jacob, Joseph or Paul saw,
4. prophecies as in Israel and the early church occurred,
5. the Spirit led many as with Elijah or Paul's missionary team,
6. the Lord often spoke through specific Bible verses,
7. circumstances proved to be God-incidences not just co-incidences,
8. often when leadings were checked with the group or the church the Lord gave confirmations and unity.

Mel Tari, Kurt Koch and others have told of the amazing revival in Indonesia. The Reformed Church Presbytery on Timor, for example, recorded 80,000 conversions from the first year of the revival there, half of those being former communists. They noted that some 15,000 people had been permanently healed in that year. After three years the number of converts had grown to over 200,000. On another island where there had been very few Christians 20,000 became believers in the first three years of the revival.

So often in times of great tribulation, political upheaval and bloodshed, the Spirit of the Lord moves most powerfully and the church grows most rapidly, as happens in many countries today.

Pacific Islands

Revival has been spreading in Pacific islands, especially in the Solomon Islands. Teams have gone from there to other countries such as Papua New Guinea and helped to light revival fires around the Pacific.

Solomon Islands, July 1970

Muri Thompson, a Maori evangelist from New Zealand, visited the Solomons in July and August 1970 where the church had already experienced significant renewal and was praying for revival.

Many of these Christians were former warriors and cannibals gradually won to Christ in spite of initial hostility and the martyrdom of early missionaries and indigenous evangelists.

Beginning at Honiara, the capital, Muri spent two months visiting churches and centres on the islands. Initially the national leaders and missionaries experienced deep conviction and repentance, publicly acknowledging their wrong attitudes. It was very humbling. A new unity and harmony transformed their relationships, and little things which destroyed that unity were openly confessed with forgiveness sought and given.

Then in the last two weeks of these meetings the Spirit of God moved even more powerfully in the meetings with more deep repentance and weeping, sometimes even before the visiting team arrived. At one meeting the Spirit of God came upon everyone after the message in a time of silent prayer when the sound of a gale came above the gathering of 2000 people.

Multitudes were broken, melted and cleansed, including people who had been strongly opposed to the Lord. Weeping turned to joyful singing. Everywhere people were talking about what the Lord had done to them. Many received healings and deliverance from bondage to evil spirits. Marriages were restored and young rebels transformed.

Everywhere people were praying together every day. They had a new hunger for God's Word. People were sensitive to the Spirit and wanted to be transparently honest and open with God and one another.

Normal lectures in the South Seas Evangelical Church Bible School were constantly abandoned as the Spirit took over the whole school with times of confession, prayer and praise.

Teams from these areas visited other islands, and the revival caught fire there also. Eventually pastors from the Solomons were visiting other Pacific countries and seeing similar moves of God there.

Western Highlands, PNG, September 1973

Prayer meetings began among pastors, missionaries and Bible College students in the Baptist mission area among Engas of the Western Highlands of Papua New Guinea in the early 1970s owing to the low spiritual state in the churches.

This prayer movement spread to the villages. In some villages people agreed to pray together everyday until God sent new life to the church.

During September 1973 pastors from the Solomon Islands and Enga students who were studying at the Christian Leaders Training College visited the Enga churches.

Revival broke out in many villages on Sunday 16 September. Many hundreds of people, deeply convicted of sin, repented and were reconciled to God and others with great joy.

Pastors in one area held a retreat from Monday to Wednesday in a forest which previously had been sacred for animistic spirit worship. Others joined the pastors there. Healings reported included a lame man able to walk, a deaf mute who spoke and heard, and a mentally deranged girl restored.

Normal work stopped as people in their thousands hurried to special meetings. Prayer groups met daily, morning and evening.

In the following months thousands of Christians were restored and thousands of pagans converted. The church grew in size and maturity (Vision magazine, 1973:4-6).

Duranmin, PNG, March 1977

Pastors from the Solomon Islands spoke about their revival at a pastors and leaders conference in the highlands of Papua New Guinea. Diyos Wapnok attended from the Baptist Mission area at Telefolmin. He heard God call his name three times in the night there and realised that the Lord was drawing his attention to some special challenge.

Later, on Thursday afternoon 10 March, 1977 at Duranmin in the rugged western highlands, where Diyos was the principal of the Sepik Baptist Bible College, while he spoke to about 50 people they were all filled with the Holy Spirit and great joy. Revival had begun. It spread through the area with vibrant new enthusiasm. Conversions, Bible studies, prayer and healings of many kinds were common. 3,000 were added to the church in 3 years. The church grew and was strengthened. This revival movement spread to other areas as Diyos and others told of what God was doing.

Sepik, PNG, 1984

In the Sepik lowlands of northern Papua New Guinea a new visitation of God burst on the churches at Easter 1984, again sparked by Solomon Island pastors. It too was characterised by repentance, confession, weeping and great joy. Stolen goods were returned or replaced, and wrongs made right.

Ray Overend reports (1985:9-10):

I was preaching to an Easter convention at a place called Walahuta during the recent Sepik revival in Papua New Guinea. The words the Lord gave us were from Isaiah 6 ...

After the last word of the message the whole church rose to its feet and clapped loudly - something completely new to me! I knew they were not applauding me. They were acknowledging to God in praise the truth of his Word... Then I sat down in the only spare little space in the overcrowded church and the whole congregation began to sing - one song after another...

Many faces were lifted to Heaven and many hands raised in humble adoration. The faces looked like the faces of angels. They were radiating light and joy. And then I noticed something.

Right beside me was a man who had heard the Word and now he just watched those radiant faces lost in praise. Then he hung his head and began to sob like a child. He was ministered to. Demons were cast out. And he received the Lord Jesus right into his heart. Then he too began to clap in gentle joy.

But who was he? A pastor came over to tell me that he had been until this moment the leader of the Tambaran cult in the Walahuta area - that Satanic cult of which the whole village lived in mortal fear - and traditionally the whole of the Sepik

The man who was second-in-charge of the Tambaran cult in that area was also converted that day while he was listening to the worship from a distance as God's love and power overcame him. Ray continues:

I will never forget June 14th, 1984. Revival had broken out in many churches around but Brugam itself [the headquarters], with many station staff and many Bible College and Secondary School students, was untouched. ... Then early on Thursday night, the 14th, Judah Akesi, the Church Superintendent, invited some of us to his office for prayer. During that prayer time God gave him a vision. In the vision he saw many people bowed down in the front of the church building in the midst of a big light falling down from above just like rain.

So after the ministry of the Word that night Judah invited those who wanted to bring their whole heart and mind and life under the authority of Christ to come forward so that hands might be laid on them for prayer.

About 200 people surged forward. Many fell flat on their faces on the ground sobbing aloud. Some were shaking - as spiritual battles raged within. There was quite some noise...

The spiritual battles and cries of contrition continued for a long time. Then one after another in a space of about 3 minutes everybody rose to their feet, singing spontaneously as they rose. They were free. The battle was won. Satan was bound. They had made Christ their King! Their faces looked to Heaven as they sang. They were like the faces of angels. The singing was like the singing of Heaven. Deafening, but sweet and reverent (Overend 1986:36-37).

The whole curriculum and approach at the Bible School for the area changed. Instead of traditional classes and courses, teachers would work with the school all day from prayer times early in the morning through Bible teaching followed by discussion and sharing times during the day to evening worship and ministry. The school became a community, seeking the Lord together.

Churches which have maintained a strong Biblical witness continue to stay vital and strong in evangelism and ministry, filled with the Spirit's power. Christians learn to witness and minister in spiritual gifts, praying and responding to the leading of the Spirit.

Many received spiritual gifts they never had before. One such gift was the 'gift of knowledge' whereby the Lord would show Christians exactly where fetishes of 'sanguma' men were hidden. Now in Papua New Guinea sanguma men (who subject themselves to indescribable ritual to be in fellowship with Satan) are able to kill by black magic... In fact the power of sanguma in the East Sepik province has been broken (Overend 1986:23-24).

In 1986 a senior pastor from Manus Island came to the Sepik to attend a one year's pastors' course. He was filled with the Spirit.

Shortly afterwards he went to Ambunti with a team of students on outreach. There they were asked to pray for an injured child who couldn't walk - and later in the morning he saw her walking around the town. He came back to his course and said: 'In my 35 years as a pastor on Manus I had never seen the power of God like that!' (Overend 1986:38).

North Solomons, 1988

Jobson Misang, an indigenous youth worker in the United Church and former student of Alcorn College in Brisbane (now incorporated in Trinity Theological College) wrote a letter reporting on a further revival movement in the North Solomons Province of Papua New Guinea in 1988:

Over the last eight weekends I have been fully booked to conduct weekend camps. So far about 3,500 have taken part in the studies of the 'Living in the Spirit' book. Over 2,000 have given their lives to Jesus Christ and are committed to live by the directions of the Spirit. This is living the Pentecost experience today!

These are some of the experiences taking place:

1. During small group encounters, under the directions of Spirit-filled leadership, people are for the first time identifying their spiritual gifts, and are changing the traditional ministry to body ministry.

2. Under constant prayers, visions and dreams are becoming a day to day experience which are being shared during meetings and prayed about.

3. Local congregations are meeting at 4 a.m. and 6 a.m. three days a week to pray, and studying the Scriptures is becoming a day to day routine. This makes Christians strong and alert.

4. Miracles and healings are taking place when believers lay hands on the sick and pray over them.

5. The financial giving of the Christians is being doubled. All pastors' wages are supported by the tithe.

6. Rascal activities (crimes) are becoming past time events and some drinking clubs are being overgrown by bushes.

7. The worship life is being renewed tremendously. The traditional order of service is being replaced by a much more lively and participatory one. During praise and worship we celebrate by clapping, dancing, raising our hands to the King of kings, and we meditate and pray. When a word of knowledge is received we pray about the message from the Lord and encourage one another to act on it with sensitivity and love.

Problems encountered include division taking place within the church because of believers baptism, fault finding, tongues, objections to new ways of worship, resistance to testimonies, loss of local customs such as smoking or chewing beetle nut or no longer killing animals for sacrifices, believers spending so many hours in prayer and fasting and Bible studies, marriages where only one partner is involved and the other blames the church for causing divisions, pride creeping in when gifts are not used sensitively or wisely, and some worship being too unbalanced.

Eastern Highlands, P.N.G, 1988-1989

Johan van Bruggen, principal of a Lutheran Evangelist Training Centre near Kainantu in the Papua New Guinea highlands reported in newsletters on the beginnings of revival in their area:

There came Thursday 4 August, a miserable day weather wise, although we had great joy during our studies. Evening devotions - not all students came, actually a rather small group. I too needed some inner encouragement to go as it was more comfortable near the fire.

We sang a few quiet worship songs. ... Samson was leading the devotions. We had sung the last song and were waiting for him to start. Starting he did, but in an unusual way. He cried, trembled all over! ... Then it spread. When I looked up again I saw the head prefect flat on the floor under his desk. I was praying in tongues off and on. It became quite noisy. Students were shouting! Should I stop it? Don't hold back! It went on and one, with students praying and laughing and crying - not quite following our planned programme! We finally stood around the table, about twelve of us, holding hands. Some were absolutely like drunk, staggering and laughing! I heard a few students starting off in tongues and I praised the Lord. The rain had stopped, not so the noise. So more and more people came in and watched!

Not much sleeping that night! They talked and talked! And that was not the end. Of course the school has changed completely. Lessons were always great, I thought, but have become greater still. Full of joy most of the time, but also with a tremendous burden. A burden to witness.

What were the highlights of 1988?

No doubt the actual outpouring of the Holy Spirit must come first. It happened on August 4 when the Spirit fell on a group of students and staff, with individuals receiving the baptism of the Holy Spirit on several occasions later on in the year. The school has never been the same again. As direct results we noticed a desire for holiness, a hunger for God's Word which was insatiable right up till the end of the school year, and also a tremendous urge to go out and witness. Whenever they had a chance many of our students were in the villages with studies and to lead Sunday services. Prayer life deepened, and during worship services we really felt ourselves to be on holy ground.

[In 1989] Our 35 new students were again fascinated by the new life they discovered among the second year students. The Word of God did the rest. During the month of March real repentance took place. One week before Easter the Holy Spirit moved mightily among the students and staff. There was a lot of crying during that week. Each night the students met in small prayer groups. The aim was to get them prepared to go out to seven small Easter camps that were planned for the Gazup area - our area here around the school.

God's Spirit really prepared them well! I have never seen and heard so much crying. Many students had listed all their sins. I must confess that some of these lists really shook me. There was witchcraft, magic, adultery, stealing, drunkenness. It once again showed me how deep and far the world has invaded the church today. There was tremendous relief as students were assured of forgiveness and were filled with the Holy Spirit.'

An example of how God used these students is the account of a young man, David, Markham Valley of the Eastern Highlands in Papua New Guinea who was studying at the Training School. He had a growing burden for his village of Waritzian which was known and feared as the centre of pagan occult practices.
During his studies he was concerned for his people who were not ready for the Lord's return. He prayed much. As part of an outreach team he visited nearby villages and then went to his own people in May, 1989. They had already written to the Training School asking for him to come to teach them. He was concerned about the low spiritual life of the church. He spent a couple of days alone praying for them.

Then as he was teaching them they heard the sound of an approaching wind which filled the place. Many were weeping, confessing their sins. They burnt their fetishes used in sorcery. This had been a stronghold of those sanguma practices. Many people received various spiritual gifts including unusual abilities such as speaking English in tongues and being able to read the Bible. People met for prayer, worship and study every day and at night. These daily meetings continued.

Vanuatu, 1961-62, 1991-92

Paul Grant was involved in the early stirrings of revival in Vanuatu during 19961-2. He writes:

> It is important to note the following components in the lead-up to later visitation and reviving:
>
> 1. A shared concern of missionaries for revival.
> 2. A significantly developed interest in the quickening power of the Spirit among west Ambai church members and leaders through teaching of the Scriptures and news of revival and the power-works of the Spirit in other parts of the world, e.g. a Series of talks on the East Africa revival, the Welsh revival, signs and wonders and healings as reported from the Apostolic Church in Papua New Guinea, and inspiring records in other magazines.
> 3. An emphasis on prayer meetings, both between missionaries and in local churches.
> 4. Regular and frequent prayers for a visitation of God's Spirit by Apostolic Churches around the world. The first Monday night of each month was observed as a prayer night for worldwide missions.
> 5. Concentrated, sustained Scripture teaching in the classrooms of the primary school where students later would experience the power of God. ...

> Beginning in the Santo church on August 15th 1962 and continuing there and in churches on Ambae (commencing in Tafala village in October) over a period of about 12 weeks the power of God moved upon young people. There were many instances of glossolalia, healings, prophetic utterances, excitation, loud acclamations to God in public services, incidents of deep conviction of sin, conversions, restitutions, and other manifestations of holiness of life...

> This visitation resulted in a liveliness not known before. Initially it was mainly among young people. In later months and years it spread among all age groups and to my present knowledge was the first

such visitation in the history of the Christian Church in Vanuatu. My gratification centred upon the following particulars:

1. The Holy Spirit had animated and empowered a people who were well taught in the Scriptures. Records show a lift in spiritual vitality in all the village churches.
2. It brought the church as a whole into a more expressive, dynamic dimension and also a charismatic gift function. They were much more able to gain victory over spirit forces so familiar to them.
3. It began to hasten the maturation processes in developing leadership.
4. The reality matched the doctrinal stand of the church. There was now no longer a disparity.
5. It confirmed to me the very great importance of being 'steadfast, unmoveable, always abounding in the work of the Lord forasmuch as you know that your labour is not in vain in the Lord' (1 Corinthians 15:58 AV).
6. It led to significant outreach in evangelism, both personal and group. ...

In the following years some of the young men and women served God in evangelistic teams, school teaching, urban witness, government appointments, and as pastors and elders to their own people. One of them has with his wife been an effective missionary... in Papua New Guinea (Grant 1986:7-10).

More recent revival movements in Vanuatu have stirred parts of the church there, such as described in this letter from Ruth Rongo of Tongoa Island (another former student of Trinity Theological College) written on 28 August 1991:

I've just come back from an evangelism ministry. It lasted for three months. God has done many miracles. Many people were shocked by the power of the Holy Spirit. The blind received their sight, the lame walk, the sick were healed. All these were done during this evangelism ministry. We see how God's promise came into action. The prophet Joel had said it. We people of Vanuatu say 'The spirit of the Lord God is upon us because he has anointed us to preach the Gospel to the poor people of Vanuatu.' Praise God for what he has done. In where I live, my poor home, I also started a home cell prayer group. We're aiming or our goal is that the revival must come in the church where I am. Please pray for me and also for the group.

Our prayer group usually meets on Sunday night, after the night meeting. We start at 10.30 p.m. and go to 1 or 3.30 a.m. If we come closer to God He will also come close to us. We spend time in listening and responding to God.

These revival movements continue to increase in the Pacific, especially as indigenous teams minister in other areas with the Spirit's fire. The church grows stronger, even through opposition. Indigenous Christians live and minister in New Testament patterns from house to house, from village to village. See G Waugh's articles and *South Pacific Revivals* for updates.

Australia

Powerful moves of God's Spirit in Australia have included the Sunshine Revival in Melbourne from February 1925 and the aboriginal revival beginning in Galiwin'ku (Elcho Island) from March 1979.

Sunshine, February 1925

Two young men in their twenties led the Sunshine Revival. Charles Greenwood began prayer meetings in his home in 1916 and the group completed building the Sunshine Gospel Hall in February 1925. A. C. Valdez, recently arrived from America, joined the group and became its leader that year. At first meetings were held on a Saturday and Sunday. Then they had a two week campaign. The hall was packed.
Charles Greenwood reported:

> During this campaign the power of God was manifested in a mighty way - sinners were converted; many believers were baptised in the Holy Spirit and healed. Soon the news spread that the Lord was pouring out His Spirit at Sunshine, and people came from near and far. Over 200 Christians from all denominations were baptised in the Holy Spirit in this blessed outpouring of the 'Latter Rain' (Chant 1984:90-91).

They established the Pentecostal Church of Australia following that campaign and public meetings were then held in the Prahran Town Hall because of the crowds. Later that year they moved into Richmond Theatre which became Richmond Temple. It could seat 1200 and had shops at the front which became their Bible and Tract Department. In 1926 A. C. Valdez believed his work there was completed and he returned to the States. Kelso Glover, also in his twenties, arrived from the States and led meetings for three weeks in a revival atmosphere. He was invited to stay on as pastor. Richmond Temple became the headquarters of the Pentecostal Church of Australia and from July 1926 they produced their national paper the *Australian Evangel.*

Galiwin'ku (Elcho Island), March 1979

Revival among aborigines commenced in Galiwin'ku (Elcho Island) from 1979. Djiniyini Gondarra ministered there where half the island became involved in the church and the whole community was affected. The pattern is similar to other revivals - prayer and expectation, the Spirit of God moving in new and powerful ways, repentance and confession on a wide scale, restitution of stolen goods and money, forgiveness and reconciliation between people, crime and drunkenness greatly diminished, renewed concern for justice and righteousness in the community, churches filled with Christians alive in the Spirit. Here too, teams have travelled to other areas bringing some of the fire of revival to ignite churches and communities with a vital Christian commitment and a strong impact on society.

What is our response to these modern day accounts so similar to the Book of Acts? Will we humble ourselves, and pray, and seek God's face, and turn from our sin, so that God will forgive us and heal the land (2 Chronicles 7:14)?

We can do that. We must. Alone. In prayer clusters. In home groups. In meetings. In constant prayer and repentance.

'Lord, engulf us in your holy fire. Burn our dross. Refine us. Ignite us, and multitudes in the land, for your glory, setting your church on fire.'

References

Burke, T & D (1977) *Anointed for Burial.* Seattle: Frontline.

Burgess, S M & McGee, G B eds. (1988) *Dictionary of Pentecostal and Charismatic Movements*. Grand Rapids: Zondervan.

Chant, B (1984) *Heart of Fire*. Adelaide: Tabor.

Grant, P E (1986) 'Visitation and Vivifying in Vanuatu', unpublished article.

Greenfield, J (1927) *Power from on High*. London: Marshall, Morgan & Scott.

Gunstone, J (1989) *Signs and Wonders*. London: Daybreak.

Hession, R (1973) *The Calvary Road*. London: Christian Literature Crusade.

Howard, P E (1949) *The Life and Diary of David Brainerd*. Baker (1989).

Hughes, S (1990) *Revival: Times of Refreshing*. London: CWR.

Koch, K (n.d.) *The Revival in Indonesia*. Evangelization Publishers.

Koch, K (1973) *Revival Fires in Canada*. Grand Rapids: Kregel

Mills, B (1990) *Preparing for Revival*. Eastbourne: Kingsway.

Olford, S F (1968) *Heart-cry for Revival*. Westwood: Revell

Orr, J E (1975) *The Flaming Tongue* (1900-). Chicago: Moody.

Overend, R (1986) *The Truth will Set you Free*. Laurieton: SSEM.

Pratney, W (1984) *Revival*. Springdale: Whitaker House.

Pytches, D (1989) *Does God Speak Today?* London: Hodder & Stoughton

Robinson, S (1992) 'Praying the Price'. Melbourne: ABMS

Tari, M (1971) *Like a Mighty Wind*. Carol Springs: Creation House.

Tari, M & N (1974) *The Gentle Breeze of Jesus*. Carol Springs: Creation House.

Wagner, C P (1983) *On the Crest of the Wave*. Glendale: Regal

Wagner, C P (1986) *Spiritual Power and Church Growth*. London: Hodder & Stoughton.

Wallis, A (1965) *In the Day of Thy Power*. London: Christian Literature Crusade.

Whittaker, C (1984) *Great Revivals*. Basingstoke: Marshalls.

Wirt, S (1975) *Knee-Deep in Love*. London: Coverdale

Vision Magazine, Australian Baptist Missionary Society, Dec. 1973.

See further updates in later issues of the *Renewal Journal,* and on *renewaljournal.com*

Reviews

Prayer: Key to Revival, by David Yonggi Cho.
Waco: Word, 1984, 158 pages.

Prayer: Key to Revival, by David Yonggi Cho, describes many ways to pray effectively. Coming out of the Korean church scene where early morning prayer meetings, nights of prayer, and prayer mountains set apart for continual prayer and fasting are common, it reflects a strong commitment to prayer still rare in the West.

Sections in the book cover motivation to pray, types of prayer (petition, devotion, intercession), different forms of prayer, and methods of prayer. It has chapters on personal devotional life, family devotions, church meetings, cell groups, prayer retreats, all-night prayer meetings, fasting, waiting on the Lord, persistence, prayer in the Holy Spirit, faith, listening to God, group prayer and powerful prayer.

This is essential reading for anyone serious about Christian living, discipleship and leadership. It is one of the best handbooks on prayer available today. Paul Yonggi Cho spends five hours a day in prayer. He requires that all his leaders and staff in their church of over 800,000 people pray for at least three hours a day. No wonder theyre experiencing revival with around 12,000 converts every month.

Filled with personal examples it is fascinating and timely. It challenges us to believe God and act on that belief as we pray. Read it for enjoyment. Study it for key insights. Apply it to ministry.

Dictionary of Pentecostal and Charismatic Movements,
edited by S M Burgess and G B McGee.
Grand Rapids: Zondervan, 1988; with corrections 1990. 914 pages.

Every church and college library should have this comprehensive single volume encyclopaedia. The 800 articles written by 65 contributors make it the best reference work on Pentecostalism and charismatic renewal available.

Both a strength and a weakness is its focus on North America with some reference to Europe. Other volumes are needed for South America, Africa, Asia and the Pacific. At least the limitations make it a manageable size.

The 300 historical and contemporary photographs enhance the text. Informative articles discuss baptism in the Spirit, Bible institutes and colleges, Catholic-Pentecostal dialogue, the charismatic movement, Elim, Episcopal renewal, eschatology, evangelism, glossolalia, healing, Holy Spirit doctrine, the Jesus Movement, missions, prophecy, statistics, and many more issues. Failures are well documented as well as the amazing spread of Pentecostalism and charismatic renewal.

Statistics cover the growth of the movement since 1900. Growth continues to accelerate with over 400 million, or one quarter of all Christians, involved by 1992. By 1990, figures were:
First wave: Pentecostalism - over 193 million;
Second wave: Charismatic Movement - over 140 million;
Third wave: Mainstream Church Renewal - over 33 million.

Concise biographies include those of David Barrett, Reinhard Bonnke, Don Basham, John Bertollucci, Jamie Buckingham, Yonggi Cho, Larry Christenson, Andrae Crouch, Nicky Cruz, John Alexander Dowie, David du Plessis, Tom Forrest, Terry Fullam, Kenneth Hagin, Michael Harper, Jack Hayford, Tommy Hicks, Peter Hocken, Melvin Hodges, Walter Hollenweger, George and Stephen Jeffreys, Kathryn Kuhlman, Killian McDonnell, Francis McNutt, Aimee Semple McPherson, Ralph Martin, Bob Mumford, Edward O'Connor, T L and Daisy Osborn, Agnes Ozman, Charles Parham, David Pytches, Kevin and Dorothy Ranaghan, Oral Roberts, Pat Robertson, Michael Scanlan, William Seymour, Chuck Smith, Russell Spittler, Cardinal Suenens, Peter Wagner, David Watson, David Wilkerson, Rodman Williams, John Wimber, Maria Woodworth-Etter,

Thomas Zimmerman and others.

It needs an index. That would make these topics more accessible! This well written, comprehensive volume will be a major reference book for years to come.

See also:
Burgess, SM & Van Der Maas, EM (eds.) 2002, *International Dictionary of Pentecostal and Charismatic Movements,* Zondervan, Grand Rapids, MI. – updated and more international.

Experiences of the Spirit, edited by Jan Jongenell.
Frankfurt am Main (also New York): Peter Lang, 1990, 280 pages.

In 1989 the University of Utrecht in the Netherlands hosted the fifth Conference on Pentecostal and Charismatic Research in Europe. The 50 participants came from ten European countries, the United States and South Africa. Experiences of the Spirit, edited by Jan Jongeneel the Professor of Missions at Utrecht, gathers 17 papers from the conference in six parts including contributions from well known charismatic authors such as Walter Hollenweger (Reformed) and Peter Hocken (Roman Catholic).

Part 1, The Search for a Pneumatology, discusses doctrines and experiences of the Holy Spirit. For example, Jan Jongeneel shows how 'The right doctrine leads the church to doxology and the right experience leads the church to go out into the world in mission.' Walter Hollenweger writes about priorities in Pentecostal research noting that 'A movement which represents more or at least as many members as all the other protestant denominations taken together can no longer be considered a fringe topic in church history, missiology, and systematic theology.' This section discusses Spirit-baptism, the charisms, and the contribution of charismatic theology to ecclesiology.

Part 2, The Message of Healing, explores theological links between vibrant revivalistic or Pentecostal spirituality and engagement for social justice and liberation. Articles cover faith healing in the Netherlands, the importance of Spirit-baptism and spiritual gifts in bringing balance to limited perspectives, and the importance of spiritual healing in the therapeutic supermarket.

Part 3, Black Spirituality, discusses South African Pentecostalism in the struggle against apartheid ideology, and argues for the significance of British Black Theologies within the African Diaspora in North America, the Caribbean, and Britain.

Part 4, The Dialogue with the Churches, notes that 'bilingual men and women are needed, who are able to interpret both the academic rational language of western theology and the oral expression of Pentecostalism.' Articles trace charismatic and ecumenical developments in France, and comment on Roman Catholic/Pentecostal dialogue. Peter Hocken argues for 'the operation of the full range of New Testament gifts and ministries. To the extent they are not given scope in the historic churches, they will appear outside, and are thereby themselves reduced.'

Part 5, Short Reports, survey developments in Czechoslovakia and in Latin America.

Part 6, Epilogue, evaluates the conference from ecumenical and missiological perspectives in papers written by staff members of the Faculty of Theology of Utrecht University. It includes suggestions for improving ecumenical commitment and communication in the interface between charismatic renewal, ecumenical developments and social engagement.

The book explores significant missiological and ecumenical issues positively, identifies unresolved problems, and indicates areas needing further research. Most papers are written by scholars involved in Pentecostal and charismatic ministry and teaching. The book strongly emphasises the mission of the church in the world.

Pentecost, Mission and Ecumenism: Essays on Intercultural Theology,
Festschrift in Honour of Professor Walter J. Hollenweger, edited by Jan Jongeneel and others.
Frankfurt am Main (also New York): Peter Lang, 1992, 380 pages.

These 26 articles were written by students and colleagues of Walter Hollenweger to honour his work. He retired in 1989 from his position as Professor of Mission at the University of Birmingham, where he had been appointed in 1971 as the first Professor of Mission in an English university. A Swiss theologian, he is well known for his pioneering work in Pentecostal studies, especially his book The Pentecostals (1972; 2nd ed. 1976; 3rd ed. 1988) based on his doctoral research at Zurich.

His Ph.D. students included Arnold Bittlinger, Peter Hocken and James Haire. Part of a tribute from James Haire is included (p. 37):

> Research students came before everyone else. Work was corrected and returned within days. Criticisms and suggestions were precise and for the aid of the researcher. ...Most of all, I remember those moments when tears came to his eyes, whether in interviews or in teaching... when the magnitude and indescribable depth of the Grace of God became apparent to him. Here was a person beyond denomination or cultural background for whom God's action was quite overwhelming.

The book is arranged in three parts.

Part 1 covers the biography of Professor Walter Hollenweger, with six articles describing the wide range of his interests and abilities. For example, his doctoral study of Pentecostalism ran to ten volumes, and he learned twenty foreign languages in those six years of research in order to read the sources in their original tongue! His study of this movement throughout the world increased his appreciation of oral and narrative theology.

Part 2 deals with historical case studies and statistics on Pentecostalism and charismatic renewal in missiological and ecumenical perspective. Articles range from the beginnings of Pentecostalism to its world wide influence, including an article by Martin Robinson on the work of David du Plessis, one by James Haire on Indonesia, and one by David Barrett on signs, wonders and statistics in the world today.

Part 3 gives missiological and ecumenical reflections on enculturation and encounter. Writers include Jan Jongeneel, Charles Kraft, Peter Staples and Peter Hocken. The various articles discuss the impact of Pentecostalism and charismatic renewal on mission and liturgy, on ecumenical theology and the ecumenical movement.

Church on Fire, edited by Geoff Waugh
Melbourne: Joint Board of Christian Education, 1991, 176 pages.

Barry Chant's review:

Over the last 30 years, the face of the church in Australia has changed dramatically. Hundreds of ministers and churches have been transformed and radically re-directed by their experience of charismatic renewal.

In both city and country, among Catholics and Protestants, in large churches and small churches, there has been a renewed baptism of fire.

In *Church on Fire*, Geoff Waugh, then Director of Distance Education at the Uniting Church's Trinity Theological College in Brisbane, has brought together stories from all over Australia of what the Holy Spirit has been doing.

The book begins with the exciting record of the revival among aborigines in the Northern Territory in 1979 and the years that followed. This is followed by numerous personal testimonies and then examples of renewal and revival in local churches.

The final section includes a number of observations on charismatic renewal by a wide range of people including such well known names as Hamish Jamieson, Arthur Jackson, Rowland Croucher and Dan Armstrong.

For anyone who wants some insight into the charismatic movement, this is a valuable resource.

(This review is reprinted by permission from New Day, September 1992, PO Box 564, Plympton SA 5038)

Additional note: Contributors to Church on Fire are -
Aboriginal Renewal: Djiniyini Gondarra, John Blacket
Personal Renewal: John-Charles Vockler, Owen Dowling, Charles Ringma, Dorothy Harris, Gregory Blaxland, David Todd, Barry Manuel, Ruth Lord
Church Renewal - Examples: Barry Schofield, John Lewis, Vincent Hobbs, Phil Audemard, Brain Francis, David Blackmore, Bob Dakers, Geoff Waugh

Reviews

Church Renewal - Observations: Barry Chant, Hamish Jamieson, Tom White, Lazarus Moore, Glen Heidenreich, Rowland Croucher, Arthur Jackson, Don Drury, Don Evans, Peter Moonie, Dan Armstrong

Church on Fire is available through the Renewal Journal, www.RenewalJournal.com

DVD Reviews

Making God Known into the 21st Century. This 14 minute, lively and well edited promotional video describes the activities of Youth With a Mission (YWAM) in Australia, including the outreaches. Loren Cunningham, the International Director and Steve Aherne the Australian Director comment briefly. The video shows the wide range of YWAM training and ministries including Discipleship Training Schools, church planting, worship, street evangelism, drama, mime and dance, and modules of study available from their University of the Nations through bases around the world, including Australia. Copies may be borrowed from YWAM bases or purchased from Australian Religious Films, 258 Sailors Bay Road, Northbridge N.S.W. 2063.

Global Perspectives. Youth With A Mission (YWAM) produced international news DVDs describing their work around the world. The 30 minute video, produced in America, is a professionally produced bulletin, interesting and informative. It gives clips of YWAM teams in many different countries, medical and mercy missions to worn torn and famine areas, outreaches at international events such as the Olympics and World Expo, and a summary of major YWAM outreaches around the world. Contact your nearest YWAM base for this valuable current resource.

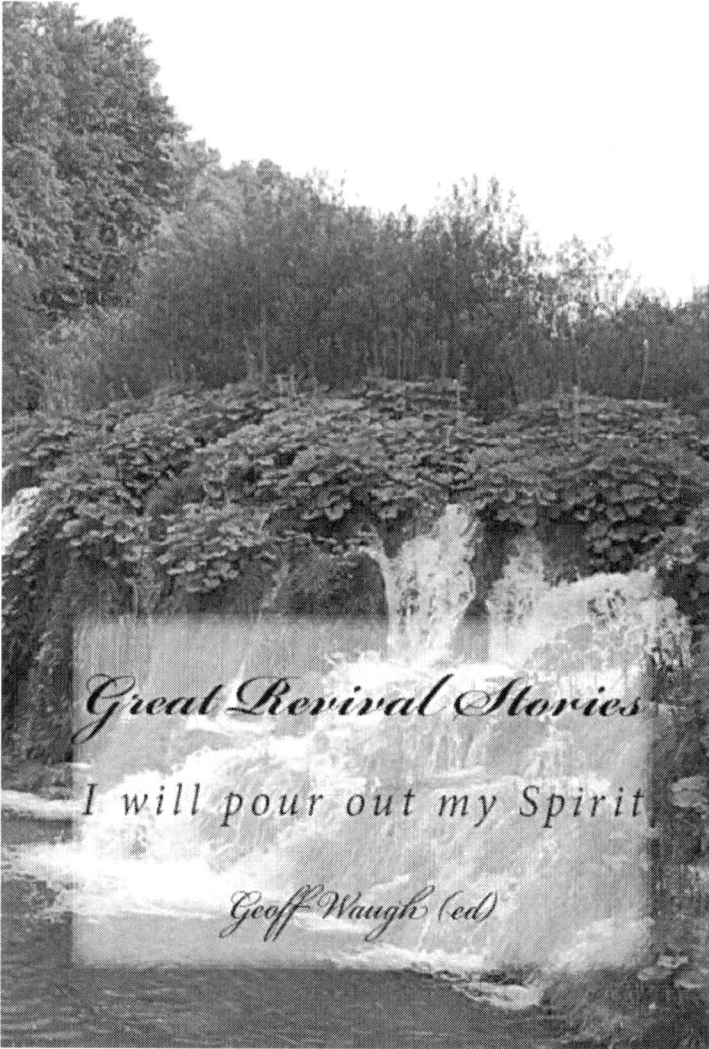

Great Revival Stories

Compiled from *Renewal Journal* articles in 2 books:
Best Revival Stories and *Transforming Revivals*
See Blog on renewaljournal.com

Renewal Journal
2 Church Growth

Contents

Renewal Journal 2: Church Growth

Cover photo: 2 Church Growth
Revival and rapid church growth in South America.

Editorial

I will build my church

Thank you for your interest in this *Renewal Journal*. Many people found it timely and helpful.

This second issue explores church growth. Andrew Evans describes the place of prayer in a church that grew from 150 to 3,500 people. Jack Frewen-Lord, Cindy Pattishall-Baker and Dean Brookes all report on significant growth in local churches. John McElroy outlines vital leadership principles in growing churches. Stuart Piggin gives an overview of local revivals in Australia, David Wang tells of revival growth in Asia, and I comment on the astounding church growth in the world today.

I've been encouraged by reports of people who have started prayer groups for revival since reading the first issue of this journal. The example of people giving one day a month for prayer and fasting, described in this issue by Andrew Evans, has been taken up by more churches. One young man in Brisbane heard of this and asked his minister if he could organise it in their church. He promptly gathered a list of over 31 people who would pray and fast for their church and for revival one day a month. They had someone doing that every day of each month.

Stuart Piggin's article in this issue tells of over 6,000 Anglicans in Sydney gathering regularly to pray for revival.

Not only are more people praying than ever before, but there are now reports of the Spirit of God moving more strongly in individuals and in churches, such as the reports at the beginning of this editorial. In church services and prayer meetings whole groups of people are being touched afresh by God. Some groups now report strong impacts of the Spirit in people's lives like we saw in the early seventies. Many are renewed. Many saved. Many have visions or are overwhelmed by the Spirit.

Hoist your sail! Fresh winds blow across the land now.

The famous evangelist, pastor and revivalist, Reuben A. Torrey, successor to D L Moody in Chicago, reported on similar moves of God's Spirit in his time. We can pray and participate in this in our day.

Here is Torrey's comment.

> The very first sermon I preached as pastor of Moody Church, Chicago, was on prayer. As I drew my address to a close I said something like this:
>
> 'Beloved brethren and sisters, how glad it would make your new pastor if he knew that some of you people sat up late every Saturday evening and rose early every Sunday morning to pray for their minister.'
>
> Those honest souls took me at my word. What was the result? When I took the pastorate, the church (which seats about 2,200 in comfort) had never been filled above the main auditorium and the galleries had never been opened. But God heard prayer, and in a few weeks the place was packed.
>
> But that was not be best of it. The power of God fell, and from that day till I left America, there was never a single Sunday without conversions. I don't believe that there has been a single day in the whole of the ten years that have since passed without somebody being converted in or about that building.
>
> You say, 'That must have been remarkable preaching!' Not at all. I was away five months in almost every year, but the work went on.

What God did for that church, he can do for yours. Pray without ceasing. Pray and believe. Pray and obey.

1 Church Growth through Prayer

Andrew Evans

Dr Andrew Evans is the senior pastor of the Assemblies of God church in Paradise, Adelaide, and was national President of the Assemblies of God in Australia.   The Paradise church has grown to over 3,500 people.

The Paradise church was one of the largest Assemblies of God churches in Australia with 200 attending when they called me to be the pastor in 1970. They had tried to get a pastor from Australia, New Zealand, and elsewhere, but had failed. As a last resort they asked me.

For seven years I had been a missionary in Papua New Guinea. The area where I worked had a population in which about 10 per cent could read and write.   Similarly, in the churches that I oversaw 90 percent of the congregations were illiterate. Therefore my preaching had to be simple Bible stories, or in simple language.

Through a series of crises God led me back to Australia. It was a difficult struggle for my family and me. While in PNG my wife contracted hepatitis and nearly died. I remember standing by her bedside praying to God to keep her alive. At times I would wake during the night and listen to see if she was still breathing. There were other complications for her at that time including the trauma resulting from a python slithering into the bedroom where she lay sick in our native material house. At her scream I ran in to find the snake above the door. I didn't know what to do, but with all my strength I hit it with a chair, demolishing the chair and killing the snake.

When we returned to Australia my wife became a little better but was still taking all kinds of drugs. This was my situation when Paradise church asked me to become their pastor. Some of the board members of Paradise church knew me before I became a missionary so were influential in my coming there.

Church decline

Suddenly I had to minister to educated Australians after seven years of working with primitive people. Besides this, some people thought the church was headed towards failure as the attendance was gradually declining.

'What am I going to do now?' I wondered. 'I have been in Papua New Guinea all these years and do not know how to preach to educated people.' I worked hard work on every sermon. After one year the church attendance had decreased from 200 people to 150. I became very concerned.

When I began as the pastor of Paradise church I read a book called 'How to have a Soul-winning Church'. The author started his church with 17 people and it grew to 2,000 through a door-knocking program. Encouraged, I tried this program. Our church people were mobilised and went everywhere knocking on doors and inviting people to church. We had special literature printed to distribute. We knocked on one thousand doors, and talked to people personally, but not one person came to church as a result of this campaign.

Another thought occured to me. We would have a healing crusade using a world renowned minister with a healing ministry. So we invited a famous evangelist. Our church advertised effeciently and distributed brochures. The brochures contained testimonies of people jumping out of wheelchairs and blind eyes opening. A banner outside the front of our church declared, 'Come and see blind eyes opened, the lame walk, the deaf hear, the dumb speak.' We were all ready for a revival.

Through this expensive crusade we received 12 converts. Not one of them stood publicly. They just signed decision cards. I regarded this method as a failure also.

Later I thought of another idea to make our church grow. I reasoned that I was just a pastor, an ordinary shepherd, not an evangelist. If I could find an associate minister who was a real evangelist then our church would surely grow. We invited an evangelist friend of mine to be my associate. He declined. So that idea failed.

Meanwhile the church kept growing smaller. Nothing we tried seemed to work. I was greatly discouraged.

Another problem for me was that the previous pastor at Paradise church was a 'ten talent' pastor. He could do anything. He could play the guitar and sing, was a really good preacher, and always had a word of knowledge for the people. The people all loved him. When he resigned they cried.

Picture the situation! This talented man left the church and I came to be their pastor. I tried all the gimmicks possible to get the church to grow, but nothing worked.

Desperate prayer

One day a man came to me saying, "I have a problem with my wife."

This couple were wonderful Christians. The wife was previously a drug addict and the husband had been an alcoholic. They both had remarkable conversions and everything went well for several years.

"My problem is that my wife wants a divorce," he continued.

His wife had begun to drift slowly back to her old ways again. I had counselled her for hours and nothing changed. Now her husband was asking, "What am I going to do? She is going to leave me."

This man wanted me to give him a word of knowledge. Instead I just answered, "I don't know. I haven't a clue."

Nevertheless I offered to help him if he would fast and pray the next Saturday with me, all day long. He agreed. The following Saturday the two of us came to the church and began to pray. My method of praying is to walk back and forth across the room and pray aloud. Praying aloud keeps your mind from wandering. It helps concentration. So we were both

117

walking back and forth across the room praying, "God help us. We don't know what to do about this marriage."

We were desperately calling upon God for help. As we continued praying, the Holy Spirit spoke to me saying, "I want you two to do this every Saturday."

I agreed, saying, "I will, but you must tell my friend yourself."

No sooner had I agreed than my partner spoke to me saying, "Pastor, the Holy Spirit has just spoken to me saying that we should fast and pray every Saturday."

"Fine. Let's do it," I said.

For the next eight months the two of us fasted and prayed every Saturday. Our prayers were not only for the broken marriage but for the church, for revival, and many other things.

The next day after we made this commitment, God put his seal upon it. As I led the first chorus during the Sunday service I felt a strong urging of the Holy Spirit to give an appeal. This was not on the program so I thought, "Let's sing a few more choruses first until the people get settled, then I will give an appeal."

But the urging was stronger than ever. I argued with the Lord, "Don't you think it is a bit early in the meeting to give an appeal? We could wait until the end of the service. That is how we always do it."

As I was mentally arguing with the Lord I saw a man get up from the back seat, walk down the aisle and kneel at the altar. I said, "All right, Lord, I get the message."

I challenged the people, "Would anyone else like to join this man?"

More than half the congregation came forward and began to cry and weep. God moved upon us in a powerful way.

The man who had come forward first was an alcoholic. He came to church that morning with a strong desire to drink again. He had been sitting in his seat fighting that desire. God met his need, and many other needs.

Then God spoke to me: "If you want church growth, you have to build a powerful prayer base. That is the foundation of church growth."

The church may have many activities but its growth will not be powerful and effective without a strong prayer base. Our trend is that of tradition. It is hard to change what has been practiced for a long time. However, it is very important to follow God's direction in the program of your church.

Church growth

After my friend and I had been praying together for about eight months the Holy Spirit spoke to me: "I don't want you to continue praying every Saturday with this brother alone but go onto the next step. Bring the entire congregation into it."

I announced to our congregation, "Two of us have been praying now for eight months, but God told us not to continue alone. Instead, we are to invite others in the congregation to join us in praying and fasting. You say you are concerned about our nation, our society, our church, but do you really care enough to give one day a month to prayer and fasting for revival?"

Out of our congregation of 150 only 31 people committed themselves to join us in prayer. Therefore we mobilised one person every day to give a whole day for prayer and fasting. This covered the entire month - 31 days. Someone was praying for revival everyday.

Immediately we noticed the impact of prayer upon our church. People began to come in. The church began to develop and grow. By the early nineties we had over 3,500 attending and 1600 involved regularly in day and evening home cells. Every year I challenge them anew to give one day a month to prayer and fasting. Whenever the members are slack in their commitment it is felt in the church.

Our church has a group of people called the intercessors. These are special people who give one day every week to prayer and fasting. About 300 members had joined this group by 1992. They pray for me every week. Wherever I go, whatever I am doing, they always pray for me. I meet constantly with the intercessors to relate prayer needs.

This is one department of the church that I oversee myself because I realise the importance of prayer. I have found that it is impossible to see church growth without a tremendous prayer foundation. Our church has grown and is now decentralised. A full time team of 20 pastors join me in pastoring Paradise church.

Dreams and visions

Many scriptures speak of evil abounding in the last days. Another stream of scriptures says that in the last days there is going to be a great revival. Some passages describe a terrible falling away, a decline, and things getting worse and then there are many scriptures that say a revival is going to take place. Both are true, and both are more obvious around us now.

Prayer prepares the way for revival. At Pentecost the Holy Spirit came in great power when the believers were praying. Then Peter spoke of Joel's prophecy, 'In the last days it will be, God declares, that I will pour out my Spirit upon all flesh, and your sons and your daughters shall prophecy, and your young men shall see visions, and your old men shall dream dreams' (Acts 1:27).

It thrills me to see so many young people sold out to God. These promises are very powerful. I am sure God has given many people great visions and dreams for the future. I encourage people, young and old, to hold onto these dreams because they come to pass in your life.

When I was a Bible school student God spoke to me through prophecy and said, 'One day you are going to preach to multitudes.' I could hardly believe this. But God planted a vision and dream in my heart.

What about the promise for the old people? They will dream dreams. That does not mean dreaming of the past, sitting in a rocking chair and dreaming of the good old days. Dreams in the Bible are supernatural and progressive.

My father is a dreamer. When he was 80 years old he came to me and said, 'Andrew, God has told me to start a church in a town called Katherine.'

There was no Assembly of God church in Katherine. This town in the Northern Territory has a population of about 3,000 people and is about 300 miles from the next town. Many people go to the northern part of Australia to get away from something - a bad marriage, a bad job, or some unpleasant experience. Katherine has many people like that.

When my dad told of his dream to start a church in Katherine I said, "You're crazy."

But my dad had a dream and began saving his pension in order to fulfil that dream God had placed in his heart. After six months my dad said, "I am going to Katherine."

"Do you know anyone up there?" I asked.

"Well I have written to four people, but none of them answered my letters."

"Where are you going to stay?"

"I don't know."

My dad got on the plane and flew to Katherine. The airport there is about 25 kilometres from the town and is located in a desert place. Upon arriving my dad stood there looking like a lost sheep. He had no home to go to, no place to stay that night. He was standing at the airport holding his bag.

An aborigine couple approached my dad and asked, "Can we help you?"

My dad answered, "I want a lift into Katherine."

"Oh, come with us," they said. So they took him in their car into town.

On the way they asked him, "Why are you coming to Katherine?"

"God sent me to start a church here."

"Do you know anyone here?"

"No."

"Do you have a place to stay?"

"No."

"We will see if we can find a place for you," they responded.

My dad went to the showground and began meetings. In two weeks his crowds grew to 120, and 37 people made decisions for Christ.

We live in marvellous days. People of all ages are part of the move of God in these last days, young and old alike. God is wanting to do something powerful and dynamic. He is blessing young people, and old, giving them revelations, dreams, visions and gifts. They are going out praying for the sick, ministering in various ways, and souls are bing saved all over the world.

This article is adapted from a chapter published in a manual of Church Growth International, Yoido P.O. Box 7, Seoul 150-600, Korea, and used with permission.

2 Growing a Church in the Spirit's Power

Jack Frewen-Lord

The Rev Jack Frewen-Lord was the Uniting Church minister at Praise Chapel, Townsville, and former Associate Director of the Methodist Young People's Department and Department of Christian Education in Queensland. Jack and his wife Leonie are actively involved in compassionate healing and deliverance ministries.

"Attempt something so big that unless God intervenes it is bound to fail" says Jamie Buckingham. That challenge is one of the texts on the office wall in Praise Chapel.

I'd like to think that was the kind of goal I set for the Townsville West Parish in 1976 when I found myself there as pastor after serving for 12 years as Associate Director of the Methodist Young People's Department and then the Department of Christian Education in Queensland.

I didn't set such a goal. In fact, I concluded that the parish was not viable with its average age of 65 and a membership of 40 in an industrial area of decreasing population. Yet ten years later we had 450 people and had helped establish an aboriginal church as well.

Creative ministry

My initial realistic agenda was to give the parish a decent burial, acknowledging its faithfulness over almost a century. My hidden agendas were more like fantasy than dreams and visions. As the Christian Education officer for the area, I saw an opportunity to experiment. I wanted to have a go at the different programmes that I had tried for years to get other parishes to do, and I wanted to prove that team ministries can really work.

So I proposed that we amalgamate the parish work and the Christian Education ministry for the North Queensland Presbytery with one office and support base. Remarkably, this idea was totally accepted by all concerned. A creative team of ministers, education officer and secretary went to work on Townsville West.

Those poor parishioners could be forgiven for wondering what had hit them. Every service had something different. Each monthly Family Service was something else again - from 8 metre plastic blow-up whales that swallowed up all the Sunday School when the lesson was on Jonah, to moving back all the heavy wooden pews to accommodate a menagerie of huge stuffed animals with children wrestling them on the floor. I wondered whether the aged spinster ladies' eyebrows would ever come down again.

We survived that first year. The team worked beautifully, sharing parish work and regional Christian Education activities together, including many camps. About then, we made some bold decisions such as focusing on the family. This seemed unrealistic as we had about four families of Dad, Mum, and children. Nevertheless we decided that church and Sunday School were for the family.

So the decree went out that no child would be accepted in the Sunday School unless accompanied by a parent. That raised more eyebrows. It quickly reduced the Sunday School to a third of its former handful.

At the same time, however, I made a commitment to introduce a co-operative Religious Education programme which catered weekly for almost all the 900 pupils of four primary schools. We did this in co-operation with other churches and the school principals. It was a more useful Christian Education programme than Sunday School. I believe it was a ministry which God honoured as Catholic, Anglican, Uniting, Salvation Army and Pentecostal people worked together in beautiful harmony. That programme is still working after 14 years.

Speaking of families, I give credit to the tremendous backing of my own family with a very capable wife (who had seven leadership positions in the church at first) and four committed and musically talented children. Their charisma and music began to draw other young people. Many came in off the street - bikie leathers, sun glasses and all.

The spinster ladies did not find it easy to accept some of the tattoed, tank-top, bare foot people who began to fill the seats at church. We encouraged the young people to love them as a real ministry. Soon these older ladies were clapping and praising as much as anyone.

It became obvious that we would not have a burial. The Body was coming alive. I can't say we were very much aware of the Holy Spirit at this time, but we knew we had received the kiss of life.

Goal setting

So it was time to set some goals - realistic ones for rebuilding a church. Our first was a five year plan to establish a biblical base through the Bethel Bible Series and to preach the Word in association with this. By the end of that five years the congregation had quadrupled with 80% involved in serious Bible study. We had many new converts.

We hosted a number of visiting ministries from within and outside Australia. One of the strangest things was that we did not invite these ourselves. They either asked if they might come, or other interstate churches asked if we could accommodate them. We did so with open arms, and were greatly blessed by the variety of ministries that kept moving us on to renewal. I believe it was a gracious provision of the Holy Spirit preparing us for his personal visitation at the right time.

When renewal begins to hit a church there tends to be hurts and divisions and walk-outs. Some people find it hard to live with the new enthusiasm. We lost only one family for this reason.

One of the interesting factors holding the church family together was the overflowing offering plates. Instead of the meagre offering easily absorbed in the bottom of the huge offering plates, now the stewards found someone following down the aisle picking up the notes overflowing and falling off. That was manna to the hungry for those faithful members who had struggled to keep a church alive with cake stalls and endless fetes.

Now we were able to consider worth while missionary gifts. We set a new goal to establish an aboriginal church, beginning as a part of our congregation and then gradually working to independence. That was achieved in 1981 when the Rev. Charles Harris, our aboriginal pastor, was added to the team. The aboriginal church became independent in 1984, well within the five year plan, and the buildings at West End were handed over to this church.

Renewal

I would say that 1981 was the time of the Holy Spirit's visitation. Again, this was totally unplanned by us. A neighbouring parish, Hermit Park, had invited the Rev. Harry Westcott with a team of elders from O'Connor Uniting Church to hold a tent mission in their church grounds. We decided to support this mission totally. We did so, to our blessing. Many of our leaders, including myself, were baptised in the Holy Spirit. That mission gave a good watering to the seeds of renewal which had been planted by our various conscious and unconscious choices.

This was a major turning point for our parish. Instead of sticking to our nicely ordered, time prescribed worship, we allowed the Spirit to do what he wanted in the services. These were exciting days with further growth in numbers. We saw many healing miracles and the release of gifts of the Spirit.

We discovered again that the church is truly the body of Christ. Jesus Christ moves in his church, his body, by his Spirit. Our identity can only lie in Christ Jesus, not in buildings or places or communities. This is strongly seen in the underground churches overseas and especially in the vibrant house church movement throughout Asia.

Home cell groups

Our next phase of goal setting was to explore church growth principles. Our leaders attended seminars and visited other churches in renewal to catch the wind of the Spirit where it blew strongest.

We added another person to our staff. In biblical language, it seemed good to us and to the Holy Spirit to separate Bruce, a young Bible College graduate, to the ministry of establishing home cell groups. I believe we were led by the Holy Spirit to make this a total programme for the whole church.

Our members were commuting to West End from all over the city of Townsville. So we had a vision of the church in the neighbourhood meeting mid-week in cell groups, evangelising in the neighbourhood, then gathering for corporate fellowship, worship, teaching and the sacraments on Sundays.

We trained and dedicated home cell leaders. Our church in the neighbourhood was launched, with 80% of the congregation meeting in home groups which we named home church. They met for worship, prayer, pastoral care, teaching and fellowship. The church continued to grow.

Buildings

Our lovely brick building on the corner became inadequate. We regularly squeezed 180 into the sanctuary built to hold 120. For a while we had two congregations there. So we decided to move to a kindergarten hall which was a converted warehouse that could hold 250. We wanted to make one congregation out of two and commit all our operation to one centre, leaving the West End property for the use of the aboriginal church.

With this extra space the church continued to grow. We decided to rename our church Praise Chapel Uniting Church Family Fellowship.

One of our early decisions in setting missionary goals was to spend as little as possible on buildings and to concentrate on people. We added a youth pastor to the team. A number of ministries were added to the weekly programme, including counselling with prayer for deliverance.

Despite our good intentions not to spend money on buildings, it soon became obvious that we would need larger premises and car park facilities. We searched for a larger warehouse, unsuccessfully.

So we finally decided that we should look for land to build on. After many weeks of earnest prayer, miraculously a five hectare block became available within the parish.

We held a dedication service in tents on the land with a commitment to build a centre to accommodate 1,000 people.

It was a daunting prospect. We faced a cost of half a million dollars with a bank balance of nothing. I must admit that my faith was severely tested. My heart is that of a pastor and I knew that almost every family in the church had a mortgage on their home.

Where was the money to come from? 'There must be some financial Christians around who would be willing to invest in Praise Chapel,' I reasoned.

So I took the project to a number of my friends and acquaintances who would be worth at least a million. The money of every single one was tied up, and unavailable. So we were back to basics!

God supplied through his faithful people in this low income congregation. Almost overnight they made $100,000 available in gifts and another $100,000 in interest free loans.

Nine months later we opened the new Praise Chapel at a cost of $600,000. 'Not by might, nor by power, but by my spirit, says the Lord of hosts' (Zechariah 4:6).

Since that time, again and again, the faithful with their meagre income have shown that the Holy Spirit has taught them to give.

Those who are faithfully committed to the principle of tithing have fully supported all our commitments.

Church growth principles

Someone studying the growth of our parish from a congregation of 40 in 1977 to 450 in 1987 would probably say we stumbled on church growth principles by accident. I prefer to believe it was openness to the Holy Spirit that led us to make right decisions at the right time. We were also able to learn from churches of various denominations that were moving in renewal.

The church growth movement of the 70's and 80's has had a marked effect on many churches in this nation. We did study church growth principles and organised seminars with international speakers. These had some influence on our thinking. Perhaps Kennon Callahan's 12 Keys to an effective church encouraged us most. That enabled us to systematise our situation and helped us set mission objectives and a realistic five year plan.

However, my own feeling is that we can over emphasise organisation. The church is not primarily an organisation, but an organism, a body of believers. Unless its moves are God breathed by the Holy Spirit, and unless there is utter dependence on the Holy Spirit, it will not move in truth and life.

By the early 90's this church had plateaued at a membership of 450. Some of the cause of this is mere organisation. We constantly need a fresh move of the Holy Spirit.

A further observation is that only a handful of members remain who were here at the first move of the Spirit among us. The turnover of population in Townsville is 80% every three years. So we have almost a new congregation every three years. That makes heavy demands to continually train new leaders.

It is easy to slacken off and go soft on the need for fresh infillings of the Holy Spirit. We are always tempted to stay in a comfort zone. We can spend a lot of time comforting the afflicted in counselling and deliverance, when there may be a greater need to afflict the comfortable.

I know Jesus said he would send another Comforter to be with us, but that does not mean he makes us comfortable. None of Jesus' leading or

129

teaching has the remotest resemblance to being comfortable. I have found him to be the stirrer of the church, and we surely need a stirrer in every age and generation.

May our Lord stir us into courageous ministry through the power of his Spirit in his church and in our lives.

3 *Evangelism brings Renewal*

Cindy Pattishall-Baker

The Rev. Cindy Pattishall-Baker, a Uniting Church minister, was a Consultant for Evangelism and Renewal in the South Australian Synod of the Uniting Church in Australia.

Evangelism can lead to renewal and on to revival of the church. I have seen this in my experience in ministry in the last sixteen years as someone committed to the renewal of people and churches.

We need to release the dedicated and already discipled people of our parishes and churches into sharing their faith with those outside the church. This is a strategy for renewal that will lead to the revival of the church in the 1990's.

Time and time again new converts begin the process of renewing the church and individuals in it. Their fresh approach to religion, their radical testimonies to the faith, and their enthusiasm to share the gospel and to live in its power, affect many others.

Does it work? Let's look at one parish I know really well where I served for seven years.

Evangelism leads to revival

Margaret Matthews, a nurse and an elder in the Cobden Uniting Church Parish, gave this account at the Conference on Conversion Growth in Launceston, Tasmania, 10-12 March, 1988. It describes her experiences of both personal and parish-wide renewal that started with evangelism.

Cobden is in the heart of a dairying district in Western Victoria, and a recent decision to expand the local factory has assured the future viability of the town. Our population of 1,450 is stable. We all know our neighbours. Our parish has two churches, both of which now have active Sunday Schools, youth groups and fellowship groups. Bible studies are an integral part of our life, catering for all levels of faith from 13 to 84 year olds. All participate in the leadership of worship. We started evening services with a more relaxed, informal worship style where newcomers felt more at ease.

Our growth story really began many years ago, when during a prolonged time of ministerial vacancy we were visited by an evangelist who challenged us to pray for revival in our church. A small group gathered together following the lines suggested: that we share the leadership, pray for the church and each other, and bring a name before the group and pray that God would prepare their hearts as we approached them and shared his Word. We saw our prayers answered and we saw our fellowship grow to 20-30 people who met under our first minister after the formation of the Uniting Church in 1977.

Like most of our generation, we clung to the concepts we had grown up with: preaching the gospel was the minister's job and bringing newcomers to the church was no longer our responsibility. We lost our sense of purpose and our direction for several years. Our numbers began to dwindle and although we continued to pray that others might come to know the Lord, we were almost back to the original six or seven of us.

A new minister arrived. Hearing our prayer for revival and seeing us do nothing actively to bring it about, she organised an evangelism workshop for our Presbytery and persuaded eight of us to go to it. For myself, it was a real step of faith. I had forgotten how easy it had been, with the Lord's help, to share my faith with friends, and now we were being asked to knock on stranger's doors – a terrifying thought!

It became our ministry to make those strangers into friends: getting to know people, listening and ministering to their needs, sharing their stories, sharing our story and God's story, depending on God to do the rest. We all came home from the workshop inspired to put what we had learned, into practice.

We set aside one night each week to go visiting on a regular basis. We first met for prayer to ask the Lord to prepare the way and to go with us, and those of our group who did not go out joined together to pray for those who did. After our visit we returned to the church to talk it over, to learn from each other's experiences, to get any hurts or knock-backs off our chests, and to share any blessings with those who stayed behind to pray.

To our surprise, after a few weeks, we realised we were enjoying this experience and started looking forward to it. We found that our little team of eight just couldn't keep up with all the people who would like us to return for a visit. There was a great thirst out there beyond our church of people wanting to know more about the Lord, about the church, or wanting to share the hurt that took them away from the faith in the past.

About twelve months later, a second evangelism workshop was organised by our own and neighbouring parishes. Now many others in the church could see the importance of evangelism and most of our elders and several of our converts attended it. By then, I had begun a Bible Study home cell for some of the new converts who had no background of Christianity, but a wonderful new faith which was to change their lives, and lead me into a deeper faith commitment.

I didn't start out to be an evangelist. I didn't have that burning desire to share my faith with everyone I met, which I found among our converts. My visiting was an act of obedience to God's will for us to share the gospel with all people. It was a stepping out in faith on the road that takes you from 'What can God do for me?' to 'What can I do for God?'

Margaret, through the witness of her converts, later sought the infilling of the Holy Spirit and today not only continues to share her faith but is a mighty preacher and dynamic Bible Study teacher. From the witness of these early evangelists and those who were converted to the faith, the parish grew by 135% on their adherents roll and by 26% in four years (1983-87) in their confirmed members' roll. In 1988, the 241 regular Sunday worshippers included 121 of the people who had faith for longer than ten years and 119 (49%) of the people having come to faith in the last five years (between 1983-88). In 1989, 94% of those converted to the faith were still regular attenders at worship (some now 6 years old in their faith).

Revival first started in this parish because an evangelist came and proclaimed the gospel. That gave others a hunger to do the same. It almost failed when a minister arrived during a prolonged vacancy and the people abdicated their responsibility to him, but it was later revived by another minister. As the converts grew in faith and hungered for a deeper expression of their faith, they sought, received and began to use their spiritual gifts. It led them into a personal encounter with the Holy Spirit. This influenced the established church to re-evaluate itself and to also grow in renewal.

Renewal that brings revival

Our strategies in the church for bringing renewal have at times been wrought with force, causing judgment, mistrust and resistance. This resistance in the church can gravely hurt those in the renewal movement. So they have at times left the churches that would not accept their way or stayed in their church and developed a ghetto mentality of 'we-they' that made it harder for others to see renewal as an option for their lives.

In past years, the renewal movement often concentrated on changing worship to allow all the spiritual gifts to be prevalent and seen by sceptics and non-believers alike, thinking that this would aid in renewing others. Signs and wonders, although reaching some and exciting them to seek renewal, also frightened many more and turned them right off renewal.

A strategy for the renewal of the church needs to be more than just a change of worship where signs and wonders can be evident. Renewal demands a more radical lifestyle and call to ministry than this. When this change is seen in others, the people in the church do respond.

Here is an anatomy of renewal that I believe leads to revival:

1. Evangelists proclaim the message of salvation and people are converted to faith.

2. The converts grow in faith and hunger for a deeper expression of their faith. They seek, receive and use the spiritual gifts leading them into a personal encounter with the Holy Spirit which influences the established church to re-evaluate itself and to also grow in the area of renewal.

3. The church then needs to understand and standardise the use of the spiritual gifts from good biblical teaching - moving the people away from experience as the authority for the use of spiritual gifts to good theology about their use.

4. Converts and those who grew up in the faith examine their lives in light of God's Word, showing a desire for deeper service to the Lord and a hunger for righteous and holy living.

Evangelism - renewal - revival

The Reformation revivals of the 1500's, the Great Awakening of the 1700's, or the South Australian revivals in the mines at Wallaroo, Moonta and Burra at the turn of this century, follow this common pattern: evangelism - renewal - revival (in that order).

First, evangelists went out and proclaimed the gospel. The gospel they proclaimed emphasised a personal encounter with Jesus Christ and an individual religious experience rather than the doctrines of the church. Many people fell under the conviction of these evangelists' proclamation of the gospel and received salvation.

As these converts grew in faith, they began to hunger for a deeper expression of their faith and began seeking, receiving and using the spiritual gifts God uses to build the church. That led them into a personal encounter with the Holy Spirit. This greatly influenced the preaching of the evangelists and their message.

When revival got to this second stage evangelists like John and Charles Wesley shifted from their basic salvation message of the early days of revival to sermons on a deeper discipleship and on walking in the power of the Spirit of God. This led to them establishing Bible studies, encouraging lay people to take up leadership roles in every giftedness of the Spirit, and it eventually led to the established church of their day re-evaluating itself and growing in renewal.

135

This process also happened in the Reformation revival where the reformers shifted from the basic salvation message of their earlier days to deeper discipleship which led to the established church (the Catholic Church) re-evaluating itself and having a revival itself influenced by such people as St. John of the Cross and Theresa of Avila, some 40 years after the Reformation.

This leads to the third phase of revival. In every succeeding generation when renewal comes, the church all over again, needs to learn how to understand and use the spiritual gifts given to them by God. So, the next phase of revival seems to be standardising the use of the spiritual gifts and how they are to be ordered and used in the life of the church. Every new generation of revivalists find themselves in unchartered waters. So it takes time to sort out problems with the use of spiritual gifts and ensure that there is sound Biblical teaching on them.

Often those in the renewal movements, excited to experience the power of their faith, rush into using the gifts (and having `the experience') rather than doing serious biblical study in order to bring others with them in good understanding. The `experience' is not enough. We need good renewal theology that is strong enough to be debated.

The last phase of revival seems to be an inner desire of both converts and those who grew up in the faith to examine their lives in light of God's Word, a desire for deeper service to the Lord and a hunger for righteous and holy living. This was very evident in the Great Awakening revival where evangelists later in the revival clearly shifted their proclamation of the salvation message to the preaching on holiness and righteous living (such as the sermons of the American revivalist of the early 1700's, Jonathan Edwards).

The history of the church, shows long periods (which sadly follow great revivals) where the gospel is reduced by many in the church to narrow relativism. Pragmatism is rife. This leads to a suspicion of the supernatural, and for a while the church loses the power of its faith from lack of belief in the Holy Spirit and the Spirit's gifts. The church in this condition seldom goes out to do evangelism but is content with social work and political statements.

Therefore, for renewal of the church to be effective today and for it to issue out into revival, we must first start with evangelism.

Revival involves mission and ministry

The following comments show how the personal encounter of the Holy Spirit by converts led the church to re-evaluate its life, moving them into renewal. It caused them to explore the use of spiritual gifts by good Biblical teaching and discipleship. That moved people away from experience as the only authority for the use of spiritual gifts to good theology about their use.

These quotes are from talks that Cobden people gave at the Launceston 1988 Conversion Growth Workshop sponsored by the Uniting Church Assembly's National Mission and Evangelism Committee.

Barbara Cowley, the Cobden Parish treasurer and a mother of two, says,

> I have always believed in God and have attended Sunday School and church most of my life. In our courting days, my husband used to come to church with me, but after we were married he always found himself too busy to come. Our two children were baptised and attended Sunday School regularly, our daughter especially so, and our son until the age of 10 when he rebelled about going.
>
> When my daughter finished Sunday School and didn't want to attend church anymore, I went to church by myself but my attendance started to drop off. At about that time my husband started exploring his faith. This encouraged me and we started attending church as a family. Since then, both our children have made decisions for the Lord at different times.
>
> Since being baptised in the Holy Spirit, my eyes have been opened to the workings of the Lord. Even though I had been involved in attending church all my life, it's only in the last couple of years that my faith has come alive in attending our Bible Study group, which has helped me grow in my walk with the Lord.

Hazel and the late Norm Maskell, dairy farmers, church elders, and Cobden Parish's original evangelists in their mid-70's, led cell groups. Hazel and Norm said,

Why did we form study or cell groups? We believed that the church would not or could not grow until our people came together to study God's Word, understand his gifts and to build each other up in faith. Those we brought to faith needed nurturing and encouraging. So our study groups came into existence one by one. These converts were more teachable than some of the older folk in the faith. Being eager to learn, they were wide open to Bible teaching and getting to know the Lord in a real way. Their growth was astounding, causing our growth too! We have seen miracles happen and now we see many of these new Christians taking leading roles in our church life alongside of us.

I have found that new Christians pray out loud, share faith, and learn far more easily than we who have been in the church for some time, because they have no preconceived ideas. Almost any Bible Study member in our church will pray on the spot publicly. They thank God for various things, confess their own shortcomings, and pray for others. Now almost half the congregation will participate in prayer or the leading of worship whenever asked to do so. The result of these Bible Study groups is that our church has not only grown in numbers, but more importantly, we understand the Holy Spirit so much better and know the Spirit to be working in our church. We older folk have learned so much and grown closer to the Lord.

Sometimes there may be difficulties for the church when it tries to assimilate not only new people into the life and especially the leadership structure of the church, but also starts re-evaluating itself in light of the testimonies of these new converts and their walk with the Lord.

Most people within our church will say `we need new blood, some fresh faces and especially we need more younger folk to keep us going.'  However, once there is new blood, fresh faces, and younger folk coming into our churches, many old timers may feel that the `new folk have taken us over and have made so many changes that we don't know what's going on anymore, so we will just stay at home and let them run it!'

Church growth in evangelism and renewal means that we, too, as individuals have to grow and be renewed. Many people resist this. Sometimes, church growth can only happen by birthing a new church that's separate from the established church. This happened both in the Reformation and Great Awakening Revivals and it did most recently in the 1970's and 1980's. However, it doesn't have to be that way.

Although the Cobden Parish had some battles and upheavals from its evangelism and renewal, division was averted by hospitality fellowship, Bible Study and shared worship. The leadership shared in hospitality fellowship, that is, intentionally inviting oldtimers in the church to meals and gatherings with converts and helping them to get to know and to interpret their faith journey to each other.

The Bible Studies started out to disciple converts. Then, as people in the church started to re-evaluate their faith journey through their contacts with the converts and hungered to know more, Bible Studies were set up for them too. Later, converts and those of long standing in the church merged many of their separate Bible Studies together where they learned to pray and care for one another.

Another important aspect of the Bible Studies, was the curriculum the Parish wrote to train people about the infilling of the Holy Spirit and the proper use of the spiritual gifts. When members discovered their own spiritual gifts, they were encouraged to take up their ministry roles within the life of the church. For converts this usually occurred by the end of their first year in the faith.

Shared worship took the form of setting up eight worship teams of six people each, chosen across generations and from each of the worshipping congregations. Each member of the team had a designated area of leadership: prayers, music, administration of the team, children's sermon, the sermon, the organisation of the service sheet, announcements and the Bible readings. They had to listen to each other's needs and they developed a style of worship that all were happy with and that was open enough to be able to evolve, as the parish needs changed.

Conclusions

We see that evangelism starts the process of renewal which brings revival. Renewal leads to a personal encounter with the Holy Spirit as the converts of the church's evangelistic outreach grow in faith and hunger for the power of their faith, seeking, receiving and using the Spiritual gifts. This renewal leads to the established church re-evaluating itself and either blockading and resisting renewal, or growing in it.

Renewal leads to discipleship training in and standardising the use of the spiritual gifts with good Biblical teaching and the development of an articulate theology that can be debated. Discipleship leads to a radical lifestyle where one has a desire for a deeper service to the Lord, a greater knowledge of God's Word and a hunger for righteous and holy living.

When the church misses one of these parts revival doesn't happen. For instance, in studying several charismatic churches, I have discovered that if a church tries to bring in renewal before it does evangelism, it often gets a huge amount of transfer growth from other churches which leads to divisions and it eventually goes into decline.

If renewal doesn't follow on into good discipleship, the church folk often get stuck on the experiences of the Holy Spirit and cannot articulate a clear enough theology so that they can take others into the experience with them in good understanding. Often these churches can become quite ingrown and in a denominational structure be quite divisive.

If discipleship does not produce a radical lifestyle, the church does not benefit others. Then it runs the risk of not only privatising a person's faith journey, but also of making one's experience the only test of the validity of other people's faith. It also means that the church remains at the level of signs and wonders instead of moving into a deeper discipleship with Jesus where one is sold out to him in complete sacrifice in holy living.

Jesus said to the doubting Thomas, `Blessed are those who have not seen and yet have come to believe' (John 20:29). Signs and wonders are for non-believers (1 Corinthians 14) but a radical lifestyle of a disciple is for the mature Christian.

Many church leaders spend so much effort in renewing a congregation from within. I firmly believe that a congregation should be renewed from without, through evangelism and the converts that receive their message.

Then evangelism will lead to renewal and revival in the land.

Some responses to *Renewal Journal 1*: Revival

A minister wrote saying how appropriate the Journal was because the Lord is moving in that area in ways described in the Journal.

Another man noted that the *Renewal Journal* 'has come at just the right time when there are stirrings of the Spirit in our own area after a long dry spell."

A lady wrote: "I believe the Lord is awakening his people because everyone I talk to has the same urgency about prayer in the churches. Many who have been sitting still for years are beginning to blossom and are encouraged and growing more than they have for twenty years in a short space of time. People are returning to the churches of their own accord - not through being witnessed to, but because the Lord is drawing them. This can only be because God's people are praying and this is enabling the Holy Spirit to work."

A man in Brisbane was so interested in the *Renewal Journal* he bought 50 copies to sell at meetings. He sold them all.

A group in Adelaide has been distributing the Journals at meetings.

These people all bought bulk orders of the Journal so they could pass copies on to their friends.

You can now obtain copies of the first issue, on revival, and all subsequent issues. It has struck a strong chord for many people.

4 New Life for an Older Church

Dean Brookes

The Revd Dr Dean Brookes is a Uniting Church minister and former Consultant for Evangelism in the Synod of South Australia.

In January 1989 I began as minister of a thirty-five year old church at Beaumont in Adelaide that had suffered numerical decline.

It had followed the typical pattern of an inner suburban church with its complex of buildings, a Sunday School of 350 children, and two packed morning services in its hey day of the boom years of Methodism in the fifties and sixties.

In those years the church was a buzz of activity. Its youth group grew as children entered their teens. Membership figures increased as the teenagers took confirmation classes. Church growth was natural and expected. It required no specific strategies. People looked for a neighbourhood church which provided worship, a Sunday School, youth program, and the accepted activities associated with church life at the time.

Gradually the neighbourhood became prime real estate. When the young people married they had to move out to newer suburban areas where land was cheaper. Predictably the congregation declined and grew older. By 1989 an average of 85 people attended the one service on Sunday and a handful of children attended the Sunday School. Many were concerned about the future of this single congregation parish, and the parish leaders had begun discussions with nearby congregations regarding amalgamation.

Re-greening in the Spirit's power

This became for me an experiment in turning a church around. Was it possible to arrest the decline and begin to build again? Would the church have a significant and effective future as well as a dynamic ministry in the name of Jesus Christ?

Early in my first year at this church I found I was also involved emotionally and could not separate my personal feelings from what I discovered and what I believed God had in store for us. Could I lead this church to new life and growth? I personally was most aware of my own need of God's help and of my need to grow spiritually as the leader of this church.

I was fortunate to be nearing the end of doctoral studies in church growth and renewal. I had also been a consultant in the related area of evangelism for eight years. Hence I came with some knowledge and experience that I believed would help my leadership of this church. However, my experience of working at length with a declining congregation was minimal. I knew that I and they would be very dependent upon the grace of God and the power of the Holy Spirit.

In the interview before my appointment the nominating committee indicated they were seeking someone of my age and experience. They also emphasised their desire to be more effective evangelistically and to reach the neighbourhood for Christ.

I intimated my bias for evangelism and sought to know whether they would be open to change and to embrace new directions I might initiate. They agreed, not knowing exactly what would occur in the years to follow.

New goals and direction

I began by getting to know the people and by learning their corporate history. Some had been in the church since its inception. Most had been there for ten or twenty years or more. Very few, if any, were new to the church in recent years. They considered themselves a friendly church but did not have in place ways of welcoming and assimilating new people.

Obviously pastoral work was important. I was led by the Spirit to visit people in their homes. In the first year I listened considerably. I also realised that the people were ready for change and much could happen in the first year. Indeed, some significant developments needed to occur as symbols of hope and as signs of God doing a new thing.

We were to engage in a stewardship program in June of my first year. Planning for this two year stewardship cycle had to begin early. So I talked with my parish council and elders about their aspirations and yearnings for the church. It was obvious there were no common goals, no specific direction, no vision to fire the imagination and to prompt people to give freely. Therefore in the April of 1989 we gathered forty people, key leaders and interested people for a seven hour session of reflection, evaluation, waiting on the Lord and goal setting.

We met on a Sunday afternoon and evening with a shared tea. At the end of the time we had established ten specific goals that we could work towards in 1989-1990. These became strategic in the life of the church and did much to harmonise people around a common direction. It gave purpose to the stewardship program which was successful and assured the church of financial resources for the ensuing years.

In the weeks preceding the goal setting I preached on the nature of the church using New Testament imagery such as the Body of Christ, the vine and the branches, and the picture of living stones given in 1 Peter 2:4-10. This supported the truth that theology is the basis of renewal. Although there are simple practical strategies that are easily overlooked, true growth is biblically and theologically founded. It occurs through the Spirit of God renewing both people's lives and the structures that enable us to live in community.

Theology of renewal

Theology became for us the very essence of renewal. How we understood and experienced God and the covenant determined our attitudes, expectations and actions.

The term 'the body of Christ' became important as a description of who we were. It affirmed three main truths about the church:

1. There is to be corporate growth in unity and maturity.

2. Growth occurs as the variety of gifts of the people, given by the Spirit, are used in complementary fashion.

3. The church is a living organism with Jesus Christ in authority as the supreme head of the body.

Emphasising a gift theology, inherent in the Uniting Church Basis of Union, we held a gift workshop in the spring of my first year. This examined the teaching of 1 Corinthians 12, Romans 12, and Ephesians 4. It had practical application and included a process by which the participants could begin to identify their special gifts for ministry.

In Ephesians, Paul describes a church in which all the members are to be equipped for the work of ministry. He does not envisage a church where only a few are engaged in ministry or where most are consumers rather than participants.

Ministry is done by the whole church, by Christians working in concert. The whole is greater than the sum of the parts.

Harmonious cooperation and the complementary use of gifts far surpasses the results of individual Christians working alone and independently.

One of the priority tasks of church leaders is to help the members discover their gifts for ministry, to develop such gifts, and to channel them into effective areas of service.

Equipping people for ministry

To enhance the pastoral ministry of the congregation a Caring Committee was appointed by the elders council. This group believed that the ministry should be according to one's spiritual gifts and not by virtue of the office one might hold.

We identified over thirty people gifted in pastoral ministry and called them together to discuss the ministry model we had in mind and to provide instruction on how to make effective pastoral visits. An eight week care workers course followed in the next year. The result is that we now have a team of people who visit members and others associated with the church. This provides a network of care in which no-one need be overlooked. The visitors meet about three times a year to discuss their ministry and to review their list of people.

Another person, gifted in administration and with deep compassion, coordinates a special caring program whereby practical help is given to those with special needs.

In our church we no longer allocate each elder to a group of members. Some elders are not gifted pastorally but have other excellent gifts. Any elder is available to anyone according to need and relationships that are established. We work on the principle that the elders are responsible to see that visiting occurs and are there to release the gifts of those who can do it well.

Other gifts have emerged under this theology. We appointed an honorary administrator who retired from the business world but who obviously brought a wonderful gift in administration. His work of about ten hours a week has involved two mornings a week at the church office. I arranged to be at the office on those mornings as that increased efficiency and communication. Opening the church office on these two days improved the church's profile and made its leaders more accessible.

Many music gifts lay dormant in our worship. We had a very good choir and a couple of proficient organists. The piano in the sanctuary, however, was rarely used. To cater for increasing numbers at worship we added an additional morning service in August 1989. This provided more options. The 9 a.m. service became family oriented and only on occasions is the pipe organ used at this service. Instead, an orchestra sometimes numbering seven or eight has provided the music.

Introducing new songs and installing a screen for use with overheads enlivened the worship and provided greater variety. Our work with musicians includes workshops for worship leaders. We have many unused gifts in this area that we wish to employ. The commencement of a regular 7 p.m. service has created other opportunities for lay leadership, especially by youth. By 1992 the aggregate number at worship had grown to about 200 and the average age is much less than it was in 1989.

We had demographic data available to us on that first planning day and we discovered that the surrounding community contained more younger people than was reflected in the church. Fifty per cent of the population in the parish area is under forty years of age. With this in mind, and trusting in God, we set about embracing the future with confidence. Now our Sunday School is growing, we operate a creche, and we have a growing youth movement.

Believing prayer is central to the renewal that is occurring. A prayer chain has operated in the church for many years. Its members, all ladies, meet over lunch once a month. Here prayer needs are shared.

Another early morning prayer group has begun as a spin-off from 7 a.m. services on Wednesdays during Lent. A number decided to meet every Wednesday at that time and so a group of ten, including men, have gathered faithfully to pray for people and for the church. A focus of our prayer is the renewal of the church and for effective evangelistic ministry. Our church also offers prayer for healing, primarily during ministry time following services of worship.

Group life has also received attention. New home groups and Bible study groups have commenced to provide opportunities for people to engage in study, to offer and receive ministry, and to enhance fellowship. These meet according to needs and availability. They very from weekly to monthly gatherings.

Ongoing renewal

At the heart of what is occuring in our church is our belief that God is continuing the renew us and, while giving ministry in the present, is preparing us to embrace God's unfolding future. We undertand that renewal is the ongoing renewing by God of the church. It is dynamic, never static. It is not an achieved state. It is not the end but the way. To be in renewal is to be journeying with God in the presence of believers.

The primary theological ground for renewal is the kingdom of God. Renewal is not the result of human effort although we are able to respond to God's renewing activity in ways which appropriate such activity. Renewal is the work of God that points to the coming reign of God in the lives of persons and community.

The kingdom of God is neither entirely present nor entirely future. It is here now, is coming, and will come. This gives perspective to renewal. It enables the church to be a community of hope. This orientation points to what is to be as a reality greater than what has been. As such it is a very powerful motivator for Christian living and ministry. It creates vision which fosters hope and incentive.

Under the guidance of the Holy Spirit we have been led to preach that the church is a community premised on the promise of what is to be. We are not simply to adjust to present reality, nor only to patch up here and there or even seek to recover what was. Renewal points to transformation, embracing the new. Hence we pray 'Your kingdom come' (Matthew 6:10).

We believe that the ultimate purpose of the church is to glorify God and to be an agent of God in establishing the unity and wholeness of all things in Christ (Ephesians 1:9-10). The church is a servant of the kingdom of God.

In witnessing to the wholeness of God's kingdom we seek to demonstrate unity, forgiveness, reconciliation and new relationships. One of the most important factors in our witness is the quality of our corporate life in Christ lest our words be empty and our theology barren. We endeavour to be spiritually renewed, our motivation enlivened by the Holy Spirit. We seek a genuine growth in holiness that releases the power of the Holy Spirit.

Our church is on the way. In some quarters we struggle with conservatism but we endeavour to listen to one another, recognising the Spirit of Christ in us all. We also use appropriate practical strategies that can be learned from church analysis and church growth. We are down-to-earth and pragmatic. But we endeavour to place God at the centre knowing that unless the Lord builds the house we labour in vain. Renewed in the power of the Spirit we wish to be living stones, built into a spiritual house of God (1 Peter 2:5).

5 Renewal Leadership

John McElroy

The Revd Dr John McElroy is senior minister of Churchlands Christian Fellowship in Perth.

When I first heard some colleagues talk about the 1990's as a 'decade of revival' I wondered if it was just more wishful thinking aimed at getting Australian churches to take evangelism seriously.

It is increasingly apparent, now, that we live in a 'kairos' moment - God's time for us. Good and evil grow side by side at what appears to be an accelerating rate.

In these times of economic and social upheaval we have the potential of an almost unprecedented audience for God's action. Our fellow Australians are seeking spiritual answers to life's questions. Many do so for the first time. Others are seeking a place to belong and want healing from the wounds of life.

At a time of such obvious need and searching we agonise to observe some congregations experiencing decline and, in a few cases, apparent death. Yet, regardless of outward appearances, wherever God's people gather in worship there is always potential for renewal.

God has a plan for the church. In the past God kept his promise. Even though it would appear whole generations lost a true knowledge of God, he sovereignly renewed his kingdom again when he found willing hearts. Today, God is looking for pure and willing hearts among those who would aspire to leadership in the church.

In preparation for revival and harvest, God is raising up leaders whose visionary zeal is matched by their integrity. Our Master is concerned not only about whether we reach the goal, but how we achieve it. Leaders today are wise to remember that the end does not justify any and every means of getting there. On earth, Christian leaders are servants of a God whose nature is integrity, justice, love and mercy. Our Lord wants his ambassadors to reflect his nature and character in the midst of providing leadership.

For some time I have noted that methods and standards vary greatly in the selection and guidance of church leaders. Within my denomination, I have often been called upon to give advice or rectify situations which are attributable to poor leadership decisions.

My intent is not to reiterate what others have written on issues facing renewal leadership. I would like, however, to underline three issues which I feel must be considered by those who desire to be leaders in renewal. These issues have come out of my experience as pastor of a renewal-based congregation within the Uniting Church and as convenor of the Christian Ministries Network of Western Australia.

Caution in leadership selection

Leadership is a key issue in renewal and revival. The apostle Paul warned against being hasty in the laying on of hands for leadership (1 Timothy 5:22). While this scripture is often quoted, the importance of its implementation is often underestimated, much to the detriment of the church. Once a person has been placed in a position of leadership that person carries an authority and influence within the Body of Christ which either promotes or hinders its mission.

I have not yet discovered one elder, staff person or leader who, at the time of being selected, was fully mature in the Lord. That is normal. Jesus picked the disciples on the basis of their potential, not their perfection. Chapter three of 1 Timothy provides an essential list of considerations for spiritual leadership. In addition to this list, I often ask the following six questions concerning potential leaders:

1. Have they undergone a period of settling in and observation?

When new people decide to make our Fellowship their spiritual home, we invite them to undertake a minimum three to six months settling in and getting to know us. During this time we ask that they join a weekly home group but refrain from signing up for, or becoming involved in, any of the ministries of the church. During this period our leaders observe their character, gifts, and apparent maturity in the Lord. This brief time of waiting clarifies not only their suitability for ministry but whether the needs and vision of the individual fit our capabilities.

2. Have they dealt with sin or strongholds operative in their lives?

In other words, are they free of habitual sin or do they require ministry, healing, or counselling which will set them free from ungodly thoughts or behaviour? Do they give evidence of anger, unforgiveness, rejection, lust, pride, hurt, gossip, or any of the acts of the flesh noted in Galatians 5:19-21? The presence of sin or strongholds does not indicate a person's ultimate unsuitability for leadership, but it does indicate: not yet!

3. Do they show evidence of having gone to the cross?

Does the nature of Jesus, particularly humility, seem to be evident and growing? Going to the cross speaks of dying to the flesh and human cleverness in our attitudes and lifestyles. Such people will show traits of circumspectness, submissiveness, wisdom, compassion, transparency, patience and prayerfulness. They are humble, teachable, willing to be accountable, and allow others to speak into their lives.

4. Do they have a growing intimacy with God?

In John 15:5 Jesus said, 'Those who abide in me and I in them bear much fruit, because apart from me you can do nothing.' To abide in Jesus speaks of an intimate relationship of prayer and communion; of two best friends who anticipate one another's moods, mannerisms and

153

responses. Abiding is the process of becoming like the company we keep. The result of intimacy is to bear certain recognisable fruit: the fruit of the Spirit, an ability to discern the Lord's voice, and a growth in our understanding of God's nature and the way he brings his will to pass.

5. Are they free of selfish ambition or worldly cleverness?

Selfish ambition is essentially the desire for recognition, power, and control. Worldly cleverness is the means of fulfilling ambition: intellectualism, deceit, power games, manipulation, partiality, and control. Some seek church leadership with hopes of lordship rather than service. Others have a mistaken notion that what made them successful in the business world translates identically to the church.

Our own enthusiasm can never substitute for godly wisdom in decision making, as stated in Psalm 127:1, 'Unless the Lord builds the house, those who build it labour in vain. Unless the Lord guards the city, the guard keeps watch in vain.'

Those suited to spiritual leadership acknowledge sooner rather than later that prayer, waiting on the Lord's timing, and following his plan are the only ways to build God's house.

6. Do they have the same spirit and vision as your team?

Are potential leaders on the right train? Are they willing to work in submission to the pastor and leaders of the local church? Do they hold views which mesh with ours, or are they at odds with our established vision, ethos, and mission?

For some reason, growing churches attract ambitious people aspiring to leadership who lack the discernment to choose the church God has actually selected for them. You must therefore look out for 'cruisomatics' flying from church to church looking for the perfect roost. Beware of those practicing a 'gift of correction' or ministries which they proclaim will 'get your church on the right track.' These are the lone rangers, free spirits, and ultimately the self-inflicted wounded whose unrepentant hearts cause untold grief.

When selecting potential leaders it is always wise to narrow the front door, so to speak, by being cautious and getting as many facts as possible on the table. Good things come to those who wait and ask God's discernment in the selection of leaders. I, and many others, have learned the hard way. It is much easier to refrain from placing a person in leadership than to admit a mistake and have to remove them later.

Unity results in synergy

Unity, especially among leaders, gives impetus to revival. It results in a Holy Spirit induced synergy.

The Macquarie Dictionary defines synergism as 'the joint action of two substances... which increase each other's effectiveness when taken together.' While synergism is most commonly thought of in the context of chemistry or metallurgy, it also applies to the church. When two churches and their leaders pray together, relationships bond, cooperation results and the net impact is greater than their previous effect as two separate entities.

The chances of revival taking place within a church, area, or city increase when there is unity within the leadership. John Wimber has noted that one of the signs of impending revival would be a call to unity. This call to unity is not an exercise of theological compromise or ecclesiastical carpentry but comes as the Body of Christ is touched by repentance, healing, and holiness.

Pat Robertson, in his book The Secret Kingdom, writes of eight principles arising from the teachings of Jesus which govern all of life. He calls these eight principles 'the laws of the kingdom'. One of these principles, which Robertson calls 'the law of unity', presents both a challenge and promise to Christian leaders in Australia.

Essentially, the law of unity states that within the Trinity there has always been agreement and harmony. Consequently, unity and harmony in Christ's Body are crucial to the unleashing of God's incredible power among us. Great creativity and power for accomplishing God's purpses are released where there is harmony.

A practical outworking of the law of unity is seen in Matthew 18:19-20 where Jesus said, 'Again, truly I tell you, if two of you agree on earth about anything you ask, it will be done for you by my Father in heaven. For where two or three are gathered in my name, I am there among them.'

Here our Lord calls for agreement based on unity. Since Jesus was among them when they gathered to consider an issue, Jesus' disciples would be expected to agree with him. As the central focus and inspiration of their fellowship, Jesus would bring his disciples to harmony if they genuinely laid aside their own preconceptions and centred on him.

The biblical accounts of life in the New Testament church further illustrate the power of unity. As the believers continued to seek the Lord together in prayer (Acts 1:14) the Holy Spirit added to their number and confirmed the gospel with signs and wonders (Acts 5:12-16).

Early in 1990 I became aware of the existence of Christian networks of encouragement in Australia, England, the United States, and South Africa. These networks focus on unity through prayer and building relationships among leaders. I had the privilege of visiting networks in South Africa and in the U.S.A.

While the setting and composition of each network varied greatly, they had five traits in common:

1. They were built on relationships between church leaders.

2. Those involved had been renewed by the work of the Holy Spirit and believed the Spirit was raising up a strong church to take the land.

3. Those involved came from a wide variety of church backgrounds.

4. All shared a Body-wide vision, putting aside competition and empire-building in favour of building up and encouraging the wider Body of Christ.

5. They showed evidence of the spirit of Joshua and Caleb, having the courage to dream and plan great exploits for God.

Inspired by what I saw, I returned to Perth and began to pray about God's plan for networks of encouragement in Australia. Aware of similar moves under way in the eastern states initiated by the Rev. Dan Armstrong and Kairos Ministries, I felt a need to bring leaders together across Western Australia. After inviting some colleagues (many of whom had worked together in organising Vineyard Conferences) to join in prayer, the Christian Ministries Network WA was formed in 1990.

Recently I have observed a marked increase in the number of interdenominational prayer meetings and in fellowship activities aimed at building relationships between evangelical and charismatic leaders in Western Australia. Politicians, judges and heads of some Bible Colleges are among those beginning to come together for prayer and fellowship. There appears to be a warming of the spiritual atmosphere over the state, similar to the Greenhouse effect.

As the impetus towards unity increases and relationships are built, I am noticing a decrease in competitiveness. Leaders desire increasing cooperation. Pastors talk about such subjects as discovering God's plan for taking our cities, networking with the wider Body of Christ, establishing the church of the city, and discovering and sharing each congregation's redemptive gift. I have concluded that unity is bringing a synergy to the Body of Christ in Western Australia.

For further reading on developing strategies for bringing revival to our communities I recommend two excellent books, Taking our Cities for God by John Dawson (Creation House, 1989) and The House of the Lord (Creation House, 1991).

Revival foundations: Jesus and obedience

I believe that one of the reasons why God withholds revival is that he knows our nets are insufficiently strong or mature to contain the catch. Historically, revivals have lasted for about a generation for this reason. Eventually the nets broke down. In the coming revival I believe God wants us to pay attention to the foundation on which we build our nets.

157

In 1 Corinthians 3:11, the Apostle Paul reminds us that 'no one can lay any foundation other than the one that has been laid; that foundation is Jesus Christ.'

We do well to remember this. Many Christians and congregations are unsure of the implications of Jesus as the foundation. We have inadvertently confused Jesus with our doctrines, liturgies, denominational trappings, and social activism. These are forms or expressions of faith and may be valid, but they are not the one and only foundation: Jesus Christ himself.

Many Christians have built their identities and loyalties on the other building materials Paul alludes to in subsequent verses, not on a personal relationship with and loyalty to Jesus. These alternative building materials may look and feel substantial. In the final analysis, however, they do not stand the test.

What does it mean to build on the foundation of Jesus? It means being cemented into him. It involves being more Christlike as his disciples and obeying all he commands (Matthew 28:18-20). To build on the foundation of Jesus is to build a church which is nourished in the love of Jesus and gives love in response (1 John 4:19). This kind of church will take the land.

John Dawson emphasises that, 'It is not primarily out of compassion for humanity that we share our faith or pray for the lost; it is, first of all, love for God' (Taking our Cities for God, page 209). Love is the greatest power the world has ever known. As more of God's love and light flood the world, darkness will be overcome.

This leads us to the vital question: What brings revival to a land? Revival is essentially a 'soft spot' in the heart of God, an act of God's grace and mercy. God sovereignly determines when and where revival will happen. Yet within the scope of God's sovereignty we can make a response. We see it in God's word to Solomon in 2 Chronicles 7:14,

If my people who are called by my name humble themselves, pray, seek my face, and turn from their wicked ways, then I will hear from heaven, and will forgive their sin and heal their land.

Perhaps the first act of humility required of us is to ask ourselves: What is our goal in evangelism? Are we seeking to make people 'churched' as members of a particular denomination with a loyalty to our ethos and traditions? Or are we making disciples of Jesus? Will the fish we catch be appropriately 'cleaned,' that is discipled to become like Jesus and serve him? How do we help new disciples go back into the harvest field to bring others into his glorious light?

In Ezekiel 34:4 we find the tasks of God's shepherds. They strengthen the weak, heal the sick, bind up the injured, bring back the strays, and search for the lost. When I consider each of these five traits I find there the sum total of what God appears to be training his church to engage in. Here is the culmination of what I understand to be power evangelism, personal evangelism, and making disciples who carry on the ministry of Jesus Christ.

Only Jesus Christ has the authority to draw everyone to himself. Only at his name will every knee bow and every tongue confess that Jesus Christ is Lord. Only as the sheep hear the Good Shepherd's voice and sense his touch as ministered through his obedient servants will they be drawn to him in revival.

There are, no doubt, many issues crucial to effective leadership in renewal. These three, however, are foundational to fostering revival. We must be more cautious in the selection of leaders. Our unity, especially in leadership, will result in a Holy Spirit induced synergism which sparks revival in the land. The church must stay true to the right foundation of Jesus and obedience to him.

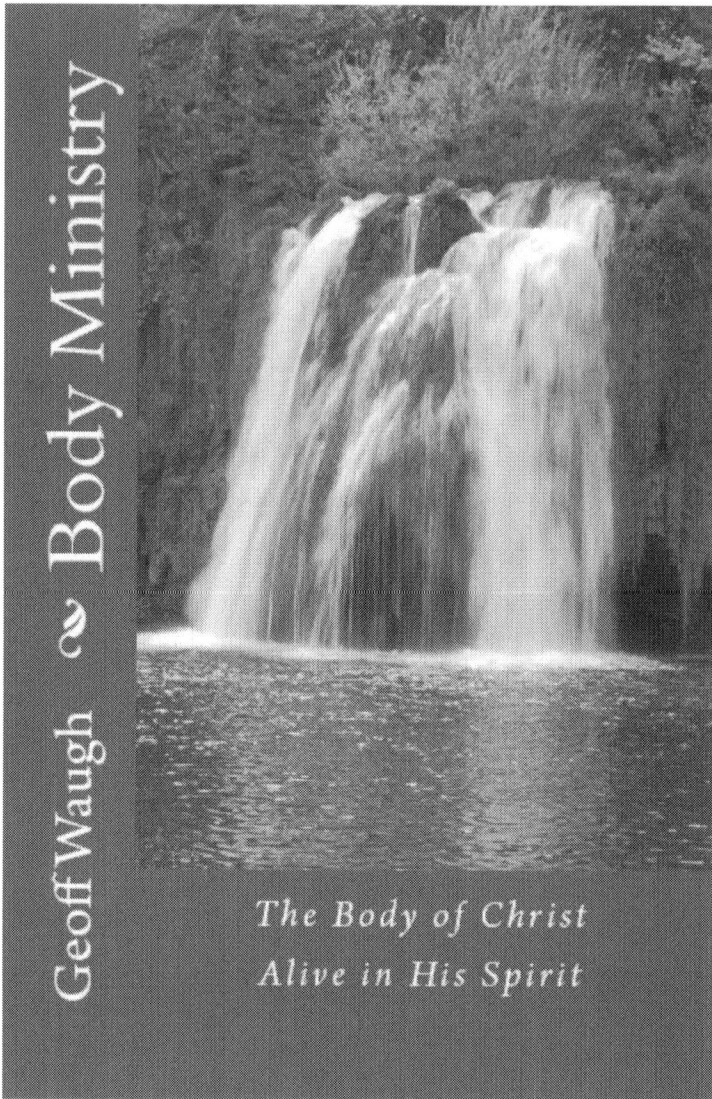

Geoff Waugh ~ Body Ministry

The Body of Christ
Alive in His Spirit

Body Ministry

The Body of Christ Alive in His Spirit

6 Reflections on Renewal

Ralph Wicks

The Rt Revd Ralph Wicks, an Anglican Bishop, was a pioneer in renewal among Anglicans in Australia. He comments on that ministry.

An event of some significance occurred in the early years of my episcopate. I had a feeling that the church as a whole was just plodding along.

There were a few bright spots among the parishes, but on the whole I thought church growth was not exciting. What troubled me more was that not many clergy were over-concerned, and if they were anxious about the situation, they didn't show it.

At the same time as I was experiencing these impressions, I was made aware of the 'Holy Spirit' movement. Pentecostal churches had been with us since the beginning of the century, but in the 1960s they had been showing a lot of vitality and considerable growth in adherents - many former Anglicans and also former members of a number of other historic churches. I was interested to discover the reason for this new phenomenon. Books by Michael Harper, Colin Urquhart and David Watson, Anglican priests in England, helped me to understand this 'charismatic movement' (charisma here refers to the Pauline list of Spiritual Gifts).

Power ministry

I wanted to know about the 'Power' ministry, i.e. the Power of the Holy Spirit. I knew God had blessed the few natural gifts I had, but there was always so much effort on my part, and I got tired. There was not much 'resting in the Lord'.

But I had a problem. My wife and I now lived in a fine house in Taringa Parade, Taringa, owned by the diocese. My wife knew of my growing interest in the charismatic movement, but was very apprehensive about this spiritual phenomenon. She said to me, 'If you get involved in this movement, I'll leave you.' So I pulled back from the charismatic movement. However, an extraordinary event was about to unfold.

I went to a clergy retreat. While I was away, my wife went, albeit reluctantly, with a friend to a house meeting to hear an evangelist and spiritual healer. I imagine the friend was endeavouring to find support for my wife, who now had cancer. During the meeting, an invitation to go forward for prayer was given. My wife, who was really a very private person, was first to step forward. Later, she told me she didn't really know what happened except friends were picking her up from the floor. She felt weepy, and asked to go home. She cried herself to sleep, not out of grief, but of joy.

The next day she had a strong desire to ring three women from whom she was estranged. Two were delighted that friendship was restored; the third, from whom my wife had not heard for months, got her phone call in first, and there was much rejoicing. In a real sense, I found a different woman in my home when I returned from the retreat. She of course looked the same, but she seemed to have grown ten feet tall spiritually.

With confidence now, I went to a conference in Sydney, led by Archbishop Bill Burnett of Capetown and Bishop Zulu, also from Africa.

Archbishop Burnett was the Episcopal Father of the Charismatic Renewal in the Anglican Communion.

The conference was terrific and I ended up being elected chairman of the Anglican Renewal Ministries in Australia, a post I held for several years.

It was a joy to organise several Diocesan Renewal conferences at Camp Cal, Caloundra. Guest speakers at various times included Vernon Cohen and Dick Wallace, Anglican priests from Melbourne. It was a privilege to have Father Terry Fulham from Darien, Connecticut, USA, at another of the meetings.

Ecumenical Renewal services at St John's Cathedral drew packed houses. The Rev. Geoff Waugh, from a Baptist-Uniting Church background, and a Roman Catholic priest, Father Vincent Hobbs, were co-convenors of these rallies, some of which were also held at St Stephen's Roman Catholic Cathedral and the Albert Street Uniting Church. These were exciting times as lives were changed, Holy Spirit power was in evidence and healings took place. A small number of diocesan priests were blessed and their ministries enriched.

Proclamation of Jesus

However, it was not all plain sailing. Some clergy regarded me as a 'weirdo' but one thing they could not deny: The proclamation of Jesus and God's gifts of salvation by grace through faith became key features of my preaching. I was reminded by Scripture that the work of the Holy Spirit is to glorify Jesus.

Of course, there are excesses in most spiritual movements. I have also known Anglo-Catholic and Evangelicals to go 'over the top', and I have experienced 'charismatic Christians' who have become quite unbalanced and fanatical.

I have been glad to have experienced the strong sacramental life of Anglicanism and the good order of liturgical worship. But liturgical worship need not be stiff. The warmth of the Spirit can melt the coldness of mere formalism. At times, 'non-liturgical' services, too, have a very helpful place in our churches.

I was invited to a conference of Evangelicals in Melbourne. I guess it was strange to have one brought up in a strong Anglo-Catholic tradition to be given this invitation. However, my role was to respond to a paper by Michael Cassidy on 'Charismatic or Spiritual Renewal'. Michael has been well known in many countries as one of the leaders of African Enterprise - an organisation concerned with a two-pronged mission - Evangelism and Community Social Development.

From Monday to Wednesday, the lectures had been superb, but more of the head than of the heart. I thought, in fact, that the mood of the delegates was quiet and subdued. So arrived my six minutes. The then Archbishop of Melbourne, Bob Dann, kept reminding me about the 'six minutes'. I put away my prepared text and simply shared with the conference what spiritual renewal meant to me: how my ministry was enriched, how I came to understand and love Jesus more. The response of the delegates was very moving to me. They rose in acclamation. I went backstage and wept. God had done something beautiful.

As I had to leave the conference immediately and return to Brisbane, I could know only second-hand that the mood of the conference changed from that moment - people were more open and friendly than before.

What has always amazed me is that Anglican leaders, yes, bishops, have almost acted as though Pentecostalism does not exist, especially when many Anglicans have moved into Pentecostal fellowships and especially since Pentecostalism is the fastest-growing Christian expression in Australia. Either they are afraid to admit that Pentecostalism has 'something'; or worse, they think Pentecostals are in some way outside the pale and not to be regarded as part of the Christian family.

Bishop Shevill once said, 'The untaught truths of yesterday become the heresies of today.' In other words, what the historic churches fail to emphasise, others pick up and go to excesses. Historic churches, by their partial neglect of the third Person of the Holy Trinity, have in part, only themselves to blame for the growth of many Pentecostal fellowships.

Parish Missions

Before and after my adventure with 'Charismatic Renewal' I felt called to offer myself to any priest who would risk inviting me to lead a parish mission. I had no particular training in evangelism but I learnt something by doing.

During my time as an archdeacon and assistant bishop, I conducted parish missions or intense weekend teaching periods in a number of places within and outside the Diocese of Brisbane. The 'local' ones were at Stanthorpe, Pittsworth, Petrie (twice), Mt Gravatt (twice), Maroochydore, Bundaberg, Nanango, Ekibin, Inala, Yeronga and Ashgrove. Outside the diocese, missions were taken at Kurri Kurri in the Diocese of Newcastle, Glen Innes in the Diocese of Grafton, Stratford in the Diocese of Gippsland, Belgrave in the Diocese of Melbourne and Biloela in the Diocese of Rockhampton.

It was a privilege to be invited by the Bishop of Singapore, Ban it Chui, to take a mission in his Cathedral of St Andrew and also a clergy retreat. The visit to Singapore was a real eye-opener. In this diocese, the 'charismatic movement' has changed church life in many parishes. I saw churches filled - especially with young people hungry for the Gospel. In one parish I visited, a cinema has now been acquired to accommodate the growing congregation.

One night while I was ministering in St Andrew's Cathedral, a young man - a Buddhist - wandered in and was converted to the Christian faith. On one Sunday, I ministered to an all-Indian congregation. For three hours, the whole congregation came singly or in family groups for the laying on of hands with prayer. A number were overpowered by the Holy Spirit - and all the time I was praying over others, two women knelt on the concrete floor beside me, praying for me. With such enthusiasm for Jesus, it is perhaps not surprising that it was hard for me to leave Singapore.

Of course, it is difficult to estimate the effect of such parish missions. In one or two places, I suspect the missions were a complete failure. My own ministry may have been defective or maybe the preparation may have been inadequate.

However, in other places, according to the rectors, lives were changed, people were converted, people were physically healed. A former rector of Maroochydore, in the Diocese of Brisbane, told me that my mission was the most significant event in his long ministry in that parish. For that I praise God and give Him the glory.

Recently I met a businessman in Nambour who confessed that he had been converted at the mission in Glen Innes. I remembered this man well. He was the last to whom I ministered at that mission.

There have, however, been a few regrets. I have known people so changed and challenged by the inflowing power of the Holy Spirit to be a real threat to parish clergy in parishes where I have ministered. These dear priests have not been able to cope with the enthusiasm of the newly converted and have found them difficult to cope with. Some of my missions have swelled the numbers going to Pentecostal churches.

It has been beautiful over the years to see wayward husbands come back to their wives and families, to see men and women freed from the burden of guilt which has plagued them for years, to see people with cancer have remission for a number of years, to know people so enthused that they form the nucleus of a new parish. I have been amazed over the years at the transforming power of Jesus in individual lives.

This article is reproduced from pages 76-82 of Bishop Ralph Wicks' book, **One Rung from the Top** *(Brisbane: Boolarong, 1993), used by permission.*

7 Local Revivals in Australia

Stuart Piggin

Dr Stuart Piggin, Director of the Centre for the History of Christian Thought and Experience at Macquarie University, lectured in history at Wollongong and Macquarie Universities before taking up his present appointment. His books include studies of Australian Church History and of Evangelicalism.

I want to advance four propositions about the history of revivals in Australia, and then comment on the prospects for revival in Australia today.

Four propositions

1. Local revivals have been frequent in Australian history

In my research I have found references to 71 local revivals in nineteenth-century Australia. And far from being impervious to revival, the twentieth-century has witnessed more revivals than any previous age. This century has witnessed the greatest growth ever in the Christian Church, and revival in Africa, Asia, and South America is endemic.

In Australia the new century began with the largest evangelistic campaigns in Australia's history. R. A. Torrey arrived in Melbourne (April 1902) following successful evangelistic tours in Japan and China. Attendances totalled a quarter of a million each week when the population of the whole of Victoria was only one million. Meanwhile, in 1902/3 a tent mission crusade throughout 200 country towns of NSW reported 25,000 inquirers.

In the 1920s there were rather spectacular revivals associated with Pentecostalism. In 1925 a revival broke out in the Melbourne suburb of Sunshine. Hundreds came under conviction of sin, were filled by the Great Baptizer, and created such excitement that people came from all over Australia to receive blessing. Out of this was formed the Pentecostal Church of Australia.

The 1930s, the decade of the African revival, witnessed scenes of considerable spiritual vitality in Melbourne. The Methodist Local Preachers Branch was very vigorous and had an impact on evangelical life in Australia. Teams of these local preachers went all over Australia and New Zealand. For many years it held a Holiness Convention each King's Birthday weekend in Melbourne. It was conducted entirely by laymen. A Baptist minister, George Hall, who trained in America under Dr R. A. Torrey and Dr Campbell Morgan, and who knew evangelical life in USA intimately, said the Methodist Local Preachers Melbourne Branch Holiness Convention was the greatest spiritual force he had ever experienced.

The 1930s also saw scenes of revival in Queensland, especially connected with the Pentecostal branch of Methodism. Revivals were reported at Woombye, Kingscliffe, and Toowoomba. One who was used in this work was Booth Clibborn, grandson of William Booth. Other effective evangelists were Gavin Hamilton, Hyman Appleman, Garry Love and Gypsy Smith. The aboriginal pastor, Rodney Minniecon, now at Griffith, was a product of the same movement.

There were revivals associated with the name of Geoff Bingham in Australia in the 1960s and 1970s, some remarkable occasions associated with the Jesus movement, particularly among young people in Melbourne, and, of course, revival broke among aborigines on Elcho Island in March 1979.

Stuart Piggin

2. Evidence indicates that local revivals have been genuine

Consider the revival at Kiama in 1864 under the ministry of the Rev. Thomas Angwin, a Methodist. His sermons revealed a knowledge of 'the deep things of God', and congregations and prayer meetings grew in number, swelled by Presbyterians and Anglicans who sought a richer fare than they were receiving in their own churches. On 'one of the later Sundays' in July 1864 the revival came:

The arrows were sharp in the hands of the King's messenger that night. They were straightly aimed, and shot with all the intensity of a love baptised with the compassion of the Christ. ... The next night there was almost equally as large a congregation at the prayer meeting. Then began what the good old people called 'a breaking down'. The communion rail was crowded with seekers. Some hoar-headed men were amongst them; a storekeeper in the town, notorious for his fearful temper and furious conduct when under its influence; some gentle-spirited women; a number of senior lads from the Sunday schools ... Night after night for the rest of the week and into the middle of the next, the meetings continued. ... It was a revival which gave workers to the Church, teachers to the Sunday School, local preachers to the circuit plan and ultimately several ministers to the Australian Methodist Church (Carruthers 1922:32).

Revival in Australian Methodism in the second half of the nineteenth century is mainly associated with John Watsford, the first Australian-born Methodist clergyman. In Ballarat in the 1860s, in Parramatta, in the inner city suburbs of Surry Hills and Balmain, and in country town such as Windsor and Goulburn, Watsford was used to ignite the fires of revival. Of a service in the Bourke Street Methodist church, Sydney, in 1860, Watsford (1901:123) reported:

To a congregation which packed the building I preached from 'Quench not the Spirit'. What a time we had. The whole assembly was mightily moved, the power was overwhelming; many fell to the floor in agony, and there was a loud cry for mercy. The police came rushing in to see what was the matter; but there was nothing for them to do. It was impossible to tell how many penitents came forward; there must have been over

169

two hundred. The large schoolroom was completely filled with anxious inquirers.

3. Revivals have raised moral standards of whole communities

The 1902/3 tent meeting crusade in rural NSW crusade which resulted in the conversion of 25,000 was nowhere more wonderful in its manifestation than in the coal mining villages of the Illawarra when 2735 professed conversion or some 15% of the region's population. The fire of the Spirit fell on each coal mining village in a work described as 'gloriously monotonous'. At Mt Kembla 131 professed conversions; Mt Keira 214; Balgownie 183; Bulli 292; Helensburgh 234 and so on. At Mt Kembla 'an intense emotion with an evident assent to the Preacher's burning words were imprinted on every face and feature'.

What about the impact on the moral tone of the community? At Mt Keira swearing disappeared and the pit ponies in the mines stopped work as they could no longer understand their instructions, a phenomenon also reported in the Welsh revival 3 years later. Asked what was the evidence that the revival was genuine, the Rev. D. O'Donnell replied that the question was a very proper one, since there should be 'works meet for repentance'. He catalogued four evidences:

> First, payment of debts. Tradesmen report the settlement of accounts they had long regarded as bad. Second, a pure language. ... It is said that in the Mount Keira pit an oath has scarcely been heard since the Mission . . . Third, a fair day's work. The proprietor of one of the mines told me that the biggest day's output of coal they ever had, followed the Mission. Fourth, attendance at Church. All the churches report greatly increased congregations and increase in the membership (Colwell 1904:630).

The great revivals of the past have always resulted in a decline in national illegality and immorality. The same is true of the Billy Graham Crusades in Australia in 1959. The number of convictions for all crimes committed in Australia doubled between 1920 and 1950 and then doubled again between 1950 and 1959 when the population increased by only one-quarter. Then, in 1960, 1961, and 1962, the

170

number of convictions remained fairly constant, resuming its dramatic upward trend in the middle and late 60s.

The illegitimate birth-rate was also investigated to get some rough index to non-criminal community standards. In the period 1955 to 1965 this index rose every year to almost double the 1954 figure, but the year it rose slowest (.06%) was in 1960. The illegitimate children not conceived in 1959 were not born in 1960!

Turning to alcohol consumption, the Bureau of Statistics supplied the following figures.

Annual Per Capita Consumption of Beer in Australia in Litres
1958-59   111.01
1968-69   113.5
1978-79   133.2

This also reveals the same deteriorating trends as we have seen in all the other social indicators. It is therefore striking to learn that the figure for 1960-61 is 100.1, that is 10% lower than the 1958-59 figure, an unexpected and dramatic fall.

4. Revival comes with social salvation to marginalised and underprivileged groups

Today's aborigines, who number about 150,000 in Australia, are experiencing revival, with some of their own movements emerging. There has been a change in the tone of communities touched by revival: less drunkenness, petrol sniffing, and fighting; greater conscientiousness in work; an increased boldness in speaking out against social injustices. At the Anglican Roper River Mission (Ngukurr) which had been reduced to a social disaster area by the granting of a liquor licence, the revival, which began in 1979, came as a form of social salvation. Sister Edna Brooker exclaimed:

'New life has come to Ngukurr. Half the population say they have turned to Christ and the transformation from alcohol, petrol sniffing and immorality is very wonderful' (Boyd 1986).

At Warburton in Western Australia 500 came to the Lord and were baptised. At Wiluna crime dropped to zero and the local publican had to put on free beer to entice people back into his pub.

So, revival comes as a form of social salvation to a needy people. In Australia the major perceived problems are economic recession and malaise; unemployment; marital breakdown and the poverty of relationships; drugs; death on the roads; environmental rape; demoralisation of the young. Revival would be the chief means of energising the Church in general and Christians in particular to address these problems.

Prospects for revival in Australia

1. Revivals are often caught rather than taught

Many people, particularly in the missionary movement, are learning about revival which is endemic in other parts of the world and are bringing what they have learned back to Australia.

Australian missionaries working in Africa learned much from the East African revival which began in Ruanda in 1931. Revival has been endemic in the Solomons since the early 1970s. Among the missionaries was George Strachan who has written an instructive book entitled *Revival: its blessings and battles*. There, for example, he answered the important question, 'Why do revivals not start?'

> Lack of real prayer is a major hindrance. For many of us prayer is of no great importance. It is just an 'extra' to a busy life. But prayer that brings power takes precedence over all else. Nothing should be allowed to steal away time spent with God in prayer (1989:55).

In 1962 Geoff Bingham, who had been influenced by the East African revival, returned from Pakistan. That year Bingham taught at a teaching mission at Thornleigh. He taught all the great truths which had crystallised for him when he experienced revival in Pakistan: the holiness of God; the tyrants which hold people in bondage, namely sin, the flesh, Satan, principalities and powers; God's wrath, the conscience, the law. He then showed how all of those have a hold over us because of guilt, but that when the guilt was taken away in the cross so the bondage is taken away.

A prayer meeting before the mission was held in the home of Fred George, a returned CMS missionary from Tanzania. About thirty people attended it. At first the meeting was fairly routine with prayer for the church and mission, and then Geoff said 'I think that the Lord wants to bring home to us now what the Lord thinks of us.' He read from Psalm 24, 'Who shall ascend to the hill of the Lord ... ? He who has clean hands and a pure heart.'

Then he suggested that those present should come to the Lord and ask him to reveal himself. They all knelt down in a circle, and then someone began to weep, and a great conviction came over all of them. Some tried to pray, but dissolved in sobs.

One who could not attend that mission because he was sick was John Dunn. At that home prayer meeting there came over John Dunn an incredible sense of his own depravity in the sight of God. He saw something extraordinary.

It was as if he were standing outside himself, looking at himself. And he wanted to flee from himself as fast and as far as he could because of the horrific sight he had of his own sin. He was crushed and broke down and sobbed convulsively, and the others around him were prostrate on the floor, broken hearted.

Then a gentle quietness came over the whole group, and then a wonderful sense of God's total forgiveness. Then they sang and sang until they were hoarse. The singing and intercession just went on and on, until someone said, 'It's half past four in the morning'. Everyone was staggered that so much time had elapsed.

2. The Theology of Revival is increasingly studied and understood

The thinking of some of the most influential evangelical teachers and preachers of the twentieth century leaves room for revival - e.g. Martyn Lloyd-Jones and J. I. Packer. Packer, for example, tells us that the Puritans did not use the word revival much - they spoke of godliness, by which they meant revival. There is an increasing study and appreciation of the writings of the church's greatest theologian of revival, Jonathan Edwards. Bingham has written over 150 books. Many of them bear on revival. Then there is the excellent study material of the Fellowship for Revival's Academy prepared by the Rev. Robert Evans, 57 Talbot Road, Hazelbrook, NSW, 2779. So there is ample opportunity for the Christian to study the whole issue and theology of revival.

3. Revival is usually preceded by unprecedented unity

Unity among Christians must involve greater cooperation between Evangelicals and Charismatics.

This will require godly leadership from those who have been given leadership roles in those branches of the Christian church. I think that there has been such a stand off between the two that I have been advancing a theology which might bring them both together on what they agree about the Holy Spirit rather than have them arguing over what they disagree about the Holy Spirit.

We all agree that the most fundamental work of the Holy Spirit is to convict of sin and to regenerate and sanctify. Let us all - evangelical and charismatic - meet together and pray for a great outpouring of these things rather than arguing over disputed matters such as gifts and exorcisms.

4. Revival comes when we move together

Revival is the river of God's love flowing freely and fully through the Church, and it may come when the existing tributaries start to flow together.

a. In late 1989 the first of the prayer meetings for a spiritual awakening within the Anglican church was held in Lindfield, a Sydney suburb. That has expanded and some 26 regional groups are now meeting to pray for revival. This involves about 6000 folk in prayer for the revival of the church and the spread of the gospel. Much blessing is being reported. There are churches which as a result of their involvement with this are reactivating their prayer life. One church reports conversions every week. At a time when the Anglican church is divided over so many issues it is great that Anglicans should be able to draw together to pray in this way.

b. The Fellowship of Revival in the Uniting Church has nurtured such wonderful Christians as Dr Robert Hillman. His life and his lectures on the ministry of intercession will continue to speak to the Church and sensitise it to its need for revival.

c. Then there are such groups of faithful souls longing for revival as Intercessors for Australia, and Aussies Afire launched by the Bishop of Grafton in 1989. There is also Fusion and Aussie Awakening, headed up by Mal Garvin.

d. Bishop Dudley Foord, an organiser of the Sydney Anglican prayer gatherings, spoke at the National Parliamentary breakfast in Canberra. This was a great opportunity to remind the nation that national regeneration or the restoration of a demoralised people is a spiritual matter primarily and only secondarily an economic matter. Then Bishop Foord and Glenda Welden, the wife of the publisher, Kevin Welden, and a member of the Christian and Missionary Alliance, attended the first international Prayer Leaders Conference organised as part of the Lausanne Commission on World Evangelisation.

The clouds are gathering. Be encouraged to pray until the inundation of the Spirit comes.

References

Boyd, Jeanette (1986) 'The Arnhem Land Revival of 1979: An Australian Aboriginal Religious Movement', unpublished paper, October.

Carruthers, J. E. (1922) Memories of an Australian Ministry. London: Epworth.

Colwell, James (1904) Illustrated History of Methodism, Sydney: William Brooks.

Strachan, George (1984) Revival: its Blessings and Battles. An Account of experiences in the Solomon Islands (Revised 1989). Laurieton: South Sea Evangelical Mission.

Watsford, John (1901) Glorious Gospel Triumphs. London: Charles H Kelly.

Dr Stuart Piggin researched the history of Australian evangelicalism and on the history of and prospects for revival in Australia. In 1991 the Centre for the Study of Australian Christianity, which fosters postgraduate research into Australian religious history in conjunction with Macquarie University, was established at Robert Menzies College at Macquarie University.

8 Asia's Maturing Church

Interview with David Wang

The world's largest revival continues unabated despite widespread restrictions and persecution. Dr David Wang, International Director of Asian Outreach, talks about why God is moving so dramatically among Asian believers, published in 1992.

Q. Is this truly a Decade of Harvest for Asia?

A. For 25 years I have been involved in Asian evangelism and mission. I must admit that there have been tines of discouragement, particularly in the latter part of the 1960s. We saw a lot of activity and effort, but not many lasting results.

However I would say that for the past 20 years we have seen a tremendous response to the gospel of Jesus Christ. This is happening not only in countries such as Korea and Singapore, which are enjoying phenomenal revival, but also in countries closed to traditional mission activities such as China and Vietnam. We're now seeing the Holy Spirit moving in dramatic ways, resulting in conversions and church growth, with regular signs, wonders and miracles.

The traditional word 'harvest' no longer seems adequate to describe what God is doing. I would describe it as 'the great ingathering'. This is even happening in traditionally difficult Thailand and Japan. I visited these countries very recently and both missionaries and national leaders were reporting breakthroughs of an unprecedented nature.

Q. Why is the Asian Church suddenly growing so dramatically?

A. We must give credit to the early missionaries who laboured, bled and died sowing the seed of the gospel. Some of the seeds laid dormant for many years. But they did take root. As God's time comes upon this continent, they are now bearing fruit. Aided by signs, wonders and miracles some are bearing a hundred fold!

Secondly, we now see an explosion of the Church led by indigenous leadership. God is raising up excellent Asian leadership. Asian workers are now evangelising, sending out missionaries and bringing in a great harvest.

Thirdly, persecution and suffering inflicted by communist or atheist regimes and other religious forces have enhanced the Church's growth even further.

But ultimately I recognise that it seems to be God's sovereign plan. He seems to have a timetable, and now is the time for the Asian Church to experience revival, renewal, growth and expansion. It is God's time for this continent.

Q. You mentioned persecution - what specific role has it played?

A. Persecution has brought out two things in the Church of Asia. Firstly, it has brought forth Christ's beauty in the lives of the believers. I know of Christians who have been deprived of everything that we consider important and are suffering deeply for their faith, yet they are living out a life of purity and simplicity in Christ. That kind of living has a great impact.

Secondly, persecution has returned the Church back to the basics of Christianity. It is no longer the clergy who are important. It is no longer the building that is important. What is important is having a fundamental relationship with Jesus Christ. Believers who have suffered persecution experience that Jesus is very real to them.

This return to the basics of Christianity and living a faithful life of beauty in Christ have resulted in mass conversions of people to Christianity.

Q. We read of thousands of these persecuted believers sharing a handful of Bibles and often having no pastor. How can the free world help to meet their urgent need for leadership and Bible-based teaching?

A. Without question this is the number one concern for every one of us who are involved in ministry into the Restricted Access Nations of Asia.

I think first of all we have to realise that ultimately it is God who gives the increase. He is also the author and finisher of this good work. We have to go back and trust Him and say, 'Lord, it is your Church. It is your body. It is your vine. You take care of it.'

This seems to be a basic philosophy for Christians in the East. When you talk to leaders in the rural areas of China they say things like, 'Another church has sprung up in that village over there. And a church of 7,000 has just exploded out of nowhere in that mountainous region.' They give thanks to God for what He has started, and commit it to Him saying, 'Lord, you continue to finish your work.' I suppose we have to learn to do the same.

On the other hand, for ministries like Asian Outreach, we do need to shift more and more from pure evangelism to evangelism-plus-discipling. I would say now that at least 50% of our efforts targeted into the Restricted Access Nations are discipling and training in nature. Other ministries are also making a similar shift. In this part of the world, it has to be evangelism-plus-discipling now.

Q. What can believers in Asia's Third World countries teach their brothers and sisters in the First World nations of the West?

A. In the West, or in the free world as a whole, I see the church identifying far more with the powerful victory of Jesus' resurrection. They want that kind of relationship. They are keen for the success, the prosperity, the good things of the Risen King. Few partake in the fellowship of Christ's suffering (Philippians 3:10). However I see the opposite in the Asian Church, particularly in countries where situations are confining and restrictive. These believers are more willing to fellowship with the suffering of Christ. To them that is the greater reward and privilege.

Recently one of our co-workers went to China with a large sum of money to bail out a Christian worker. She had been sentenced to five years of hard labour in a very poor province of China. A few days later my co-worker returned with the money. That woman refused to be bailed out. She said, 'Pray for me, but don't get me out of this situation. Here is where the sinners are. Here is where the criminals are. Here is where Jesus Christ would have come. Now He has sent me. So please don't bail me out.'

Q. Dr Paul Kauffman, the founder of Asian Outreach, has been quoted as saying, 'For the cost of sending out one Westerner to the mission field, five Asians can be sent.' Should we be sending more Asians?

A. Yes, and no. Looking over the last 15 years I do see the Asian Church moving from a 'bless me' position to a 'bless the world' position. They are now ready not only in attitude but also in capability. Christians in Korea, Taiwan, Hong Kong, Singapore, Malaysia, Japan and even Thailand or Indonesia are now in a position where they can pray, they can send, they can give and they can go. I am seeing more and more of the Asian Church changing from being missionary-receiving to becoming missionary-sending.

However, I do want to sound a warning. Third World mission is not the rising star and the answer to ushering in the return of Christ. We have our share of weaknesses and problems. We are just as culturally insensitive. We suffer our share of egocentric nationalism. We stumble over the same things that Western missionaries have stumbled over. Perhaps we are even more arrogant! I think the key is for Western and Asian churches to both send out missionaries. Together let's co-operate in learning, teaching, sharing, caring and shouldering - in a relationship of interdependence - the Great Commission responsibility.

Q. Should we be sending Asian missionaries even to the West?

A. This is something we have to really work at on both ends. We, on our end, have to stop being nationalistic. Thus far I see far more Korean missionaries going to Koreans in overseas countries, or Japanese missionaries going to Japanese, or Chinese missionaries working among the Chinese diaspora. I would like to see Asian missionaries going to wherever the need and the response are the greatest, be it in the West, be it Africa, be it Latin America or be it anywhere.

It is also time for the West to realise that mission has undergone a fundamental change. It is no longer 'from the West to the rest'. Mission is now a universal endeavour of God's Church. People of various nationalities have to learn to work side by side to spread the Gospel. So if it's time for Asian missionaries to go to the West, well, let's do it.

Q. Are we seeing Asian leadership with such a global view?

A. I do see Asian leadership taking more and more of a strategic role in world evangelism. Some are even holding highly recoginsable positions, such as Dr Thomas Wang heading up the AD2000 Movement.

But as a whole, the Asian Church is currently producing localised leaders who are effective in their own culture, among their own people. Only a few are also gifted with multi-cultural flexibility and availability. However, I believe that in days to come we will see more and more Asian leaders who are bigger than their own church, or their own denomination; bigger even than their own nationalities. Because they are totally for the kingdom, they will take a vital role in Christian leadership worldwide.

Q. How will Asian leadership be different?

A. Over the last one hundred years Christian leadership has been primarily trained with a Western theology. This theology has a strong emphasis on the Gospel as the knowledge of God, and the wisdom of God. But there is a general lack of understanding and application of the Gospel as the power of God - see 1 Corinthians 1:24. Thus the propagation of the Gospel has been mostly information based, and somewhat 'powerless' in a warfaring sense.

Now we're seeing an influx of Asians - along with Africans and Latin Americans - into the overall leadership of the Church. Because of their cultural and historical backgrounds, they have a far better understanding and application of the Gospel as the power of God. Signs, wonders and power encounters are more common to their thinking and lives. I see this having a balancing effect, enabling the Church to make great advances into the world of darkness.

Q. There are some who believe that this 'power of God' belongs to another age. Yet we hear many stories of signs and wonders in Asia leading to mass conversions. Is God doing something different in Asia?
A. God is creative. He doesn't have to repeat himself in any way. But I do

see that He has a pattern of operation when it comes to breaking up new ground, opening up new countries.

He allows new signs, wonders and miracles to take place to create tremendous impact. Because Asian cultural influences include a traditional dominance of spiritism and spiritual activities, God has to use signs, wonders and miracles in a very, very phenomenal and outstanding manner to demonstrate that there is no other god but Himself.

I believe He also wants to demonstrate to people in the West that He is a God of power, a God of might. He is the Great Physician. Unfortunately for many, God is our last resort, and not the first and only resort. Therefore we don't go to Him as desperately and frequently as our Asian brothers and sisters, seeking Him regularly for supernatural intervention. A Biblical principal is that the more you ask the more you receive; the more you knock, the more the doors are opened; the more you seek, the more you will find. That perhaps is one reason why we see more signs, wonders and miracles in Asia. They knock more. They seek more. They ask more.

Q. If God is raising up His Church through mass conversions and is refining it through persecution, where is God taking His people?

A. As I see the events happening all about us, I summarise the work of the Holy Spirit as 'Immanuel and Maranatha'.

Firstly, I see God being with us. God is not only being with us in a theological way, a historical way, in a hearsay way: 'I hear that God is doing this and this and this... wow!' But God is with us in a very 'Immanuel' way: personal, current and relevant. And you know it: you sense it, you hear it, you see it, you touch it.

I am sensing that God's Spirit is taking His people to a realisation of the reality of Christ. Jesus is very real. As I fellowship with Christians in China, I don't hear people saying, 'We heard about,' or 'We read about,' but rather 'I experienced Him, I touched Him - He touched me, He revealed Himself to me, I saw Him, and also He healed me.' He is Immanuel in a first person, hands-on manner.

On the other hand I am seeing 'Maranatha'. Christ is coming back very soon. I think I have never seen the world so shaken up, so disrupted, so changed to the point where everyone is in a state of confusion, flux, and uncertainty. Countries and peoples who previously were not particularly open to the Gospel are becoming receptive. With that kind of openness, the Church is presented with an unequalled opportunity: publish the good news, and proclaim the Gospel 'till He comes.

That's where I see He's taking His people. He is giving His people a strong sense of the reality of Immanuel. He is also giving us a strong awareness of Maranatha. Something really big is going to happen very soon.

Q. How can West and East work together to support and encourage each other?

A. In my 25 years of ministry I have seen some basic changes in the relationship between the Asian and Western Church.

In the beginning there was a total reliance on the Western missionaries for personnel, provision and prayers to meet the needs in Asia. Everything seemed to be reliant on the West. Then I saw the pendulum swing to the other extreme. One general mood was 'Missionaries, go home!' Even missions echoed such a cry. Total dependence swung to total independence.

Now I see a new and more balanced phase: a phase of interdependence. I think both the Eastern and the Western churches have matured to accept the validity of each other, with each other's strengths and weaknesses. I see them valuing each other's giftings. I see more and more a symbiotic relationship developing where we say, 'You rely on me and I rely on you.' We now recognise that we need each other to survive, to prepetuate.

I do not call this relationship a partnership. Partnership is often an arrangement of convenience. I would like to see more of a marriage relationship developing, which is not an arrangement of convenience but of mutual commitment and trust. It is a body relationship.

I have seen Asians receiving Westerners, and I pray that Westerners will increasingly receive Asians.

Q. What has been the burden of prayer upon your heart, above all else, about Asia?

183

A. In Asia I have seen churches grow from nothingness into, perhaps, the biggest churches in the world today, such as Yonggi Cho's church and now the Hope of Bangkok, and several others such as the Full Gospel Assembly of Malaysia. I saw them when they were small, and now they've grown tremendously. As I look at this kind of phenomenon, the thing that encourages me greatly is to see the birthing and the growing up of a church.

The thing that concerns me is that often the church started as an organism and ended up as an organisation; started as a corporate body of believers and ended up as a corporation.

My prayer for Asia is that I want to see the basic, beautiful gospel of Jesus Christ proclaimed, and a simple, pure bride of Jesus Christ prepared. That's my prayer.

This article is used with permission from Asia Report, *March/April, 1992 (G.P.O. Box 3448, Hong Kong). Read further information on Asia in subsequent issues of the* Renewal Journal.

9 Astounding Church Growth

Geoff Waugh

Dr Geoff Waugh, founding editor of the Renewal Journal, researched church growth and revival, especially in the twentieth century and beyond. His books include Flashpoints of Revival, Revival Fires, *and* Anointed for Revival. *Further details are on www.renewaljournal.com*

The last decade of the twentieth century was seen as a decade of evangelism and harvest. It capped a century of astounding church growth.

We can thank the Lord for it, and pray all the more earnestly for over two thirds of the world yet to be won to Christ. Praying makes a huge difference. We co-operate with God in prayer as the Spirit of the Lord moves in mighty power in the earth.

More people are praying now for revival than ever before. You can be one. So can your prayer group and your church.

Mission statistician David Barrett, researched the magnitude of the prayer movement, noted that be the end of the twentieth century more than 170 million Christians were committed to praying every day for spiritual awakening and world evangelization. In addition, more than 10 million prayer groups focus on those priorities. Over 20 million Christians worldwide believe their primary ministry calling is to pray daily for revival and for fulfilment of the Great Commission.

Such massive praying, including yours, is linked with incredible church growth around the world.

Peter Wagner's research described Latin American Evangelicals growing from 50,000 in 1900 to over 5 million in the 1950s, over 10 million in the 1960s, over 20 million in the 1970s, around 50 million by the end of the eighties and 137 million by 2000. Over 100 new churches begin every week. Now the church in Latin America grows at over 10,000 every day, or 3.5 million a year.

Africa saw church growth from 10 million in 1900 to over 200 million by the early eighties, with 400 by 2000. Christians grew from 9% to 50% of Africa in the twentieth century. Around 25,000 to 30,000 are added to the church daily in Africa, an estimated 10 million a year.

China, with 1 million evangelicals in 1950, has seen growth to an estimated 100 million. In 1992 the State Statistical Bureau of China indicated that there were 75 million Christians in China (Asian Report 197, Oct/Nov 1992, p. 9). David Yonggi Cho now estimates 100 million Christians in China's 960 million population amid incredible persecution. Current growth rates are estimated at 35,000 a day or over 12 million a year.

South Korea, a Buddhist country in 1900, had 20% Christian by 1980 and 30% by 1990 with estimates of 50% by 2000. David Yonggi Cho heads a church of over 800,000 members with over 25,000 home groups and over 12,000 new members every month. They have sent out 10,000 missionaries and commenced many other huge churches.

An official report of the former Soviet Union in 1990 acknowledged that 90 million of its 290 million inhabitants confessed allegiance to a church or religious community (Worldwide Photos Limited, Renewing Australia, June 1990, p. 38). Christians estimate that over 97 million are converted in Russia, that is one third of the population (Pratney 1984:273).

Geoff Waugh

One quarter of Indonesia is now reported to be Christian. These islands have seen many revivals and people movements such as in 1965 amid political turmoil when over 100,000 animistic Muslims became Christian on the island of Java alone. Revival continues there.

Reports indicate that more Muslims have come to Christ in the past decade than in the previous thousand years. 'New believers are immediately tested to a degree incomprehensible to us. Many are imprisoned and some have been martyred by governments or relatives. Yet the persecution seems only to strengthen their determination and boldness. In one country, where all Christian meetings are illegal, believers rented a soccer stadium and 5,000 people gathered. Police came to disperse the meeting and left in confusion when the Christians refused to leave' (United Prayer Track News, No. 1, Brisbane, 1993).

1700 unevangelized people groups worldwide in the mid-seventies had been reduced to 1200 by 1990, and further reduced to 5,500 in 1993. David Wang of Asian Outreach estimates that these unreached people groups can all be reached by 1997.

The 'Jesus' Film, based on Luke's gospel, has been seen by an estimated 503 million people in 197 countries, and 33 million or more have indicated decisions for Christ as a result. It has more than 6,300 prints in circulation and around 356,000 video copies. The world's most widely translated film, Jesus, has been dubbed into more than 240 languages, with 100 more in progress (National & International Religion Report, May 3, 1993, p.1).

The CBN-TV (Christian Broadcasting Network) 700 Club with Pat Robertson reported 6 million conversions in their work worldwide in 1990, which was more than the previous 30 years of results combined.

John Naisbitt, secular sociologist and author of 'Megatrends' (1982), has co-authored 'Megatrends 2000' (1990) in which one chapter forecasts religious revivals in the nineties including widespread charismatic renewal. He notes that one-fifth, or 10 million, of America's 53.5 million Catholics now call themselves charismatics, emphasising a personal relationship with Jesus Christ.

David Barrett research has uncovered the massive growth of the

187

number of pentecostal/charismatic Christians. His figures indicate growth from its beginnings in 1900 to 550 million by 2000. Pentecostal/charismatic Christians are now more than one third of all practicing Christians in the world today, just one indication of how the Spirit of God is moving.

The Assemblies of God, the largest Pentecostal group in the world, grew from 4.5 million in 1975 to over 13 million by 1985 and 16 million by 1990. By the decade of the nineties it was the largest or second largest Protestant denomination in 30 countries.

Much of the amazing church growth results from visitations or outpourings of the Spirit of God. Leaders, pastors or evangelists are surprised and often overwhelmed. Rapid church growth has happened before, but never on such a large scale as now.

Such amazing growth is accompanied by fervent prayer, and usually grows out of earnest praying. People repent and turn to God. Lives are changed in large numbers. It makes a significant impact on society. Signs and wonders are common, as in the New Testament.

Revival and church growth

Church history and current revivals include times when God moves in great power. Revivals often result in rapid church growth.

* The early church saw it. Read Acts! At Pentecost 3,000 were won in one day. Soon after that there were 5,000 more. Then great multitudes of men and women. They had the reputation of turning their world upside down (Acts 17:6).

* Missionary expansion continued to see it. For example, Patrick in Ireland and Augustine in England saw strong moves of God and thousands converted with many signs and wonders reported.

* The Moravians saw it. On Wednesday 17 August 1727 the Moravian colony in Germany was filled with the Spirit at their communion service. Their leader, 27 year old Count Nicholas Zinzendorf, said it was like being in heaven. Within 25 years they sent out 200 missionaries, more than all the Protestants had done in two centuries.

* The American colonies saw it. 50,000 were converted in 1734-5. Jonathan Edwards described the characteristics of that move as, first, an extraordinary sense of the awful majesty, greatness and holiness of God, and second, a great longing for humility before God and adoration of God.

* 1739 saw astonishing moves of God in England. On 1st January the Wesleys and Whitefield and 60 others, Methodists and Moravians, met in London for prayer and a love feast. The Spirit of God moved powerfully on them all. Many fell to the ground, resting in the Spirit. In February 1739 Whitefield started preaching to the Kingswood coal miners in the open fields with about 200 attending. By March 20,000 attended. Whitefield invited Wesley to take over then and so in April Wesley began his famous open air preaching (which continued for 50 years).

* John Hunt, a pioneering Methodist missionary in Fiji, wrote in his journal about revival there in October 1845. The Spirit fell on the people in meetings and in their homes. There were loud cries of repentance, confession, long meetings, simultaneous praying aloud, and some being overwhelmed. 'Many cases of conversion were as remarkable as any we have heard or read of: many of the penitents had no command whatever of themselves for hours together, but were completely under the influence of their feelings. ... During the first week of the revival nearly 100 persons professed to obtain the forgiveness of sins, through faith in Jesus Christ. Some were exceedingly clear, others not so clear' (Birtwhistle 1954:133).

* Jeremiah Lanphier, a city missioner, began a weekly noon prayer meeting in New York in September 1857. By October it grew into a daily prayer meeting attended by many businessmen. By March 1858 newspapers carried front page reports of over 6,000 attending daily prayer meetings in New York and Pittsburgh, and daily prayer meetings were held in Washington at five different times to accommodate the crowds. By May 1859, 50,000 of New York's 800,000 people were new converts. New England was profoundly changed by the revival and in several towns no unconverted adults could be found! Charles Finney preached in those days.

* During September 1857, the same month the prayer meetings began in New York, four young Irishmen commenced a weekly prayer

meeting in a village school near Kells. That is generally seen as the start of the Ulster revival of 1859 which brought 100,000 converts into the churches of Ireland.

* Throughout 1859 the same deep conviction and lasting conversions revived thousands of people in Wales, England and Scotland. One tenth of Wales became new converts. Charles Haddon Spurgeon, the Baptist prince of preachers, saw 1859 as the high water mark although he had already been preaching in London for five years with great blessing and huge crowds in a church where people prayed continually and had seen continual growth.

Twentieth Century Awakenings

* From October 1904 Evan Roberts in his twenties, formerly a miner and blacksmith, saw God move powerfully in answer to his and others' persistent prayers. 100,000 were converted in Wales during 1904-5. Churches filled from 10 a.m. till after midnight every day for two years, bringing profound social change to Wales.

* William Seymour began a Mission at Azusa Street in Los Angeles on Easter Saturday, 14 April 1906 with about 100 attending, both blacks and whites. It grew out of a cottage prayer meeting. Revival there drew people from around the nation and overseas and launched Pentecostalism as a world wide movement.

* Revival in Korea swept the nation in 1907. Presbyterian missionaries, hearing of revival in Wales, prayed earnestly for the same in Korea. 1500 representatives gathered for the annual New Year Bible studies in which a spirit of prayer broke out. The leaders allowed everyone to pray aloud simultaneously as so many were wanting to pray. That became a characteristic of Korean prayer meetings. Revival continues there now.

* The famous cricketer and missionary, C T Studd reported on revival in the Belgian Congo in 1914: 'The whole place was charged as if with an electric current. Men were falling, jumping, laughing, crying, singing, confessing and some shaking terribly. ... This particular one can best be described as a spiritual tornado. People were literally flung to the floor or over the forms, yet no one was hurt. ... As I led in prayer the Spirit came down in mighty power sweeping the congregation. My

whole body trembled with the power. We saw a marvellous sight, people literally filled and drunk with the Spirit' (W.E.C. 1954:12-15; Pratney 1984:267).

* The famous East African revival began in Rwanda in June 1936 and rapidly spread to the neighbouring countries of Burundi, Uganda and the Congo (now Zaire), then further around. The Holy Spirit moved upon mission schools, spread to churches and to whole communities, producing deep repentance and changed lives. Anglican Archdeacon Arthur Pitt-Pitts wrote in September, 'I have been to all the stations where this Revival is going on, and they all have the same story to tell. The fire was alight in all of them before the middle of June, but during the last week in June, it burst into a wild flame which, like the African grass fire before the wind, cannot be put out' (Osborn 1991:21).

* God moved upon the mountain town of Soe in Timor on Sunday 26 September 1965. That night people heard the sound of a tornado wind and flames above the Reformed Church building prompted police to set off the fire alarm. Healings and evangelism increased dramatically. Hundreds of thousands were converted. About 90 evangelistic teams were formed which functioned powerfully with spiritual gifts. The first team saw 9,000 people converted in two weeks in one town alone. In the first three years of this revival 200,000 became Christians in Timor, and on another small island where few had been Christians 20,000 became believers.

* God's power visited Asbury College in Wilmore, Kentucky, on Tuesday 3 February 1970 at the regular morning chapel commencing at 10 o'clock. The auditorium filled with over 1,000 people. Few left for meals. By midnight over 500 still remained praying and worshipping. Several hundred committed their lives to Christ that day. Teams of students visited 16 states and saw several thousand conversions through their witnessing in one week. Over 1,000 teams went out in the first six weeks.

* The Jesus Movement exploded in 1971 among hippie and counter culture youth in America in the early seventies. Thousands were baptised in the ocean. Vital new groups like Calvary Chapel led by Chuck Smith emerged and multiplied rapidly. Newspapers of the movement included the Hollywood Free Paper which grew from a circulation of 10,000 to over 150,000 in two years; Truth merged with

Agape and printed 100,000. Right On! grew from 20,000 to 100,000 circulation (Pratney 1984:231).

* In 1971 Bill McLeod, a Canadian Baptist pastor, invited the twin evangelists Ralph and Lou Sutera to speak at his church in Saskatoon. Revival broke out with their visit which began on Wednesday 13 October. By the weekend an amazing spirit gripped the people. Many confessed their sins publicly. Meetings had to be moved to the Civic Auditorium seating 2000. This spread to other churches as well.

* In September 1973 Todd Burke arrived in Cambodia on a one week visitor's visa, later extended. Just 23 years old, he felt a strong call from God to minister there. By the end of September he had seen hundreds healed and saved. A virile church grew rapidly, later buried after the communist coup of 1975. By 1978 a million Cambodians had been killed. Still the desimated church survives, and is growing again.

* In 1979 John Wimber began pastoring a fellowship which his wife Carol had begun in their home. Their Vineyard Fellowship grew rapidly with their prayerful worship, powerful evangelism and a growing healing ministry. On Mother's Day in May, 1981, a young man gave his testimony at the evening service and called on the Holy Spirit to come in power. Revival broke out at that service as hundreds were dramatically filled with the Spirit. In the next four months they baptised 700 new converts. The church grew to 5,000 in a decade and commenced many other Vineyard fellowships.

* The church in China continues to see God's strong move amid great persecution, torture and killing which still continues. David Wang tells of a pastor imprisoned for over 22 years who left behind a church of 150 people scattered through the hill villages in northern China. On his release in the 1980s he discovered the church in that area had grown to 5,000. Three years later it had trebled to 15,000. Evangelists who saw 30-40 converted in each village they visited in the eighties now report 300-400 or more being converted in their visits. Some villages are experiencing a visitation of God where the whole village becomes Christian.

* Nagaland, a state in the North-East of India, began to experience revival in the 1960s and has continued in revival. By the early 1980s 85% of the population had become Christians (Mills 1990:40).

* Missionaries were expelled from Burma in the 1960s but the church continues to grow. A baptismal service at the Kachin Baptist Centenial Convention in 1977 saw 6,000 people baptised in one day.

* During the 1980s the 200 missionaries of the Philippine Missionary Fellowship each organised daily prayer group meetings at 7.00 p.m. to pray for the growth of the church. They report that within a couple of years this directly resulted in the formation of 310 new churches (Robinson 1992:13).

* Revival has been spreading in the Pacific islands, especially in the Solomons since July-August 1970 when God moved powerfully in the nation, especially in meetings with Muri Thompson a Maori evangelist. The Spirit came in power, producing deep and loud repentance, much confession, signs and wonders, and transformed churches. Teams have gone from the Solomons to many other countries, sparking many other revivals.

* Engas in the Baptist mission area of the Western Highlands of Papua New Guinea had a fresh outpouring of the Holy Spirit from Sunday 16 September 1973, as the village pastors preached in their services after attending meetings during the previous week led by visitors from the Solomon Islands. Many were saved. Many were delivered from evil spirits. Many were healed. The church grew rapidly.

* The Huli speaking people of the United Church in Tari in the Southern Highlands of Papua New Guinea also experienced revival from August 1974, with much confession, many tears, and deliverance from spirit powers. That revival spread to surrounding areas also.

* On Thurdsay afternoon 10 March, 1977 at Duranmin near the West Irain border of Papua New Guinea, Diyos Wapnok the principal of the Baptist Bible College spoke to about 50 people. They were all filled with the Holy Spirit and great joy. Keith and Joan Bennet of Gateway were there. 3,000 were converted in the next three years. They had daily prayer meetings in the villages and many healings and miracles.

* Aborigines on Galiwin'ku (Elcho Island) experienced revival from Wednesday 14 March 1979. Djiniyini Gondarra had returned from holidays that day and people met in his manse for prayer that night

where the Spirit fell on them, as at Pentecost. They met all nght and many were filled with the Spirit and many healed. The movement spread rapidly from there throughout Arnhem Land.

* In the Sepik lowlands of northern Papua New Guinea a visitation of God burst on the churches at Easter 1984, sparked again by Solomon Island pastors. There was repentance, confession, weeping and great joy. Stolen goods were returned or replaced, and wrongs made right.

* Jobson Misang, an indigenous youth worker in the United Church reported on a move of God in the North Solomons Province of Papua New Guinea in 1988. For 8 weekends straight he led camps where 3,500 took part and 2,000 were converted.

* The Evangelist Training Centre of the Lutheran church in the Eastern Highlands of Papua New Guinea had a visitation of God on Thursday night 4 August 1988. Crowds stayed up most of the night as the Spirit touched people deeply, many resting in the Spirit, others praying in tongues. Students went out on powerful mission igniting fires of the Spirit in the villages.

* On Saturday 6 May 1989 the Spirit of God fell on Waritzian village in Papua New Guinea's Eastern Highlands. For three days the people were drunk in the Spirit. Healing and miracles occurred. On the Monday they burned their magic and witchcraft fetishes. The area had been a stronghold of spirit worship. Students from the Lutheran Training Centre were involved that weekend.

Harvest in the 1990s

* In the 1980s Christians in East Germany started to form small prayer groups of ten to twelve persons to pray for peace. By October 1989, 50,000 people were involved in Monday night prayer meetings. In 1990, when these praying people moved quietly into the streets, their numbers swelled to 300,000 and the wall came down (Robinson 1992:14).

* In the former U.S.S.R. there were 640 registered Pentecostal churches and many more unregistered. By the eighties 30,000 young people were meeting together in Poland to seek for the power of the Holy Spirit (Pratney 1984:273). Those numbers continue to expand in the

nineties.

* Pastor Giedrius Saulytis of Vilnius, the capital of Lithuania, tells how after his conversion in 1987 he commenced a church which had 15 people in 1989. In 1993 that church has 60 home cells with 1,500 attending services, 800 being registered members. They have started three other churches, one of which now has 1,000 attending. Every week preachers from their church preach 20 times in 12 different cities in Lithuania (Church Growth, Spring 1993, p. 19).

* In a 1991 crusade in Leningrad 70,000 out of 90,000 attending made commitments to Christ. Russian delegates to the July, 1991, charismatic leaders conference in Brighton, England, reported on the amazing growth of the church in Russia (ARMA Brisbane Newsletter, Sept/Oct 1991).

* A Moscow conference with Pastor Cho of Seoul, Korea, held in June, 1992, at the Kremlin and a plaza nearby, attracted over 40,000 participants. Among them were 15,000 new converts (Church Growth, Winter 1992, p. 12).

* Chaplains in the Gulf War told of thousands of conversions and baptisms among the American troops from September 1990 to January 1991. 10,000 conversions were reported.

* Christians in Iran have recently grown in number from 2,700 to over 12,000 according to Abe Ghaffari of Iranian Christians International. An additional 12,000 Iranian Christians live in Western nations. Disillusionment with harsh Islamic law has opened Iran to the Gospel (United Prayer Track News, No. 1., Brisbane, 1993).

* Harvest has begun among the Kurds who have been hounded into refugee camps where Christians have helped and comforted them. The first Kurdish church in history has resulted. Many Kurds are open to the Gospel (United Prayer Track News, No. 1, Brisbane, 1993).

* In 1990 a bloodless revolution freed Mongolia from Russian rule. Within two years more than 500 people became Christian in that formerly resistant nation. A young girl was the first in her area to accept Christ. Now she reports that 70 others are meeting every week with her.

* The church in the Sudan is suffering under Islamic edicts. Missionaries are expelled, pastors imprisoned, and Christians persecuted. Despite the persecution there has been phenomenal church growth reported, especially in the south and the Nuba mountains region.

* A church leader wrote from Asaba, Nigeria, in 1992, telling how their church had increased from 700 to 3,200 within 6 months. A team of just over 100 went on outreach, first in Sokoto State where they started 5 churches involving 1,225 converts within 3 months. Then they went to Bomu State where 3 branches were planted with over 1,000 converts in all. Many Moslems were converted. He added,

> When we reached Kano which is a Moslem state, we were able to preach for 2 weeks. Suddenly, the 3rd week, we were attacked, beaten and our property looted including our Bibles. Out of the 105 persons with me, 85 of them were kiled, 17 mercilessly maimed (hands cut off). Only three escaped unharmed. I was beaten to unconsciousness, and imprisoned for 6 months without a hearing. After returning home, I was sued by some of the families of those who died in the outreach. Finally, I am particularly grateful to God that the Church of God is marvellously marching on in these three states. Praise the Lord! (*Church Growth*, Autumn 1992, p. 23).

* The church in previously resistant Nepal in the Himalayas is growing steadily. David Wang tells of a former Lama priest nicknamed Black Bravery, who has been an illiterate pastor for 15 years. By the nineties he led 43 fellowships with total of 32,000 people. Another pastor in a remote area has 40,000 Christians in his region. Most conversions in Nepal involve casting out demons to set people free (Asian Report, May/June 1991).

* In October-November 1990, one small island in Indonesia saw 30,000 converted and 45,000 were baptised in another region in January-February 1991. This growth is among former animistic Muslims.

* Ruth Rongo from Vanuatu told of three months of evangelism ministry in 1991 where the power of God touched many villages and

shocked the villagers with miracles just as in the New Testament. The church grew rapidly. Ruth was then involved in a prayer group which met after the Sunday night service. They began at 10.30 p.m. and prayed every week to 1 or 3.30 a.m.

* John and Barbara Hutton were missionaries with the Huli people of Tari in Papua New Guinea. In April, 1993, Barbara wrote, 'We have recently been to P.N.G. again. We were blessed to be part of a Youth Camp. I have never seen such exuberant and joyous worship among the Huli people before. There is a fresh move of the Spirit occurring. The highlight of the trip was the baptism of 100 young people in Tari when the Holy Spirit fell on the group before they even stepped into the water. A youth group of 6 there just last December was about 400 strong before we left late January. God moved through Huli university students home on holidays.'

* Eric Alexander of the Bible Society in India wrote in 1993, 'I was in Amedabad in the month of February and was delighted to see a great revival in the Church there. I was surprised to hear that 30,000 people have accepted the Lord Jesus as their personal Saviour in the Diocese of Gujarat (Church of North India). Thousands of new converts are in the Methodist, Roman Catholic, Salvation Army and Pentecostal churches. There are thousands and thousands!' (Sharing Australia, SOMA Newsletter, March 1993, p. 2).

* Fresh touches of God's Spirit have been felt in Australia in 1993. It is only a beginning, but thank God for every touch of the Lord.

During May and June the Christian Outreach Centres experienced a strong move of the Spirit, with much repenting, and many resting in the Spirit or drunk in the Spirit for hours, or days. Many have received visions and prophetic insights, including young people and children in the schools. Beginning at their headquarters in Brisbane it spread to their churches. It brought a new zeal for evangelism and outreach.

Gateway Baptist Church moved into its new 1500 seater auditorium in 1993 (the former Queensland Expo Pavilion from Expo 1988), with around 2,000 attending and more involved in their 40-50 prayer groups, cell groups and outreach groups than ever before. It is the South Pacific Centre for the AD 2000 Prayer Track.

Many Uniting Churches now move in renewal and have had to build large sanctuaries or move out into school halls. O'Connor in Canberra, Churchlands in Perth, Praise Chapel in Townsville, and others in Brisbane have experienced significant growth. The Uniting Church in Queensland has conducted seminars in 1993 for church leaders on the principles of ministry in large churches.

Networks of small home churches are also forming now. Perth, Canberra, Sydney and Brisbane all have clusters of house churches or emerging networks which are linked for fellowship and accountability. These too are increasing in Australia.

Informal prayer groups as well as organised prayer groups of churches and Christian organisations continue to multiply as never before. This is true in Australia also. Much of this prayer involves a new commitment to repentance and revival.

Pray always

Every revival move is born in prayer - personal prayer, prayer cells, prayer groups, prayer meetings, prayer in church, prayer in the car (with your eyes open!), prayer in bed, prayer with friends, prayer on the phone, prayer with people of other churches, pastors of different churches praying together, combined churches prayer meetings.
David Bryant, founder-president of Concerts of Prayer International, suggests practical steps we can take in response to the phenomenal developments around the world (National & International Religion Report, May 1992, pp. 7-8):
1. Believe that God wants revival. Pray with faith and vision.

2. Join a small prayer group. Share the vision. Set the pace.

3. Work at integrating the prayer movement. Consider four 'C' areas:
closet prayer - personal prayer life;
cluster prayer - in small group settings;
congregational prayer - when an entire church meets to pray;
concerts of prayer - inter-church prayer meetings and rallies.

4. Seek out 'pools of renewal' in churches and organisations in your area, especially those praying for revival. Find ways to flow together and encourage one another.

5. Be equipped in your prayer life. Many resources are available (including this journal!). Share these resources together.

6. Get involved in a communication network. That will keep you informed. Note the renewal resources listed in this journal.

7. Visit places where prayer is flourishing. Talk to the leaders and bring reports to your own group.

8. Most importantly, don't give up. We inherit the promises by faith and patience (Hebrews 6:12).

* Peter Wagner reported an example of prayer in Latin America. Arturo Arias, the pastor of an 800-member church Centro Misionero El Sembrador in El Salvador, spoke at a meeting of church leaders in Guatamala. Wagner writes:

> He told us how his church has received an unusual burden from God for extended prayer and that they responded by scheduling a 24 hour prayer meeting. They received such a blessing from God that they then attempted a 48-hour meeting. God continued to pour out His presence and power. Could they extend it and keep the church open for 7 days and nights of continuous prayer? They did, and the anointing increased. The day before Pastor Arturo left for our meeting his church had concluded a 10-day continuous prayer meeting!

> As he finished his address he said, half in jest, that his people were so enthusiastic about prayer that they were asking, 'Can we have a month long prayer meeting?' I immediately approached him privately and said, 'How about challenging the Centro Misionero El Sembrador to become the first church to commit to an all-month-24-hour-a-day prayer meeting through October 1993?'

> Arturo Arias replied, 'I can easily speak for my church on this matter. Consider it done! We are committed to 31 days of continuous prayer next October! What a challenge to the rest of us! (*Prayer Track News*, Sept-Dec, 1992)

So, pray without ceasing. We live in a time when more people are praying and more people are being reached for Jesus Christ than ever before. May God find us responsive as we watch and pray.

References

Birtwhistle, A (1954) In His Armour. London: Cargate
Burke, T & D (1977) Anointed for Burial. Seattle: Frontline.
Koch, K (n.d.) The Revival in Indonesia. Evangelization Publishers.
Mills, B (1990) Preparing for Revival. Eastbourne: Kingsway.
Osborn, H H (1991) Fire in the Hills. Crowborough: Highland.
Pratney, W (1984) Revival. Springdale: Whitaker House.
Richardson, D (1981) Eternity in Their Hearts. Ventura: Regal.
Robinson, S (1992) 'Praying the Price'. Melbourne: ABMS
Tari, M (1971) Like a Mighty Wind. Carol Springs: Creation House.
Tari, M & N (1974) The Gentle Breeze of Jesus. Carol Springs:
Wagner, C P (1983) On the Crest of the Wave. Glendale: Regal
Wagner, C P (1986) Spiritual Power and Church Growth. London: Hodder & Stoughton.
Wagner, C P (1992) Prayer Shield. Ventura: Regal.
Watt, E S (n.d.) Floods on Dry Ground. Marshall, Morgan & Scott.
W.E.C. (1954) This is That. Christian Literature Crusade.

Reviews

This issue of the Renewal Journal looks at some Australian books.

Heart of Fire by Barry Chant
Adelaide: House of Tabor, 1984, 382 pages.

Dr Barry Chant has written the only comprehensive history of Pentecostalism in Australia. The 1973 edition, updated and expanded in 1984, makes fascinating reading. Every college and Christian education centre should have one. Every minister and leader in renewal needs to be aware of its story and heed its advice.

The revised edition includes twelve sermons by Pentecostal pioneers and has twenty pages of historical photographs. It also tells of the beginnings of charismatic renewal in denominational churches and in inter-church activities.

Subsequent printing and the revised edition enabled the author to correct any errors in the account and add valuable information. He wrote, 'Not everyone appreciated the 'warts and all' approach. To those who have complained that I have been too 'honest', I can only answer that I know of no other way to write. On the other hand, there have been widespread comments of appreciation, including many from outside the Pentecostal movement, for 'telling it like it is'.

It tells the story of failure as well as success, of God's grace and power amid human weakness and faithfulness. Pentecostalism has been and continues to be controversial. It must be. Wherever God's Spirit moves in power the evil in us and in society is confronted. Pentecostalism itself is confronted, for like every movement it can lose its heart of fire and needs constant renewal.

Dr Andrew Evans, General superintendent of the Assemblies of God writes,

> Barry Chant is one of the leading Pentecostal ministers in Australia. ... This book, I would consider as being one of the best that he has written. It is a unique record in which he has set down in accurate detail the history of the Pentecostal movement in Australia from its beginnings until now. It is the only one of its kind in print. I find it to be inspiring and filled with many interesting anecdotes. It also has an element of teaching in it; if the Pentecostal churches were to study it in depth it would help them in the future from making some of the mistakes of the past.

> I have been personally blessed as I have read this outstanding account and it is my special joy to commend this book to those who are interested in what God has done and is continuing to do through the Pentecostal movement.

The Spirit in the Church by Adrian Commadeur
East Keilor: Comsoda Communications, 1992, 143 pages:

A book about Catholic Charismatic Renewal in Australia reviewed by John Wilson, in Jesus is Alive, February 1993.

What? Another book on the Renewal? Aren't our prayer groups' tables already over laden with books? But hold on a minute. How many are locally produced and with the common touch as we know it? How many leave us with the feeling, 'Wow, we really have got something here!'

The author of **The Spirit in the Church** outlines the story of the Renewal in Australia with special reference to his involvement in Melbourne following his eight years as a Redemptorist student. He takes us back to the 1970's when the 'new thing the Lord was doing' was like new fire among us. This is a timely reminder of our younger and fervent days.

The reader is taken on the spiritual journey with Adrian the young man and 'New Australian' who makes discoveries about the Lord, about the Church, about Scripture, about himself. It is also the story of many of us who have been around since those days. This reader knows personally many of the circumstances and personalities mentioned. This gives the book authenticity. Adrian explains the workings of the Holy Spirit and the consequent happenings in the prayer groups and beyond. He explains with precision and sensitivity.

We may read here of the authoritative backing given to the Renewal by recent Popes and National Bishops Conferences. We read of Covenant Communities, of miracles and above all of joy in the midst of a Church otherwise in turmoil.

My question after reading the book was: 'What other section of the Church in our day has contributed as much as the Charismatic Renewal to the Church?' What a treasure we have, is my final reaction to reading this book. And perhaps the challenge to each of us is to appreciate ever more the treasure of Charismatic Renewal as we have it now, lest we say with shame later on, 'Surely Yahweh was in this place and I never knew.' I am referring to the fact that the Lord has done marvellous things already for those prepared to see. What might He do in the future?

Available from the author, 15 Holly Green Court, East Keilor, Vic 3033, Phone/Fax (03) 337 2051. Cost $12.50 posted.

Streams of Renewal, edited by Robert Bruce
Sydney: Uniting Church Board of Mission, 1991, 92 pages.

Here is a book of inspiration and encouragement concerning charismatic renewal in the Uniting Church, especially in New South Wales.

Part I, the first 22 pages, includes a summary of the developments of the healing and charismatic streams in the Uniting Church, written jointly by Don Evans, Don Drury and Robert Bruce. It is an invaluable historical record of these significant developments.

Part II gives the personal journeys of twenty people (photographs included) whose lives have been deeply transformed by these streams of renewal. Some of these people have become well known nationally, including Sue Armstrong, Don Evans, Harry Westcott, Audrey Drury, Con Stamos, Alan Robinson and Peter Savage.

Are you looking for a book to give your friends about the significance of charismatic renewal in Australia? Here's one. It's available at $6 ($8 including postage) from the Uniting Church Board of Mission, PO Box E178, St James, NSW 2000. Ph (02) 285 4584.

Word and Spirit by Alison J Sherington
Published in Brisbane by the author, 1992, 38 pages.

Reviewed by James Brecknell, in *Journey*, November 1992:

Alison Sherington's *Word and Spirit* has the potential to bring healing to Christian disunity concerning the role of the Holy Spirit. The booklet is subtitled Coming to Terms with the Charismatic Movement, 'and is intended as an encouragement to be both faithful to the Word and open to the Spirit.'

Word and Spirit addresses many of the questions produced by confusion about the Word of God. Confusion seems so unnecessary in the light of Alison Sherrington's writing. She shows that the truth of God is clear.

Her booklet clarifies topics such as the role of experiences of the Holy Spirit, problems of terminology, the desire to be baptised and filled with the Spirit, and the modern position on spiritual gifts.

The author reinforces the need for the people of God to have the right attitude to the Holy Spirit. She writes that we need to be open to God, and this means being ready to change, ready to understand the empowering of the Holy Spirit as a means for glorifying God. We should seek the Giver more than the gifts of the Holy Spirit, and the gifts are for his glory. Openness enables a living knowledge of the unity of Word and Spirit.

Living in the Spirit, by Geoff Waugh
126 pages, 1987 (2nd ed., 2009), Renewal Journal publications.

Review by Bishop Owen Dowling:

Many Australian Christians have experienced renewal in the Holy Spirit. Yet it would be true to say that those church members enthusiastic about renewal are often a small group within a parish, frustrated because the parish, in its overall life and direction, does not seem to be renewed.

The Joint Board of Christian Education originally published this book of eight studies on the Holy Spirit and the Christian life called *Living in the Spirit.* The author is Geoff Waugh, then Director of Distance Education at the U.C.A.'s Trinity Theological College in Brisbane.

The assumption is that each study will take two hours, but the suggestion is made in the excellent guidelines at the beginning of the book that the course may be spread over sixteen sessions with only half the material in each chapter being attempted at each study session.

I find the study material to be balanced in theological emphasis and exceptionally well organized and presented. A relatively large group, say a parish camp as a whole, or a group meeting in the parish centre, could handle the studies, with small group activity taken as part of the operation of the whole to allow closer interaction. On the other hand I can see that the handbook would work well in a smaller home group, though I would recommend the sixteen study approach in this case.

There is a balanced approach to the controversial matter of the gifts of the Spirit. I find myself opposed to that kind of teaching which treats the list of gifts of the Spirit in 1 Corinthians 12:8-10 as an exhaustive list - the 9 gifts - because Paul alters the list when he gives it again in verse 28 of the same chapter. *Living in the Spirit* takes a wider perspective on the gifts, following Robert Hillman and his list of 27 Spiritual Gifts (see his book of that title also published by the J. B. C. E.). Hillman finds biblical evidence for 27 spiritual gifts which we should expect to see operative in the church, and rightly divides them (following 1 Peter 4:10-11) into Speaking Gifts and Serving Gifts.

The study techniques used in the book are specific and helpful. There is a good understanding of group dynamics, and exercises provided where possible answers are listed so that group members have something to start with. Bald questions without any suggested answers are often daunting; the method here seems to be one of easing people in to dealing with biblical material, and sharing their own experience along with this. Some study books go one way or the other - all on biblical references, or all experiential; this book combines both.

One feature I like of the studies is the 'Voices from History' section, with apt quotes from members of the Body of Christ from such writers as Tertullian, Augustine, Gregory the Great, Francis of Assissi, Charles Finney and David du Plessis. The studies thus connect into the wider life, thought and practice of the church family, and are the richer as a result.

Those seeking to lead their parishes down a path of spiritual renewal with strong practical overtones and outcomes should look carefully at *Living in the Spirit.*

Renewal Journal

These reviews of the first issue of the Renewal Journal are written by Revd Dr Lewis Born, a former Director of the Department of Christian Education and Moderator in the Uniting Church in Queensland, and the Revd Prof. James Haire, former Principal of Trinity Theological College and Dean of the Brisbane College of Theology.

Rev Dr Lewis Born wrote:

Renewal is no longer a matter of speculation. It will be recorded as one of the most significant faith history phenomena of all time. The Global Village factor makes this revival the most comprehensive international social and religious phenomena ever known.

To those who remain untouched or unexposed to renewal theology and events may I suggest that Geoff Waugh's editorship of the Renewal Journal is a good step towards being more informed and possibly persuaded to the point of being involved, even to being a corrector of its course.

Future students of both social and church history will be surprised, both at the facts and at those who slept through them. Professor Walter Hollenweger (Missiology, Birmingham) has stated, 'a movement which represents more or at least as many members as all other Protestant denominations taken together can no longer be considered a fringe topic in church history, missiology and systematic theology.'

Among those who still sleep are members, clergy and leaders of orthodoxy who see themselves as defenders of the faith against this threat of enthusiasm and 'unnecessary extremes' to traditional faith, practice and theology. Tradition and orthodoxy need to be re-defined. If New Testament Christianity is the orthodox, then what claims to be twentieth century orthodoxy may be labelled by future theological historians as in fact deviant.

No doubt some of the renewal theological emphasis runs into error, if not enthusiastic heresy. Some of its worship forms and practice are too subjective and unbalanced for my limited taste. There are many charlatans. But who would claim that contemporary 'orthodox' faith and practice were free of phonies and heresy?

Contemporary renewal is one of the most significant events in the history of Christianity. Don't do a 'Rip Van Winkle'.

Rev Prof James Haire wrote:

Dr Geoff Waugh, an expert in Renewal Studies over many years, has begun editing an important Australian Journal which is unique in that it gathers together renewal material from the many church groups throughout Australia and overseas.

The first issue was published in the summer of 1993 and has articles ranging from an historical view of revival movements throughout history by Geoff Waugh himself to more specific accounts or revival experiences in Arnhem Land among the Aboriginal people of Australia by Dr Djiniyini Gondarra.

There are also significant articles by Stuart Robinson, J Edwin Orr, and material from John Greenfield. In this issue all of them are centred on the theme of revival. In addition, there are reviews of recent books on Pentecostal and Charismatic movements.

The Journal is breaking important new ground by linking renewal with ecumenical fellowship primarily throughout Australia. For that reason it is quite a new contribution in this area.

I warmly commend this fresh and ground-breaking enterprise. It looks as if it will play an important part in the Christian Church throughout this country.

Renewal Journal
3 Community

Contents

Renewal Journal 3: Community

Cover photo: 3 Community
Church and community group in Ghana, West Africa.

Editorial

Pray always
2 Thessalonians 5:17

I recently visited Elcho Island, east of Darwin in the far north of Australia, with a team of 15 for their annual Thanksgiving Weekend on the anniversary of the revival there in 1979. God's Spirit moved most strongly that weekend, I believe, when we waited on the Lord together, with Aboriginal leaders responding sensitively to the Spirit's leading. We worshipped and prayed. Small clusters of people prayed for those who sought prayer, and God touched them gently and strongly.

The small communities there impressed me. Many people pray constantly, for hours a day, still. In some of those remote places the presence of the Lord is strong. The fires of the Spirit burn.

We can all do that - in our home groups, house churches, and meetings. We can wait on the Lord in worship and prayer and respond to his Spirit among us.

Revival fires are blown by the wind of the Spirit across this great south land of the Holy Spirit, and across the world, igniting thousands of communities of the King.

God's Spirit now moves like gusts of wind blowing and like waves breaking over us. It can be turbulent.

Many people report that their lives have been profoundly disturbed lately. Props and false securities are being shaken. False foundations crumble revealing what is built on the Rock.

This issue of the *Renewal Journal* explores some of the emerging developments as human structures are shaken and eternal issues emerge. In radical small communities people are learning to be the church, to pray in faith, to use spiritual gifts, to serve one another, to reach out in love. Increasingly, small groups are becoming the church in the home and the work place for many people. Some are linked with congregations. Some are house churches.

Communities of the King multiply. God is raising up a new breed of people committed to him and to one another, loving and serving in the power of the Spirit.

The articles in this issue of the Journal describe that. Charles Ringma, Dorothy Harris and Tim McCowan call us to discipleship in community life. Shayne Bennett and Adrian Commadeur report on charismatic communities among Catholics. Ian Freestone, Spencer Colliver and Col Warren outline emerging patterns of house churches and Barbara Nield examines the amazing growth in China's house churches. Brian Edgar tells of renewal in a Bible College community and Darren Trinder reports on Spirit waves in Christian Outreach Centres across Australia.

I examine these major trends in the church and in revival in these books:
The Body of Christ, Part 1: Body Ministry
The Body of Christ, Part 2: Ministry Education

Jesus said, "I will build my church and the gates of hell will not prevail against it." He is doing that. His church still advances globally, in the power of his Spirit for the glory of God.

1 Lower the drawbridge: bring social justice home

Charles Ringma

The Rev Dr Charles Ringma taught at the Asian Theological Seminary in Manila and Regent College in Vancouver and was the founding Director of Teen Challenge in Australia. He reflects on Christian community in our homes.

**while we seek to practice social justice
to bring about a more just society,
we can also lower the drawbridge and
bring this ministry into our own homes**

If you had seen her in a crowd you would have been none the wiser. She probably would not have arrested your attention although she was attractive. Deena was a prostitute supporting a drug habit. Her small inner-city flat was her place of work.

Deena's life was spinning out of control with a failed marriage, a small child in tow, poor health, hassles with the police, an expensive drug habit to maintain, and an increasing sense of loneliness and despair. At this point our paths crossed through my involvement in regular street work.

After several conversations it became obvious that Deena did not need a hospital or a psychiatrist. She did not need a treatment centre or a drug rehabilitation program. Rather, she needed a place of safety in which she could start again and rebuild her life. So Deena eventually came to live in our home.

Caring Charismatics

In this we were not alone. One way in which Charismatics and Pentecostals, particularly during the 1970s, sought to demonstrate their concern for others was by taking them into their communities and homes. This was one way to help broken and wounded people who were not only on the fringes of the church but also on the fringes of society.

There were many reasons for this development.

1. Charismatic renewal was not yet heavily institutionalised. The focus was on people more than programs. Ministry took priority over buildings and projects.

2. The empowerment of the Spirit was celebrated as equipment for service, not as an enhancement for personal wellbeing and self-development.

3. The new discoveries of renewal brought the church into closer contact with the wider community. This happened through the use of theatres, general community buildings, and the creation of drop-in centres and coffee shops as ways of reaching out to non-church people, especially youth.

4. Renewal had not only brought new life to church members but had also brought new people into the church.

5. Inspired by such books as David Wilkerson's *The Cross and the Switchblade*, Christians touched by renewal believed that something could be done through the power of the Holy Spirit for people with life-controlling problems.

For these and other reasons the church seemed to be closer to the person in the street.

Christian community

There are several reasons why 'caring Charismatics' became involved in these types of initiatives.

1. One factor was that, unlike the traditional churches, Charismatics were not overwhelmed with seeking to maintain massive institutional structures. They were therefore free to explore other ways of expressing their social concern.

2. Another factor was the rediscovery of small groups in homes where people could share their lives, pray for one another, discover and use spiritual gifts, and involve friends in informal activities.

3. A similar factor which helped to direct the particular expressions of their concern was the renewal's rediscovery of community. Christians in the 1970s believed that being church had something to do with being together and sharing life. As a consequence both institutional and informal Christian communities were established as well as house churches.

What characterised this impulse towards Christian community? It was not introversion and

escapism. The purpose of sharing life together was not simply to celebrate God's gift of new life in Christ. Nor was it simply to care for one another. Instead, this life together, consisting not only of spiritual fellowship but also of sharing resources, sought to provide a context into which we could bring those needing help and encouragement.

Furthermore Christian community was seen as providing a way to make the good news in Christ more visible. This does not mean that the life of the community takes priority over the Word of God. It simply means that Christians sharing life together could demonstrate something of what it meant to be part of the body of Christ.

An underlying idea was that if others could see Christians sharing life together in common

worship and service then they would gain some idea of what the Christian life was all about.

Some might see this as a high risk strategy. They may believe that it is better for 'seekers' to be exposed to the purity of the preached word. However, those practising a community approach of life together believed that 'seekers' should see something of the warts and all life style of Christians.

The intake process

So Deena came to live in our home. She was not the first and certainly not the last. Nor was she the most difficult. During a period of fifteen years, my wife Rita and I have invited a range of young people into our home.

The most difficult were not drug addicts or prostitutes but those with major psychiatric disturbances. But for them all, the invitation to live in our home was not a haphazard process. Early in the piece we had learned some valuable lessons from young people who needed help but in fact took advantage of our generosity.

This caused us to develop a simple but multipronged intake strategy.

First of all, Rita, Jenny (a wonderful Christian fellow traveller who shared our home), the children when they were older, and I would discuss and pray about taking in a certain person.

This person was then invited to share some meals with us over a period of several weeks and was then invited to stay for a weekend. The purpose was to build some relationship. Our concern was to determine whether our situation best served this person's needs or whether he or she required a more structured environment such as a rehabilitation centre.

Certain guiding principles emerged.

1. Our home was not a crisis centre nor a youth refuge. It was an extended family practising hospitality to people who were invited to stay with us for a period of time.

2. The invitation to join us did not depend on the person being a Christian. In fact, the opposite was the case. Nearly all those who shared our home were not Christians when they joined us. Nor were they made to understand that they had to become Christians during their stay. What was made clear, however, was that we were Christians,

that we sought to honour Christ in our life style, and that we practised certain disciplines which included devotional times.

3. We attempted to make it clear that the person was not a client, a patient, nor a family member, but a guest of the family. The focus, therefore, was not rehabilitation nor psychiatric counselling. We offered a safe place in which the person could re-evaluate his or her life and begin to rebuild it.

Within this context, counselling was informal. The key strategy was to encourage the person to begin to live a life of responsibility and integrity.

A theology of hospitality

A set of theological ideas undergirded our practice of hospitality to Deena and other troubled young people who came to share our home.

It should be noted, however, that the ministry of hospitality was not a formal ministry for us. It was simply a part of living life. We were all involved in other areas of ministry.

1. One of the broader concepts that guided our action was that God calls his people to demonstrate to others the quality of love that God has shown to them. Put differently, God wants us to reflect to others something of the kindness and goodness he has shown to us.

While there is an emphasis in Scripture that this care for others should be demonstrated within the community of faith (see Deuteronomy 15:1215; Galatians 6:10), there is a corresponding emphasis that this requires a wider application.

In the Old Testament both those within the community and those who were strangers and aliens were to be treated with similar fairness and justice (Deuteronomy 24:1718). The reason for responding in this way was because God is his great goodness had liberated his people from slavery. They were commanded to treat aliens with similar generosity and goodness.

The New Testament also requires this. Not only is there a persistent emphasis on caring for brothers and sisters in the faith (Romans 12:13; Galatians 6:2), but acts of service must also be extended to those who were outside the Christian community (Luke 6:3435; Galatians 6:10).

217

2. A supporting theme is the emphasis in Scripture on the ministry of hospitality (Genesis 18:15; 19:12; Judges 19:1520; Job 31:32; Matthew 25:3446; Acts 9:43; 16;15; 1 Timothy 3:2; Hebrews 13:2).

A key inspiration for this type of ministry is a concept central to the work of Mother Teresa in India. It is that when we minister to the poor and needy we are somehow ministering to Christ himself. This idea comes from Matthew 25:3446. It is also supported by other passages of Scripture. The statement that 'whoever welcomes one such child in my name welcomes me' (Matthew 18:5) conveys a similar idea.

We can also put this a little differently. By inviting a needy person into our lives we are involved in a process of seeing that person grow into wholeness. Where that leads to a Christian commitment we are seeing that person's awakening to the Christ who was already there calling him or her to the fullness of life he has for them.

In this sense a guest, no matter now broken that person may be, is a very special person. While the temptation is to become fixated on this person's needs and problems, the challenge of Matthew 18:5 (welcoming Christ) is to focus on what is yet to come into being and to emerge in that person.

So the practice of hospitality for people with life-controlling problems involves receiving them in hope and to trust for the emergence of Christ's life within them. This can be an exciting adventure.

3. A third ideological foundation for this kind of ministry is Isaiah 58:6-12. Some themes in this significant passage should be noted. The most basic is that God desires us to convert our spiritual disciplines into strategies of social concern. Fasting can be expressed in seeking to set oppressed people free and to practically care for their needs.

A related theme is that genuine ministry is a two way process. Working with the wounded makes us all the more aware of our own needs and imperfections. We too need further healing. As we serve others God promises that our own 'healing shall spring up quickly' (Isaiah 58:8).

Finally, working restoratively with individuals means that not only will their individual lives be renewed but that potentially families and communities will also be transformed (Isaiah 58:12). A healed person can mean a healed marriage, family, or wider set of social relationships.

A rhythm of restoration

Our ministry of hospitality was supported by these theological ideas. They also helped to guide our practical application in living together.

1. A basic issue in our praxis was that the normal rhythm of our life as an extended family could act as a way to orient our guest towards more normal behaviours and attitudes. Most drug addicts, prostitutes, or people with life-controlling problems live highly irregular lives with little routine or structure. We found the experience of a more disciplined life style helped to orient them towards a more realistic approach to life.

2. A related idea is that life involves responsibility. Deena was not with us for a holiday. She was a guest of the family with corresponding benefits and responsibilities. Along with all the others she had her part to play in the functioning of the household. For all of us this meant cleaning, food preparation, shopping, cooking, and gardening.

The idea behind the involvement of all of us was that no one was more important than someone else and all had responsibility. Coupled with the joy of working alongside of each other, this had the effect of reinforcing the idea that we have to act responsibly in life. Life is not merely a number of arbitrary forces. I am not simply the victim of my circumstances. Life is also what I make of it and how I choose to live.

3. A further idea is that hospitality involves creating free space for the guest. Simply put, we are not there to entertain and look after Deena twenty-four hours a day. The home is neither a prison nor a fun parlour. This means that Deena has the responsibility to manage some of her own time. It also means that she has time for reflection and solitude.

Personal space for reflection is particularly critical. Many people with life-controlling problems are people who are in flight. They find it difficult to face their pain and disappointments. Yet, however slowly this may occur, these do need to be faced so that like a boil they can be lanced.

The framework then for the rhythm of restoration was realism, responsibility and the creation of a free space.

Journey to wholeness

The outworking of restoration varied according to each person. No one makes the same journey on the way to wholeness. But there are some common factors.

The first issue that usually occurs early in a person's stay is the temptation to return to the old and the familiar. Because the shape of the new is not yet clear there is a pressure to revert to old habits. This occurs even when a person was thoroughly sick of their previous life style and desperately wanted to change.

Clearly, when this pressure takes place the person must take more time in order to begin the rebuilding process. This critical transition phase requires that the other household members provide much encouragement and quiet intercessory prayer for the person.

A second feature is that the guest begins to question whether the new is really possible. This is the crisis of hope. Questions emerge. Can I really make something better of my life? How can I overcome my past problems? What will my new life look like?

In this phase the guest usually begins to probe the spirituality of members of the household to see if that may possibly provide the bridge to the new life. Questions are asked. What does prayer mean to you? What does it mean to have faith? What is Jesus supposed to do for you?

At this point it is important that time is given for these questions to be explored properly. A guest should not be pressed into an easy decision for Christ. In our experience, people took many months to settle these issues.

Once a person came to faith in Christ and began to grow in his or her discipleship, issues of restitution and reconciliation with others began to emerge. This was usually followed by questions of future life direction.

Somewhere within the space of the year that a person on average stayed with us there would come various crises of faith. These crises usually led to the realisation that further inner healing and renewal were required.

Facing the world

Our home was not the end of the road. It was the beginning of a further journey for people. This journey would also take them beyond our situation. Our place was only a temporary stopping place. It attempted to provide a place of safety and normality in which people like Deena could begin to rebuild their life.

It made no attempt to provide anything magical. Nor were easy solutions offered. The invitation, instead, was to face life realistically and responsibly. Living with Christians gave these people a close look at what the Christian life was all about for us. It allowed them to observe and to ask questions. It furthermore allowed them to explore what Christian spirituality might mean for them and what answers the Christian faith held for their lives.

We made no attempt to live a special life in front of these people. We were ourselves. We also made time for our own special family needs and for the other priorities in our lives. We made no attempt to make our home a little haven for people. They, like us, had to come to terms with the real world. So as time went on the issues of employment, where to live, vocation, calling and further life direction became issues of discussion, reflection and prayer.

Just as the intake was a careful process, so leaving us was a series of moves that gave Deena increasing responsibility. Beginning moves for her to create a life of her own included more free time, weekends away with family and friends, and eventually employment with the additional choices a steady income provided.

A final reflection

God calls the Christian community to be salt and light in a dark world. The church is to be God's instrument of transformation. That transformation, however, must be conceived holistically and it must take place at various levels.

While on Sunday the church is the gathered community, during the rest of the week it is the scattered church. As such, Christians find themselves in families, neighbourhoods, and in a great variety of work situations where they are to be God's instruments for good, reconciliation and reconstruction.

This means that Christians are involved in all of life. They work with the poor and in areas of policy and economics and get their hands dirty in areas of micro-reform.

What we must keep in focus is that we lack credibility when we pontificate on the big issues but never become practically involved with individuals and their needs. Here the example of Jesus is practical and to the point. His was the task to usher in the kingdom of God and to build the new community of faith. But Jesus also made time to heal and care for those who came to seek him out. Thus, while we seek to practice social justice to bring about a more just society, we can also lower the drawbridge and bring this ministry into our own homes.

2 Called to Community

Dorothy Mathieson and Tim McCowan

Dr Dorothy Mathieson was the Australian Coordinator of Servants to Asia's Urban Poor, and lived and worked in the slums of Manila in the Philippines and travelled internationally. She and her husband George continue to care for people in counselling and prayer.

Dr Tim McCowan served for eight years with Servants to Asia's Urban Poor in Manila

Only the Spirit can bring forgiveness, love and patience, so essential to community building

We are called to community with one another and with the poor in the slums.

This is one of the principles of a group of cross-cultural workers called Servants in Manila, Bangkok, Phnom Penh and other Asian cities. We are trying to respond to God's heart for the poor. We have embarked on a journey of vulnerability discovering gradually how increasing intimacy with the Father leads to opting for the poor and the despised, not for the systems of power and control. Only the Spirit can empower this.

Servants' principles are not just abstract Guidelines but living realities, forged in the context of the joy and struggles of welding teams together and living with the poor.

Incarnation calls us to the poor, to live with them, learn from them, discover the poverty of our rational, materialistic worldview and stance of western accomplishment.

Simplicity calls us to live focussed lives, discovering the freedom of releasing as many resources as possible to God's agenda of lifting up the downtrodden.

Servanthood reminds us that followers of Jesus must live as he lived, as a servant. Then we will be eager to empower and liberate the poor through relinquishing our own agendas, expertise and control.

Holism calls us not to function with a limited mandate in the context of a complicated poverty and injustice. What is the gospel to the starving mother, the prostitute supporting her extended destitute family, the community worker jailed illegally? We are called to preach the word, show compassion, plant churches, heal the sick, but also to do justice. The whole gospel for the whole person means the Spirit must be allowed to operate so the good news comes truly in word, deed and in power.

Community challenges us to forgo our cherished individualism and private agendas and to discover how others are totally necessary for our survival, effectiveness and spiritual growth. But it is here that we founder. We need a clear theology of community and we need to flesh out what this means for us.

Tim McCowan of the Manila team has worked on this:

Servant's Community: Theological Basis

Christianity is a communal faith. 'Individual Christianity is a contradiction in terms' (McAfee Brown, The Bible speaks to you, 202).

We cannot live the Christian faith in a vacuum, or without others. This belief is based on the following theological foundations.

1. God is 'a community'

As Christians we believe God is a trinity of persons, called Father, Son and Holy Spirit. An intimate communion of three making one. Distinct but unified. A community, selfsufficient yet desiring to reach out and include others in their extravagant love.

2. God's image

According to the evangelical German theologian, Karl Barth, we most accurately reflect God's character and image when we are in community. God 'created man in his own image ... male and female he created them.' The image of God is not so much 'our rationality' or volitional capacity, but our communality. God's image therefore is only properly reflected when we are together in our differences and complementarity. Art Gish in his classic, Living in Christian Community (p. 21) says that the phrase 'Let us make man in our image' indicates that the fellowship in the Godhead created the manwoman community to reflect God's concern for fellowship and communion. The human 'we' identity is to be a reflection of the divine 'we'.

3. God is a covenant maker

God delights to make covenants to show his concern for 'peoples' rather than just individuals. All his covenants, although made with individuals, are focused on affecting his people or the nations. They embrace communities, not simply individuals.

4. Jesus is a community builder

Jesus intentionally called a group of disciples, and gathered them together into a community. They were to be 'with him and to be sent out' (Matthew 10:1; Mark 6:1; Luke 9:1, 10:1). Jesus' central teaching was to the so called kingdom or reign of God. But

if it is true that God's reign concerns history ... we who live nineteen hundred years after the event [of Jesus' living, death and resurrection] must share in its power, not merely by reading of it in a book or hearing it in a verbal report, but by participating in the life of that society which springs from it and is continuous with it ... The centre of Jesus' concern

225

was the calling and binding to himself of a living community of men and women who would be the witnesses of what he was and did. The new reality which he introduced into history was to be continued through history in the form of a community, not in the form of a book (Lesslie Newbigin, *The Open Secret*, pp. 57-58).

He called them to leave their families and previous vocation and stay with him. They lived together, shared a common purse, and adopted an alternative lifestyle from the surrounding society. He also sent them out in pairs to preach, heal, cast out demons and invite others to join their wider band. He therefore formed them into a 'community in mission'.

5. The church is a community

Throughout the New Testament, the church is described in communal terminology. It was a community of believers, centred on Jesus Christ, more than an institution. The Reformers, living in a time of 'Corpus Christianum', sought to define the church by its various functions, i.e. the teaching of the Word of God, the administration of the sacraments, and right discipline. Yet this misses a fundamental point. The church does not consist of those who merely do certain things, but by those who are 'in Christ'. It is a fellowship of persons, entirely without an institutional character. It is the body of Christ; the family of God; a chosen race, a royal priesthood, a holy nation, God's own people (1 Peter 2:9).

Tim applies these biblical principles to Servants.

Servants' community in Manila is:

1. A 'missionary band'

We are expatriates in a foreign land, called and committed to a single, broad missionary mandate. We are not a community just to share our struggles and a few possessions, but to engage in holistic mission amongst the urban poor. Like the Moravians before us, we are a 'community in mission' that seeks to find empowerment for ministry through our communal life together. In other words, we are bifocal, aiming to keep community and mission holding hands. We live separately, but come together two days a month, in order to be sent out again. This is our missionary spiral, if you like.

2. A valiant attempt

Trying to engage in strategic ministry whilst living with the urban poor, plus maintaining a viable communal life, places us in an unavoidable tension. We often feel torn between the calls of our squatter neighbours and our own community. Where is the priority? Not wanting to lay down hard and fast rules, and keeping our bifocal vision, means we have sadly seen some fall through the gaps. We are still not sure how possible it is for us to ride this gigantic wave of the Spirit, who calls us with such amazing patience, to trust him for 'the impossible'.

3. A fragile association of ragged radicals

Every Servant starts off as an idealist. We are all very different, but we all come out generally to see the slums transformed. Pretty soon we realise that most squatters are set in their ways, and are not so open to being changed. When all our plans have filled the waste bin, we discover just how much we need each other in the team. Maybe our self esteem or a particular project is in tatters, so that our frustration level is up and our energy level is down. These are the times when we come into 'teamtime' wounded, bruised and broken. This is why we are unashamedly committed to each other, to be burdenbearers, available to be agents of the Lord's healing for each other.

4. An 'open circle'

Servants is not a self-perpetuating community. Our real empowerment for mission comes not just through our corporate life together, but our corporate worship life. In our fragility and brokenness, we unashamedly open ourselves up to our Healer, Redeemer and Lord. The depth of our need goes beyond 'the water' each of us can contribute. We need 'the living water' that only he can give. He is the reason for our leaving family, friends and earthly treasures, and embracing the pain and joy of serving the 'little ones'. Beside the extravagant generosity of our God, we are mere grateful beggars, trying to encourage some others to accept his gracious invitation.

5. A 'little leaven'

Servants is a small daring minority, that seeks to be an agent transforming both the squatters and their slum communities. Although we boldly cling to such a grand vision, few outsiders know of our existence as a community. It is 'hidden' and seemingly insignificant to any social analyst. We are seeking not to multiply our organisation, but our distinctive ethos and values. Slowly, yet wonderfully, this leaven is spreading through 'the dough'. Others (both Filipinos and Westerners) are now joining us as we follow the Lord into difficult discipleship amongst the poor and marginalised.

6. An unfinished story

We have made many mistakes on our journey as a 'community in mission'. We don't claim to have the whole truth, or to be on our last chapter. We are on a big learning curve, wanting to keep listening to the Lord, each other, the poor, and our brothers and sisters in the wider body of Christ. We're not builders laying concrete footings, but sojourners putting down a few tent pegs, that we may just have to pull up tomorrow. Our structures, our leaders, and our composition have all changed, but the One who calls us on is faithful and he will accomplish what he has set out to do (1 Thessalonians 5:24). We don't wish to put ourselves up as the only model of mission amongst the urban poor, but to be faithful to the vision and invitation that the Lord has given us in this small corner of his world. Please pray for us.

Community only possible through prayer

The theology is sound; the derivative principles are inspiring. But the gaps created by the reality of community living are glaringly obvious. We discover that our desperate inadequacy for the huge task reveals not only our own weaknesses but those of other team members. After the first thrill of involvement, we reach the awful conclusion that we don't like one another, doubt the others' callings, disrespect their motivations.

Closeness lowers the barriers, then we fear losing control. We dissolve, become belligerent, too passionate for side issues, too reformist about others, too accusing of our own shortfalls. The more and more we try to create unity, we destroy it. The high call to self-sacrifice that community issues jars against our pervading personality preferences, impressive education, theological training and expertise.

Only the Spirit can bring forgiveness, love and patience, so essential to community building. And it is happening, but it's so fragile. We have to abandon ourselves to the dynamic of the Spirit, not to legislation or to past successes. What will the Spirit reveal next .... in me .... in us .... in new directions?

As we respond to his painful and joyful refining, we can build ourselves into communities which the poor can see and say in amazement, like the earliest observers of the faith did, 'See how they love one another.'

Some responses to the *Renewal Journals*

God moves in many ways, including the multiplying of these emerging small communities of committed people. Thousands are praying as never before. Reports continue to come of God's Spirit stirring.

All across this land the Spirit of God is leading people to wait on the Lord in worship, prayer and faith, then minister in the Spirit's power. This journal strongly encourages that.

A lady in Belmont, Victoria wrote, 'We thoroughly enjoy reading the *Renewal Journal* and have started a prayer group for revival.'

A husband and wife in Newtown in Victoria were blessed by the *Renewal Journal* and as a result they started a prayer group for renewal in their Reformed Church.

A young man in Brisbane bought extra copies of the *Renewal Journal* to distribute to his leaders' group at his church and has urged them to spend more time seeking the Lord together.

You could pass your copy of the *Renewal Journal* on to others to bless them.

You can now obtain republished copies of the *Renewal Journal.* It has struck a strong chord for many people.

3 Covenant Community

Shayne Bennett

Leaders of the Emmanuel Covenant Community in Brisbane included Moderator Shayne Bennett and Founder Brian Smith (photo). Shayne Bennett wrote as an elder of the Emmanuel Covenant Community.

I will never forget January 1975. I was in Melbourne as the representative of a youth prayer group to attend a national conference on charismatic renewal. It was a time when the charismatic renewal was riding on the crest of a wave. Thousands of people had gathered from across the country as well as overseas to hear a line up of exciting speakers. They represented many denominations and the gatherings were marked by an incredible sense of joy and freedom.

During this conference, Fr Vince Hobbs, Brian Smith and John Carroll, three leaders from the Catholic Charismatic Renewal in Brisbane, began to share a vision of developing covenant community. They also took the opportunity to speak with Ralph Martin, one of the conference speakers, who was also a leader of a charismatic covenant community in Ann Arbor, Michigan.

The Statement of Community Order Document (Section B.1.) explains that 'A covenant community is a group of Christians who have been led by the Lord to express their love and commitment to him and to one another as part of a divine call or vocation. They do this through a public life-long commitment called a covenant.'

A time to begin

I still remember Brian Smith coming to me at the conference saying, 'I really believe now is the time to build community.'

The idea of charismatic communities was not new. We had been in contact with them from as early as 1972 when Brian Smith first went to the United States. The hesitation about moving towards community was always a question of timing and maturity. Until now, no one was ready to step out and make that first move. That was about to change.

On their return to Brisbane, Brian Smith and John Carroll with their wives and families began to meet with two other couples to pursue this sense of call. In February of 1975 the four couples washed each others' feet as a sign of their commitment and as an expression of their service to one another, not just in spiritual matters but in the whole of their life circumstances.

A new foundation was being laid which others would soon be invited to join. These couples shared their vision with the people of the prayer group at Bardon, which was the principal meeting place for Catholics involved in charismatic renewal with about 400-600 attending.

Responses varied. Some were excited at the new initiative because they had been looking for an opportunity to be more committed and for a way of including their children in this charismatic experience. Others were cautious and questioned this new direction.

After some weeks the community had its first intake. Thirteen families expressed a desire to be part of this new move of the Spirit. In the first year the community grew to nearly 200 members.

I observed the community from the beginning, preferring to remain part of the youth prayer group that had also begun to develop a strong sense of community. I had some suspicion about how this Brisbane Covenant Community (as it was then called) was going to develop. Would it begin well and simply become another prayer meeting or would it actually begin to achieve the goal of building a Christian way of life?

By the end of the first year it was obvious that the community was not only talking about a way of life, it was actually living it.

Early in 1976 our youth group of around 30 people decided that our call was to a community way of life and that it was better to join with the Brisbane Covenant Community than attempt to go in our own direction.

After a few months formation our group made covenant, committing ourselves to follow the Lord in the context of this people called the Brisbane Covenant Community.

A time to build up

The first years of the community were life the beginning of a great adventure. It was the time of laying the foundation stones. The dynamism of the charismatic renewal had flowed into the community. Charismatic gifts played an important role in bringing depth and richness into our praise and worship.

As well as gifts that we'd come to appreciate in prayer groups, we realised there were so many more gifts that we hadn't thought about as charisms. As we shared life together as a community, other things became important.

Different ministries with children and young adults began to emerge as well as gifts of administration and various roles of service. Our horizons were broadening. We grew in our appreciation that charisms were given for the building up of the body.

We had a growing consciousness that this Christian community lifestyle was important both for the church and for the world. Cardinal Suenens had already begun to articulate the need for the church to offer pilot projects as a pre-figuration of the kind of human community for which the world is searching so painfully... From a human point of view, it might seem paradoxical to make the future of the church dependent upon small Christian communities which, no matter how fervent, are but a drop in the ocean... But if we consider the spiritual energy released by every group which allows Christ to fill it with the life of the Holy Spirit, then the perspective changes, for we are putting ourselves in the strength and power of God (A New Pentecost, pp. 151-153).

If the Church is to fulfil its mission, communities which demonstrate this Christian way of life are an integral part of that mission.

A study conducted by Fusion, a Christian organisation committed to evangelisation in the Australian context, spoke of Australians as 'people who think in terms of the concrete rather than the abstract, and very often thought forms that are used to express the Christian message are alien to them... What Australians need is a model. Once it's seen in action they are quite capable of recognising its meaning' (Fusion 1986).

This challenge to be a Christian community for the church and for the world was somehow at the heart of our mission.

One of the other hopes which was born out of this community life was a longing for reconciliation between Christians. While the founding members were predominantly Catholic, there were also two Anglicans among them. This experience of sharing life together, coupled with the general enthusiasm of the 70s with regard to ecumenism, caused the community to hope that through the charismatic experience and a committed way of life it might find a way through the problems and divisions of a separated Christianity.

In late 1976 the name of the community was changed to the Emmanuel Covenant Community and with the change of name was a growing confidence that God really was with us and leading us in building this way of life. From the point of view of structure, the community lifestyle encompassed four main expressions, as outlined in the Emmanuel Statement of Community Order Documents (Section B.5.):

1. The General Community Gathering which is a meeting of the whole community to worship, to receive teaching and to maintain a common vision and fellowship;

2. Small group meetings are opportunities for share the Christian journey and receive encouragement and support;

3. Formation teaching courses are conducted to provide teaching on the spiritual life and everyday living as well as giving a clear orientation on the life of the community.

4. Social life in the community plays an important role in developing a genuine and balanced Christian lifestyle.

While these basic structures were important, the community had to offer more if it was to be a model to the church and the world. One of the most important developments in this area was the formation of clusters.

In 1978, members of the community began to move geographically closer together so that the community dimension would take more concrete expression. Community had to be demonstrated in practice, not just in theory. As families and single people moved closer together, more and more opportunities presented themselves for the building of authentic Christian community. These included travelling to work together, sharing mowers, supporting people when they were sick, providing practical care for widows, and other expressions of support.

Localised community expressions also enabled Emmanuel to be more effective in its local outreach and to contribute something to the wider community. Taking initiative at the local level to hold football games, Australia Day celebrations, picnics in the park, and Christmas carols were but a few ways that we endeavoured to share our lifestyle and contribute to our local community.

These were bridges of friendship which were built in local neighbourhoods to let others know we were ordinary human beings and not aliens from another planet ready to capture them and take them with us (which was one rumour circulating about us). Time and good will helped to break down some of the initial fears that were encountered when developing clusters.

A time to reach out

While the initial concentration of energy in Emmanuel was in trying to become that which we claimed to be – a Christian community – we didn't cease to reach out to others in local parishes, at national conferences, and in assisting other groups in both Australia and New Zealand in their desire to develop community.

In February, 1980, when I was conducting one of those outreaches to northern Queensland, I received a phone call asking me to serve as an Elder of the community. 'An Elder is a leader in the community who together with a body of Elders exercises a governing role in the community' (Statement of Community Order Document, Section D.3.).

My first response was a sense of awe as I reflected on God's call in my life. The second awareness that I had was the sense of responsibility in leading and caring for this people that God had called into being. The prophet Jeremiah came to mind and his exclamation to the Lord when he protested that he was too young. 'Say not, "I am too young." To whomever I send you, you shall go; whatever I command you, you shall speak' (Jeremiah 1:7). I was 25 years old at the time, married for three years with one small daughter. In the days ahead, that scripture gave me a lot of strength.

In November of 1980 the Emmanuel Community began its most ambitious missionary outreach. Responding to requests for assistance, three teams of five people travelled to six south east Asian countries to conduct leadership and training programmes for the Catholic charismatic renewal. I led the team which went to West Malaysia and Indonesia.

For each one of us who participated in these outreaches our lives would never be the same. Asia and her people had taken deep root in our hearts and in the coming years God would give some of us many opportunities to return, to live amongst the people and assist them in the development of their own covenant communities. Today there are at least six covenant communities in Malaysia with new groups forming year after year.

Our outreach to Asia was not just a matter of going to Asia and giving out. We received more than we could ever hope or imagine. This was true for Emmanuel as a whole, especially when Asian brothers and sisters would visit us. In sharing life together, we were changed by their humility, love and commitment to Christ. Through our contact with them we became aware of our own poverty.

This experience of our own poverty was to be relived over and over again as future teams would go to Papua New Guinea and Fiji sharing life with the people and growing in love and understanding of their culture and way of life. For Emmanuel, the key to outreach is living the life.

The people who participated in these outreaches were not experts but ordinary people who gave up their own holidays and paid their own way. What they had to do share was not so much what they had read in books but what they had experienced in trying to live the Christian life day by day in the context of a community. These were things that people could relate to, whether they lived in the highlands of Papua New Guinea on in the coastal villages of Fiji. Through outreaches like these the community grew to realise the importance of being faithful to the challenge of living the Christian life day by day.

A time to die

The first ten years of the community, although facing many challenges, were rather like when the apostles walked with Jesus and never ceased to be amazed at what he could do. Then just as the apostles were called to a baptism of suffering, so were we although I don't think we really anticipated what we were about to experience.

Our baptism into Christ encompasses his life, death and resurrection. All of these elements are important. What is it like for a community to be baptised into the death of Christ?

For Emmanuel, there was no single event but rather a series of them which brought about a real sense of dying in the community. At a very human level, people were tired of living such a committed life year after year. It was demanding and the cost was high. People struggled with their commitment and asked the question, 'Is it worth it?'

At around the same time ecumenical tensions arose as well. We found ourselves struggling with the same ecclesiological problems that the wider church was experiencing. Despite our early hopes and many years of hard work, we had to admit our own limitations and faced the fact that it was not possible to build the ecumenical community we had once dreamed about.

Added to this was the breakdown of international relationships amongst covenant communities resulting in divisiveness and resentments. The once young and healthy community was suffering through its own sin and human limitations.

Perhaps the greatest test of trust was to come on 1 February, 1988. We had just celebrated Eucharist at our community office when we received word of an urgent phone call for Brian Smith. No one could have anticipated his words as he emerged from his office: 'My daughter Teresa has passed away.' The next twenty-four hours would reveal the truth of Teresa's brutal rape and murder.

The question on everyone's lips was how could God allow this to happen. Like many other people in the community, I had known Teresa since she was a little girl. She was a real character, full of fun, life and faith. That evening as Brian and Lorraine Smith were interviewed on national television, they spoke of their forgiveness for Teresa's murderer. As the Emmanuel community attempted to comfort Brian and Lorraine, so too did they comfort the community by continuing to speak of forgiveness and the need to surrender to God's will.

While Teresa's life had a wonderful impact on the lives of many, I would dare to say that her death had a greater impact. There is no doubt that she was a servant of God in both her life and in her death. As we trusted in God to raise Teresa, his servant, from death into fulness of life within him, it somehow gave us all a little more courage to believe that God would raise Emmanuel from its despair and bring it to new life.

A time for healing

The resurrection for which we hoped was not immediate but it did happen. It did not come as a result of good planning or skilled leadership but purely through the action of the Holy Spirit. Members of the community were renewed in their commitment. There was a new enthusiasm to move on. It was a different enthusiasm from that of the beginning. It was one marked by realism and a desire to give in to the will of God.

This was especially evident among the young people in the community. While the community is now clearly Catholic and not ecumenical in its entity, the heart to work towards Christian unity still remains an important charism.

A fruit of the difficulties experienced between communities internationally has been the development of two international associations for communities.

The first is the International Brotherhood of Communities (IBOC) which provides a meeting place for all the different expressions of covenant communities around the world. It is ecumenical in its expression and seeks to encourage leaders of communities as they respond to God's call.

The second group is the Catholic Fraternity of Charismatic Communities and Fellowships. Inaugurated in Rome in November 1990, the Catholic Fraternity had very humble beginnings. While fewer than 40 delegates from 13 communities gathered for the inaugural meeting, we experienced a conviction that God intended to do great things from this small beginning. More than 200 covenant communities from around the world have sought information on becoming part of the Fraternity. The Emmanuel Community in Brisbane was not only a founding member of the fraternity but did much of the preliminary work which culminated in a formal recognition by Pope John Paul II. This is the first time a canonical approval has been given by the Vatican to any charismatic group.

Conclusion

As I look back over my years of involvement in the Emmanuel Covenant Community, some things are clear to me. The contribution of covenant communities to the life of the church and the world must come out of brokenness and humility rather than pride or arrogance. The path to humility is the way of the cross and whether we like it or not, Jesus calls us to embrace it. 'Whoever does not take up his cross and follow in my steps is not fit to be my disciple' (Matthew 10:38).

We are not people who have it all together, but people who are on a journey, people who experience the same trails and temptations as anyone else. Unlike our early years when we thought we were going to save the whole world, we have come to find that our only boast is the cross of Christ. The cross is our redemption. As we surrender to the cross, so too do we dare to hope in the resurrection.

References

Fusion (1986) 'Understanding and Reaching Australians', a Position Paper.

Suenens, Cardinal *A New Pentecost*. Harper, 1984.

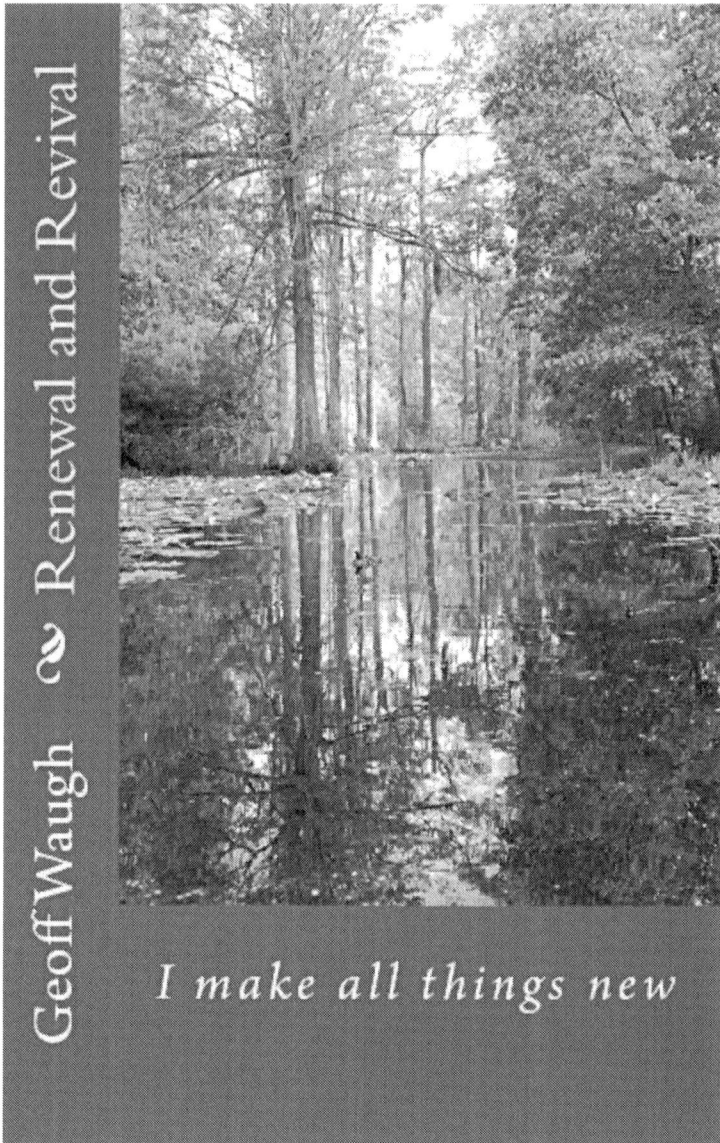

Renewal and Revival

Compiled from 2 books: *Renewal* and *Revival*
Renewal Journal articles by Geoff Waugh

4 *The Spirit in the Church*

Adrian Commadeur

Adrian Commadeur comments on charismatic renewal and Christian communities. This account of his discoveries, following eight years as a Redemptorist student, is adapted from Chapter 4 of his book The Spirit in the Church.

---

each has a sense of belonging,

plays a significant role in the community,

and is accountable to someone else

The gift of the Holy Spirit, with accompanying charisms, has the purpose of empowering the Christian to witness to the death and resurrection of Jesus.

This has been the experience of many in the charismatic renewal, both to desire and to be able to share the good news of Jesus Christ within the Christian community and to the world. While it belongs to the very nature of the church to proclaim the gospel, I grew up with the notion that the church was there to keep Catholics fervent, and reach out to the pagans in Africa or Asia to evangelise them.

Since the coming of the Holy Spirit in a fresh personal Pentecost, the call to evangelisation has stirred me strongly. At times I have responded according to my ability.

Life in the Spirit seminars

One of the early leaders of Renewal in the United States, Steve Clark, developed a series of

teachings in 1971. It was based on early Church practice of introducing catechumens or serious inquirers into the community of faith.

On the basis of the perceived needs of those seeking the baptism of the Holy Spirit, the series consists of seven weekly sessions of teachings and discussions and prayers. Life in the Spirit Seminars have been used worldwide to bring people from either unbelief to faith, or from belief to deeper faith and the release of the Holy Spirit.

The seminar is an effective means of spiritual growth through teachings on basic Christian themes and daily biblical reflections between weekly sessions. A participant's book including daily Scripture readings and prayers is made available to each person. More than one million copies have been printed.

For the team presenting the Seminar a Team Manual was prepared, showing in detail the method of conducting the seminar and the contents of each of the teachings. By 1974 already 100,000 copies were in use.

The Life in the Spirit Seminar has been, and continues to be, a most effective way of bringing people into a new and personal relationship with Jesus Christ by means of the release of the Holy Spirit. It is a marvellous way of renewing faith, clarifying the basics of doctrine, incorporating people into a community of faith and love, and introducing them to the power and gifts of the Holy Spirit which enables them to become more effective witnesses to the risen Jesus.

For nonbelievers, especially young people who have not heard the gospel (even though it may have been presented to them either at school or in church), it is an introduction to Christianity. For those who have been lukewarm in faith, or uncertain of their beliefs, it is a renewal, especially through an introduction to the person of Jesus. To those who search for a deeper life of faith and prayer, it is a fulfilment of the heart's desire. For all, the Life in the Spirit Seminar is a fulfilment of the promise of Jesus, `You will receive power, when the Holy Spirit has come upon you' (Acts 1:8).

Prayer groups

Prayer Groups are a wonderful means of evangelisation and introducing new people to a fuller life in Christ and the Spirit. There are approximately 450 Catholic charismatic prayer groups around Australia. They meet in churches, church halls, meeting rooms, school rooms, chapels and homes.

They range in numbers from as few as three or four, to around 300. The average size of the 90 groups in the Melbourne Archdiocese in 1991 was 25 participants. On special occasions like a healing Eucharist, there can be twice the normal number in attendance. If a conservative estimate of 20 people per meeting were accepted, then some 10,000 Catholics meet every week in charismatic prayer groups around Australia. Some 20,000 could be said to be active Australia wide.

While Covenant Communities are the major alternative, prayer meetings are the normal local expression of the Catholic charismatic renewal. This means that the prayer meeting should be a significant place for evangelisation into the local church community.

Renewed parishes

Across the spectrum of the Church there are now a number of exciting examples of renewed parishes where people flock to join in worship, fellowship, Christian formation and service. One of the major tensions that Catholic Charismatics must resolve is their commitment to their prayer meetings and to their parishes.

On the one hand, the prayer meeting often provides for warmth of fellowship, ministry in the power of the Holy Spirit, strength and conviction in praise and worship, and teaching that is based both on Scripture and on the spiritual experiences of the speaker. In addition, there are times of social activities and regional and national conferences, retreats, seminars and similar `celebrations'.

On the other hand the parish provides for Sunday and weekday Eucharist, the sacraments such as reconciliation, and pastoral care in sickness. Parish activities are multifaceted and provide for schooling, caring, sporting, social and adult education activities. In this way the different needs of the charismatic parishioner are met.

Ideally both these needs should be met in the parish that is renewed in the Spirit, in which there is a spiritual vitality that can attract others to its worship and lifestyle. On the one hand, people are satisfied with a deeper spiritual journey through the prayer meeting. On the other, the necessary and the obligatory elements of the faith are satisfied.

Certain principles apply in all parish renewals. It seems that there needs to be a sovereign

initiative of God and a parish clergy and leadership open to the Holy Spirit. One of the principal methods seems to be the formation of the Parish Group (Cell) System, to enable informal formation at a personal level.

The pastor at St Boniface's, Fr Michael Eivers, outlines six factors that are keys to the success of the cell system.

* The cell system must initially be directed by the pastor and continue to have his support.

* Cells are community related, and reach out to people in the members' neighbourhoods and work environments.

* Cells are self-multiplying groups.

* The cell system is the parish way of life, not just another program.

* Cells are highly evangelistic, missionary groups.

* Continuous training and motivation of cell leaders is critical (Perini, p. 9).

I hope that in Australia there will soon be parish priests with their parish teams, who will dare to renew the sacramentalized and evangelise unbelievers in the power of the Holy Spirit and through the cell system.

Covenant Communities

One eloquent expression of the inspiration of the Holy Spirit in charismatic renewal has been the formation of Covenant Communities.

Covenant Community is a group of Christians who have been led by the Lord to bind themselves to Him and also to one another in the form of public commitment. Its call is to live a Christian lifestyle, in family and single life, through openness to the charismatic gifts, worship and prayer, sharing and teaching, and support for one another (Emmanuel Covenant Community, Brisbane).

As early as 1971 the first members of prayer groups in the USA felt the call to bind themselves together in a shared lifestyle. It may have been relatively easy to do so for students and graduates of the various universities. They had both the idealism and the freedom to commit themselves to one another, without such other commitments as family or mortgages.

Some of the earliest communities were True House, led by Joe Byrne, and People of Praise, led by Kevin and Dorothy Ranaghan and Paul de Celles, in South Bend, Indiana, near the University of Notre Dame, and the Word of God, led by Ralph Martin and Steve Clark and others, in Ann Arbor, Michigan, around the University of Michigan.

On visiting them in 1973 I was impressed by the strength of numbers and commitment to the cause of renewal of the Church through a return to the lifestyle of the early Christians. Even within each community there seemed different levels of commitment. Many lived in households and some shared their goods and possessions, including their socks!

Australian communities

A number of Covenant Communities have developed within the charismatic scene in Australia. They range up and down in numbers and influence. If some have a lower profile they still have qualities shared by most other communities. There are also signs of new or renewed religious communities which give rise to hope for new sparkling life and ministry of the Church in Australia.

The Brisbane based Emmanuel Covenant Community was formed in 1975, with four men and their families responding to the call to bind themselves together in Community. First members and leaders of the Community were Brian Smith and John Carroll, with their wives, Lorraine and Penny, and their families. As early as 1976 Emmanuel became affiliated with other communities, notably in the United States, and later to others around the world in an International Brotherhood of Communities (IBOC), and in The Catholic Fraternity of Charismatic Covenant Communities and Fellowships (1990).

Associated with Emmanuel in Australia are a number of Communities that have been helped by them in their establishment. These include Bethel in Perth, Hepzibah in Canberra, Melbourne and Adelaide, and Disciples of Jesus in Sydney and Melbourne. Other communities include many small groups of people who have committed themselves to the Lord and to one another, but have not grown in strength or numbers. Although the membership of most Communities includes a majority of Catholics, a number of Communities could be said to be ecumenical such as Servants of Jesus in Sydney.

Membership of Catholics, Anglicans, Protestants and perhaps some Pentecostals requires sensitive leadership and acceptable common activities. Within ecumenical Communities, Catholic fraternities have at times been structured, to enable a specifically Catholic identity to be expressed, especially in the liturgical life of the Community.

Communities commit themselves to be of service in the Church and to the world. At times they do outstanding work either through large organised groups such as the National Evangelisation Team (NET) or through small teams of evangelists who travel within or outside of Australia to preach the gospel. Many Communities have developed a specific ministry such as to the poor, for unmarried mothers, or visiting the lonely.

Charismatic community lifestyle

Most of the Communities share a basic lifestyle which is expressed in certain practical ways. Membership of the community is demonstrated by participation in:

* general community gatherings.

* smaller groupings for discussion, sharing, and support.

* a Christian formation program for family and single life.

* informal gatherings for social activities.

* teaching and evangelistic outreaches according to the opportunities offered or initiated.

* leadership exercised by a group of elders, the number of which is determined by the needs and size of the community and supported materially and financially by the members.

* members seek to live in close geographical proximity for easier fellowship and support.

* traditional Eucharistic and liturgical prayer.

Communities are making a significant contribution to the renewal of the spiritual life of the

church. They promote a commitment to the Lord Jesus Christ and a mutual love of members of the community. Extensive teaching programs and pastoral oversight have strengthened the life of faith and sharing among their members. Numerical strength and the pooling of resources have been made possible. This has enabled leaders to be constantly in touch with leaders worldwide and so have maintained bonds and standards of renewed community life.

Fraternity of Covenant Communities

On 30 November 1990, a significant event occurred in Rome. On that date the Pontifical Council for the Laity promulgated the decree which inaugurated the Catholic Fraternity of Covenant Communities and Fellowships. The decree noted that Covenant Communities from Australia, Canada, France, Malaysia, New Zealand and the United States were 'motivated by the desire both to assure greater dialogue and collaboration among themselves and to deepen their communion with the Successor of Peter as an essential element of their Catholic identity.'

The decree recognised the Fraternity as a Private Association of the Christian Faithful within the Catholic Church. It expressed the hope that this recognition would consolidate and promote the Catholic expression of the charismatic movement, might increase its spiritual fruits and encourage intensified apostolic activity in the work of evangelisation.

At the inauguration, Brian Smith from Brisbane, was elected President of the Executive of the Fraternity. He noted that the declaration was the most significant event in the history of the charismatic renewal since the 1975 Holy Year international conference and the acknowledgment it received from Pope Paul VI at that time. He said, 'It is the first time that the Renewal has had formal, canonical recognition by the Vatican.'

Communities of life and service

A further expression of the charismatic renewal has emerged in the church. Groups of committed people have established themselves as communities of life and service. These include the establishment of houses of prayer, teams of service, or new religious houses or communities of lay people married or single with a focus on such ministry as street kids or contemplative prayer. Localised and adapted to cultural and religious circumstances, these communities add greatly, but often unobtrusively, to the life of the church at large. All of them would consider themselves to be part of the main stream at the heart of the church.

One of these communities of life and service is the Holy Spirit of Freedom Community. Frank and Lu Feain lead this community with three houses in Melbourne and Perth, have a circle of collaborating tertiaries to support them financially, materially and spiritually and work for homeless `street kids'. This community brings the love of God to drug users and victims of domestic abuse, through `friendship evangelism.'

Another group is the House of Prayer at beautiful Carcoar, NSW, conducted by Helen and Neville Bowers and serving both the charismatic renewal and the local diocese. The ministry includes the provision of retreats, seminars and days of prayer.

Another significant development over recent years is the number of Schools of Evangelisation. Young people especially, receive formation in mature Christian living, and practical training in the skills of sharing the gospel with others.

The church exists to evangelise

All of the expressions of Catholic charismatic renewal demonstrate the creative activity and

ministry of the Holy Spirit. While some may judge one form or lifestyle or expression superior to another, all expressions of charismatic renewal aim to assist in the growth of personal holiness and to serve the church and world with the proclamation of the gospel.

In conclusion, the experience of successful prayer groups and communities shows that a dynamic lifestyle where each has a sense of belonging, plays a significant role in the community, and is accountable to someone else best attracts new believers, and keeps them as effective members of the church community.

References

Blum, Susan (undated) 'A Parish Where Everyone Evangelizes' in *New Evangelization 2000*, issue 5.

Perini, Pigel (undated) 'New Evangelisation in an Ancient Basilica' in *New Evangelization 2000*, issue 7.

---

5 House Churches

Ian Freestone

Captain Ian Freestone wrote as a Church Army Captain working with the Ruach Neighbourhood Churches in Sydney. Original Renewal Journal article, 1994. For further information see Ruach Ministries on www.ruach.org.au

Out of a desire to see a fuller expression of Christian community in the church and out of a passion to see unbelievers come to Christ and become part of his church, several of us began a network of house churches.

We often refer to them as neighbourhood churches, firstly, because not all of them meet in homes and secondly, because we are wanting to encourage each house church to have a neighbourhood vision for outreach.

God spoke prophetically to us at that time saying, 'You don't grow a church from the outside in but from the inside out. The house church is the basis for growth and the key to growth is faith.'

That was in 1990. It has been a difficult road at times since then and we still have a real sense that we are on a journey. We join with many in believing that revival in this nation is imminent, if not upon us, and what is needed are structures that can cope with an influx of new Christians. The establishing of house churches provides one means for us to ride on what the Lord is wanting to do.

Why House Churches?

There is a growing realisation that our present church structures are inadequate to meet the demands of a changing society. It is doubtful whether they are flexible enough to cope with a major outpouring of the Spirit of God. Ralph Neighbour, a pioneer and proponent of cell group churches, has called for a 'second Reformation'. He suggests that present church structures are woefully inadequate: It is sad, but true: the church structure we have duplicated over and over in this century is shockingly inefficient! The buildings are empty for most of the week. The members aren't equipped to minister to hurting people. Everything centres on activities within the church buildings' (1990:14).Unless we are prepared to critically examine the structures in the church, we will continue to be inhibited in our God-given mission: to be Christian community in such a way that we might 'know Christ and make him known.'

John Smith recognises our failure in the Australian Church to reach ordinary people for Jesus: 'To the average Australian, the church always has been, and still is, a foreign culture. Nor has there been sufficient attempt to change that image...The church is a subculture from abroad: it still has a distinctly colonial air about it. ... If we are ever going to communicate to the majority of Australian people, we will have to make some savage changes to our church agenda' (1988:214-215).

What we need therefore in the church are bridge builders: people willing to work towards new models of church life and ministry (Kaldor 1988:23). The church in the house is one of those bridges. Yet it is more than a bridge. In our opinion it is the most appropriate context for the expression of Christian community. We share Robert Bank's belief that 'on biblical and contemporary grounds the Home Church is fundamental to any quest for renewal' (1986:39).

The problem with our present church structures is that we have developed what Howard Snyder calls an edifice complex. He suggests that we have patterned the organisation of the church on the temple model. We have confused the building the church meets in as the church itself instead of seeing the church as the people of God. In a powerful critique of present day church buildings, Snyder points out that our church buildings are a witness to our immobility, our inflexibility, our lack of fellowship, our pride and our class divisions (1975:69-73).

Ross Paterson makes some provoking comments concerning Chinese House churches: 'Churches which lost their buildings and their corporate life (after the cultural revolution) became centred around and rooted in the family, as meetings had to be held in homes... This lack of structure has proved of enormous benefit to the church in China' (1989:195).

Many have sought to introduce small groups within churches to address our crisis in the West but, as David Prior states, there is 'disillusionment with the widespread proliferation of such groups.' He adds, 'This is in no sense to decry the real benefits which individuals have undoubtedly received as members of prayer groups, Bible-study groups, etc., it is simply to underline their inadequacy in terms of discovering what a local church is intended by God to become' (1983:9).

Robert Banks, as part of his argument to say the same, quotes C. M. Olsen: Although small groups have been utilised as a church renewal scheme, they have rarely been legitimised as a full expression of the church. They have been conceived as an adjunct for the personal growth of the participants... Meanwhile the 'real' church gathers in the sanctuary at eleven every Sunday... the small group is relegated to serving as a means to a larger end... In this role it cannot become anything more than a halfway house' (1986:15).

Theologically, church buildings can be no more than convenient places for God's people to meet in larger numbers. We talk about church as something we 'go to' for an hour or two once a week. We say that it is important to 'go to church' to fellowship with God's people. But often the nature of the church service and the way things are structured actually work against the kind of 'koinonia' the Bible speaks about. As Snyder insists, 'Church buildings are not made for fellowship... homes

are.   And it was in homes that early Christians met to worship'
(1975:71).

According to the New Testament, the most common place for 'church'
was in the home.   Kevin Giles makes clear the point that you can only
begin to unravel the workings of early church leadership when you
understand that the background to the epistles is church in a house
setting (1988).

It seems that the temple courts provided the believers with a place for
large-scale public witness while the needed community life could be
developed through the home: 'Every day they continued to meet in the
temple courts.   They broke bread in their homes and ate together with
glad and sincere hearts' (Acts 2:46).

The church in the house was not an extension of the real thing, an
appendage to what we would know as a formal Sunday gathering.   Nor
was it a deliberate 'church growth strategy' of the apostles to fulfil the
need for fellowship and encouragement outside the main body of the
church.   The church in the house WAS the church!

They did all of what we try to do inside our church buildings (and
more) and with much greater effectiveness.   As others have noted, the
absence of church buildings was not a hindrance to the rapid expansion
of the church; instead, in comparison to the situation after AD 200, it
seemed a positive help.

There are numerous people in the New Testament, both men and
women, who are said to have held church meetings in their homes.
Among them were Priscilla and Aquilla, Gaius, Nympha, and Philemon.

The concept of the church in the house is not a new one.   Throughout
the history of the Christian church there is evidence of God's people
meeting in homes for church.   Over many years and in many different
lands God has been calling his church home.   This is illustrated in
recent days in the Basic Christian Communities in Central America, the
revival taking place in Communist China, the growth of ICTHUS
fellowship in London, and Faith Community Baptist Church in
Singapore, as weas the number of independent house churches that
have begun worldwide.

How the Lord is leading us.

* Within the house church everything happens. It is the church! Bible teaching, fellowship, worship, breaking of bread, exercising of gifts, collection of money for God's work, pastoral care, and reaching out into the community all take place through the ministry of the house church.

* House churches are not seen as an extra on top of the real thing, that is, church on Sunday. On the contrary, the house church is the church; the nucleus of the church's life and ministry.

* They are networked together in a 'pastorate system.' The house church is the church, but the house churches also meet together at times for a Celebration Service in a rented hall. This is not to try to 'do church' but to simply celebrate in all that God is doing through his church. These celebrations happen in districts at least once a month and then every few months the districts join for a combined celebration. These gatherings of praise and worship are helpful to remind the neighbourhood church member that he or she is part of a wider community of God's people. This provides both for the intimacy in a home-church context as well as a regular opportunity for a combined celebration.

* Each is led by an unpaid pastor. These pastors meet regularly with the pastorate leaders for training and encouragement.

* The members of a house church comprise the total family. All age involvement is encouraged.

* It is a commitment beyond the two hours spent together. House church members are involved in interacting meaningfully outside the meeting time.

* Retreat centres are used so that 2 or 3 house churches can go away together. These are times of refreshment, restoration, empowering and equipping.

* All the house churches are urged to reproduce another house church thus avoiding the tendency to just get bigger and become just another independent church.

* There is an emphasis on creative ministries in the house church and in celebration services. This has led to the writing of many home-grown community worship songs that have been recorded.

The development of House churches is a strategy God is giving to grow the church from the 'inside out'. We believe that if the basic unit of the Christian community became the church in the home, then many could be reached with the Good News of Jesus.

Notwithstanding the above, house churches are not to be established merely as evangelistic ventures.   The house church system is not simply a program or a technique to win the unconverted.   The emphasis is to build biblical Christian community that leads to a powerful witness to Jesus in the neighbourhood area. House churches are begun to enable the Body of Christ to be the body of Christ. They are set up to 'be the church' in the place in which they are planted.

This new wineskin of house churches that the Lord was revealing to us did not arrive in a spiritual vacuum but in the context of a community which had been on a journey of renewal. This should be a warning to any group which thinks they can simply transport the house church vision into their own context without being mindful of the necessity for spiritual renewal as the foundation for real growth.

A house church whose members have not tasted of the new wine may have new structures but little spiritual life. The journey of renewal will be critical for any group desiring both new wine and new wineskins.

References

Banks, Robert and Julia (1986) *The Home Church*. Australia: Albatross.

Giles, Kevin (1988) *Patterns of Ministry amongst the First Christians*.

Kaldor, Peter and Sue (1988) *Where the River Flows*. Australia: Lancer.

Neighbour, Ralph (1990) *Where Do We Go From Here?* USA: Touch Publications.

Olsen, C. M. (1973) *The Base Church: Creating Community Through Multiple Forms*. Atlanta: Forum House.

Paterson, Ross (1989) *Heartcry for China*. Great Britain: Sovereign World.

Prior, David (1983) *The Church in the Home*. Great Britain: Marshall Pickering.

Smith, John (1988) *Advance Australia Where*. Australia: Anzea.

Snyder, Howard (1975) *The Problem of Wineskins*. USA: IVP.

Watson, David (1978) *I Believe in the Church*. London: Hodder and Stoughton.

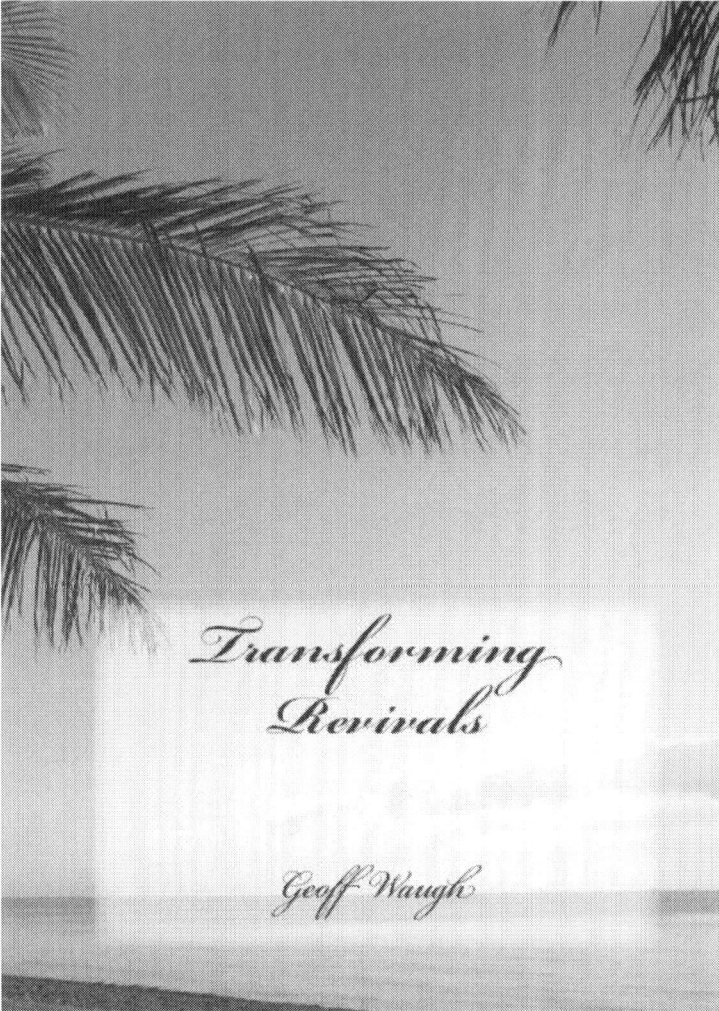

Transforming Revivals

Renewal Journal articles on transformation

6 Church in the Home

Spencer Colliver

Spencer Colliver, a former elder and coordinator of home groups in the O'Connor Uniting Church, Canberra, and Co-ordinator of networks of home churches wrote extensively about house churches.

In this environment all the people of God

will be released into the fullness of the Spirit.

A group of enthusiastic young married couples had been engaged in an intensive coffee house outreach ministry to other young people. They were jaded and disillusioned by the lack of encouragement they received from the churches to which they belonged.

I was invited to lead them in a caring and sharing group. At the end of six months of weekly meetings and other activities the bitterness had largely disappeared, but by this time all of them had stopped attending their respective churches. They invited me to work with them indefinitely. For nearly three years the weekly meeting was 'church in the home' for them. It built and strengthened their faith until most of them moved away from the city to other places where they became active in other groups or churches. That experience of home church had strengthened their faith in Christ and his church.

The house church or church in the home is neither new nor revolutionary. Wherever the people of God have been genuinely open to the Holy Spirit their lives have often found their most potent expression in small groups.

The early church had its essential life in homes. Their intimate experience of being the people of God was in households. There they 'devoted themselves to the apostles' teaching and fellowship, to the breaking of bread and the prayers' (Acts 2:42). In his letters to the churches Paul refers several times to the church which meets in the house. Early church history confirms that the most common meeting place for Christians was in the ordinary domestic setting of a house. Going to church in the first and second centuries meant going to someone's home.

A small group

There are powerful biblical, historical and sociological reasons for contending that the life of the Christian disciple is more completely expressed and fulfilled in a small group in an informal domestic setting than in a large assembly and hall.

Jesus' final command was to love one another (John 13:3435) and his final commission was to go and make disciples (Matthew 28:1820). We may proclaim the gospel to thousands but we make disciples in small groups in the furnace of daily living. We can only truly love one another in the context of an understanding, sharing relationship.

The strength and influence of the revival under John Wesley and George Whitefield was

conserved and focused through the class meetings of twelve which Wesley organised. David Prior (1983:40) notes, 'By 1742 in Bristol (i.e. four years after his Aldersgate Street experience of assurance of salvation through trusting Christ) there were 1,100 people divided into classes of 12 each, each with a leader. ... Class members began "to bear one another's burdens" and naturally to "care for one another."'

The class meeting has been described as the keystone of the entire Methodist edifice. Wesley expressed a personal need for a small group with whom he could unburden himself without reserve. No circuit, he said, ever did or ever will flourish unless there are small groups in the large 'society'. In later years, Wesley would not accept an invitation to conduct an evangelistic program unless house groups were already established to which new converts could be directed and nurtured.

The current move of the people of God into small groups and communities is widespread from the United Kingdom to South Africa to the grassroots communities of South America, from Zimbabwe and Uganda to China, Singapore and Korea. Wherever the Bible has been taken seriously and the Spirit poured out people have more frequently found their essential life with a small group of other Christians.

The large congregational meeting is the place for public worship, declaration and teaching. It is instructive to note that the people of Israel were taught the law in their families (Deuteronomy 6) and the expression of their corporate unity as the people of God was when they went up to Jerusalem four times a year for celebration and festival.

If we were to take seriously the model which Jesus gave us we would be concerned with forming groups of 1215. In order to obey his command to make disciples there needs to be a grouping or social context which stimulates personal awareness and understanding of one another and gives opportunity to observe closely the behaviour, the attitudes, and the feelings of one another. Jesus called the twelve to be with him. They walked, ate, slept and kicked the dust of Galilee together. In the discipling of a small group he modelled intimacy and fellowship.

Within that group of twelve Jesus had three who were even more intimately related with him. He took them with him on special occasions such as at the Transfiguration and the raising of Jairus' daughter. Jesus made small forever beautiful when he said that 'where two or three are gathered in my name, I am there among them' (Matthew 18:20).

When we review the biblical statements about our relationship with one another and reflect upon what has been termed mutual ministry it is difficult, if not impossible, to see how we can respond genuinely to these Scriptures except in a small, continuous, ongoing, intimately related group.

Jesus' command to love one another is emphasised again and again in the epistles. In fact is was this quality of life which caused others to recognise the Christians as Jesus' disciples. 'To be Jesus' in love and compassion is the greatest witness. In order to do that you have to be close to people.

A shared life

We are called to a shared life. Loving cannot be at a distance or in personal remoteness. Nor can it be expressed only to God in our times of worship and meditation 'for those who do not love a brother or sister whom they have seen, cannot love God whom they have not seen. The commandment we have from him is this: those who love God must love their brothers and sisters also' (1 John 4:19b20).

What does it mean to love and to share? And what are the impediments to the shared life? God cares about the way we treat each other because we are members of his family. The vertical relationship with God is given flesh and blood in our horizontal relationships with one another.

The expression 'one another' and similar terms are keys to the shared life. The Scriptures in which they are found give substance to the attitudes and behaviour which express love. They detail love in action. They deliver us from the sentimentality, lust and triviality of today's use of 'love'. It involves reciprocal relationships.

There are some 18 categories involving 'one another' in the New Testament. Love one another is most common; it occurs 12 times. Many other categories are familiar: accept/welcome (Romans 15:7), comfort/instruct (Romans 15:14), forbear/bearing with (Ephesians 4:2), live in harmony/have unity of spirit (1 Peter 3:8), confess sins to and pray for (James 5:16), submit to/be subject to (Ephesians 5:21), be kind, tender hearted and forgiving (Ephesians 4:32), serve/become slaves (Galatians 5:13), practice hospitality/be hospitable (1 Peter 4:9).

These and many similar expressions show how 'the whole body, joined and knit together by every ligament with which it is equipped, as each part is working properly, promotes the body's growth in building itself up in love' (Ephesians 4:16). Our task, under the Holy Spirit, is to build up each other.

Paul was convinced that the Christians in Rome were so complete in knowledge that they were 'able to instruct one another' (Romans 15:14). We must conclude that building one another up is too important a task to be left to the leaders. It is not the exclusive task of apostles, prophets, evangelists, pastors and teachers to build up the body of Christ. They need to train and equip God's people to do the building.

It is one thing to be a pastor; it is a more demanding but more productive task to train another to be a pastor. I may be only a 'one talent' person as a pastor but I would expect that a five talent pastor would show me how not to bury my one talent but use it for my Master.

The charismatic renewal has enabled many people to enter into mutual trust and share in a more open, vulnerable and accountable way. Yet the rich results of renewal found in deep personal sharing are still rare. What causes this plateau of involvement with one another?

Obviously there are personal reasons why leaders and people do not wish to share. We are afraid that confidences will not be respected. We are conditioned to hide our deepest feelings and cover up our negative attitudes, to put on a mask and keep up appearances at all costs. Some of us will not share with others because we are afraid that when others know us as we know ourselves they will not like or accept us. Some have an understandable fear of falling under the influence of people who will exercise power or control over their lives.

Churches emphasise the individual and personal character of salvation which then is worked out mainly in a private devotional life. This provides opportunity for discord and disunity with a fear about the consequences of a shared life. We may agree in doctrine but never share at the deeper levels of attitude and feelings.

Structural impediments built up over decades of church tradition and organisation inhibit the growth of sharing, loving relationships. Church life inhibits intimacy and community. The principal hindrance to the shared life is the big weekly meeting on a Sunday; it hinders if that is the primary expectation for the gathering of the people of God. Sharing of life is minimal and many want it that way; but others come with a desire to be open to one another and with a burden they long to share. The structure of the meeting does not allow for that.

There is nothing intrinsically wrong with the large gathering for teaching, public declaration and worship, but it is not the context or framework within which love and sharing can grow no matter how much people desire it. That happens in the structure of the small group.

If I am to achieve a life style and Christian behaviour consistent with the New Testament I have to be placed in a situation where I can share to the point where I can understand others, and they me. I need also to be held accountable for my Christian growth by brothers and sisters who hold me precious in the sight of the Lord Jesus. In such a group there is time and space for everyone to minister to one another and so fulfil the priesthood of all believers (1 Peter 2:9) without depending on a 'chief priest'.

A multi-gifted ministry

Being in a small group does not guarantee that automatically the quality of life will reflect the New Testament. Some groups may come under the domination of leadership either from the central church staff or from a controlling person. The small group can also become a microcosm of the large gathering with people only minimally involved. This was the case in Bible study groups where we sat and listened with only minimal interaction, usually at impersonal levels.

Leadership is essential, of course, but that of the servant who seeks to release everyone in the group into the practice of their gifts the charisms which the Holy Spirit is waiting to bestow. The renewal has opened the possibility of the gifts of the Spirit for all, not only for those trained and ordained. Making disciples involves bringing all the people of God into an understanding and practice of their gifts.

John Howard Yoder (1987:18) traces the movement of the 'multi-ministry' of the early church to the 'mono-ministry' of later times. He writes of the 'slower, more complex tasks of evoking, nurturing and coordinating those gifts.' Each of those verbs has a crucial process surrounding it and few groups have come to grips with these essentials of making disciples.

Ernst Kasemann (1964:70) elaborates this further noting that 'the multiplicity of charismata are constitutive of the body of Christ, "the body consists not of one body but of many." ... This multiplicity does not cause the body to disintegrate but makes its true unity possible. ... The church cannot find her order in uniformity or rationalisation. Neither must she give so much prominence to individuals among her members that others are overshadowed and condemned to passivity.'

Churches in renewal often shift the modelling of the exercise of gifts from the pulpit to the platform. The 'healing line' in which a few people exercise the gifts of the Spirit has not encouraged the full release of all to minister. A manifest personal gifting together with ordination creates a sense of awe and the feeling that ordinary people can never make it.

When a congregational setting is the principle place of ministry it is difficult for people to understand how to go about, for example, praying for healing at work or in the neighbourhood. In teaching the disciples Jesus modelled healing and deliverance right where people were, on the street, in the market place, out in the country, as well as in synagogues.

John Wimber has emphasised, 'If your church is too large to accommodate this type of learning you probably need to break it down into smaller units for equipping' (1986:13). Wimber goes on to say that his first experience in exercising all the gifts of the Spirit occurred in a small group. The small unit, however, is not only for equipping but also for ongoing practice.

That ongoing practice or continuous and full exercise of the Spirit's gifts leads into a consideration of the difference between home groups functioning as supplementary to the congregational meeting and house or home churches which operate as independent units but which may come together for celebration.

A multi-church ministry

Home churches opt to move in the direction of multi-church rather than mega-church. This is the case in a number of places in Australia and in England.

The home group has been an important addition to the life of many churches in renewal. It offers opportunity for the personal nurture, caring and sharing of the members of a congregation which is not possible during the Sunday morning service. The meeting, usually for two hours during a week night and usually excluding children, includes worship, sharing of personal needs, prayer for one another, study of Bible passages often set by the minister, and discussion. From time to time groups organise events aiming to touch non-Christians, but primarily the groups are for the support of members.

The home church, however, takes full responsibility for its life. Everything that you would expect to happen in church happens in the church in the home. The implications of this kind of church in terms of church order, leadership, membership, adherence to core doctrines, times of meetings, accountability, management of monies, and training of members are all matters which are beyond the scope of this chapter.

In personal contact and review of house churches in the United Kingdom and participation in Australian home groups for 15 years and latterly in a home church, I note the following.

1. There is in the home church an intention and vision to be the church. The vision may not always be well articulated because it is constantly unfolding, but there is a strong commitment and responsibility for its realisation. In many respects it is a church planting exercise with all the uncertainty and tentativeness associated with such a project. People coming out of a church focused primarily on maintaining its life are not prepared to handle all the questions which arise. However, once they are free of a set tradition and structure there is all the freshness and vitality of a first generation experience. This freshness in the Spirit is maintained in several ways as listed here.

2. There is an intention to foster the full participation of all members in the release of the gifts of the Spirit. The gifts and the anointing of the Spirit are granted as the Spirit determines (1 Corinthians 12:79). They are given to people to serve the body, not just for the realisation of their

ministry (1 Peter 4:10‑11; Ephesians 4:7‑16). Within a framework of orderliness everyone or as many as possible contribute to the expression of life in the Spirit in the body (1 Corinthians 14:26‑33; Ephesians 5:15‑21; Hebrews 10:24‑25). In the discipling of people there is encouragement to overcome fear and cultural reticence to enable them to express what God is doing in and for them. Everyone then shares the encouragement; no one is left out.

3. The outward expression of the body and inner growth flows over in service to the immediate community. The home church is neighbourhood based. David Prior (1983:89‑102) explores the importance of listening for the 'pain' of the neighbourhood and the need to be Jesus in that situation and do the works of the Father. The house churches of Brighton Circuit, Brighton, England, make themselves available to the street in which they are located. They seek to be servants in meeting whatever needs are there. This may be the hardest place to express Christian care and to demonstrate the good news. Those helped and healed share the good news in their locality as did the demoniac of Gadara (Mark 5:18‑20).

4. Each home church seeks to reproduce itself in one to two years; to grow and divide. When growth occurs new issues emerge. Discipleship and Christian foundation courses are developed and people trained to conduct them. New leadership is grown for the new groups and for their overall direction; the pain of separation dealt with. This church planting life style creates an impetus to growth in personal and group life constantly refreshing life in the Spirit. When we remember that over 70% of Australians acknowledge there is a God but over 80% do not have any Christian commitment we see a world outside of our comfortable group life to be won for Jesus.

5. Full use is made of people with theological training and other expertise as resource people and facilitators. Members who have special gifting are given opportunity to receive further training in order to equip others for the work of the kingdom. Some home church clusters, as indeed some denominational churches, establish their own Bible schools and courses to encourage all their members to be biblically literate. When members show they have particular capacity for, say, counselling they are given opportunity and financial help to undertake any courses available. The aim is not only to enable all people to exercise their gifts responsibly but to develop them so that the body is effective in its work and ministry.

6. As home churches grow in number some kind of service and resource centre may be necessary. In one United Kingdom situation 30 house churches are linked together with 600 people who gather for celebration and public outreach in halls and community facilities. The administrative and resource centre is in a shop front in the main commercial area. All the house churches acknowledge the leadership of the total enterprise but this commitment is given by covenant; it is not mandatory. Authority to act flows from the groups. This kind of structure, rather than imposed uniformity, is more likely to lead to unity.

7. Essentially the home church is based on a 'tent making' model so that financial resources are freed primarily to build living stones, support ministries in needy areas and developing countries, provide some support for part time ministries and mission, and to keep expenses for salaries and buildings to a minimum, in contrast to most churches which pour their financial resources into buildings and full time salaries.

8. In keeping with the unity of the Spirit home churches seek to foster relationships with other Christian groups and churches. In no way does the home church become separatist in character though it will be independent in function in order to stimulate full involvement of all members. There is an aggregation of Christian presence in the community which grows from neighbourhood to suburb to district to region to nation, gathering in streams of different kinds to the swelling river of witness.

A way ahead

In terms of church history it may be said that all of this has been tried before and fallen into decay. Perhaps so, but at the birth of groups and churches in those earlier days and for a considerable time afterward such movements served their generation in the onward sweep of the kingdom of God.

Such groups always emerged in times of renewal or persecution, often challenging the status quo. If they eventually atrophied and died this is no reason why in a new generation these ideas cannot be reworked. To merely retain a present tradition which is no longer relevant to the challenge of this day is most inhibiting. We constantly encourage people to take the step of faith. Failure is not the end of the story, nor ever will be in the kingdom of God.

The renewal of the people of God calls for full participation to go on to adulthood. To keep people sitting in hundreds facing in one direction, going through the same procedures, listening to the same person over years, keeps them in childhood and resists the Spirit of God who is calling all to freedom, service and servant-hood.

Finally, what if the worst were to happen in Australia as has happened repeatedly both in the past and in the present, and the church were persecuted and had to go underground? How would we prepare and equip the people of God? Or more optimistically, if we see a mighty outpouring of the Spirit of God on this land, would we be ready to gather and conserve the harvest? Either way, given a five year opportunity to prepare the army of God, how would it be done now?

While we speak with awe of mega-churches where thousands gather, we should remember that the cell group has always been the energising element in any successful mass movement. The historian Herbert Butterfield says, the strongest organisational unit in the world's history would appear to be that which we call a cell; for it is a remorseless self-multiplier; it is exceptionally difficult to destroy, it can preserve its intensity of local life while vast organisations quickly wither when they are weakened at the centre; it can defy the power of governments; and it is the appropriate lever for prising open any status quo.

Whether we take early Christianity or sixteenth century Calvinism ... this seems the appointed way by which a mere handful of people may open up a new chapter in the history of civilisation' (Banks 1986:233234).

The experience of house churches in China is a graphic illustration of this principle. What may have served us well in a stable society will not stand the test of an increasingly destabilised and uncertain future. The home church will not be an ancillary unit to the congregation but its basic foundation. In this environment all the people of God, not just a few, will be released into the fullness of the Spirit.

269

References

David Prior (1983) *The Church in the Home.* London: Marshall Pickering.

Ernst Kasemann (1964) *Essays on New Testament Themes: Ministry and Community.* S. C. M. Press.

Robert & Julia Banks (1986) *The Home Church: Regrouping the People of God for Community and Mission.* Sydney: Albatross.

John Wimber (1986) 'Releasing Lay People', *First Fruits Magazine,* Anaheim: Vineyard.

John Howard Yoder (1987) *The Fulness of Christ: Paul's Vision of Universal Ministry.* Illinois: Brethren Press.

---

7 The Home Church

Colin Warren

The Rev. Dr Colin Warren wrote as the Uniting Church minister at Rangeville, Toowoomba and Founding Director of Freedom Life Ministries. This article is adapted from his doctoral dissertation with Fuller Theological Seminary.

Main line churches in Australia reach mainly the middle class. We need to recognise there cannot be a dogmatic ordering of the church with respect to forms of worship, language used, and leadership style, if we are going to minister meaningfully to the poor, the rich, and all between. A homogeneous target population must be determined, and different methods of presentation used to meet the needs of each group.

Unity, not uniformity

The particular homogeneous group we are reaching consists mostly of well educated people. When people come from other social levels, they are welcomed warmly. A few remain; mostly they drop away. We despair for allowing this to happen, but I see it as axiomatic that this should occur, unless we analyse why it is happening and do something constructive to alter the situation.

It does not matter how much those from a different homogeneous group are welcomed, they will feel that they are square pegs in round holes. They have different types of conversation, different interests, speak differently, watch different TV programmes, and the children relate differently to their parents. To reach different homogeneous groups, we must develop a diversity of approaches, recognizing different needs in the areas of fellowship, preaching, and concentration span, and tailor our approach to meet the need.

It is quite reasonable for the leader of a highly educated or mentally alert group to lead from behind, using inductive methodology, but a group that does not have the same mental capacity will prefer to be with one who leads them more directly. Similarly, when counselling the first group, non-directive methods could be used more successfully than with the second group, who frequently would be helped more by a directive counsellor.

All of this indicates the need for diversity of approaches, and the need to recognize that to have unity in the church, we do not need uniformity.

Yet, denominations geared to a parish system often prohibit planting unique styles of churches if it infringes on another parish's boundary. We need a radical change that permits forward looking parishes to exercise vision that allows for obedience to the commission that Christ gave to the church.

We are organizationally geared to a maintenance ministry, not a growth ministry. This means that our churches try to encompass different homogeneous groups within the one congregation and then feel despair when they cannot hold them.

New Testament pattern

Is there a way through this dilemma without causing division? I believe there is. It lies in the concept of the home church that was so successful in the apostolic days. Historical research indicates the probability that as the Jewish synagogue was a gathering together of a group around the Torah, so originally there was a gathering of house churches around the synagogue, with persons to have oversight of these house churches.

In the New Testament, *oikia* and *oikos* are virtually used synonomously, and have the same range of meanings as in secular Greek, and the Septuagint. The most frequent use is in:

a. The literal sense of house (Matthew 2:11; Mark 7:30).

b. The metaphorical sense of family, household, or family of God (Matthew 13:57; John 4:53; 1 Corinthians 1:16; 2 Timothy 1:16).

In the primitive Christian community, the family of God concept can be seen as a strong possibility in the house churches that were established, where the family of God was seen to include slaves and other workers who belonged to a Christian household and formed the nucleus congregation of a house church, where the house was the meeting place (Acts 11:14, 15, 16, 31, 34; 18:8; 1 Corinthians 1:16).

It is important to recognize that it was a missionary situation, and the establishment of house churches was of great significance for the spread of the gospel. The early church took over the natural order of life of the community.

In a similar way, churches today in our secular society are in a missionary situation. The crucial thing is to spread the gospel. There has to be an organizational structure for the church, but that structure must be subservient to the spreading of the gospel. Pragmatic needs require that the church will always be living in the paradoxical situation where it is an anti-organizational organization. Its structures must not hinder people from being brought into the Kingdom of God.

Circumstances alter cases. The message of the church has not and will not change, but the way we package that message must change to meet the existential situation. In Australia, we seem to have reversed this process. We have changed the message to accommodate the beliefs of our society, and have considered to be suspect anyone who seeks to change the status quo with respect to the method of presentation.

People groups

Church Growth studies show that there are homogeneous people groups in any society. Churches have frequently disregarded this reality, which at first glance appears to run counter to the scriptural teaching that in Christ we are one (Galatians 3:28).

The homogeneous unit principle does not deny this, but recognizes that within this oneness, there is also diversity due to many factors which can inhibit close and lasting intimate relationships. A series of home churches can be commenced by a mother church which caters for specific groupings of people who always feel that they are on the fringe of the normal grouping for that particular location.

An example could be where evangelism wins young people who have been involved in the alternate life scene and have experienced the drug, occult, permissive sex culture. Parents of 'straight' young people have a natural and legitimate fear their sons and daughters may be attracted to the permissive culture before the old habit patterns of the alternate life style young people have been broken.

The relearning of behaviour patterns often involves a long education process. New Christians do not necessarily drop their former behaviour patterns immediately. In many cases, they are fourth generation pagans and have known no other behaviour in terms of role models. A home church can conveniently bring together such groups of people and begin the discipleship process to a Christ-like way of life.

Another example may be a group of business executives. These are often under enormous pressure in the work situation and these pressures can produce difficult dilemmas in terms of ethical decisions and can involve them in serious family problems when work pressures destroy family life. They need to be able to talk to those who know and understand their needs. Because of the responsible position they hold that affects the lives of many people under them, total confidentiality must be maintained. They can only share their burdens with those who can be trusted. Often this can only be with those who carry similar burdens and who can adequately support them in these situations.

The home church can provide a setting for the fulfilment of this need. Many other groupings of people do not fit into the normal church in Australia and so do not attend worship, but frequently would like to do so. Their position on a resistance-receptivity scale would change, if given the right opportunities.

Paul's concepts

Paul spoke with greater relevance and meaning to the community of his day than we do to people from the counter culture, and other unreached groups. Paul as a social thinker, has much to teach us about reaching those yet untouched by the church. He revealed much about the internal dynamics of his communities. They lived alongside the philosophical schools of his day and the mystery religion communities. There was nothing novel or unusual about the appearance of the Christian communities, as communities. Their novelty was their message and the radical freedom they offered.

Robert Banks (1979:65) identifies three major components in Paul's idea of freedom:

1. Independence from law, death, and alien powers.

2. Dependence on Christ and the Spirit.

3. Interdependence with others and the world.

The purpose of that freedom was so that the Christian could live a life of righteousness, conforming to the way of Jesus, which was the way of the cross (Luke 14:25-27).

Paul led his converts into a personal relationship with one another. He showed that the gospel had a shared communal aspect to it so that to embrace the gospel, was to enter into community (Rowthorn 1986:9).

The converts gathered together in private homes and shared community (Romans 16:5). It is because Paul saw Christians as belonging to both a heavenly church and a local church that he saw them as being in a continuing personal relationship with one another which was far more important than an institutional relationship. These churches had their roots in the household unit and took some of its characteristics.

Paul emphasized their unity with Christ, and refers to the church as the body of Christ. For Paul, worship involved the whole of a person's life, every word and action, and was inclusive of the whole of a person's time on earth. The purpose of the church was for the edification of its members through ministry to one another.

If we in our day can catch this vision, the need for increasing the size of buildings with the coming of new converts would be minimized. We could have a central church, sending out suitable lay persons to win and disciple in their homes those who find it hard to fit into the church scene.

Paul saw the gifts of the Spirit as being for the community and they were set in a frame work of love (Ephesians 4:12, 1 Corinthians 12:7). The community of believers had at its centre the key of fellowship expressed in word and deed. For him, the focal point of reference was the relationship between the members of the body.

In our situation, this could best be accomplished in the informal, intimate relationship of a home. In Paul's day, distinctions along national, social and sexual lines were becoming blurred. A broadening in the notion of citizenship was taking place. He thought more in terms of the things that unite people than the things that divide them.

Paul saw women functioning differently from men, but he saw them as full members of the Christian community. Although he placed some restrictions on them, he also accorded them prominence, particularly in the teaching and exhortation areas. He recognized functional diversity within the community.

Paul dissolved traditional distinctions between priests and laity. He emphasized corporate responsibility, at the same time allowing inequality in the Christian community within unity. His communities were theocratic in structure. Because of the different gifting of each person, each was able to participate with authority in its activities.

The churches recognised a diverse distribution of gifts, but no hierarchical or formal structure. There was leadership, but there was also the freedom under that leadership to exercise the Spirit's gifts. The body as a whole determined whether behaviour was in order (1 Corinthians 4:29) within the fellowship of worship. Paul's communities were participatory societies, where authority was distributed throughout the whole group.

Rather than set himself over these Christian communities, Paul stood with them in all that he did. His authority was God's gift to him, given in his Damascus road experience. It was an intrinsic authority from the Holy Spirit, evident to all. It did not need to be legislated.

This is the authority that I believe God the Holy Spirit will invest in the people who will lead home churches. They will be chosen in the same way that Paul and Barnabas were chosen, as the Spirit led the church (Acts 13:2).

Laity can build the church

We tend to forget that those whom Jesus sent out to evangelize the world were trained on the apprenticeship model, not in theological colleges. Neither should be denigrated, but it should be recognized that both can successfully be used when operating in the power of the Holy Spirit.

Rangeville Uniting Church has been training a group of lay persons in preparation for sending them out, in the same way Jesus sent out his disciples. In Jesus' day, they were called out from ordinary occupations. We can expect God to do the same today.

The great commission has not changed and if we truly believe that God is going to win the world, there will not be enough clergy to handle the harvest. In our situation, the church buildings are now inadequate. We do not want to invest further resources in buildings, but in people. We are ready to send out lay persons to plant churches in their homes.

The desire is to target those groups not being reached. If some consider that lay persons would not be theologically adequate for the task, we need to remember that the first prominent theological thinkers on behalf of the church were lay persons of great ability; men like Tertullian, Cyprian, and Augustine. It is good to remind ourselves that revolutionary movements like the Cathars, the Waldensians and the Lollards were spearheaded by the laity. They developed a great preaching activity and urged a return to the Bible.

The Reformation in Europe, like the previous Conciliar movements, was mainly a movement of the laity, as was the Reformation in England. In the middle ages, the urge for reform sprang mainly from the laity. In the Reformation on the continent, it was the laity who provided the main driving power.

John Calvin was one of the most conspicuous examples of a layman who was a self made theologian. Many other examples could be given of the key role of lay persons in the significant advances of the church. The church government needs to see the laity as an essential part of the church, rather than an insufficiently tapped source of cheap labour.

To treat ordinary church members as immature, is to keep them immature. The laity, more than the minister, are immersed in a hostile world and can minister out of a first hand knowledge of the current pressures on the ordinary person. The clergy must allow themselves to be taught by the laity.

Lay pastor as counsellor

Some would say that the counselling role of the home church pastor requires that a person be trained. What if the candidate has not filled this expectation? That would be the preferred option, but many clergy have little counselling training also. Untrained, caring support can be effective. We must use the tools available. Carkhuff (1969:10) states that: 'While professional programmes have failed to produce tangible evidence of their translation to client benefits or, indeed, evidence that they are concerned with researching their training efforts, assessment of lay training programmes have yielded positive results.'

He goes on to point out that lay counsellors appear to have a greater ability to:

1. Enter into the milieu of the distressed.

2. Establish peer like relations with people being helped

3. Take an active part in the client's life situation.

4. Empathize more effectively with the client's style of life.

5. Teach the client within the client's own frame of reference.

6. Provide the client with an effective transition to higher levels of functioning within the social system.

In the helping professions, the key ingredient for an effective helper is the capacity to empathize with the one seeking help. The counsellor who protects him/herself by remaining clinical, may be able to handle a greater number of clients because of less stress, but his/her effectiveness will be minimized.

The preparedness for self disclosure and making oneself vulnerable breaks down barriers in the one who is seeking help. I have found that those we would appoint to a position of lay pastor have already been trained in counselling to the level necessary to be very effective. They have already proved this.

Holy Spirit gifts

I am not advocating a technique or a gimmick, but I am urging a new approach to taking advantage of results of Church Growth studies on homogeneous groups, and the use of God given gifts of the Spirit among the lay people of our church, who are prepared to recognize and come under duly appointed authority.

The structure that I am proposing to link the mother church with satellite home churches is one which I believe suits our particular case, given the rules and regulations under which we must work in the Uniting Church of Australia.

Other situations may adapt these principles in other ways. I suspect that modifications would be necessary to suit specific cases.

The laity have a ministry to the world, and a ministry to the church. In the home church model, they can exercise both of these roles. To do this, they need the support of the whole church, which includes the clergy who can assist them to release their Holy Spirit gifts.

References

Banks, Robert (1979) *Paul's Idea of Community.* Lancer.

Carkhuff, Robert (1969) *Helping and Human Relations*, Vol.1. Holt, Rinehart and Winston.

Rowthorn, Ann (1986) *The Liberation of the Laity.* Morehouse-Barlow.

8 China's House Churches

Barbara Nield

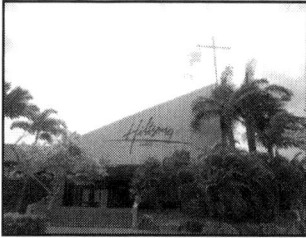

Mrs Barbara Nield taught at the Garden City School of Ministries in Brisbane. This article is adapted from a Church Growth essay she wrote in her M.A. studies.

The prodigious growth of the house church movement in China is one of the greatest phenomena in the 20th century. Various observers of these Chinese Christians maintain that this move of the Holy Spirit is gathering people into the kingdom of God at the rate of 35,000 daily, and 12 million yearly (Paterson 1989:23; Waugh 1993:47).

Although it is difficult to obtain accurate statistics, approximations show that, whereas in 1949 there were between 800,000 and 1 million Protestant believers in China (Paterson 1989:103; Kang 1990:79; Kauffman 1991:6) and 4.5 million Roman Catholics (McGavran 1989:1) by 1989-1991 there were possibly as many as 50 million in the house churches.

Carl Lawrence, however, estimated there were 75 million and a Japanese Christian editor who spent 6 months investigating the Churches throughout China in 1989 estimated 100 million (McGavran 1989:1).

The State Statistical Bureau of China completed a 2 year survey of religious believers in 1992 and the unofficial figures indicate 63 million Protestants and 12 million Roman Catholics (Asian Report 197,

1992:9). The Three Self Patriotic Movement (TSPM) maintained there were 5,000 official Churches and 5 million believers under its auspices in 1989 and these figures were unaltered in 1992. This means at least 50-58 million - the majority of believers - attend the house churches (Paterson 1989:71). Most of the growth has occurred in rural areas where 80% of the population lives.

These figures do not only represent quantitative growth since growth has been sustained for almost half a century and is still increasing. There must be highly significant qualitative factors operating in the Chinese Church to achieve such phenomenal growth.

My purpose is to evaluate the key principles that have contributed to the effectiveness of the house church movement in China. I will examine the historical context and the revival context which emerged from it. Both of these contexts involve dynamic theological and spiritual elements at work in the burgeoning Church.

Christianity and colonialism

The growth of the Church in China cannot be divorced from the historical and political events of the 19th and 20th centuries. Church growth in general 'is closely conditioned by both history and anthropology' (McGavran 1980:153).

The arrival of the Protestant missionaries of the 19th century coincided with the victories of western colonialism. 'Missionaries and colonialism in China were inseparable, at least in the minds of the Chinese' (Kauffman, 1975:82).

In 1869 a Chinese official retorted to the British Ambassador: 'Take away your opium and your missionaries and you will be welcome' (Kauffman 1975:83). The Boxer Rebellion of 1900 is an example of violent aggression against Western influence including Christianity. 189 missionaries and children were martyred as well as an even greater number of Chinese Christians (Francis 1985:23).

Therefore between 1949-1966, after almost 100 years of unwelcome foreign harassment, the Communists vigorously targeted and attacked Christianity primarily because of its identification with imperialist exploitation (Paterson 1989:40).

Barbara Nield

Chinese indigenisation

Not only was the timing of the introduction of Christianity into China fraught with difficulties, but the manner in which it was propagated aroused considerable discontent among the Chinese Christians. Western missionaries were challenged quite early to adopt the concept of indigenisation.

The principle of self-responsibility and self-support for mission-planted Churches was advocated in 1841 by Henry Venn, secretary of the Church Missionary Society. By 1851 the concept had been formulated as the Three Selfs: self-supporting, self-governing, self-propagating' (Shenk 1990:29).

In 1856 John Nevius, a Presbyterian missionary, set out this plan for indigenisation:

1. All Christians should work for a living and evangelise their neighbours;

2. Ecclesiastical organisation should only be developed as the Christians deemed expedient;

3. Churches must be self-supporting;

4. Churches should use local architectural designs;

5. Church buildings should only be constructed when affordable;

6. The Chinese church should both send and support its own evangelists;

7. Strong emphasis must be given to prayer and Bible training (Kauffman 1975:91).

The self-supporting, self-governing and self-propogating principles became the theme for the First General Conference of Protestant Missionaries in China, held in Shanghai in May, 1887.

The Chinese Church, too, was beginning to realise the need to be independent of the foreign missions. In 1906 the Rev. Yu Kuochen of

283

Shanghai established a small independent Chinese Church (Shenk 1990:32). It represented a voice of protest against the strategies of the missions.

On a larger scale, the True Jesus Church, commenced in 1917 in Tientsin and Peking by Chinese pastor Paul Wei, soon gained nation-wide prominence. This Church emphasised witnessing, tithing, and local Church government. A strong belief in the supernatural power of God to heal, deliver and empower believers was also a catalyst in its expansion throughout China (Kauffman 1975:93).

The tension that existed between the two parties resulted from different interpretations of the meaning of 'self'. The western missionaries believed in indigenous leadership, evangelism and self-support, but within the framework of western traditions, forms and structures.

On the other hand the Chinese Church leaders desired to express their faith in Jesus in Chinese cultural forms and patterns. This drive for homogeneity, the principle of establishing the gospel in every people group - panta ta ethne - without circumcising inherently good cultural practices, is a natural and spiritual desire which the Bible endorses (Matthew 24:14; 28:19; Romans 16:26).

In the imperialistic climate of China it was very important to the evangelistic thrust of the Chinese Church to be able to preach the gospel and establish people into the Body of Christ in culturally relevant ways to offset the distasteful provocation of colonialism. The Chinese Church leaders therefore expressed their disapproval in 1922 in the following statement at the National Christian Conference held in Shanghai:

We wish to voice the sentiment of our people that the wholesale, uncritical acceptance of the traditions, forms and organisations of the West and the slavish imitation of these are not conducive to the building of a permanent genuine Christian Church in China (Shenk 1990:32).

Missions and Churches subsequently made genuine attempts to affect change, and establish Chinese leadership in the Church. There were positive signs of the Church becoming indigenous. Powerful Chinese preachers and evangelists were used to win many converts. Others, such as Wang Ming-Tao 'stood for adherence to the Scriptures and withstood heresies and false teachings' (Paterson 1989:41).

In 1926 Watchman Nee established The Christian Assemblies, also known as The Little Flock. These were locally autonomous churches without any central organisation. Prominence was given to Bible study and teaching, and the movement produced excellent Chinese evangelists and Bible teachers (Kauffman 1975:94).

Sino-Japanese war

However, the period of the Sino-Japanese War (1937-1945) brought further instability and suffering to the Chinese people, and the momentum of change was impeded in the centrally organised churches (Shenk 1990:33; Francis 1985:23).

At the same time, though, conditions in the eastern provinces caused an exodus to the inland regions where the gospel increased and spread.

This was due to the timely intervention of God himself for in places such as the northern province of Shantung he was sovereignly orchestrating his church.

In the early 1930s, Shantung experienced a supernatural visitation of the Spirit of God, characterised by deep repentance and public confession of sin by both believers and new converts, accompanied by signs and wonders in healing, speaking in tongues, and casting out demons. People from all denominations were affected.

This visitation impacted the church across China, resulting in Bible conferences and a rapid increase in church membership (Kauffman 1975:92). 'To many (in China) the churches and their faith seemed the only stable element in a distraught and changing world' (Latourette, cited in Kauffman 1975:93).

God used the suffering of the people to prepare the church for the intensity of persecution that was soon to follow.

Intervention of the Spirit of God

An excellent model of the Spirit's preparation of the church for the onslaught of Communism is afforded in the truly indigenous group known as The Jesus Family (Ye-su Chia-ting). Under the Holy Spirit's direction, this commune:

* Had no central control - therefore , unlike denominations under central leadership, could not be easily controlled by the Japanese or the Communists.

* Refused to accept any foreign funds, on the basis that God was their source and they should exercise faith for his provision. Churches with foreign funds were liquidated in 1949.

* Had no church buildings. The buildings they owned were used for worship, but simultaneously used to produce their agricultural products - providing the livelihood of the commune.

* Encouraged their people to allocate a separate area in their homes for worship - a marvellous preparation for the ensuing forced worship of believers in the house churches.

* Had a dynamic faith in the supernatural ministry of the Holy Spirit which was a normal part of the worship of the commune, and proved to be an essential expectation of the persecuted church.

This church began in 1920 under the leadership of Ching Tien-ying. He established a commune in Shantung Province using land left to him by his great grandfather. The fellowship spread through the north of China and into the interior. He established agricultural policies, progressively tithing from 10-90% of the harvest annually.

During the famine of 1942 the commune gave 90% of the harvest to the poor and still met their own needs.

Later the Communists needed one acre per family for life support, yet The Jesus Family was able to feed 500 people from 43 acres and still give away 90% of the produce (Kauffman 1975:95-97).

Effects of initial Marxist/Communist rule

In 1950, under the leadership of Mao Tse-Tung and the Marxist/Communist regime, the Christian Manifesto called on the Christian church to expose and oppose the effects of imperialism, feudalism, and bureaucratic capitalism, and help promote an independent, democratic and patriotic China (Paterson 1989:54-55).

However, the Three Self Patriotic Movement (TSPM) was established in 1954 by the government to mediate between itself and the church. The name was a prostitution of the 'Three Self' principles espoused by the Christian missionaries of the previous 100 years, since the blatant agenda was to secure from the Christians a total commitment to Communist/Marxist policies, and therefore a united, patriotic China. Where the Bible and patriotism conflicted, loyalty to the party line was to be paramount. Chinese evangelical Christians saw the TSPM as the Party's controlling mechanism of the church.

Since the government viewed the TSPM as the voice of the Protestant Church, pastors and churches who refused to be associated with the movement were vehemently attacked, and many were imprisoned and tortured. Wang Ming-Tao, an eminent Peking Pastor, was arrested in 1955, imprisoned, and subjected to brainwashing and mental torture. He was not released until 1978. He was typical of the fate of many devout Christians of this period who refused to compromise with the State (Paterson 1989:42). Watchman Nee was also arrested in 1952 and never released.

Non-compromising Christianity

By 1958 all Christian meetings not authorised by the government were dissolved. Many Christians stopped attending the TSPM churches because they had become primarily centres for political indoctrination. The house church movement came out of the cauldron of this attempted politicising of the church. During this period, believers began to meet quietly in their homes for mutual encouragement, prayer, and sharing of the Lord's Supper. These meetings were a reflection and extension of the traditional Chinese social emphasis on family life (Paterson 1989:78).

These house churches (1954-1966) became the fertile soil out of which explosive growth occurred.   They provided the climate for the preservation of 'grass roots' evangelical Chinese Christianity, and through attention to the basics - Jesus Christ, crucified and risen again, the power of corporate prayer, and the mutual edification of the Body of Christ - laid a firm foundation for growth.

Another factor influencing the success of this movement in the early stages was its roots in the cultural basics.   The Chinese church was now truly indigenous.   At the same time, the Holy Spirit had been progressively teaching believers to hear and respond to his voice and minister in his power in preparation for the years of the Cultural Revolution, when the church was mercilessly and relentlessly persecuted.

Persecution: context for revival

During the decade 1966-1976, the Red Guards (representatives of the hardliners of the Communist Party) embarked on a ruthlessly cruel campaign to eradicate religion.   For Christianity it meant:

* Confiscation of all Bibles and Christian literature;

* The stifling of all remaining institutionalised Christianity;

* Closure of all church buildings;

* Public humiliation of Christians through physical and emotional assault;

* Martyrdom;

* Imprisonment in labour camps, factories and farms;

* Suicide of some Christians;

* A denial of faith in Christ for some;

* Betrayal of fellow Christians by some.

Barbara Nield

Yet, the gospel spread to areas without any previous witness, due to the exile of believers to remote farms and labour camps (Paterson 1989:45-46). Amazingly, even Red Guards, impressed by the lifestyle of the believers, turned to a saving knowledge of the Lord Jesus Christ during this time.

Many Chinese believers testify to the fact that the church was purified in the fires of this persecution. Only those who were wholeheartedly committed to Jesus withstood such fierce opposition. One woman believer said 'If a person joins us, we have a real Christian' (Paterson 1989:94).

Suddenly, believers needed each other more than ever before. Meeting in small groups, mostly in homes, they learned the value of the unity of the Body of Christ, the edifying effects of fellowship with other Christians, the power of prayer, the priceless value of the Scriptures, and the comforting presence of the Holy Spirit in their midst. The lessons of the preceding years were now bearing fruit in their dire need for mutual strengthening and encouragement.

The Chinese church was developing a quality of lifestyle and attitude that many Western Christians have never experienced. As they were leaderless in many instances, they began to appreciate the doctrine of the priesthood of all believers.

This is the true meaning of revival - a fresh and deepened commitment of believers to Jesus Christ as Saviour and Lord. Christians who know him in this measure have a hope that transcends all hopelessness in this life. Although it was very dangerous to witness openly to the Lord at this time, many believers did so. The church primarily grew from conversions as people observed the way Christians endured persecution, and saw their lifestyle under extreme pressure.

By 1977 a more moderate set of pragmatic policies was pursued by Deng Ziaoping in the early years of his second term in office. The more liberal faction of the Party campaigned for the Open Door policy for the West - to help foster much needed industrial reforms.

Christians were released from prison for political expediency. China wanted to boost her trade and diplomatic relations by impressing the

289

West with a policy of religious freedom and attention to human rights issues (Paterson 1989:49-50).

During the decade 1978-1988 the house churches saw great multiplication growth (McGavran 1989:1), and initially enjoyed relative peace. Consequently, the Christians boldly evangelised, worshipped and taught in large meetings. Outstanding reports included one city where 60% of the population became Christians, and a city of 160,000 where the majority are Christians, living in 13 communes (Paterson 1989:82).

David Wang (Paterson 1989:163) reports of another situation in which the majority of the citizens of an entire county became Christians in 1988. A Pastor had been imprisoned in 1963, when there were only 170 believers in his county. When he was released in 1986, there were 5,000 believers. Two and a half years later, the church had grown to 56,000 believers.

Evangelism: the result of revival

Conversions on a huge scale are the result of aggressive evangelism, characterised by a bold proclamation of the Gospel, accompanied by signs and wonders in the power of the Holy Spirit. Believers who learned to operate in the power of the Spirit in the secret meetings of the house churches now boldly proclaim the saving, healing and delivering power of Jesus Christ.

This is specialised evangelism that works through the supernatural intervention of the Holy Spirit into particular situations. Itinerant evangelists devote their lives to preaching the gospel from province to province. They constantly risk imprisonment and harassment from the authorities, but they are passionate in their ministry and are seeing much fruit for the kingdom of God.

The church encourages the ministry gift of an evangelist, and also emphasises the individual's responsibility to witness, both in word and lifestyle. Anthony Lambert (1989:8) says the house church model for effective witness in China today is

the simple, apostolic proclamation of the Gospel, combined with sacrificial life-style and suffering. This ... is remarkably effective in reaching the masses of the people. ... The church is growing by leaps and bounds from the grass roots upwards.

Influence of radio ministry

One other form of evangelism in China deserves special mention. The Christian radio ministry has progressively impacted unbelievers all over China. During the years when the country was closed to the outside world, the Far East Broadcasting Company received virtually no feedback on the influence of their programs on the Chinese. However, after 1979, letters received from inside China reveal that Christians are being nurtured, encouraged and strengthened by the broadcasts. More than 50% of the responses are from unbelievers seeking information about the gospel.

The following figures show the increase in written responses each year between 1978 and 1988. The overall decadal growth rate is a staggering 9,000%. The responses totalled only 177 for the entire period between 1969 and 1978, but sharply increased after China and the United States resumed diplomatic relations in 1979.
1979 - 3,000 responses.
1980-1986 - 10,000 responses a year.
1987-1988 - 16,000 responses a year.

Given the fact that there are many who still cannot respond because of the danger, the radio ministry is of immense value to the cause of the gospel (Paterson 1989:115-116).

Reasons for growth

Vital theological convictions have produced significant spiritual emphases in the house churches.

Theological elements

1. Recognition of, and dependence on signs and wonders.

As early as 1917, Chinese believers recognised the sovereign, supernatural power of the Spirit of God to heal the sick, perform miracles, and deliver from demonic oppression. I believe it is significant that this revelation coincided with the drive of Chinese Christians to become indigenous.

Western believers presented the Gospel from a Western theological perspective - appealing to people's rational processes. Faith was based on the message proclaimed in words. The preached word has been emphasised exclusively, and Jesus has been well presented as 'Christ the wisdom of God'.

However, the Chinese - and other Third World peoples - are more acutely aware of the dimension of the spirit world. Therefore, 'Christ the power of God', acknowledged in the preaching of the Word with accompanying signs and wonders, is the way God demonstrates his supremacy over all false gods (Wang, Asian Report 194, 1992:9-10).

Chinese Christians expect the Holy Spirit to declare the Lordship of Jesus through supernatural acts as a normal occurrence. This theological absolute is the common thread evidenced throughout the house church movement. I am convinced this is the fundamental reason for its preservation and outstanding growth. Within the house church movement itself 'most Christians still recognise signs, wonders and miracles as the number one factor resulting in church expansion' (Wang, Asian Report 198, April, 1993:7).

2. Revelation of the Lordship of Jesus Christ

The primary priority of Chinese Christians is encouraging and maintaining a personal relationship with the Lord Jesus Christ.

Persecution has driven the church to the basics of the faith, and a very real experience of the presence of Jesus in their lives. Their faith is in Jesus who is present now in the believer, and is returning soon. Therefore, effecting reconciliation between him and all who desire salvation is a matter of urgency.

3. A Theology of entering into Christ's sufferings

A theology of suffering has issued from the fires of persecution. Christ Jesus suffered for them, therefore they willingly enter into the fellowship of his sufferings (Phil.3:10), and consider it a privilege to identify with him as his representatives in situations of persecution where they can demonstrate his great love for sinners.

David Wang tells of a woman Christian worker in a poor province of China sentenced to five years hard labour who refused to be bailed out by fellow Christians. She saw imprisonment as a divinely appointed opportunity to minister the gospel in the labour camp. Her only request was that Christians would support her in prayer (*Asian Report* 194, April, 1992:7).

4. A belief in the power of prayer

All the activities of the house churches flow from a base of intensely fervent prayer. Intercession occupies a major portion of their church meetings.

Whole congregations unashamedly weep as one before God, and the entire group of believers sustain a unity of focus, adding their passionate 'Amen' to the pleadings and supplications of their fellow Christians (Balcombe Video, 1993).

One Chinese pastor, returning from a conference in a western nation, said 'Our brothers in the West know how to plan, but we know how to pray' (Paterson 1989:189).

Persecution drove them to prayer, and now persistent corporate prayer is frequently sustained for three to four hours in any one church gathering.

5. Belief in the church as a spiritual structure

No other structures except the Body of Christ are necessary in this movement. The vast majority of house churches do not own any property, but meet in homes, old buildings, and even, in at least one instance, a cave.

What is important is the spiritual membership of the group. Inherent in this doctrine is their faith in the priesthood of all believers. Leaders do not dominate the church, but encourage all members to live pure lives, and take their rightful place in the Body of Christ (Paterson 1989:189).

6. Recognition of the Scriptures as the Word of God

The Bible is highly esteemed among Chinese Christians. They will go to any lengths to obtain a copy, sometimes travelling for days to make contact with a courier, and risking detention by the Religious Affairs Bureau (RAB) for obtaining 'foreign supplied' Bibles. In other places, one copy is circulated among members who are responsible for hand-copying the text. The lack of sufficient Bibles, along with limited sound Biblical instruction, unfortunately leaves many places open to heresy. Pastors refuse to send their potential ministers to seminaries operated by the TSPM, because of the strong political content of the courses.

7. A responsible belief in the mission of the church

These house churches take seriously the church's mission (Matt.28:18-20). This is attested to by the spiritual harvest they are experiencing. Every Christian is encouraged to witness, and the ministry of the evangelist is given a high profile (Paterson 1989:189).

Ensuing spiritual elements

Definitive spiritual emphases have emerged from these theological convictions in the house churches today in China. For ease of comparison, they are presented in a simple table. They represent Church Growth principles at work supernaturally.

Theological Elements	Spiritual Elements
Recognition of, and dependency on signs and wonders	* sensitivity to the Holy Spirit in evangelism * exercise of spiritual gifts
Revelation of the Lordship of Jesus Christ	* presentation of the basics of the gospel * emphasis on personal relationship with Jesus Christ for conversion growth * commitment to personal witnessing * sustained vitality in worship

Entering into Christ's sufferings	* selfless Christianity * boldness in witnessing * focus on eternal values
Belief in the power of prayer	* sustained, persistent, fervent prayer * total dependence on God's miraculous intervention to preserve his testimony
The church as a spiritual structure	* supportive, caring community * every believer essential to the Body of Christ * emphasis on lay ministry * importance of corporate fellowship
Recognition of the Scriptures as the Word of God	* high view of Scripture * an insatiable hunger for God's Word * willingness to risk personal safety to obtain Bibles
Responsible belief in the mission of the church	* personal evangelism * fearless preaching of the whole Gospel

The greatest benefit to the church in China is the unity gained from a truly indigenous church functioning in the power of the Spirit.

In addition to this principle of indigenous unity, the following phases of Church Growth advocated by Eddie Gibbs (1986:43-45) are all strongly contributing to the current growth of the church in China and are evident in the theological and spiritual elements.

1. Mobilising the witnesses.
2. Equipping the people of God for ministry. This is encouraged, but at times hampered through lack of suitable materials and teachers.
3. Creating a climate of receptivity. This has been a work of the Holy Spirit, using the persecution of the church and the expulsion of Western missionaries to focus the church on the real issues.
4. Effecting regeneration.
5. Incorporating into the Body of Christ.
6. Involvement in the ministry of Christ.

Conclusion

The Chinese house churches have flourished under the dynamic direction of the Holy Spirit. This growth occurs within a climate of official hostility to Christianity. The strategies of the Spirit have developed a truly Chinese church independent of any foreign control or influence, free to propagate the gospel in terms easily understood by its fellow citizens.

These churches are constrained by the present suffering to present the gospel as a matter of urgency, compelled by the love of Jesus Christ for lost sinners. The whole church seriously applies itself to evangelistic mission, and gathers the converts into a nurturing community to build them up so that they can take their rightful place in the Body of Christ.

Despite the remarkable growth of the Christian church in China, there is still much work to do. The best figures reveal there are 100 million believers in this country of 1.289 billion. When we consider that China is one fifth of the population of the world, and 33.5% of the world's population is Christian (Barrett 1993:23), the church in China is faced with a formidable task to fulfil the Biblical mandate to preach the Gospel to every people group.

They have pressed on by the power of the Holy Spirit in the past, and will continue to do so in the future as they combine his supernatural enabling with their tenacious devotion to the task at hand. Fired by their constant knowledge of Jesus Christ present in his power they proclaim Maranatha, the Lord is coming.

References

Balcombe, Dennis (1993) 'Harvest Time For China', Video, Mount Gravatt: Garden City Christian Church.

Barrett, David B. (1993) 'Annual Statistical Table on Global Mission: 1993', *International Bulletin of Missionary Research*, January, 1993, pp.22-23.

Chao, Jonathan (1988) *Wise as Serpents Harmless as Doves.* Pasadena: William Carey Library.

Francis, Lesley (1985) *Winds of Change in China.* Guidelines For Effective Service. Sydney: OMF.

Gibbs, Eddie (1986) 'Power Won't Flow From Principles', *Global Church Growth*, July/August/September, 1986, Volume xxiii, No.3. pp.43-45.

Hunter, Kent R. (1990) 'Whatever Happened To The Homogeneous Unit Principle?', *Global Church Growth*, January/February/March, 1990, Volume xxvii, No.1, pp.1,4.

Lawrence, Carl (1985) *Against All Odds: The Church in China.* Basingstoke: Marshall Pickering.

McGavran, Donald (1980) *Understanding Church Growth* (Revised). Grand Rapids, Michigan: Eerdmans.

------- (1989) 'What is Happening in China?' *Global Church Growth*, April/May/June, 1989, Volume xxvii, No.2. pp.1,4.

Kang, Wi Jo (1990) 'Korean Minority Church-State Relations in the People's Republic of China', *International Bulletin of Missionary Research*, April, 1990, Volume 14, No.2., pp.77-82.

Kauffman, Paul E. (1975) *Confucius, Mao and Christ.* Hong Kong: Asian Outreach.

------- (1991) 'China's Opposing Attractions', *Asian Report* 190, Volume 24, No.3, May/June, pp.3-7.

Lambert, Anthony (1989) 'The Mandate of Heaven: An Analysis of the Present Overall Situation in China', *Global Church Growth*, Volume xxvi, No.2 pp.7-9.

Paterson, Ross (1989) *Heartcry For China*. United Kingdom: Sovereign World.

Pierson, Paul E. (1985) *Historical Development of the Christian Movement - Class Syllabus.* Pasadena: Fuller Theological Seminary.

Shenk, Wilbur R. (1990) 'The Origins and Evolution of the Three-Selfs in Relation to China', *International Bulletin of Missionary Research*, Volume 14, No.1, January.

Wagner, C. Peter (1976) *Your Church Can Grow.* Ventura: Regal.

Wang, David (1992) 'Asia's Maturing Church', *Asian Report* 194, Vol.25, No. 2, March/April.

------- (1993) 'China/Hong Kong: At The Crossroads', *Asian Report* 198, Vol.26, No.1. March/April.

Wark, Andrew (1992) 'Reaching and Teaching', *Asian Report* 196, Vol. 25, No. 4. July/August/September.

Waugh, Geoff (1993) 'Astounding Church Growth', *Renewal Journal*, Number 2, pp. 47-57.

9 Renewal in a College Community

Brian Edgar

The Rev. Dr Brian Edgar is a Uniting Church minister and lecturer in Theology at the Bible College of Victoria. He describes a unique time of renewal at the college in September, 1993.

The Holy Spirit may at times break down existing patterns of prayer and worship in order to renew his people.

Sometimes this is because of inadequacies in the attitude of those worshipping, as in Isaiah 1:10-20. There God is tired of the sacrifice and worship of those who do not repent.

At other times the working of the Holy Spirit comes simply to give a renewed vision of the majesty and holiness of God, to refresh devotion and commitment, and to lead people to a new understanding of his nature. This is a part of the continuous renewal of which Paul says, 'let the peace of Christ rule in your hearts ... and the word of Christ dwell in you richly; teach and admonish ... and with gratitude in your hearts sing psalms, hymns and spiritual songs to God' (Colossians 3:15-16).

Such a time of renewal took place over three days in September 1993 during second semester at the Bible College of Victoria (B.C.V.). This special and unplanned period became a time of renewal, growth, conviction and great blessing.

B.C.V. is an interdenominational, evangelical college training people for ministry in Australia and overseas. There are about 180 full time students and almost as many more part time students. Ever since its foundation in 1920 individual, group and community prayer and worship have been an important feature of the community life of the college.

The priorities of the college are expressed as 'Knowing, Being and Serving'. This means knowing God in personal relationship; being transformed to become more like the Lord Jesus Christ as Spirit filled people of compassion, faith, vision and power, living holy lives in the personal and social realms; and serving God in the world, developing gifts for ministry for building up the church, meeting the diverse needs in society, and proclaiming the gospel to unreached people.

As a consequence of this commitment, time is regularly given over to prayer. Students and faculty pray in daily chapel services, in fellowship groups, in lectures, at meal times, in faculty groups, in pairs and room groups on special prayer days and nights, and in prayer cells for specific issues including healing, evangelism, community life and student ministries. People pray, sometimes with conviction and joy, at other times with doubts and fears.

Continually there are testimonies to the blessing of the Holy Spirit. Prayer is programmed as an important part of college life and God honours that commitment, but on occasions God wants to do something different.

A desire for God

The recent time of renewal began with the group responsible for preparing for a regular day of prayer. Others had a growing conviction that God's Spirit wanted to move in a new way. One student, reflecting the feelings of many, said, 'My heart had already been prepared to meet with God - and I was not disappointed. For some time I had recognised the hunger in my heart and my need for God to refresh and renew my weary spirit.'

A number of people felt a desire for the presence of the Holy Spirit. Various experiences indicated that the Lord wanted students to be involved in all night prayer to prepare for the day of prayer for the whole college.

Many would agree with the student who said, 'For the last two years it has been an increasing prayer of mine that God's Spirit would move across this nation, and more recently that I would experience more of God's fulness in my life.'

Significantly, a desire for God to work in this country in a dynamic way is connected with a willingness to allow God to work in a new way personally.   It is difficult to communicate what one has not experienced.

One student observed that although none of those who met the Lord on that day would claim the necessary qualities for spiritual leadership in this generation, nonetheless a start was made, for 'when God raises up spiritual leaders, He first judges them so that they may depend on Him alone' (Holland 1993:1).

The presence of the Spirit

On Tuesday 21 September about 140 of the college community gathered together in the chapel for prayer.   A time of teaching followed the praise and worship.   The teaching was brief, about 20 minutes, low key and even understated.   Then as people were invited to pray or receive prayer, the effect was as tremendous as it was unexpected.

What had been planned as a 50 minute session became a four hour response to the presence of the Holy Spirit as he touched people's lives and moved them to prayer, repentance, reconciliation, testimony, praise and commitment.   It is difficult to describe this; it needs to be felt.

All who were present found that this was a special time.   The college community comprises diverse groups of people from a wide range of denominations and traditions of prayer and worship. Many of them are prayerful people but most had never experienced a time like this.

The Holy Spirit convicted, empowered, challenged, encouraged and renewed people. Forty or more sought prayer. They had a tremendous ministry together.

The day's program was transformed, replaced by the plans of the Spirit. Significant personal matters were dealt with that day and in the days that followed.

One student acknowledged, 'God was convicting me of my doubt in the Holy Spirit's power to work in and through my life. ... I knew I had once again to give the Holy Spirit permission to consume those parts of my life that had been preventing me from loving God more completely.'

For many, the infilling of the Spirit meant that they were overcome - sometimes with grief and repentance, at other times with joy, often with weeping, and often with relief and rejoicing.

The ministry continued over the next couple of days. People were reconciled. They shared in prayer. They ministered to one another and were counselled.

Two days later, when the college community was gathered together, an opportunity was given for people to share testimonies of what God had done over the past few days. One hour became two, then three and four hours, as they praised, prayed, and gave testimony to the experiences of the Spirit.

It was a time for hearing how people had been challenged about their prayer life, their relationship to the Lord, their relationships with others, personal attitudes, and ministry challenges. Again there were tears and rejoicing.

Lives had been changed, barriers broken down, resistances overcome, forgiveness granted, and blessing received. Although lectures had been planned, they simply did not happen that day. Such was the intensity of the moment that no one wanted to leave the chapel.

Lessons of the Spirit

Four points stand out as concluding observations, although many other things could be said.

1. Historic connections

There is a connection here with the noted revival which took place at Asbury Seminary in the U.S.A. in 1970 and which had far reaching effects throughout America (Coleman 1970).

The speaker at the start of the day of prayer was the Rev. Mark Nysewander who was visiting B.C.V. with the Rev. Richard Stevenson. Both are part of the Francis Asbury Society (U.S.A.), a society focused on renewal through the Holy Spirit. Mark had been present as a student at the revival at Asbury Seminary in 1970 and is continuing that ministry through the Francis Asbury Society.

2. Future influence

This experience at B.C.V. may or may not spread to other people and places, but whether it does or not, it will continue to mean a lot to those who experienced it. Many future ministries will be enriched by this personal experience.

Knowing through experience what God can do in renewing a community is essential for communicating this to others and for preparing them for it. The historic connection between revivals may continue as students and faculty better understand the power of God to move people and as they become more confident in ministering in his name.

3. A gentle ministry

It should be emphasised that the ministry exercised over these days was described as 'a gentle ministry' with 'no hype'. Others were 'surprised by the quietness' of the time shared together. It is no insult to those leading worship beforehand or to those involved in teaching to say that the worship and teaching were not extraordinary in any way.

There have been more articulate, more dynamic, more profound sermons preached at B.C.V. than these. The worship was more restrained than it has been at other times, but this time the effect was different from all other times. Clearly, the issue was not human hype, enthusiasm or ability, but the providence of God who initiates and controls.

4. An openness to the Spirit

While no one can command the activity of God, it is clear in retrospect that there was a willingness on the part of many people, students and faculty, to be open to whatever God had to offer and a commitment to not allowing programs to interfere with the work of the Spirit.

This openness had surprising implications. While many were looking for a wider renewal in Australia, God wanted to work closer to home, with those who were praying.

God deals first with his messengers and challenges them to be the kind of servants he wants them to be.

References

Coleman, R., ed. (1970) *One Divine Moment*. New Jersey: Fleming Revell.

Holland, H. (1993) 'An Extraordinary Day of Prayer' in *Ambassador*: Official Journal of the Bible College of Victoria, No. 151, p. 1.

See also comment on the Asbury Revival in *Renewal Journal* (1993) #1, pp. 44-45; #2, p. 51.

10 Spirit Wave

Darren Trinder

Selections edited from A New Way of Living, *Nos. 67, 68, June - October, 1993, the magazine of the Christian Outreach Centres. Manifestations like those described here occurred in revivals throughout history, including Pentecost.*

First God has to shake up the church and then

He uses these people to shake up the world.

One could have been forgiven for thinking they had just walked into a huge wine tasting event, where someone forgot to tell the samplers to stop. But the wine these people were imbibing didn't come from any earthly vineyard. This was pure Holy Ghost vintage wine.

People were everywhere some standing, some sitting, some stretched out on the floor. It looked more like pandemonium than regular church.

What prompted every church meeting to run at least one hour overtime as the crowd continued in praise and worship?

Put simply, the Holy Spirit was doing something different. Although the phenomenon was so new and unique, to those caught in its flow it seemed so natural.

When the fires of Pentecost fell in Acts 2 not only did the 120 begin speaking in other tongues, but obviously they were very affected in a physical sense.

The sceptics of the day who witnessed the event were saying, 'They're drunk. These followers of Jesus are drunk.' From this we can safely deduce that the 120 were staggering, laughing, dancing, linking arms and singing. In other words, they were generally having a good time in the Lord, who had just visited them in a mighty manifestation.

Mansfield, Brisbane

So it was in the week beginning 2 May, 1993, at Christian Outreach Centre, Brisbane.

Some staggered drunkenly, others had fits of laughter, others lay prostrate on the floor, still more were on their knees while others joined hands in an impromptu dance. Others, although showing no physical signs, praised the Lord anyway, at the same time trying to take it all in.

People who had never prayed publicly for others moved among the crowd and laid hands on those present.

'When we first saw it in New Zealand early in April we were sceptical,' said Nance Miers, wife of Christian Outreach Centre International President, Pastor Neil Miers. 'I've seen the Holy Spirit move like this here and there over the years. But this was different. In the past it seemed to have affected a few individuals, but this time it was a corporate thing.'

Neil Miers himself was physically affected, along with several other senior COC pastors, early in this Holy Ghost phenomenon. Later he viewed the series of events objectively.

'It started in New Zealand and then broke out in New Guinea, and now it's here. If I know the Holy Ghost, it will break out across the world wherever people are truly seeking revival. 'For the moment this is what God is saying to do, and we're doing it. It's that simple.'

But despite the informal nature of the events, Pastor Miers, adopting his shepherd role, was careful to monitor the situation.

'There are some who are going overboard with it; just like when someone gets drunk on earthly wine for the first time. The next time it happens they'll understand it a little better.'

God is doing many things. He's loosening up the church. He's working deep repentance in certain individuals, and healing deep hurts in others.

Just like the outpouring in Acts, it was the public ministry that followed which really changed the world. First God has to shake up the church and then He uses these people to shake up the world.

Splashes of this revival have touched people's lives throughout the Christian Outreach Centre movement around the nation and the world.

School students

Students who usually spend lunch times playing football or talking with friends lined the door of the chapel waiting for praise and worship sessions to begin.

Chaplain at COC College, Mansfield, Koula Konstantinos, said that compulsory chapel times which normally lasted 30 minutes were extending to two hours. The voluntary chapel times at lunch times were consistently attended by 50 to 60 students.

'Students go back to class drunk, some just crying with the Holy Spirit doing work in their lives,' she said. 'I have been told by one primary teacher that the behaviour has changed in the actual class room. We've had recommitments, baptisms in the Holy Spirit, habits being broken off their lives. I just see real excitement.'

Koula said the peer pressure which normally quenches a student's desire to reach out to God was being reversed. Many students wanted to forego other subjects in favour of having chapel all day. She said entire classes are responding to altar calls for recommitments to Jesus.

Redcliffe, Brisbane

It could be a children's worker's dream! What do you do when most of your class at children's church is lying on the floor for up to 1 1/2 hours under the power of God?

Phil Radnedge, superintendent of Redcliffe COC's children's church, said some of the happenings on Sunday mornings over the past few months defy logic, but he welcomed it as a true move of the Holy Spirit.

'On a number of occasions our senior section (grades 47) has been completely overcome by joy,' he said. 'Normally shy and selfconscious children have laughed uncontrollably for hours at a time as they danced and jumped from one end of the classroom to the other.'

Phil said that even though the outward manifestations were exciting to see, it is the work that God is doing within the children which is vital. As one of his children explained, 'God is making me bigger inside so I can love Him more.'

One confused parent approached Phil wondering why her once shy, introverted little boy had become confident and assertive virtually overnight.

'It has been my privilege to see lives radically transformed since this move of God began,' Phil said. 'Parents are speaking of children who can't put their Bibles down; other children are praying more now than at any other time in their life. These children have developed a great hunger for God.'

Innisfail, Queensland

The outpouring of the Holy Spirit in Innisfail COC was just as tangible in the Teen Church and Children's Church meetings as it was in the adults.

One young boy who comes from a broken marriage was prayed for at the Teen Church meeting. Up until then he had been very hardhearted, but after the meeting his mum commented that she had a new son. He even gave her a kiss for the first time when she picked him up from high school on Monday.

Another teenager got on the drums and played the most powerful solo. The teen leader turned to the boy's sister and commented, 'This must be the Holy Spirit.'

The girl replied, 'I should know. I've heard him practice and he can't play like this.'

Others laughed, some wept, some danced, some just lay on the floor and could not get up. Some looked a little drunk and started singing, 'We're not drunk as you suppose, we're just filled with the Holy Ghost!'

But the teen's leader, Charlie Dalla Vecchia, noticed the greatest wonder: 'No one wanted to stop when it came to go home now that's a miracle!' he said.

Port Macquarie, NSW

Pastor Alan Deeks reported:

On Sunday 16 May our morning meeting started as usual at 9 am

The similarity to any other meeting ended there. People were caught up in a powerful move of the Holy Spirit that had some crying deep tears as God moved upon them, and others were laughing and falling around as if they were drunk.

We were unable to fit in a time of communion and certainly no preaching was necessary as the Holy Spirit continued to move. Apart from the few who had to leave, nobody left at the usual ending time for meetings.

A teenage girl had to be carried from the meeting. Several have had to be helped from the church by other people.

A similar experience occurred again that night, but with a greater emphasis on repentance and crying to God for souls.

The following week the numbers at our midweek prayer meetings doubled, and a great sense of the presence of the Holy Spirit was experienced by those praying.

People no longer seemed to be concerned at the length of the meetings, and we have gone way overtime now on almost every occasion since the first Holy Ghost meeting. People are reluctant to leave in case they miss something.

There is a fresh expectancy in meetings and in people's lives, and a sense of excitement of what God is doing.

Taree, NSW

As the people of Taree COC prepared for three days of intensive prayer and fasting in early May, they were unaware of what was about to happen.

Pastor Ron Jones returned from a District Chairman's Camp in Brisbane and shared about the new move of the Holy Spirit. The supernatural power of God was unleashed. People came from surrounding towns to be part of the action.

During the three days of prayer and fasting the church doors were open 24 hours a day. One family from out of town slept over so they did not miss what God was doing. This encouraged other people to sleep over as well.

People prayed around the clock, many becoming involved in intercession for lost souls. Deep travail and groanings were heard, similar to natural childbirth.

At many times over the three days laughter broke out, sometimes with as many as 200 people involved. Many were 'slain' supernaturally in the Spirit and rested in God's power for hours on end. Many wept uncontrollably. Others were prayed for on the floor and set free from demonic oppression. Several couples, on the brink of despair and certain divorce, had their marriages restored.

Pastor Ron Jones said that as word spread, people from surrounding districts such as Forster, came to have a look. He said many caught the outpouring of the Spirit and took it back to their respective churches.

'Many of the local interested visitors were supernaturally touched. Whether the talk was good or bad around town, it certainly reaped a crop of hungry people and those thirsty for the things of the Spirit,' he said.

'We have had pre-church prayer meetings where everyone present was drunk in the Holy Ghost, church meetings where the power of God fell so dramatically that people were slain in the Spirit in the back row of the church with no one laying hands on them.

'The past weeks have caused great revival among the people,' said Ron. 'Enthusiasm and spontaneity overflow in each meeting and we have had an enormous interest shown in church by increased numbers of youth as well as adults.'

Newcastle, NSW

Glenn and Jayne Wilson, youth leaders at Newcastle COC, were among the first to experience the Holy Spirit's outpouring there. For the first time in five years Glenn found himself 'slain' under the anointing. He said that as well as finding a total peace flooding his soul, a burning desire for God was also reignited that night.

Another man experienced a supernatural boldness which sprung from his new relationship with the Holy Spirit.

'Before this new move of the Holy Spirit I used to pray for people reluctantly, and then apologise straight away for my shortcomings,' he said. 'Talk about lacking confidence! Since receiving this new anointing, I find that the Holy Spirit stirs up inside me so strongly that I just have to pray for people or lay hands on them. The Holy Spirit can give you a love for people that will empower you for sure!'

Several women have explained that they have been released from deep hurts which they had harboured for years.

Another lady found herself sharing Jesus with people with an ease and desire which she thought she could never know. 'I can't help myself,' she said. 'A new boldness and a heart for people who do not know the Lord seems to continue to grow inside me.'

Families are also being restored. One man, Allen, spent nearly an hour at the first night of revival on the floor of the Newcastle Centre, weeping and repenting before God until a tremendous sense of freedom and joy flooded his spirit.

'I have been yearning for a deeper relationship with my wife and children for many months, even though there was nothing lacking in our marriage,' he said. 'That night, however, the Holy Spirit gave me such a love for my Heavenly Dad that I couldn't get enough. Within minutes the Holy Spirit had made my love for God my number one priority and shown me that my wife and kids needed to be second. I told this to my family and peace just flooded our relationship. By putting the Lord first, He has blessed our family so much.'

A spokesperson for the Newcastle Centre said that the church, as a family, was also being renewed. She said there was a new sense of unity and freshness being imparted by the Holy Spirit.

'There is genuine repentance,' she said.

Many visions and prophecies have been shared. The prayer meetings are both exciting and powerful, and we're all getting a desire for God and a burden for our city.'

Hornsby, Sydney

Passion seems to be the number one word on people's lips at Hornsby COC since the new move of God started, according to spokesman Begin Markham.

Begin said there had been an undeniable change in people's attitudes and they now attended meetings out of a strong desire to meet with God, rather than to perform a duty.

'There is a desire to be full constantly with the Holy Ghost,' he said. 'After the tears, laughter and crying out to God, the fruit remaining is a passion for God Himself not the spectacular, but a hunger for the presence of God and a passion to dive into the Word of God.

Comments from other people at Hornsby COC include:

* During a prayer meeting I was crying out for souls, and my heart turned to my 16 year old son who was in prison. I had never cried for someone else so much before. When I arrived home from that meeting, the telephone was ringing, and it was my son. There was an urgency in his voice. He wanted to start his life from scratch and was fed up with drugs and alcohol, which were responsible for his detention. God has

moved powerfully. My son has been released early and is back at school, and came to church last week to ask God for help!

* One night I had a terrific Bible study prepared for the home cell which I lead but I felt the Holy Ghost ask me to share about passion. Tears came from my eyes as I heard what God was saying through me and I remember thinking, 'This is bigger than me!' By the end of the meeting I had repented of ridiculous attitudes, but the meeting did not end there, for me. It continued until midafternoon the following day. It was easy to give over sinful attitudes and the like, and God gave me more of the Holy Ghost in return. The Lord did some terrific surgery, and I have been free ever since.

* God showed me a vision of myself walking through a fire, holding the Word of God in my hand. Everything around me was being consumed by the fire, except the Word of God. I came through the fire, and the only thing which remained was the Word of God in my hand. I have a greater passion to serve God, and a greater fear of God in my life. I know that I will never be alone again the Holy Spirit is my close friend and is always there. As I felt the Holy Ghost's love for the lost I was totally broken on the ground in tears.

Canberra, Australian Capital Territory

On 9 May, Canberra COC hosted a guest singer. As she began a song about the prodigal son, the Centre's pastor, Len Russell, started to sob loudly.

Afterwards he got up and shared with the congregation. People responded to the altar call where the power of the Holy Spirit came and people were slain and filled with laughter.

One man was so drunk in the Spirit that he had to be driven home. He was still drunk two days later and still laughing in the Spirit.

The ladies' prayer and Bible study group was completely taken over by the Holy Spirit. A lady was so drunk that her husband had to leave work to drive her home. Other ladies had to sober up to drive and pick their children up from schools.

There have been visions of castles, moats, and draw bridges with rusty chains, referring to the lives of Christians bound up by habits or sin. As these areas have been surrendered to God, and after much weeping, conquering these areas became easy.

Caroline, a lady who has had constant back pain since a car accident five years ago, is now free of all discomfort and was filled with holy laughter.

Warrnambool, Victoria

Marcus was a 10 year old with a major supply of shyness and according to his mother Linda, he hardly spoke a word even at home.

But it seems God has done such a work inside Marcus that he is now displaying a totally new personality to his family and friends.

'He even prays for me!' said Linda. 'If I say that I've got a headache, he'll come up to me and start praying fullon, loud, faith prayers. It has carried over into other areas of the home. He is being very helpful and cooperative and very open he doesn't mind just talking and sharing.'

The transformation in Marcus started at a Victorian COC Youth Convention in June where Stewart Moncrieff was a guest speaker, and continued later at Warrnambool COC.

Pastor of the Warrnambool Centre, Charlie Bartkus, said he was as surprised as the family at the dramatic change.

Apart from clapping, dancing and laying on the ground laughing, Marcus was displaying a boldness which defied explanation. All this from a 10 year old boy who never clapped or smiled in church before, and who avoided looking other people in the eye.

Melbourne, Victoria

Pastor Louise Swan wrote:

In Melbourne, the outpouring of the Spirit began on Mother's Day, 9 May. From the outset amazing manifestations of the Spirit began to happen.

A young man, normally very 'with it' and 'together' fell under the power of the Spirit and began to laugh uncontrollably for three and a half hours. The next month he spent most of the time either staggering around with a stunned look on his face or slain in the Spirit for most of each evening. Often periods of the same laughter overwhelm him. Normally a rather aggressive driver, he drove home from church all the way at 40 km/h and gave way to everything.

Much emotional healing is taking place as some onceconservative people are being transformed through laughter.

One young girl fell to the floor as my husband Barry and I prayed for her release from excruciating back pain. After about a minute of agonising pain and tears she began to laugh, and spent the next hour and a half laughing and free of all back pain.

One young married man fell under the power of the Spirit and lay on the floor for over three hours. He has been totally transformed by the experience.

A lady walked in the front door after a meeting at Melbourne had begun, stood back doubtfully and decided that the church had finally gone 'too far'. No one came near her, but the Holy Spirit hit her and she crumpled to the floor, laughing uncontrollably.

A Chinese lady, who had watched sceptically through one of the first revival meetings, asked us to pray for her at the next meeting but did not want hands laid on her. She had decided that if it was God, He would have to show her. We began to pray (no hands!) and within half a minute she had crumpled over from the waist in laughter, and then dropped to the floor laughing and crying at the same time. She lay prostrate on the floor for a half an hour repenting of her unbelief, and then got up and testified to everybody of her experience.

One young girl, whose mother had died the previous year, spent an entire evening sobbing with grief on the floor. The next meeting saw her filled with Holy Ghost laughter and she laughed for hours. Her face was totally transformed, as also were her emotions. She went home from the meeting and wrote an anointed song about the outpouring of the Spirit. It has blessed hundreds already.

Many have had visions while under the power of the Spirit or while in prayer. These have included visions of the lost in their hopeless state, visions of hell, visions of revival in all nations, visions of dramatic healings, of bodies coming back to life.

Sometimes people lying together, slain in the Spirit, have had combined visions where all have been watching the same happenings. Each has emphatically confirmed what the other was saying and continued the description.

Marriages have been miraculously restored and many other relationships are being healed. One couple was about to separate and also leave the ministry. The miracle of restoration has to be seen to be believed! They are more in love with one another now than they have ever been, and it happened almost overnight as the Spirit fell on them.

New songs are flowing out of the revival. These have ignited fresh passion for God in the hearts of the people.

Perth, Western Australia

Church services in Perth Christian Outreach Centre no longer hold a routine format, but rather the Spirit is leading and the power of God is having a dynamic effect.

It was Mother's Day when revival began moving in a way that no one had seen or expected before. Some people began to laugh while others wept. Since then meetings have been held most nights of the week with people hungry for more of God.

People's hearts and attitudes have and are being changed. Conversations are about the Lord, no one really seeming to care for the everyday events and cares of life. People have been set free from habits such as smoking.

Visions and dreams have been experienced by many people. God's Spirit has moved, changing people in a sovereign way.

Busselton, Western Australia

The fire of God is also sweeping across the city and country areas of Western Australia. Pastor Helen McInnes from Busselton Christian Outreach Centre said, 'People have been inwardly healed and delivered.

316

We have not had to counsel, but instead the presence of God has come and is moving. He is greatly purifying and cleansing.'

The main result has been that people are seeking God. God is revealing his glory, and revelation is coming to people about the true meaning of obedience and surrender.

Even though there are outward manifestations, it is the internal work that is eternal. Best of all, this is just the beginning.

Manifestations of the Spirit

Here is a guide for those people who are wondering what the fuss is all about.

1. A passion for God: Men and women are yearning for more of God Himself (Psalm 42:12) and for His Word (Job 23:12). There is an eagerness among people to gather with other Christians (Psalm 69:9) and to pray (Acts 12:5). Much of this prayer is intercession for souls. There is much travailing and prevailing (Galatians 4:19).

2. Repentance: People are turning away from sin and dead works and turning to God (Acts 20:21, 2 Cor. 7:910).

3. Restoration of relationships, renewed love: A new unity is sweeping groups of people. Broken relationships are being restored through humility and an openness to the needs of others (Galatians 5:22, Isaiah 58:12).

4. Overwhelming joy: People touched by the Spirit are genuinely happy (Acts 8:8). There is singing (Ephesians 5:1819), dancing (2 Sam. 6:14), shouting (Psalm 5:11) and clapping (Pslam 47:1). Laughter is sometimes uncontrollable (Pslam 126:6).

5. Inexplicable peace: People are finding God's peace as the Holy Spirit sets them free from grief, confusion, stress, anger, frustrations, hurts and other bondages (Isaiah 53:3, Malachi 4:2, Luke 9:11).

6. Dreams, visions and prophecy: Just as the prophet Joel foretold (Joel 2:28) when the Spirit is poured out many will see revelations with their spiritual eyes (Acts 2:17). Prophecy and other gifts of the Spirit are common occurrence (Acts 2:1718).

7. Healing: Some people are receiving healing in their minds and their bodies (Isaiah 53:3, Malachi 4:2, Luke 9:11).

8. Boldness: Self-consciousness is being swallowed up by a holy boldness (Acts 4:31). People are finding that sharing the Gospel is easier than before.

9. Direction: Some are receiving from the Holy Spirit clearer guidance with respect to their ministry, their work, their families and other areas of their lives (Proverbs 3:56).

10. People slain in the Spirit: Even the sceptics are finding themselves on the floor at prayer meetings, sometimes for hours (Revelation 1:17).

11. Crying: There have been tears of joy and thankfulness and repentance (Psalm 136:56).

12. Drunkenness (in various stages), daze, stupor: Men and women of undoubted character have been seen staggering around as drunk people as they have come under the influence of the Holy Spirit (Jeremiah 23:9, Acts 2:13, 15). People have seemed to switch off mentally and physically as God reveals things to them in the Spirit (Numbers 24:4 and Acts 10:10).

Since these reports have been gathered, similar phenomena were reported world wide, including reports associated with the 'Toronto Blessing', Pensacola and refreshing and revitalising of churches in many lands.

Review

Book and DVD Review

Viva Christo Rey! Book by Rene Laurentin, Waco: Word, 1982. Video/DVD originally by Catholic Charismatic Renewal.

The book by Rene Laurentin, *Viva Christo Rey!* (Word, 1982) tells the amazing story of God's work among the poor of El Paso and Juarez on the border of Mexico and Texas.

People there who live in cardboard homes without electricity or running water, without employment, have found in the Holy Spirit an abundance of joy, grace and riches which few people today enjoy.

A charismatic Catholic prayer group took the gospels seriously, and decided to provide a meal for the people who scavenge their living from the city dump. They were prompted by Jesus' command to share food with those in need. They provided food for 150 people at Christmas, but over 300 turned up, and then brought their friends. The food did not run out and there was enough left over to give to various orphanages.

So began a ministry of love and care which has grown for over forty years. The sick are being healed, both medically and through prayer. The hungry are fed, and food has never run out in twenty years. Employment has been provided in cooperatives. Better housing has been built.

Fr Rene Laurentin writes that 'most importantly, they have found in the Holy Spirit the source of the spiritual conversion that has made for more humane living through converted action. The Holy Spirit, too, has given them a capacity for renewal, a capacity rarely found among intellectuals, who are so often lost in things, in learning, and in the orchestrated power and influence that earned the rich the reproach of Jesus. The gospel is still the good news proclaimed to the poor.'

One prayer group decided to do something in obedience to Jesus. Miracles have followed.

The one hour enthralling DVD (copy of a video) of the same name, Viva Christo Rey! (Hail, Christ the King) provides a stirring documentary of early beginnings and recent developments. It was produced jointly by the Catholics and Assemblies of God.   (G.W.)

Renewal Journal
4 Healing

Geoff Waugh (Editor)

Renewal Journal
4 Healing

Contents

Renewal Journal 4: Healing

Cover photo: 4 Healing
Grant Shaw leads healing teams in Australia and globally here with nurse Leah Waqa who prays for the sick and has raised the dead in Vanuatu in the South Pacific.

Editorial

Wholeness in Spirit, Soul and Body

The cover photo shows Grant Shaw with Leah Waqa. Grant Shaw and I attended the Sunday service at the Upper Room church in Port Vila, the capital of Vanuatu in the South Pacific. There Leah, a nurse, told how she had been dispensing medicines at the hospital that week when parents brought in their young daughter who had been badly hit in a car accident, and showed no signs of life - the monitor registered zero – no pulse. Leah felt unusual boldness, so commanded the girl to live, and prayed for her for an hour, mostly in tongues. After an hour the monitor started beeping and the girl recovered.

Grant joined me on Pentecost Island in Vanuatu. South Pentecost attracts tourists with its land diving – men jumping from high bamboo towers with vines attached to their ankles. Grant prayed for a jumper who had hurt his neck, and the neck crackled back into place. That young man and his father both gave their lives to the Lord right there in the village. Grant prayed for a son of the paramount chief of South Pentecost. He was healed from a painful leg and later he invited the team to come to his village to pray for the sick. No white people had been invited there to minister previously. More were healed there in Jesus' name. The full account is in *South Pacific Revivals* by Geoff Waugh (2010).

Healing is a tough subject, especially if you or your loved ones are sick!

Attitudes to 'the healing ministry' and theologies about healing vary greatly. At one extreme lies the claim that everyone can and should be well, and if you have enough faith in God you will be healed; at the other extreme lies the claim that healing, if it occurs, now happens through medical science.

People at the first extreme tend to avoid medical help, trust in God alone for healing, and deny any 'lying symptoms'. However, they usually acknowledge the importance of healthy food, exercise, rest and positive attitudes – which people at the other extreme also acknowledge.

The truth, I believe, doesn't just stand somewhere in the middle, but in both. God heals. His healing power is always at work in us with every heart beat, every breath. Life is his gift to us. Healthy living contributes to good health. Oranges and Vitamin C tablets promote health. So do healthy attitudes. So does prayer, and faith.

We know that being healthy is good, not bad. We go to a doctor or we take medicine because that can help overcome sickness and restore health.

Most of us pray for healing, for others and for ourselves. We usually appreciate others praying for us. We pray for others in many different ways.

It may be the general 'God bless them' prayer or our wish for their well being. It may be the more specific 'Heal them, please God' or 'Lord lay your healing hand on them'. It may be the still more specific prayer with a person as we lay our hand on them in Jesus' name. It may be the even more specific prayer or command, led and anointed by the Holy Spirit, through various gifts of the Spirit including healing, miracles, faith, prophecy, words of knowledge or wisdom, discernment of spirits, or tongues and maybe interpretation.

And sometimes we don't pray for healing, but it happens anyway!

More difficult to understand is when we do pray for healing, we do have faith, we 'trust and obey' and yet healing does not happen, as far as we can see. We have to acknowledge that we don't 'see' very far yet. There is mystery in healing, as there is in living. We don't understand the mystery of life, nor do we understand a lot about eternal life.

However, we know that God gives life, and sustains life. We can learn more about how to co-operate with God, including learning how to pray more effectively, believe more truly, and love more fully.

Healing is complex. Most healing takes time, but intervention through prayer or medicine can speed up the process, sometimes dramatically. Healing also involves the whole being – spirit, soul and body (1 Thessalonians 5:23). These are inter-related.

We can learn more about blockages to healing such as unforgiveness, unbelief, unhappiness, and unwillingness to yield fully to God. These can be removed in a loving, caring environment.

One major discovery in charismatic renewal, and in similar ministries, has been the reality of God's healing grace revealing the Father's love, such as through compassionate prayer in Jesus' name in the power of the Holy Spirit. This ministry of love and compassion increases everywhere now.

Those who live and worship in places or among people where there is love, compassion, forgiveness, faith, courage and support for one another are especially blessed. All these facilitate healing. As we yield to the Spirit of God among us, these graces abound, and so does healing. This is part of the Lord's purpose and commission for his church – to be a loving, caring and healing community.

We believe that Jesus healed, especially in compassion for people. He commanded and taught his disciples to preach the good news about the reign of God, heal the sick and cast out evil spirits. Jesus is the same – yesterday, today and forever. His commission is the same still. We are learning again to humbly and courageously obey him in the power of his Spirit. There is more to learn and do yet.

This issue of the *Renewal Journal* aims to help you do that. David Lithgow, Jim Holbeck, John Blacker, Colin Warren, John Warlow and Spencer Colliver tell of their discoveries and understanding of healing. Sue Armstrong and Trevor Faggotter describe revival movements which also include healing through prayer.

The next issue of the *Renewal Journal*, Number 5 (95:1), looks at Signs and Wonders including an overview of their place in the church throughout history and their explosion in revival movements today. Subsequent issues cover topics such as worship, prayer and compassion. These take on new meaning and expression in renewal ministry.

The *Renewal Journal* carries articles on renewal and revival across all churches and in the community. Pray as you read! May God bring healing to the land as we repent and believe the good news of God's great grace.

1 Missionary Translator and Doctor

David Lithgow

Dr David Lithgow and his wife Daphne were Bible translators and medical missionaries with Wycliffe Bible Translators for over 30 years, mainly in the Milne Bay Islands of Papua New Guinea. These edited selections from newsletters tell a little of their work for the Lord.

In one place it seemed that everyone turned to the Lord and was baptized in the sea. The same happened on two more islands.

Rev. David Kuwab burnt lots of magic paraphernalia which was brought to him.

---

* Seven sick people were prayed for in Jesus' name, and all were healed. Other people kept their sick relatives hidden inside their houses, preferring to trust their own magic and spirit cures. No one among these people was healed. This has been a demonstration of the power of Jesus.

* A woman who had been crippled for years got up and walked immediately, and was doing normal garden work in a week. The people here were convinced that Jesus is the Strong One, and this report spread through the whole area.

* The Lord has worked some surprising miracles, like multiplying the one remaining antibiotic capsule for treating an infection to become twelve – enough to complete the cure.

* After the studies and worship services many of the people came for prayer for the Lord's cleansing from sin, and to receive the Holy Spirit. At Wabunun they came in a continuous stream, many weeping, for one and a half hours.

* The Lord moved powerfully through healing miracles and casting out evil spirits, demonstrating that his power is greater than that of local spirits and magic.

The Word and Work of the Lord

David and Daphne summarise their life together including work in the Muyuw, Dobu and Bunama languages of the Milne Bay Islands:

We had been leaders in the Evangelical Union of the University of Queensland since 1950, Daphne studying Science and David doing Medicine. In 1954 Daphne left for Ubuya Leprosy Treatment Centre near Milne Bay in Papua New Guinea. There she learnt the Dobu language and trained Papuan staff in laboratory work. When Daphne returned, David had graduated and was a Resident Doctor at Townsville General Hospital. We married in August 1957.

In February 1958 we left for Fiji where David was a doctor for the Methodist Mission Hospital serving Indian people. This entailed learning the Hindustani language. Our first two children, a daughter and son, were born there.

David, as the only doctor continuously on call, worked hard meeting physical needs of the people, but had little time to get to understand their spiritual needs. He felt helpless when faced with demon possessed Hindu patients, and could only prescribe sedation.

The work of Wycliffe Bible Translators and Summer Institute of Linguistics (W.B.T. and S.I.L.) was just beginning in Australia. Here we felt was a way of meeting people's deepest needs – living with them as they live, learning their language and customs, and bringing God's Word to them right where they are.

In 1960 we returned to Australia, and David found work at the Greenslopes Repatriation Hospital. In the next two years we welcomed two more sons. We became members of W.B.T. and in May 1963 we flew to Ukarumpa, the S.I.L. Headquarters in the Eastern Highlands of Papua New Guinea.

In the first few years while getting started in language work David was also the group doctor. In 1963 an allocation site was found at Wabunun village on a long sandy beach on the south-east coast of Woodlark Island off Milne Bay. Wabunun was home for the children from 1964 to 1972 in their house built of bush materils – split black palm floor, platted bamboo walls, and sago leaf roof. Daphne taught them correspondence lessons until they were 7 or 8 years old, after which they were in Children's Homes for schooling at the Ukarumpa base.

From 1970 onwards the children all stayed at Ukarumpa for schooling, and we were able to travel around the language area, 150 miles by 70 miles, mostly on the big Muyuw outrigger sailing canoes.

The churches throughout this area had selected young men who came to Wabunun where we trained them as teachers of Muyuw, and sent them back with reading primers and duplicated portions of translated Scriptures. They all achieved some degree of success. Two of these teachers who were barely literate themselves had taught all the young adults to read as well as some of the older folk. They had established the church which worshipped together every Sunday morning – or when they thought it was Sunday, because they had no calendar.

In 1972 the **Muyuw New Testament** translation was virtually complete, so we moved to Dobu Island to help in the Bible Society project to retranslate the **Dobu New Testament** into modern Dobu. There the house had a sawn timber floor, bush materil walls and an iron roof.

From 1978 to 1982 we were settling our teen-age children into life in Australia while we worked as the Wycliffe Bible Translators representatives in Queensland. Every year David returned to Dobu to keep the literacy and translation program moving.

In 1978 our doctor advised against David returning to Papua New Guinea because of incipient cancer. It seemed David could expect about another two years of normal health. Our plans were examined closely but there seemed no need to change any of them. We also sought healing through prayer in Jesus' name. Since then David has had better health then he had before. After such a sentence of death, every day is valued as a special gift from the Lord, and it gives an added sense of urgency to the task.

From 1982 we were at Dobu or Diwala Translation Centre, helping with the translations and doing literacy work. In 1985 the *Muyuw New Testament* was revised and reprinted. We travelled in S.I.L.'s new 24 foot boat with the minister, Rev. David Kuwab, who had been the main translation helper. We visited every island and village selling Scriptures and hymn books, and re-establishing literacy work where it was needed. Near the beginning of this trip the Lord moved powerfully through healing miracles and casting out evil spirits.

The new *Dobu New Testament* was dedicated in 1986. It is now used widely alongside the old Dobu Bible. Over 10,000 copies have been sold. As the Lord worked in Muyuw, he has also worked strongly in the Dobu speaking area, leading individuals and groups to renounce traditional magic and to trust in Jesus' name for salvation and healing.

In 1991 the *Bunama New Testament* was printed and dedicated. It was distributed by three groups of three Bunama speakers who gave Bible studies from the new Scripture in twenty different villages. In almost every village there were people who sought the Lord's salvation – older folk, young men, girls, school children. We were amazed at the many different ways in which the Holy Spirit spoke to people's needs.

Preach the Good News, Heal the Sick, Cast out Demons

David describes a few events on mission patrols:

Muyuw Patrol, 1985

The 600 *Muyuw New Testaments*, first printed and sold in 1977, are worn from heavy use, tattered and discoloured. Some have lost their cover. People were eager to buy new ones for themselves and their children. Those who had no money traded canoe paddles, shells, ebony carvings, turtle-shell ear-rings, or baskets of food.

The main Muyuw translator Rev. David Kuwab, who is now Superintendent Minister, with his wife Dasel came with us on the seven week's patrol by boat to all the inhabited islands and villages where this language is spoken. On one island Rev. Kuwab baptised ninety people and married five young Christian couples.

At another island an old man asked if he could take his wife with us on the boat to the next island where they wanted to get strong Papuan magic. Hospital staff had told his wife that the basis of this sickness was witchcraft, so they could do nothing and said she should go home and get Papuan treatment. All Papuan treatments had failed and they wanted to try stronger traditional magic. Rev. Kuwab and I went to her house and prayed for her. We asked if she believed Jesus could heal her, and she said 'Yes'. So we helped her to her feet and started her walking. Soon she walked unaided doing heavy work in the food garden.

At the Government Administration Centre the wife of the Provincial Member for Health had been bed-ridden for three years. They believed this was from witchcraft. He had employed all the local methods to appease the witches and cure the sickness but she only got worse. He asked us to pray for his wife and we did so. When Kuwab asked if she believed Jesus could heal her he got a lethargic response. Daphne visited this woman to pray with her daily. She was improving, so the Provincial member asked Kuwab and me to pray for her again. After prayer this time, she got up and walked. We noted that she was quite anaemic and gave her iron tablets and advice on diet and encouraged continuing prayer and trust in Jesus. Rev. Kuwab warned them strongly against reverting to Papuan magic.

On our last day at Woodlark a man brought his mentally disturbed wife. Rev. Kuwab had told them to stop doing anti-witchcraft magic and to pray in Jesus' name. The previous night they had done that and she told us she was now all right. They agreed to another prayer but as soon as Jesus' name was uttered she screamed and stiffened and talked of bad things put in her abdomen by a witch. I rebuked the evil spirit in Jesus' name and we prayed strongly. When Kuwab asked if she believed in Jesus she gave a definite 'No'. I felt led to pray in the Spirit. Kuwab asked her again and she now said that she believed Jesus could save her. She seemed normal, though lethargic, when we left. She did recover.

One day was free to visit another village so the deacon took me there by canoe. We were not able to tell the people that I was coming, so the deacon and I prayed for the Lord to prepare the people. Normally they would have been scattered in the bush, in their food gardens, or at creeks and beaches getting fish and shell-fish; but we found almost all the people sitting in the church. One Tuesday each month they have a devotional meeting. This was that meeting.

They had just finished their devotions so they invited me to speak about the New Testament, hymn book and other Muyuw books. They bought them eagerly. Then the youth leader showed me their study paper on the Holy Spirit from a youth convention and asked me if I could help them understand it. So after a lunch break we went into the church again. I read and explained the Muyuw Scriptures about the Holy Spirit and they responded very positively. Many asked for prayer for the filling and empowering of the Holy Spirit.

There was much sickness in another village, especially children. They have no medical help. I had few medicines suitable for children. We gave them what medicines we had and prayed for all the sick. As in all places, they bought New testaments eagerly. Many people came under conviction of sin, coming forward for prayer for Jesus to cleanse and forgive them.

At the Sunday service at Wabunun, where we as a family had lived and worked for eight years, after Scripture had been expounded Rev. Kuwab invited people to come for prayer for sickness, or cleansing from sin, or for the Holy Spirit. People came forward in a solid stream, some weeping. Kuwab's own son, now a grown man and getting into bad ways, came forward with bowed head and his father prayed for him. Kuwab had never before prayed for people under such conviction of sin and desiring salvation.

After a Bible study for preachers and leaders the next day more people came forward for prayers. It took half an hour to pray for them all. On the third and final day, after a straight Bible study no appeal was made but during the final hymn people began to come forward for prayer, mostly sick folk who had been brought from more distant places.

West Woodlark Patrol, 1989

We visited the islands of west of Woodlark in October. After two days of rough weather we limped in with a broken rudder attachment. The Lord provided an ex-plumber on the island who had some tools in his village house and was able to fix it.

We really admire the teachers of the English Curriculum Government Schools. Through their work many children become literate in English and Muyuw, but as not all children go to school there are many illiterate teenagers and adults who now want to learn to read. To try to meet this need we trained 26 new village literacy teachers.

Four places with a total of over 1200 people were still without any medical service despite government efforts to get Aid Post Orderlies to work there. We heard that people of one island were saying, 'You don't recover if you pray but you will recover if you use magic.' When we arrived at that island 80 people were sick with malaria, some desperately ill. All recovered with prayer and chloroquine treatment. The people of one island complain more about having no minister than they do about having no medical help. For most, the value of Christian leadership is rated very high.

As well as *Muyuw New Testaments* and hymn books we took *Kiriwina and Dobu New Testaments* for sale. We found that the Holy Spirit's blessings are not restricted to one way of ministry or to one language. People from a number of languages live at the commercial centre for Woodlark Island. The new United Church minister does not know Muyuw but has a powerful and effective ministry through the Dobu language.

The dialect on one island was a mixture of two main languages. There we found the strongest church on all of these islands. However, a matter of concern is a prophetess who is visited by a spirit from time to time and gives confusing teaching, but she has a large following.

After we returned from the Woodlark area Daphne stayed in our house at Dobu catching up with household matters and weeding our yam garden while I did a survey of another area with Peter from Holland. He and his doctor wife are looking for a language in which to begin translation work. Family in-fighting which is worsening, destruction of villages, and criminal activities among some of those people are causing widespread concern. The police recently made a large number of arrests. There are, however, faithful Christians there in the United, Catholic, and Seventh Day Adventist Churches.

On the patrol we had hard hiking in rain and flooded rivers, then sea travel to return. I had been having intermittent malaria and some other problems, but improved during the patrol and returned feeling strong and fit.

Bunama Patrol, 1991

The *Bunama New Testament* is now with the people, and the Lord blessed the distribution patrol. Of the 600 printed only 40 were left unsold.

I went with the nine Bunama speakers in the distribution team. We spent two days in preparation, praying and studying 1 Timothy, the book we were to use for village Bible studies. Then we set off in groups of three, each group to a different village.

The emphasis was on teaching, and at some stage in most places at the end of a session the team leader or the local pastor would invite people wanting help from the Lord to remain behind. The manifold working of the Holy Spirit was amazing to all of us. Together with the local pastors we prayed in pairs for the people who requested help. Several times the boat captain was teamed with me. Two years before he was illiterate but Daphne taught him from a Dobu primer. Now he reads the Dobu Bible and his prayers were spiritually sensitive and powerful.

Even among the most distant of the dialect groups they understood the Bunama Scripture and teaching quite well and many of them responded to the Lord. They all had individual and different needs, and the Holy Spirit worked in their hearts.

In another place a team leader was hesitant about making an invitation and did so rather tentatively. Later he felt rebuked for his reluctance because many responded. He discovered the agony of soul of one woman who needed the Lord's help, as well as seeing two boys of 10-12 years who had waited back in the distance but were strongly convicted of their need for forgiveness.

There were failures too. — After church one Sunday a number of people went back inside the church and sat quietly. Too late, the members of that team realised they were probably wanting help. — Often after uplifting experiences, team members and local people would sing all night. This was good for the local people but I felt it left team members unable to give of their best the next day. — Some pastors felt that hospitality required them to give betel nut and tobacco to team members, and most felt that good manners required them to use it. Three of the team members were smokers and most used betel nut to some degree. I feel that this drug can dull a person's spiritual sensitivity. — When under pressure near the end of the trip I hurt someone by an outburst of anger, and my apology may not heal all of that hurt.

Half of the team members and some of the village pastors are people the Lord had touched in Dobu Bible studies as we have visited these areas in previous years. It is wonderful to see the Lord's work being multiplied.

All team members spoke clearly against the use of traditional magic and spirit practices. This is a break-through and a key to the Lord's blessing on their ministry. Ten years ago it was considered wrong to mention these things in church.

In the second week the engine of our boat was getting harder to start, taking up to an hour with the crank handle. So before trying one day we prayed and it started first crank. Next morning a team member prayed for the engine. It started by battery power just with the starter button. It has kept starting that way ever since.

The language used at another village was not Bunama and I was undecided about calling there, but called in anyway. There were lots of people about, and they wanted a Bunama Bible study. A team member led it and made an invitation at the end. I could see six young men hanging back in the shadows and listening from a distance. They responded, each with a strong desire to leave his old ways and be a true Christian. The pastor was away, but his wife was delighted. She told us that those young men had been a heavy burden on their hearts.

Our trip finished on the island where it began. They wanted a Bible study from Bunama New Testament and afterwards several of them bought it. The response for prayer was mainly from men aged 25-30. Some were so moved by God's Spirit that they could hardly speak.

Woodlark and Marshall Bennett Patrol, 1994

This trip took three months. Revival is now spreading through these islands.

We arrived soon after a mission led by a United Church minister. During the mission at the main population centres hundreds sought salvation through Christ and were baptised in the sea, surrendering their equipment for magic and sorcery. One witch admitted having killed over twenty people, and she collapsed physically as the power of the Lord came on her.

Two local ministers travelled with us on the S.I.L. boat, continuing this ministry to the more remote places. Rev. Bili Wilson went with us to the Lachlan Islands and the eastern end of Woodlark. Rev. David Kuwab, co-translator of the Muyuw New Testament, was with us in visiting the rest of Woodlark and the Marshall Bennett Islands.

The people gave Rev. Bili Wilson and us their full attention for five days so we gave them the Good News and sold lots of Scriptures. They responded in an amazing way. On Friday I gave the main study in the church and invited people during the last hymn to come into the fenced section near the pulpit for prayer. That area was soon full and most of the rest of the congregation were crowding forward. Rev. Bili and the Pastor worked as one team; Daphne and I as a second team.

On Sunday people were invited to give up their equipment for doing magic, so after church the older men brought wood, gum, ginger, stones, and bones and eagerly released it to be burnt. Rev. Bili, using a metaphor, said, 'If you have any *death* in your house bring it here and burn it.' On Sunday afternoon Rev. Bili baptised 18 young adults in the sea.

There was widespread response to the Lord. Hundreds more were baptised in most places, and lots of equipment for magic and sorcery was burnt. Hundreds also sought prayer for special needs. One woman came to Rev. Bili Wilson and said, 'This is my heaviness – I am a witch.' Then she collapsed, and two other women held her on her feet while we asked the Lord to take away this evil spirit and give her the Holy Spirit.

We went to another island where the enthusiasm was the greatest yet. Older folk there, as well as the young folk, are very keen for the Lord. There was another baptism of many people in that area. Two leaders prayed for each candidate before their baptism. Afterwards the newly baptised Christians stood in a line and all who wished to do so shook each by the hand and gave words of encouragement or prophecy as the Spirit led. The biggest prayer need of the young people was to learn to read so as to read the Bible and hymn book. We prayed for them, gave them primers, and instruction for those who can read to help them daily in their homes. I also told them that betel nut gums up their brains.

There is a strong Pentecostal church in one island we visited. They had just finished a mission. They all speak Holy Spirit tongues and have no tobacco, betel nut, traditional mortuary feasts or kula trading. Whether they are right or not on these issues, it frees them to worship the Lord with such joy that I have never seen before. Their faces shine with a happy peaceful radiance. When you meet them along the road they talk enthusiastically about the Lord and his return.

They baptised 42 people on Sunday, many of them being United Church followers who will continue in the United Church. The United Church there follows the Pentecostal worship pattern in most ways. I preached at the United Church mid-day service. The singing praise session at the start turned into a congregational prayer meeting, all praying together. It seemed they would never stop!

We were delayed a day leaving there by a cyclone. Everything got wet. At least it was cool when the cyclone was around. After it cleared it was terribly hot. On almost every trip we caught fish including some big ones. One pulled my attaching knot undone and got away with the whole line. If you have any weakness in your tackle you lose all those big ones, and your tackle.

At the next island it seemed as though everyone turned to the Lord and was baptised in the sea. It was the same in two more islands.

Frightening gossip preceded us in some places. People were told that if they are baptised in the sea and then commit sin again they will die. Some people wanted to stay with the ways of worship and life practices to which they were accustomed. These people saw the revival movement as a new and different religion.

However, in each of the opposition strongholds ten to twenty people sought baptism and new life in Christ. One was a healing magician who found that after practising his art he had terrible dreams, so he wanted to be rid of his magic. Another man testified in church that he was finished with his various sorcery practices.

Rev. David Kuwab's youth was spent in the midst of sorcery and magic. He dramatically explained the use of items for magic and sorcery and physical poisons as he threw them into the fire, shouting, 'These are Satan's things.' The people showed no sign of embarrassment; just relief and joy. The young people sang praises to the Lord during the long baptism procedures. Mature Christians prayed for each person before they were taken down into the water, and another Christian prayed for them when they came back to the shore.

When the Gospel of Christ was proclaimed in one place a famous spirit healer was one of the first to respond. He was quite willing to give up his healing and killing practice. He told Rev. Kuwab, 'I have only used sorcery to kill bad people, never good people.'

Spiritual hunger generated a great demand for Muyuw Scriptures. We had to get fresh supplies, and we still ran out of New Testaments at the last island. The new large print New Testament was very popular with people of all ages. In a population of some 4,000 people we sold 700 New testaments, 150 hymn books, and 300 booklets on Spiritual Warfare which Rev. Kuwab had translated.

The Marshall Bennett Islands at the end of a three months trip were exhausting. That is where we ran into opposition. There is no medical worker for over 2,000 people. The three main islands are flat-topped craggy limestone, 500-600 feet in elevation with no water supply where the people live on the tops of the islands, except what falls from the sky. There are few good anchorages.

With no medical services the people have depended heavily on healing magicians. On one island there was hostility between members of the church, and many were suffering from malaria, coughs and scabies. The plight of some small children was pathetic. We were carrying medicine for malaria and pneumonia but nothing for scabies. Rev. Kuwab worked hard to help the church leaders overcome their differences through the power of Christ.

Although people were resistant there, at one smaller preaching place 60 were baptised. At another place 20 were baptised and gave up their magic.

We had planned and prayed for the Woodlark trip for a long time. Since 1963 we have been praying that God's Word would bear fruit among the Muyuw people.

What is now happening exceeds our greatest expectations. To our Lord Jesus be the glory.

2 My Learning Curve on Healing

Jim Holbeck

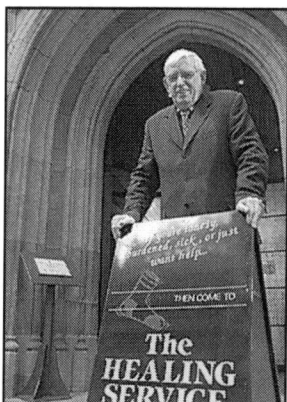

The Rev. Canon Jim Holbeck, an Anglican minister, wrote as the leader of the Healing Ministry at St Andrew's Cathedral in Sydney, 1988-2006, where he succeeded Canon Jim Glennon who commenced the weekly Wednesday healing service in 1960.

Sign at Cathedral door:

If you're lonely, burdened, sick, or just want help then come to the HEALING SERVICE

---

when God's answer comes

it will always be to his greater glory

and to our greater good.

Having entered into my early twenties with virtually no experience of church life, and thinking that religion was absolutely irrelevant, I have completely changed my mind. I am engaged in what I once thought absurd and far from reality.

That I should be writing such a chapter as this shows that changes and healing through God's Spirit can take place in today's world.

The change began with my conversion at the age of 23. I came to realise that Jesus Christ was the Son of God who had died for my sins on the cross and who was now alive. I had seen the change he made in members of my own family who had 'accepted Christ as Saviour' as they put it. Then a few people I knew asked Christ into their lives and I began to see change in them.

I was encouraged that Christ could change people radically. Surely the world would be completely changed as people heard the good news and responded to it! But no! I was soon to learn the sad fact that some people can hear the message that had excited me and transformed my life, and be totally unmoved by it.

The message of the possibility of healing by God's Spirit in today's world also excited me, and I hope it will not leave you unmoved. Here are some of the lessons the Holy Spirit is teaching me as I journey on the learning curve regarding healing.

Healing is accelerated through conversion

One of the first things I noticed with many of those who became Christians was their general improvement in health. Some would have carried a heavy burden of guilt. As they received forgiveness in Christ, the burden was lifted to a large degree. In fact, many people have come to me for counselling for some physical or emotional or relationship problem and have been introduced to Jesus and accepted him as the Lord of their lives. From that point, the healing they had been seeking in various ways became a reality in their lives.

It makes sense that the greatest healing of all is spiritual healing because it open up the body, mind and spirit to the Lord's power. I believe that we should be aiming at presenting the gospel to every person who asks for healing. After all, what is the use of their gaining all the healing in the world if they are still going to lose their souls?

We are not always given the opportunity to present the gospel to individuals who seek healing, however. Some may allow us only a limited time to talk with them and pray for them. What should our response be to such people? Here's another lesson I have learned.

God heals unbelievers

Sometimes God brings healing to those who aren't committed Christians. We might like to argue theologically about whether he should or shouldn't, but in the meantime he does anyway!

One of the results of unbelievers receiving healing is that they can realise that Christ is alive and well in his church, and in gratitude they give their lives to him. Not all do, though. I notice in the New Testament that of the ten lepers who received healing only one returned to thank Jesus. The others, nonetheless, were still healed.

There are many who come to our weekly Wednesday Healing Services in the Cathedral who are not believers, but whom the Lord heals. Many who come to receive healing meet the Healer, Jesus Christ himself. Their healing made them realise that God is alive, and that he loves and cares. So they responded to his love as they saw it revealed in the cross of Christ and as they experienced it personally through their healing.

God wants to heal the real problem

Often the Holy Spirit gives some insight into the real problem when we talk with people in a prayerful environment, having invoked the Spirit to do his work of revealing and giving wisdom. We are humbled to again realise that the Holy Spirit is indeed the real Counsellor who longs to set people free and who may reveal problem areas in people's lives.

I was once confronted with a woman who was extremely agitated because her husband had been overlooked for a position she felt he should have gained. Not knowing how to get her to be quiet so that we could talk sensibly about it, I suggested we pray! As I prayed she gave a long sigh. When the prayer finished I looked up to see a completely different woman. She was, rather, the same woman with a completely different countenance. Where, a few moments before, there had been extreme agitation, there was now an incredible serenity. She said quietly, 'God has shown me that my whole attitude is wrong. Thank you so much for your help.'

She left a transformed woman in an encounter that lasted no more than five minutes. During the following months she continued to be at peace. In my prayer, I was asking that God would be with us as we talked and that he would give us wisdom. Not one word of counsel did I offer her. God the Holy Spirit, the Counsellor, healed her as she opened up to him.

Many counsellors use the expression 'the presenting problem' to describe the situation that the counsellee presents as being their problem. But often they don't know what their real problem is. Their presenting problem is only their own perception of their need. The Holy Spirit, however, knows exactly what the root cause is and is able to reveal causes, not just symptoms. I find that this sort of thing is happening more and more in the ministry of those involved in counselling.

Christians may have deep problems

As a brand new Christian I used to think that once we became Christians all personal problems would disappear. I was astounded to begin to associate with people who had been Christians for thirty years or more but had all sorts of personal hangups and were so unloving and critical.

On my first venture into an ecumenical training class to prepare for a Beach Mission, I found those relatively younger Christians very wary of me, an Anglican, at a time when few Anglicans were involved in such ministries. I thought we were 'all one in Christ Jesus' and that we would have wonderful fellowship together. I was taken aback at such suspicion. Thank God, that depth of suspicion has lessened over the years.

Then as I began to read more of the New Testament I saw that even Christian leaders sometimes don't act Christianly. Paul in his letter to the Philippians had to rebuke two fine servants of Christ, Euodia and Syntyche, and tell them to be reconciled. On another occasion he had to correct the apostle Peter for conduct that was not helpful for the Christian cause in Galatia. It showed me that we are always going to be human no matter how Christlike we become. There will always be within us the potential for sin or insensitivity or error.

More recently I have realised we are the product of so many influences including the things said or done to us during our lifetime. Sometimes we may be aware of some of those factors. Often we are not. Some of us as Christians may be as totally committed to Christ as we are able to be, yet there may still be problem areas.

Praise God, the Lord is interested in healing even the damage we have suffered in the past, to enable us to reach more potential in him. Admitting we have some problems is not a sign of weakness or spiritual illhealth. Rather, it may be a sign that greater healing is in progress. The person who has seemingly got it all together, who is dependent upon no one, who never seems to be affected by the difficulties around them, may be the one who needs the greater healing.

Healing is a lifelong process

In Romans 12:12 Paul writes about the transformation that God brings to us as our minds are renewed. Sometimes we don't realise how the world has squeezed us into its mould, even in terms of our thinking and worldview. That has been so for many of us regarding healing and spiritual gifts. If we have a worldview that dictates that God doesn't heal today, then that becomes a tremendous barrier to receiving healing. If we believe that God can bring healing to damaged emotions, but not healing of bodies, there is little motivation to reach out for such physical healing.

Our understanding of all the 'unsearchable riches' we have in Christ is meant to grow as we continue to know him. Some of us have experienced some degree of physical healing through prayer. This has increased our capacity to believe that God can do more. The testimony of people I respected as mature Christians who had been healed of lifethreatening illnesses through the healing ministry at St Andrew's Cathedral in Sydney made me look more deeply into the whole area of healing.

I came to see that the Lord is interested in healing us not only spiritually so that we can live in heaven, but that he also wants to heal us emotionally and physically to equip us to live for him on this earth. The 'unsearchable riches' are always more than I am able to comprehend or appropriate. Part of maturing as Christians may involve appropriating more of those 'unsearchable riches' which are ours in him. That will take more than our lifetime.

Healing comes through cooperating with God

I recently preached about being doers of the word as well as hearers. For example, if God commands us to forgive others, then we must act upon that word and do so. As one woman in the congregation heard those words she prayed, 'Lord, do I need to forgive someone?' Immediately a person came to her mind. She was aware of the hurt this person had caused her years ago. She prayed a prayer thanking God for bringing this to her mind, and before God she forgave that person. She then asked God to forgive her for holding resentment against that person for so long. Just then she was filled with an incredible warmth which lasted for hours. When she phoned to share this with us some days later, she was able to say how free she felt knowing that these deep wounds had been healed. She cooperated with God as he brought her this insight and received a great healing as a result. One wonders how many people could know greater healing if they cooperated with God's nudges rather than ignoring them.

Psalm 139 has meant a great deal to Christians for generations. Recently we have discovered its significance for the healing of memories, or for healing of past hurts. The Psalm reminds us in a powerful way of God's omniscience, omnipresence and omnipotence. David states that God knows all things, and then turns that truth into a prayer. He asks God who searches all things to search him, to know him, to test his anxious thoughts, to see if there is any offensive way in him, and to lead him in the everlasting way.

David wants God to share that knowledge with him, so that he might act upon that insight. Because God knows the root cause, as well as the present symptoms, he knows the real areas that need healing. In many counselling situations these days, this fact is recognised with a prayerful reliance on the Spirit of God to bring any revelation necessary for a person's healing.

Healing comes in the Lord's way and in his time

Paul wrote in Colossians 4:2, 'Devote yourselves to prayer, keeping alert in it with thanksgiving.' He knew we need to keep our spiritual eyes open, to see how God answers our prayers. If we're really honest, we have to admit that so often in our prayers we've got it all worked out as to how best God might answer them. It will be in this way, and at this time. We often pray, expecting that God will answer in the way we think best. But his way may be quite different from what we imagined. His timetable may be much slower than ours. As Isaiah wrote so long ago, God's thoughts are not our thoughts, neither are his ways our ways. We might add, neither is his timetable our timetable.

This is especially so in healing. Often we have people come to our services for physical healing and through his word God shows them their need for salvation. They are saved, and then much later find the healing. Others miss the answer to their prayers because they are impatient. When it hasn't come according to their timetable they get resentful and hinder the healing that was coming to them in the days ahead. We may be sure that when God's answer comes it will always be to his greater glory and to our greater good.

Conclusion

Unfortunately, or should I say fortunately, there is no conclusion! Being on the learning curve with the Spirit of God means that we have to be open to new insights the Spirit brings.

When those who have studied healing for decades say that ultimately healing is a mystery, it's not because there are no truths that can be learned. Rather it's a statement that comes from the humility of learning that no matter what we think we know regarding healing, there are more lessons to be learned. I'm grateful for these lessons I've learned over the years, but I'm looking forward immensely to those that the Spirit of God will teach us in the days ahead.

From the Introduction to *Healing the Sick,*
by John G Lake, 1951, 1986

Among the tens of thousands who have been miraculously healed by the Lord under our own ministry in over 70 nations of the world, only a small fraction of them have been individually prayed for. Most of them have been healed through their own faith which came to them while meditating on the Bible truths we presented from the platform or from the printed page. ...

Those who carefully read and act upon the truths we present here obtain a broader understanding and a more solid faith than those who hear only occasional teaching on the subject of healing.

Many who have attended our crusades, but failed to receive healing, have later been miraculously healed while reading this book.

God sent his word and (it) healed them (Ps 107:20).
The gospel is the power of God to everyone that believes (Rom 1:16).

When believed and acted upon, any promise of God is transformed into the power of God.

Every promise of God contains the power of God necessary to produce what it promises, when it is believed and acted upon.

God's promises are life to those that find them, and health to all their flesh (Pr 4:22).

3 Spiritual Healing

John Blacker

The Rev. John Blacker is the founding Director of ARM - Australian Renewal Ministries.

John and his wife Valma travel extensively to pray for people and encourage renewal and revival.

Spiritual healing is complex and mysterious.
There are no simplistic answers.

Jesus healed the sick and commissioned his church to heal the sick. That ministry is still a vital part of the church's mission.

These past twenty years have been the most rewarding of my forty years of public ministry, and the most controversial. It thrust me into a healing ministry. God's calling in my life, along with a changed theological perspective, opened the way for my involvement in this ministry which was so much a part of Jesus' life and work.

Each year, as an itinerant preacher and teacher in healing and wholeness ministry, I visit numerous groups and serve in many churches, mostly mainline ones. The healing ministry is growing everywhere as the church is renewed in faith and obedience.

Faith accepts the evidence

I am often asked, 'How did you get started in the healing ministry?'

My answer usually contains the three elements of conviction, desire and practice.

The **conviction** of Jesus Christ's immutability, the one who is the same forever, came as I discarded certain dispensational teachings. That false emphasis claims that the healing ministry instituted by Christ was not meant to continue in our time; that it lasted only till the end of the apostolic age. I came to understand that if the command of Jesus to go and heal the sick was valid two thousand years ago, it must be equally valid today. If he retained the power to save souls it is hardly likely that he would have lost the lesser power to heal.

When I became fully convinced that Christ's power to heal was unchanged and that he really does heal now, I wanted to help people this way. The **desire** to be able to touch people with peace and a sense of wellness, which had been in me since I was a very small child, began to stir deeply and insatiably within me.

In **practice**, I saw God's power being released through the 'laying on of hands' causing visible physical change in people. My mind and spirit took a gigantic leap of faith which accepted the evidence before my eyes. The process can only be described as traumatic and revolutionary. I went through a theological and philosophical change. This all issued in a reawakening of what I now believe was a God inspired childhood desire to touch and heal.

I did not have long to wait to begin the practice of expectantly praying for the sick. A group of Full Gospel Businessmen visited the church where I was the pastor. They came, at my request, to conduct a healing seminar. As they ministered God's grace in power I watched with tremendous excitement and anticipation. These lay people placed their hands on those who were seeking release from pain. They were convinced that it was all occurring through faith in Jesus Christ who is the same, yesterday, today and forever. They believed in a God who really does make it happen.

Then, full of anticipation and brimming with hope, I asked if I could 'have a turn'. I recall with thankfulness that my friend Doug McFadgen readily agreed that I should pray. Not having had any previous experience or model to follow I began to put into practice what I now believe, and others who know me concur, is an authentic healing ministry. Some more recent examples of this style of ministry have confirmed it also.

As I reflect on those early renewal beginnings with a sense of wonder, love and praise, I do not have words to adequately express my thanks to God who gently and generously educated me in the presence and power of his Spirit. He showed his predestined calling to heal by releasing the gift of faith in me so that I might practice his healing ministry among hurting, bruised and broken lives.

Health is natural

Extraordinary scientific advances in many areas of medical research and health care have been accompanied and balanced by an increase in holistic health practitioners. Spiritual healing, as illustrated in Scripture and other historical literature, comes into this arena of a holistic approach to healing.

Most spiritual healers and practitioners of holistic medicine take the view that the causative factor present in many forms of human disease and dysfunction is found in systems imbalance. Holistic practitioners aim to restore such imbalances through natural or supernatural powers.

My own point of view is that health is natural but disease and dysfunction are unnatural. My aim, therefore, is to release by faith into suffering lives the appropriate supernatural power so that whatever has caused imbalances in physical, mental and spiritual ways will be overcome and corrected.

Today's rediscovery of the Christian healing ministry marks a return to a fundamental part of our Lord's teaching. The number of individuals and church groups practising spiritual healing through sacramental rites, laying on of hands, anointing with oil, and the prayer of faith is increasing every day. Praise God, miraculous healings reminiscent of biblical examples occur with greater frequency. Through the revival of the Christian healing ministry we have been immeasurably blessed.

Today, more clearly than ever before, I see the healing ministry of the church as an authentic answer to the agnostic belief that Christianity is mere legend, or only a philosophy, or solely an historical event finished two thousand years ago. To know the healing Christ is to see Christianity as what it is meant to be; a dynamic, living reality.

The whole person

Spiritual healing as demonstrated by Jesus deals with the care of the whole person, body, mind and spirit. It calls people to salvation and to closer relationship with God. However, not all who are healed seek salvation, and not all who are healed in spirit are also healed physically.

Some claim that when healing through prayer does not occur there will be psychological damage. Also it is suggested that those who are not healed will tend to blame themselves or doubt the reality of their faith. We have found this to be a false understanding. Those healed in spirit know that an unhealed body is no more the will of God than a sinful world is his will. Both result from universal human failure, corporate faithlessness and mass disobedience. Centuries of unbelief and sin cannot be instantly dispelled. The thunder of human doubt and misunderstanding cannot be immediately silenced.

Nevertheless, I am convinced that total health is the primary will of God, and I will not cease to proclaim that Jesus is the Saviour of our bodies and minds as well as our spirits. Therefore, while total healing may not immediately occur, or not ever during some people's earthly life because of unknown or alien factors, nothing can impede God's healing of the spirit. This is the basis of true wholeness. None who turn to God remain totally unhealed.

Repentance opens the door

Faith unlocks the door to God's power but repentance opens it. This dimension of remission from sin presents a great obstacle for some people who find it difficult to believe that what Jesus said must simply be done.

The testimony of those who have seen and felt the incredible effect of his words concerning repentance cannot be ignored. If we emasculate his teaching, selecting only what we want to believe and rejecting what we would prefer to discard, we find ourselves left with a powerless ideology instead of a dynamic religion.

Our own sin is one of those aspects of Christianity which most of us would probably like to forget, or even deny. But the destructiveness of sin in our lives, and the full salvation of God's forgiveness are central to Christ's teaching. This lies at the heart of the church and is an essential part of the healing ministry. To deny our sin is to deny our salvation, for we cannot be saved from what we do not have.

The list of our sins is long. We cannot describe it all here. The more obvious sins of the flesh are pretty well known. They should not be minimised. However, the sins most frequently overlooked are the sins of the spirit: hostility, resentment, anger, fear, jealousy. These most flagrantly violate the law of love issued by our Lord. To break this law is to commit an offence against God. We then suffer the consequences of physical and mental disease as well as spiritual sickness. The best health insurance cover I know starts with the declaration, 'O God, I repent and am heartily sorry for this .... , my sin.'

The force of humility

Having noted that unrepentance can mitigate against spiritual healing, and having pointed to some common sins of the spirit, I want to single out pride as the greatest culprit.

The saints of history all put their finger on pride as the most common of sins which beset us. It is also the most dangerous because it is insidious and far reaching in its effects. It may not be inaccurate to claim that pride is actually behind and responsible for all other sin.

Michelangelo was painting the Sistine Chapel when he was approached one day by an admiring inquirer who asked the famous painter, 'What is the first article of the Christian religion?'

The answer came quickly, 'Humility.'

'And what is the second article?' asked the eager questioner.

'Humility,' Michelangelo replied.

Desiring to press the point further, the inquirer asked, 'Sir, what is the third article?'

'Humility,' came the unhesitating reply from the great man of God.

Pride has nothing to do with self respect which our Lord surely meant us to have and to maintain or he would never have issued his second commandment. Pride means the sort of self aggrandisement which precludes humility. Humility is the basis of our relationship with God.

Without humility we cannot have true faith for faith involves complete confidence in someone other than ourselves. Whatever other virtues we may possess, if we do not have humility we are lost. However grave our faults, if we are humble enough to confess them we can be saved and healed.

Willingness releases spiritual energy

God has made us volitional beings. We choose. Because of this volition the psalmist suggests that we need to be willing in the day of God's power (Psalm 110:3).

As I have ministered through twenty years to thousands of people with laying on of hands I have concluded that little happens in the way of transformation in the lives of those prayed for until there is an act of will which enables the release of God's healing power. When we surrender ourselves in obedience and submit willingly to God's mercy and grace, then healing power can flow.

This is especially so for those who pray for others. God uses willing humans as means of his mercy and grace. There is that fine moment, I believe, when by faith we consciously let go and let God make it happen.

It seems logical, and is supported from my own experience, that when those praying are willing to be a channel of God's grace and those being prayed for have a wholehearted readiness and willingness to receive, then healing is most likely to happen, provided the willingness is accompanied by humility and repentance.

Not everyone prayed for is totally healed. However, significant numbers testify that something good has taken place. There are often visible signs of God's power on them or feelings present which signify changes for the good. There may be a sense of heat or warmth, tingling, some euphoria, or physical adjustments felt. These are often indications of divine healing being manifested through the Holy Spirit.

Also, different people exercise different gifts of healing (1 Corinthians 12:28). In my own ministry there is most evidence of healing where structural problems exist, where there is pain because of injury and where there is stress. Other kinds of healings occur but these areas respond most in my ministry. It appears that different ministries of healing flow through different people with particular healing gifts or powers.

Spiritual healing is complex and mysterious. There are no simplistic answers. We need to maintain a proper and balanced biblical approach and not treat it lightly or tritely. To draw back from a ministry of healing is to quench a major dimension of God's kingdom among us.

I am convinced that God does want all people to enjoy health in every area of life (John 10:10; 3 John 2). So we should use every good means at our disposal to receive and impart this wholeness.

4 Deliverance and Freedom

Colin Warren

The Rev. Dr Colin Warren wrote as a Uniting Church minister and former Principal of Alcorn College in Brisbane and Founder of Freedom Life Ministries. He ministered with teams who counselled and prayed with the sick and afflicted.

Christ has paid the price to set us free, but many Christians are not free. They are bound by compulsions or problems such as fear, grief, hurt, anxiety, suicidal thoughts, anger, lust, hate, sickness, or other emotional disorders.

Yet, many Scriptures promise freedom. Here are some:

'So if the Son makes you free, you will be free indeed' (John 8:36).

'For freedom Christ has set us free' (Galatians 5:1).

'Now the Lord is the Spirit, and where the Spirit of the Lord is, there is freedom' (2 Corinthians 3:17).

Many people in need of counselling, however, are not free. Why are there so many Christians who are not free? Does it mean that we cannot take these Scriptures literally? Or is there another answer? Our experience has shown that freedom is possible and we can take the Scriptures at face value.

The answer lies in taking Jesus seriously. The Christian church in many places, particularly in the western world, has not accepted the threefold task given to it by Jesus, that is to preach the gospel, heal the sick, and cast out demons (Matthew 10:78; Mark 6:13; Luke 9:12).

The area that most often needs attention to set people free is the area of the emotions. Paul's prayer in 1 Thessalonians 5:23 says, 'may your spirit and soul and body be kept sound and blameless at the coming of our Lord Jesus Christ.' Our whole being is involved.

This can be represented by three concentric circles. The inner circle represents the spirit, the core of our being. Outside of that the middle circle represents the soul consisting of mind, emotions and will. Outside of that again the body is represented by the outer circle.

When we accept forgiveness obtained for us by Jesus on the cross and open our lives to God, God the Holy Spirit enters and dwells at the core of our being. No evil spirits can enter the core of our being when we are born of the Spirit of God. They can, however, afflict us to a lesser or greater degree at the levels of our soul and body. A result of that affliction is that we lose the fullness of freedom offered by Jesus.

All is not lost, however. Jesus gave power to the church to remove the offending intruders. This power was given to the twelve when he sent them out and also to the seventy two who came back rejoicing because the demons submitted to them (Matthew 10:78; Luke 10:17).

Can a Christian be demonised?

The answer is both yes and no. Demons cannot take over the spirit of a Christian. They can, however, invade the soul and the body. Many beautiful Christian people have problems in the areas of their emotions, minds, wills, and bodies. These are areas that evil powers can invade. This robs many of God's people of the total freedom obtained for them at such cost by our Lord. This state need not continue because Jesus gave the church power to remove demons and set the captives free.

A common false idea is that a person can only be demonised as the result of deliberate involvement with the occult. Evil powers or spirits have other opportunities to oppress a person beside occult involvement. Some of these need to be understood so that we can minister God's healing and deliverance to the oppressed.

These ills or oppressions do not always involve demonisation, so we need to avoid the opposite errors of seeing demons in every situation or of ignoring them altogether. We cannot attribute all pain, sickness, infirmity, or other ills to demonic spirits. Ministry in this area requires the use of gifts of the Holy Spirit including discernment of spirits, and words of knowledge and wisdom (1 Corinthians 12:810) coupled with training in this spiritual field to ascertain if spirits are responsible.

Demonic oppression may be caused in many ways

1. Deep hurt in interpersonal relationships

A woman confined to bed with severe pain was referred to us by her doctor. She did not respond to pain killing drugs and had experienced severe emotional distress. After receiving counselling, which included casting out several spirits, she was able to leave her bed. Approximately two weeks later she asked for further counselling. On that occasion she was set free from other spirits which included those of infirmity, pain and sickness. Immediately the major areas of pain left her. When I met her approximately four weeks later she was free from pain, was filled with a new joy of living and was seeking to help others in need.

If we allow fear, anger, hurt, grief, loss, hate, bitterness, jealousy, rejection or other emotional areas to fester in our lives, or if through circumstances we cannot control they gain a foothold in us, that can allow evil powers to oppress us with a spirit associated with that particular emotion.

2. Inherited problems from forebears

These may be seen as having only a genetic base. Yet they are often also of a spiritual nature. I have frequently found that such things as sickness, as well as other disorders, have come because of an ancestor's involvement in behaviour which has passed on a curse to future generations.

One such case is of a successful business man whose life was made difficult by internal physical problems requiring three operations. When he came for prayer several spirits were oppressing him. These were bound to the truth revealing that his grandfather's relationship with people involved in Luciferian rites had given Satan permission to oppress this man. When the spirits were cast out his condition healed and he was able to have a much closer relationship with God in his prayer and devotional life. This is just one of many such cases.

3. After severe accidents or sickness

Sometimes people are vulnerable to oppressing powers of evil after serious accidents or illness. Spiritual forces of sickness, grief or infirmity may find entry.

A woman in her late sixties had been totally deaf in one ear and partially deaf in the other. When she was twelve years of age abscesses had burst in both ears leaving her hearing seriously impaired. At first I thought that her physical impairment was an automatic result of the abscesses. However, I was constrained by the Holy Spirit to bind and cast out the spirit of deafness. She subsequently went to her specialist and had further tests. These confirmed that her previously totally deaf ear was now hearing.

4. Deliberate sin

Probably the most prevalent area of deliberate involvement and continuing addiction applies to sexual sins. If a person is habitually involved with such things as pornographic literature or videos, sex outside of marriage, or masturbation, those actions give unclean spirits legal right to afflict the person in that way. We have ministered to many people with these problems whom God has graciously set free.

5. Transference from another person

Given certain conditions a person can be infected with spiritual oppression affecting someone else. An example of this is when a person is in a fear provoking situation with someone who has a spirit of fear oppressing him or her. This can be the condition in which the spirit of fear multiplies and infects the other person also.

6. Involvement with the occult

We are experiencing large numbers of people who have had a deliberate openness to or involvement with the occult. One example is of a seventeen year old girl who from the age of ten had been gradually getting deeper into occult things. This addiction led to Satan worship with its ugly rituals and sacrifices including eating the flesh of things sacrificed. She was trapped into something she could not escape, thinking there was no power that could deliver her. She came for help and claimed Jesus as her Lord. The spirits were then cast out and she has learned how to live a victorious Christian life and helps others to be set free.

7. The result of a curse

Curses may not be just empty words. Demonic oppression can be the result of a curse placed on a person either deliberately or unwittingly by someone else where harm is intended and declared against another.

We ministered to a man in his late twenties who from earliest childhood had sexual desire toward males. He had never allowed this desire to be gratified but had suffered greatly from it. He had no desire for women. We have discovered many times that this so called genetic problem was in reality a spiritual problem. In his case, after three unsuccessful attempts to help him, we were told through a word of knowledge to pray and fast for some days. It was then revealed that the problem was the result of a curse on the family from a former generation. Such was the strength of the curse that we were told it would be two years before he was completely free, even though prayer ministry with him was successful.

8. Oppression by astral travel

Invasion may occur by those involved in astral travel who deliberately seek to enter another person. This requires the breaking of spiritual, emotional and physical ties, and the doorways to the spirit need to be sealed to prevent re-entry.

A university student came for counselling because she had the eerie feeling that she was being watched when she was in her home. As we prayed a name was given to one of the team. The student knew that the person named was involved in astral travel and had taken an unnatural interest in her though she did not encourage him. Through prayer, authority was taken over this spirit, the chains binding her to him were broken and the doorways of entry were closed and anointed with the anointing oil of the Holy Spirit. She had no further trouble.

These problems have all been dealt with on many occasions through prayer and deliverance ministry by teams sensitive to the Holy Spirit. People can be set free.

Freedom from principalities and powers

Our western worldview of rationalism has hidden from us the real meaning of much of Scripture. This is being rediscovered now.

An example is Ephesians 6:12, 'For our struggle is not against enemies of blood and flesh, but against the rulers, against the authorities, against the cosmic powers of this present darkness, against the spiritual forces of evil in the heavenly places.'

We have not understood the significance of this for winning the world for the kingdom of God. Many Scripture passages indicate there are hierarchies of demonic powers. I have described how evil spirits may be cast out of people and this sets them free to be the persons God created them to be. However, if we are going to carry out the great commission under the authority of Jesus to whom all authority has been given in heaven and on earth (Matthew 28:1820), then we will need to use the means God has given us to do so. That will involve waging war on the principalities and powers of evil including conflict with world authorities of Satan and the territorial spirits controlling demonic powers over countries and cities.

The Holy Spirit convicted our church of this some years ago. We entered into prayer for eighteen months before God have us the names of the principalities and powers over our city. Then, after a day of prayer and fasting we were told by the Holy Spirit to have a further week of prayer and fasting. At the close of that week God revealed the names of these powers and how to bind them. This was done.

Since that time many people came inquiring about salvation and for counselling. The Lord has taught us that although it took the whole church to be in prayer for eighteen months before these strong spirits could be bound initially, those Satanic powers need to be bound daily.

All Satanic powers were totally defeated by Jesus' atoning work on the cross. If we do not take advantage of the victory Jesus won then we as a church are not using the weapons God has given us in the power of the Spirit to win the world for Christ. This is why Jesus spoke of binding the strong man and plundering his goods (Matthew 12:2829). As we bind these territorial and ruling spirits God's power is able to pierce the darkness and the convicting power of the Holy Spirit brings many into the kingdom of God.

Caution! Do not attempt to bind principalities and powers until the church has had sufficient prayer and God the Holy Spirit has given permission and instructions. The degree of prayer required will vary with the strength of the powers being bound. This varies with each situation, hence the need to be guided by the Holy Spirit. These powerful forces can cause great affliction to the unwary.

Real freedom through the authority of Jesus Christ our Lord in the power of the Holy Spirit will come when the church fulfils its threefold commission given by Jesus to preach the kingdom of God, to heal the sick and to cast out demons.

Jesus Christ is Lord. He reigns. Just as we can respond to his reign for our salvation, so we can respond for healing and deliverance in the power of his Spirit in our lives and in the world.

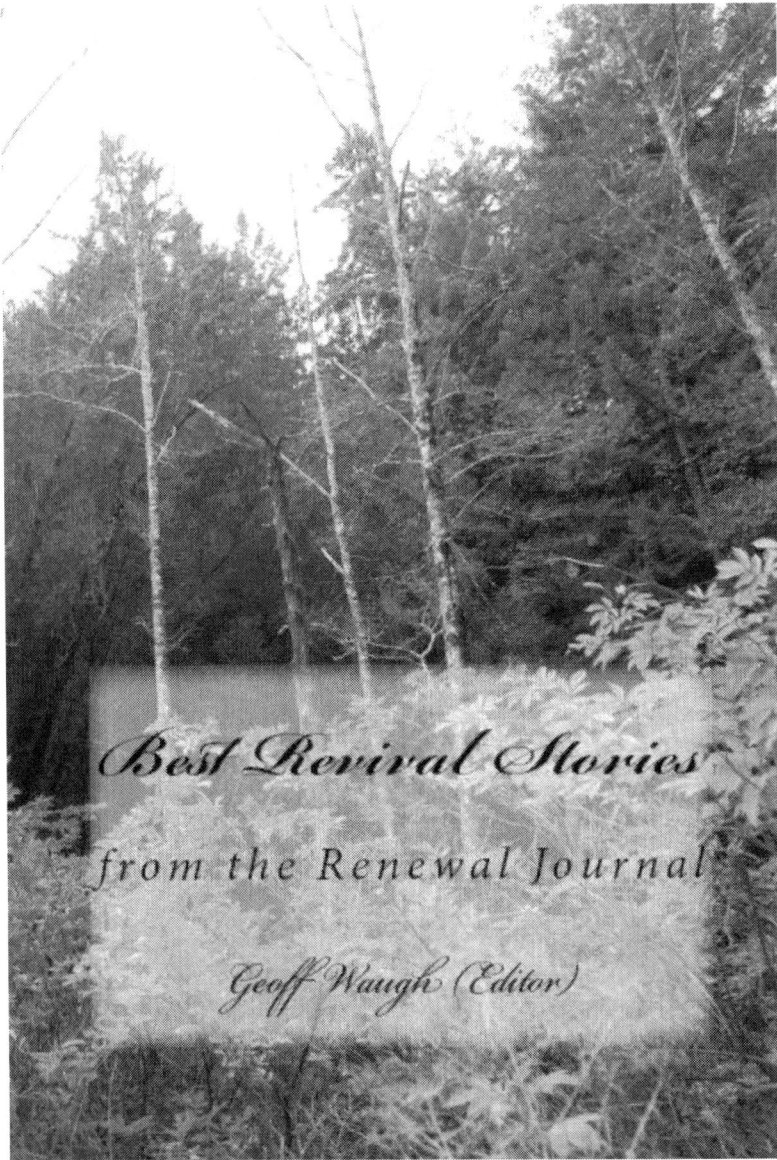

Best Revival Stories
from the Renewal Journal

5 Christian Wholeness Counselling

John Warlow

Dr John Warlow is a Christian psychiatrist working in Brisbane within a professional and charismatic context for the healing of the whole person.

After years of prayer, vision and planning, we have established a place of healing the whole person from a Christian perspective. It is called the Christian Wholeness Counselling Centre

This is a place where Christians and non-Christians can be seen by Professional Counselling Consultants from a number of disciplines, including Psychology, Social Work, Occupational Therapy, the Pastoral area and Psychiatry. It is a place where our passions are to strive for excellence in the area of psychiatry, psychology and the social sciences, and counselling within the context of a Biblical theology.

The psychiatric, psychological, social and spiritual issues are addressed within a framework of professional Christian counselling, facilitating one's journeying toward wholeness. We acknowledge the spiritual dimension of the person in addition to the physical, psychological and social dimensions. We invite clients to integrate the spiritual aspect of their life within a Christian counselling context.

It is also a place where professional counsellors can develop their skills, integrating their Christian beliefs with their professional practice. The centre helps to equip and train Christian counsellors and the church in Christian counselling and pastoral work. All this is done in an ethical manner with integrity and compassion.

Here, the problems relating to the whole person can be addressed. These include personal, emotional, psychiatric, behavioural, physical, spiritual, social and family, educational, career related, stress, and trauma related problems. The problems can relate to the whole person so the avenues for healing are focussed on each part of the person.

In essence, helping the person to face their failures and their pain in the presence of God and from there to move on to practise the presence of God is the spiritual pathway to healing. Healing comes not only in practising the presence of God, but also in walking alongside with a fellow human being, and in conjunction with a supportive church network. Thus, healing does not come in a vacuum but is done in the context of the priesthood of all believers, the presence of God and being part of the body of Christ.

Integrated approach to healing

Spiritual healing or prayer in itself often is not the only thing which needs to happen for healing. People often need other interventions. That may be medication, marital therapy, or some of the other forms of professional interventions. God never made us just to be spiritual, although the spiritual is central. God also made our bodies and our minds which often groan.

Our bodies and brains may need medication, and our minds therapy. These are provided in many forms at the Christian Wholeness Counselling Centre. They include: Individual Therapy, Group Therapy, Family Therapy, Marital Therapy, Child Therapy, Adolescent Therapy, Cognitive Behaviour Therapy, Psychodynamic Psychotherapy, Pastoral Counselling, Psychiatric Treatment, Educational Assessment, Career Guidance, Grief Counselling, Crisis Counselling, Trauma Therapy (EMDR), Stress Management, Anger Management, Conflict Management, Assertiveness Training, Communication and Social Skills Training.

The likelihood of success in healing depends on how motivated or desperate the person is to change, the extent of how much they feel they can be involved in changing compared to how hopeless they might feel, and how severe their problems are in terms of physical, psychological, social or spiritual ones.

The longer the problems have been going on, even back into previous generations, the harder it seems to be for change to occur. Intervention may include prayer for inner healing, breaking of past bondages, and on-going medication or counselling support. For some healing happens at a faster rate, for others it may take a number of years.

Healing is significantly enhanced if, in the context of coming to the Centre, a person can be free to be real and open in the Body of Christ. Thus the importance of close fellowship is vital. The church itself is a major organ for healing.

In summary, Christian Wholeness Counselling looks at the whole person in the context of their relationship with God and the church, and their own social network. It acknowledges that our bodies are yet unredeemed. It acknowledges that at times God does work in miraculous ways, but normally tears will not be dried or taken away until we reach heaven.

Healing follows a sequence. Here are essential steps on the pathway to wholeness.

Admit and be Real about Failure

START HERE: The place for healing to begin is where one walks alongside another – one step beside and one step behind. In that posture, the person is strengthened to be able to face the pain, their failures and their sin. This often seems to be the hardest part but is where healing starts.

As the darkness is brought into the light, then that which was hidden can be addressed. Where many find it hard to walk on a road to healing, is this very first step of even acknowledging the problem. For true healing this needs to be acknowledged to oneself, to God and to another human being. Admitting and being real about one's failures and sins is the place to start. The Christian Wholeness Counselling Centre allows this to occur in a place where the issues of the whole person can be addressed.

Believe and Receive Forgiveness

THE 1ST STEP: Having faced and, to some extent, owned the problems, the first step of healing on a spiritual dimension is to return to the rock from which one was hewn, to receive the things which God has done. This step to healing is through a repentance, a returning, a step of faith rather than by the primary strivings of our wills and our own efforts.

This step is one of believing and receiving God's forgiveness. It happens initially at conversion, and needs to be repeated frequently. As we remember and return to what God has done, rather than trying to strive to better ourselves, change can come. It is through this step that one returns to the rock from which one was hewn, to receive the things which God has done to stand in one's true position.

YOUR POSITION: Where is the position to which we need to return? What has God done which is healing? What is it that is there for healing, even when we have failed and fallen? God has done four major things for us in this area: he has provided us with his presence, he has placed us and set us apart for himself, he has given us his purposes, and he has provided all we need. This enables us to say, 'I am yours and you are mine', even in our pain or failure as well as in wholeness.

First, God's presence is with us: Emmanuel. Although we can quench the Holy Spirit, we have been sealed with him as he has been stamped on to our hearts. For those who are truly his, we cannot rub off that stamp. Even though the prodigal son felt no longer worthy to be a son, the Father thought otherwise. Even in our darkest moments, the darkness cannot turn off the light. Even in our lowest periods, God is beneath us. Even where sin abounds, grace abounds all the more. Healing comes as we realise God has not abandoned nor forsaken us, but is there for us right in the context of our pain. God owns us despite our sin.

Second, God has placed us close to himself. He has given us an identity of being a child of the Father with his Spirit indwelling us. Being identified with Christ in God lifts up the head of the shameful and weary traveller.

Third, God has purposed us to relate with him in intimacy, in Jesus by his Spirit. This gives us a reason for living which nothing can touch, even in the context of suffering. God's purposes remain constant despite our unfaithfulness. This leads the wandering person to have a God-given clarity and perspective on where they have come from and where they are going. So, even in our groaning, with all around seeming to overwhelm us, God's purposes can still be fulfilled. All things can work for good. His good is our intimacy with Jesus. Our imitation of Jesus can grow. Our conformity to him can be renewed. Our sense of companionship and closeness to God can deepen.

Fourth, God has provided for us his forgiveness and his freedom, leading us to his fullness.

Our lives and experiences so often betray what God has done, leaving us feeling hypocritical, shameful, and in effect no different from what we would be if we were non-Christians. Our lives more often than not are lives of the wilderness rather than those of the Promised Land.

The tendency then is to believe much more in our failings and feelings than in what God has done because the two do not seem to match up. Having faced our own sins and failures and returned to what God has done, we can stand in his grace, mercy, and forgiveness.

In the context of facing the reality of oneself, the head of the wounded and fallen can be lifted up and can see another reality, the reality of God and what he has done. Through being real about these realities a new perspective and new direction can again be followed. So the shameful may stand upright, in grace and access to God; the lost may belong; the fallen and failed may get up, yet again.

Choose to Respond to Freedom

2ND STEP: From this position, we can move on in the freedom which God provides. Receiving the provision of God's freedom leads us to relate with God in the fullness of his Spirit and walk in wholeness and healing. Only as we receives what God has done in our life can we move on to practise the presence of God in the context of our humanity.

But how do we receive and respond to this freedom? Where does this freedom come from and where does it lead? How do we take this second step? This is where the mystery of God's provision applies.

Because he has placed us in Christ, we also died with him and have been raised with him.

We know, however, that we are very much alive and our sinful nature abounds. How is it then that we continue to sin? A major reason appears to be not only the abuse of God's grace, but the unbelief of what God has done. The unbelief is partly because the reality of our experience shouts louder than the reality of what God has done.

Thus in Romans 6, Paul provides 3 steps to receive and respond to this freedom.

* First (v 6), we must know and remember what God has done. We must realise that we have been crucified with Christ. We should have been warned of this when we became Christians.

* Second (v 11), we must believe this and reckon ourselves to be dead to sin and alive to God in Christ Jesus.

* Third (vs 12-13), we must then yield ourselves to God and not to our own sinful desires.

Our bodies are very much alive but our self-centred nature has been crucified with Christ. However, it is only as we know this, it is only as we believe this and as we then put this into practice that we appropriate and apply what God has done. As we take these steps in the face of our selfishness, a Godliness can slowly and falteringly develop. There can be a renewing of our minds and a conformity to Jesus.

This is a gradual walk and needs to be applied to each situation. As we do this, as we present our bodies and our minds as a living sacrifice, to be renewed by God, then we can move on to practise the presence of God, to fellowship with God and to love others. Then we can start to move into true Christian wholeness.

YOUR PRACTICE: As we respond to God and to what he has done, we can move our position into the practice of Christian wholeness and healing. Wholeness was defined best by Jesus when he said, 'Love the Lord your God with all your heart, and with all your soul, and with all your mind and with all your strength ... Love your neighbour as yourself'. So as we struggle with issues, we start to bring into God's light and into God's presence these problems and, together with God and a fellow traveller, we can move on.

The pains and hurts of the past and the present can be cast on God; we are now not alone. As they are faced, the past which lives in the present can be let go on and released. Forgiving others starts to become possible. Changing thoughts, perceptions and behaviours in relation to oneself and others can begin again. Er go on again. Love arises. The salvation which God has worked in us starts to become worked out. So we are freed to respond and to relate with God.

In the context of pain and sin, we can actively relate with God and in doing so can actualise and realise the presence of God in their humanity. Being very real, we can start to interact with God, to imitate Jesus and to slowly experience some kind of intimacy with the Trinity. We can start to live who we are, to walk by the Spirit and not just to be born of the Spirit.

Shame and guilt no longer hold their power. We are free to leave our self-centredness to live a God-centred life. We are free to respond to God even as the Psalmist did, in ruthless reality. We can now move from the isolation and aloneness of darkness into abiding in God.

This is not 'airy fairy' or living in some supernatural spiritual cloud. This is relating to God and being free to do so as a very real human being. Having reconnected with God, hope revives and we can once more go to others to love them and to bring God's healing to them. There is power to go to those who have hurt us, in our families especially. There is power to be real about the pains which we have received from others and yet to go and to seek and touch our offenders with the wounded hands of Jesus.

Spiritual warfare can be done. This is practising the presence of God. This is the narrow road which brings life. This is knowing God and showing God. This is being filled with the Spirit. This is the narrow path that leads to life, and healing.

RETURN TO THE START: Yet so quickly practising the presence of God seems to disappear yet again in our sins and failings from which we have just come. And so, returning to the reality of our failures, we can AGAIN turn to our position in God and from there move on to practising a God-centred way of life. This is not sinless perfection, but a spiral – from practising the presence of God to falling back into sin to repenting, to walking on with God. As we do this, it is more than going round in circles. We spiral up on a journey, as with wings like eagles, slowly rising in sanctification. As we take hold of God in this way, God takes hold of us and as we open to God, God fills us with his Spirit.

This is the spiritual aspect of healing – abiding in God, and is something which we need to encourage in each other. However, when things get too hard, a place like the Christian Wholeness Counselling Centre can further facilitate healing. Consultants cannot of themselves do the work, but in closeness to the suffering clients, and in the presence of God, all three in a healing triangle can walk the road to true healing, to wholeness, to Shalom.

Summary: a sequence of healing and wholeness

START HERE: "I **A**dmit and am **R**eal about my **F**ailures."

1ST STEP: "I **B**elieve and **R**eceive God's **F**orgiveness."

YOUR POSITION: God's Presence, Placing, Purposes and Provisions.

2ND STEP: "I **C**hoose to **R**espond to God's **F**reedom."

YOUR PRACTICE: "I **D**o live and **R**elate with God in the **F**ullness of his Spirit."

RETURN TO THE START.

See also: christianwholeness.com

6 A Healing Community

Spencer Colliver

Spencer Colliver, a former elder and coordinator of home groups in the O'Connor Uniting Church, Canberra, and Co-ordinator of networks of home churches wrote extensively about house churches and home groups.

In the midst of our human frailty we can experience a wholeness in the Holy Spirit which transcends our weakness.

'Stand in faith for your healing,' they exhorted him. They had prayed for his healing with sincerity and compassion, but the long road of days, weeks, months, perhaps years, of 'standing in faith' stretched ahead. Who would stand with him?

During those days when doubt and uncertainty assail the heart of faith, who would be there to encourage and pray with him again and again until the conflict was clearly over?

If ever there is need of a small company of Christian friends and pilgrims, it is in such cases. How often the physical dis-ease is a symptom of loneliness, resentment, or buried anger. The care of others in a close knit group, ministering the grace and forgiveness of Jesus can dispel the loneliness, melt the anger, and affirm the healing process.

The small group needs to learn the Christian graces of perseverance, longsuffering, gentleness, faithfulness and hope for others. Those who have entered deeply into a small group experience will know the personal pain, doubt and fear borne on behalf of one another. You stand in faith for a brother or sister. Like the four men who let down their friend through the roof to the feet of Jesus, you bring your brother or sister again and again to Jesus.

Caring communities

Recently a good friend of mine died of a brain tumour. He had experienced several years of remission of what was an inoperable condition. This remission was a direct result of prayer for healing. During the subsequent years, to a large extent he stood alone in his church and there was little experience of a surrounding healing community. Would it have made a difference? I do not know. I do know, however, we have often failed in our healing ministry because there has been no community of Christians in daily, weekly, close-knit support. To be in community means to have all things in common – even our pain and sickness.

Cures are to be looked for, not only in the sick person, but also in the community. R. A. Lambourne (1963: 110) expresses it this way: 'So a man who has a congenital defect about which he is chronically embittered, may be saved by the loving service and prayers of another person or group and yet retain his congenital deformity, whilst one of the group who has been involved may be relieved of a peptic ulcer.' Experience has shown us that those with such defects may also have significant healing through persevering, persistent prayer.

The recorded experience of God's direct intervention in healing over the past twenty years has often been the accounts of healings received through the ministry of the healing evangelist. Books on healing were initially a description of the way God intervened in healing in a wide variety of physical, emotional and spiritual conditions through that healing ministry.

Subsequent literature has come to grips with biblical principles of healing and methods of preparing all the people of God to pray for healing and exercise the gift of healing, but little has been said or taught about the importance of people being immersed in a healing community.

It is good that those at the healing meeting are asked to stand in faith for the person prayed for, but what happens after the meeting has concluded? Many are completely healed and may well stand alone, but not all. What community will these have to sustain their faith as the healing work goes on?

In some fellowships, healing teams are used so that the individualistic approach is modified. The teams are prepared to handle whatever may emerge, whether it be physical healing, deliverance from demonic oppression, or the healing of past hurts and broken relationships. Wholeness of life is the focus. Yet the need for continuing care may not be met.

A person from a strong Christian fellowship who experiences the healing grace of God can depend upon the support of that fellowship. There the healing process will be strengthened in the combined faith and mutual commitment to one another.

It is quite a different experience for people with a history of broken relationships and little personal discipline to find a community of people who will lovingly guide the formation of their Christian life and growth in faith. They need a caring community committed to support them.

Committed communities

The formation of Christian life and character – the whole area of Christian discipleship – needs a long period of painstaking care from the committed community. A young woman convert with a history of broken foster homes and drug taking experienced significant healing, but her life habits and attitudes formed over many years needed to be changed. She usually stayed in bed till the afternoon. For months an older woman would travel across town to her one-room flat, wake her, and see her washed, dressed, and out into the everyday world.

We long and pray for these alienated people to be brought into the Kingdom. Yet we recoil from some of the long term implications of lives which need to be made in the image of Christ. How beautiful that we are not alone. The Holy Spirit grants his gifts of knowledge, wisdom, discernment, courage and healing. We also have one another, if we can genuinely find oneness of purpose and love or common unity. That is community.

Christian community is an ideal we cherish but find difficult to achieve. In the many communities to which we belong – a sociology dictionary lists some ninety – we submit only a small portion of our lives. An ultimate goal of Christian community is to have all things in common. However, in our Western church we have absorbed a materialistic individualism which results in a rejection of strong commitment to group values. A pietistic approach to the Christian life emphasises our individual personal relationship to God and tends to devalue the group relationships.

The instructions to the New Testament churches were primarily for groups, not individuals. 'Saints', commonly used in the New Testament for Christians, occurs there 62 times and 61 of these are in the plural form. We belong together.

Church communities need to provide a structure and opportunity for people to so relate with each other that these relationships show them how to become healing people. Christians in small groups in sensitive communication with each other a more likely to be aware of the needs of the wounded.

To a greater or lesser extent we are 'wounded healers'. Our own wounds give a sense of identification with the wounded. We have all known, for example, how loneliness and loss bite into our emotional stability. James Lynch, in *The Broken Heart: the medical consequences of loneliness* (1979: 181), says, 'The lack of companionship, the sudden loss of love and chronic human loneliness are significant contributors to serious disease (including cardiovascular disease) and premature death'.

He adds that 'the true revolution of our times is the disappearance of friendship and that has gone hand in hand with the loss of community'. Those who lack the surrounding comfort and support of an intimate community lack one of the most powerful antidotes to stress and disease. In a neighbourhood group members can be immediately responsive to emergent need. The immediate awareness of need and the continuing healing issues out of fellowship; the formation of a new lifestyle from the witness of what Jesus has done in the lives of others.

How often, too, the healer need healing. Pressure and stress need to be discerned, understood and prayed for in the whole group.

No group will be free of every ailment and oppression, but what a joy it is to have fellow pilgrims to be part of one's whole life. In the midst of our human frailty we can experience a wholeness in the Holy Spirit which transcends our weakness. One of our friends, dying of cancer and surrounded by her own healing community, entered into a wholeness not experienced previously.

As Lambourne (1963: 110) puts it, 'This type of situation is exemplified by the dying patient who makes of dying, as of life, not just "one damned thing after another", but a "reasonable, lively and holy sacrifice", a time of growing in wisdom and stature. Those who are near, serving, easing the pain, enter, if they wish, into the wholeness into which the patient by faith has entered ... so the community in acts of healing, relieving suffering, and suffering together, enters the communion of saints, the community of those made whole.'

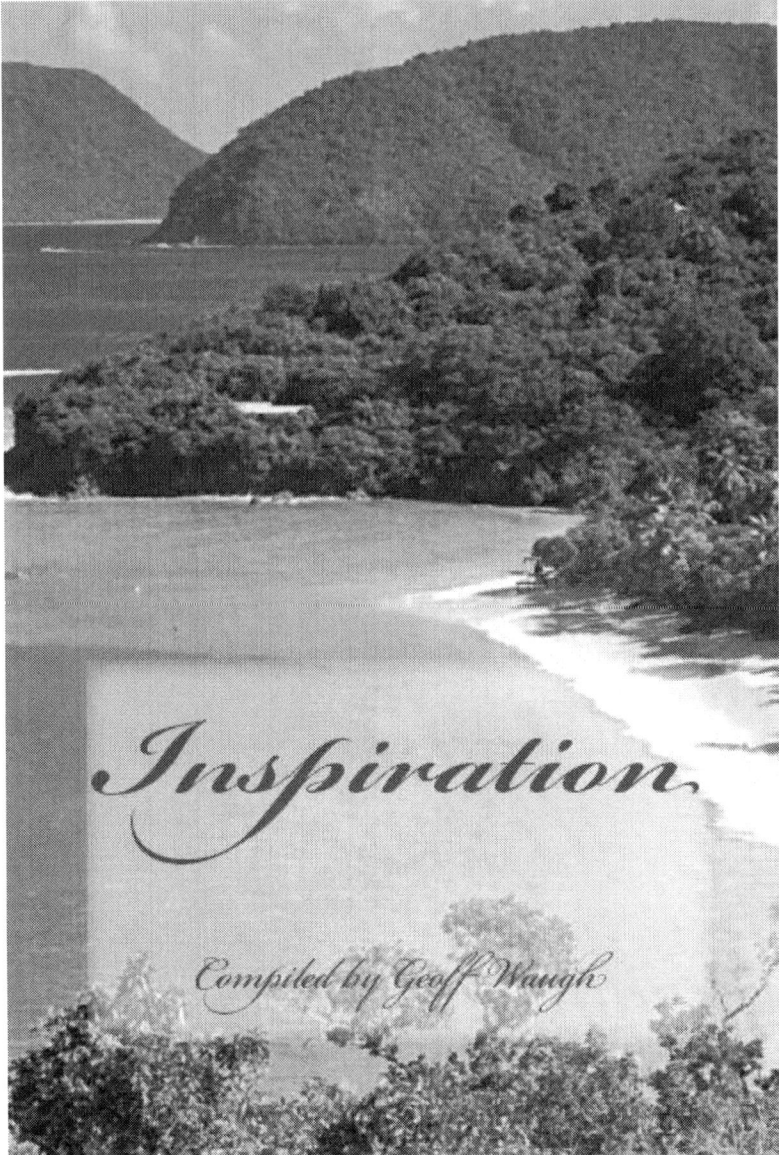

Inspiration
See renewaljournal.com

7 Divine Healing and Church Growth

Donald Mcgavran

Dr Donald Mcgavran was the founding Dean of the School of World Mission at Fuller Theological Seminary. His seminal books Bridges of God *(1955) and* Understanding Church Growth *(1970, 1980) pioneered scholastic books on church growth. This ground-breaking paper, presented to the Christian and Missionary Alliance Missionaries at Lincoln, Nebraska in 1979, contains powerful case studies.*

The problem of church growth faces all of us. Many of us are working where we have had little growth. Wherever our churches are sealed off, ethnically, economically, or educationally, the people from other classes of society do not ordinarily join us. This very common problem affects not just the Christian and Missionary Alliance. You have less of it than some other missionary societies. This problem has faced me. For the last 25 years I have been thinking of this on the world scene. For 25 years before that I was thinking of it in the Indian context. So for about 50 years I have been considering this difficulty.

As I have been reviewing church growth around the world, I have seen that it frequently correlates with great healing campaigns. That is why I am speaking about Divine Healing and Church Growth. Where the church is up against an insuperable barrier, there no matter what you do, how much you pray, how much you work, how much you organize, how much you administer for church growth, the church either does not grow, grows only a little, or grows from within, not from without. Under such circumstances, we need to lean heavily on that which is so wonderfully illustrated in the New Testament, namely the place of healing in church growth. You remember the two villages of Lydda and Sharon where it is recorded in the book of Acts that all Lydda and Sharon turned to the Lord. Two whole villages in a day! When did that happen? When Aeneas was healed by Peter. This great in gathering was preceded by a remarkable case of divine healing.

American missionaries, who have grown up in a highly secular society, usually take a dim view of divine healing, considering it mere charlatanism. After long years of sharing that common opinion, I now hold that among vast populations, divine healing is one of the ways in which God brings ruen and women to believe in the Savior. Missiologists ought to have a considered opinion on the matter. They should not brush it off cheaply and easily. Administering for church growth in part means arranging the stage so that divine healing can take place. Look at the evidence of divine healing. Withold judgment until the evidence has been reviewed. There is much more evidence than I am able to present in one short address.

My considered recommendation is that missionaries and Christians in most populations ought to be following the biblical injunction to pray for the sick (James 5:14-15). When notable healings have taken place, great efforts should be made to multiply churches. When healings have taken place in your denomination or any other denomination, when the Pentecostals mount a great healing campaign, then say to yourself, "This is the time to strike, while the iron is hot."

I now lay before you a few cases of divine healing that have come to attention from various sources. The first is a case of healing carried out by American Presbyterian missionaries. I quote a report from India about the operation of these ministers, visiting India for a brief period.

Everyday there was preaching in the evening and teaching in the morning. They lived with us as brothers. They visited and preached in 24 of the 278 churches we have. The work of the Holy

Spirit was experiences throughout the preaching ministry. Reverend Little was blessed with the gift of healing power. All those who came to the gospel meetings with a real longing for healing were wonderfully healed. Every night Reverend Little had to minister for more than four hours. People who were healed came forward and witnessed about their healing. Hundreds of people were healed. Thousands were able to accept Jesus Christ as their Lord. People were made whole physically, mentally and spiritually. Some of our pastors were healed from serious illnesses, including Rev. J. Thompson, Rev. S. Yesunesan, Rev. E.J. Victor and Rev. Moses Israel. Those who were suffering from chronic diseases were healed. A woman who was suffering from asthma for 21 years was healed. A man who was deaf for more than 40 years was healed. So many blind people were able to see. Lame people were healed. People who were suffering from bleeding were healed. Reverend Wilson shared how more than 2 weeks after Little and Wallace had departed, he would visit a church and find people still praising God for the healing they had received. He discovered that there were a number of Hindus who had received Jesus Christ as their Lord and Saviour among the thousands who experienced salvation. It was customary for Dick Little to ask the people to renounce their gods before repenting .and accepting the Lord Jesus into their lives. Apparently a number received their healing as Christ Jesus came into their hearts.

The second come from the CMS Newletter. This is written by the General Secretary of the famed Church Missionary Society whose headquarters are just across the Thames from Parliament Building in London. Here is what is published:

Perhaps there is no more impressive example in recent years of healing than Edmund John, younger brother of the Archbishop ofTanzania, with his great healing mission over a 3 year period of ministry form 1972 to 1975. Not only were vast numbers of people healed, exorcised, moved to open repentance, led to or brought back to Christ in great gatherings, but also in quiet, ordered proceedings. All that happened was related to the central apprehension that Jesus is Lord; and amazing response for the lax Christians and the newly drawn Muslims alike. John's death at the end of the astonishing blaze of ministry to his people left behind in many places a church spiritually and numerically strengthened.

The third is from Bolivia, from a United Methodist. This man studied at the School of World Mission in Pasadena and went back to Bolivia a convinced church growth man. His letter is addressed to me personally. In it he says:

It is most striking that the district of our church which has really broken new ground in growth is our very own Lake District where we have worked for 16 years. This is the rural Aymara Indian district. This growth really began to gather momentum during our absence and has been strongest during the last year. So new is this that we do not yet have proper statistics on what has taken place. The mother church of the district in Ancoraimes, our mission station, has increased its Sunday morning attendance six fold. They hold week meetings that have usually average 250, this year have averaged over 600. For the first time in the history of our work, a majority of approaching consensus has turned to Christ in a single community, practically the whole village became Christian. This was shown dramatically on May 31, 1973, the traditional fiesta date, when the community celebrated their first community Christian Fiesta. Of the 170 families, 160 have turned to Christ; five our of six zones of the community, which is called Turini. The lay pastor of the Ancoraimes church, Juan Cordero, was the key man in this movement. Mum's the word, please do not say anything about this. Dr. McGavran; mum's the word on the following factor. Preaching has been accompanied by healing. Over and over this has been the case. The lay pastor has been practically mobbed on occasion, but he has stood his ground and has virtually obliged interested persons to hear him out on the gospel before he will pray for healings.

The fourth case of healing followed by growth is one in which the gift of healing was exercised by a layman, a recent convert, not by the minister or missionary. In Tamilnadu, India, the Evangelical Church of India, planted by OMSI of Greenwood, Indiana, has grown from a few hundred in 1996 to more than fifteen thousand in 1982. During 1983 the church expects to plant fifty more churches - one a week.

After 1970 growth was accompanied by healings and exorcisms. What convinced multitudes to follow Christ was that with their own eyes they saw men and women healed by Christ's mighty power. Evil spirits were driven out in His name. The Holy Spirit was at work.

The fifth is from the Mekane Yesus Lutheran denomination in Ethiopia.

Eighty three percent (83%) of our congregations give healing from illness and exorcism as reasons for their growth.

In summary, it is clear from these five cases and much more evidence that the growth of the Church has often -- not always, but often -- been sparked by healing campaigns.

There are 200,000 East Indians in Trinidad. In 1950 a couple thousand were Christians, the sons and grandsons of people converted by Presbyterian missionaries. Except for those, very few Hindus or Moslems then living in Trinidad had become Christians. In the late fifties there was a healing campaign, and when the educated Indian community, which had scorned Christianity, saw their own people healed in Jesus' name, they said, "Here is power!" Hundreds became Christians.

The seventh case is a remarkable one from India. Suba Rao was the headmaster of a government school --a member of one of the middle castes and a wealthy man. He had laughed at baptism. He had hated missionaries. He had thought of the church as an assembly of the *low* caste.

One of his near neighbours and close friends fell sick. For two years his sickness was not healed and gradually wasting away. He went to many doctors to no avail. One night while Suba Rao was asleep, the Lord Jesus appeared to him and said, "Will you will go and lay your hand on that man's head and pray in My name, I will heal him." Suba Rao woke up and laughed, thinking, "What a funny dream" and went back to sleep. The next night the Lord Jesus stood by his side and said, "If you go and lay your hand on that man's head and pray for him to be healed, I will heal him." Suba Rao woke up; he didn't laugh this time and he didn't go back to sleep, but he didn't lay his hands on the sick man either. He said, "That's impossible!" The third night the Lord Jesus appeared to him. He got up at once and went to his neighbour. He laid his hand on the man's head, prayed for him, and in the morning the man said, "I feel much better. Do *it* again." the man was healed. Suba Rao threw out his idols. He started to read the Bible. He started a Bible study class among his neighbours. But he still ridicules baptism. He has not joined and church. But he proclaims himself a follower of the Lord Jesus. The healing of people *in* Jesus' name became his chief occupation. Joining the church, which there is composed very largely indeed (98%) of the lowest castes of Indian society is, he thinks, an impossible (and perhaps an unnecessary) step for him. Still the Lora Jesus heals men through him. (Mark 9:39).

What do healings of this kind -- repeated thousands of times -- mean for us, living in the world today? "Like a comet blazing across the skies, this faith healer suddenly appeared among the small churches planted in this land in the last 20 years." News notes to this effect have reached sending churches in America again and again in last 20 years, from many different lands and many different denominations. The biblical saga continues. In one congregation of none, under the faith healer's prayers, marvellous cures occurred, crowds gathered, thousands attended, members of important wealthy families were cured, the press carried front page articles on the events. Night after night discarded crutches were gathered. Night after night the testimonies of the blind who now see, the paralyzed who now leap, the deaf who now hear were most impressive. Faced with the enormous power of the riser and reigning Christ, men and women in increasing numbers confessed Christ, turned from sin and other gods, were baptized and incorporated into new and old churches. A new era developed, churches began to multiply in many denominations. Baptists grew, Methodists grew, Lutherans grew, Pentecostals grew, and on and on. The evangelization of this country took a great leap forward. Events like these occurring in many lands have caused heated discussion among American Christians.

During the last 100 years, Western Christians have been heavily secularized and saturated with scientific thinking. They believe diseases are caused, not by God's will, but by germs. And these diseases are cured by drugs; malaria by quinine, colds by Contac, atherosclerosis by open heart surgery. As Christianity has spread throughout the world, missionary physicians have proved enormously more effective than the mumbo jumbo of witch doctors, herbalists, faith healers of the animist world. The missionary doctor gave the patients penicillin and offered prayer to God for their cure. They were cured.

The Christian doctor would say it was not by unaided prayer but by using the medicine that God has given to mankind. This Christian interpretation of the healing process and the part played by unaided prayer and faith differs from the rationalists view, and yet it holds that, as a matter of fact, God does not act independent of physical means. That, my friends, is the atmosphere in which we all live. Secular man believes that there is no God; the causes of illness which can be measured and manipulated by men are the only reality. These causes can be physical, chemical or psychological.

To such 20th century thinking, faith healing is at best mistaken and at worst charlatanry. The faith healer is either a self-deluded enthusiast or a clever manipulator of men. If people claim to be cured, maybe they were not really sick in the first place, or have temporary feelings of well being induced by the excitement of the moment due to crowd psychology. The "healed" may even be planted t the faith healer to build up his reputation. The power of hundreds of thousands who believe alike and express their belief vividly is a real factor in human affairs and has been used by politicians, merchants, priests, and magicians from time immemorial. Westerners and Eastern secularists are highly sceptical about any power available to man other than what man himself generates by one mean or another, Faith healing causes lifted eyebrows and superior smiles.

To most people in Asia, Africa, and Latin America, however; disease is inflicted by spirits. It is cured by super-human powers regardless of what people in America think.

Witches eat up the life force of other men. An angry neighbor casts an "evil eye" on a woman and she grows weaker day by day. A wandering evil spirit devours a baby and the baby dies. A demon causes an illness which no medicine can cure. Western medicine may help some people, but Africa is full of mysterious powers which the white man does not know, and only those who know the secret source of black power can heal African affliction. These evil powers must be overcome by superior powers.

In Spanish America the Curandero has great power. His incantations, potion, sacrifices, and medicines marvellously heal the sick. In Asia, Africa, and Latin America, perhaps 98 out of 100 persons believe that superior power drives out inferior power. In Europe and North America the impersonal, mechanistic system of scientism fails to satisfy millions. Therefore, they, too, eagerly believe I the occult, extra-human powers. Satan worship flousrishes. The mysterious influence of magic words, rites, robes, stars, yogis, and gurus fascinates many people in Europe and North America. Christians in North America and Europe have a special problem with faith healing. Why? Because their religion wars with their science.

Faith healing unquestionably occurred in biblical times. The New Testament Church rode the crest of a tremendous, continual manifestation of faith healing. One of the may passages reads as follows:

Now many signs and wonders were done among the common people and by the hands of the apostles, more than ever, believers were added to the Lord. Multitudes, both men and women, so that they even carried out the sick into the streets and laid them on beds and pallets, that, as Peter came by, at least his shadow might fall on some of them. The people also gathered from the towns around Jerusalem, bringing the sick and those afflicted with evil spirits and they all were healed (Acts 8:12-16).

Yes, Christians have a problem in the Western society. Their sciences war with their Christian faith. Divine healing was an essential part of the evangelization as churches multiplied across Palestine and the Mediterranean world. What are we Christians to make of all this? Is there something here that we can use?

Many educated Christians have been more secularized than they realize and are antagonistic to divine healing. They write it off as superstition and fraud; it leads people away from sound medicine and counts many as healed who are still sick. They say divine healing is a massive deception. They think that divine healing is using God for our own ends.

Some educated Christians say that in addition to the human mechanism and material means which God uses, He sometimes acts in sovereign power. He retains the right to act outside His laws which we know in order to use higher laws which we do not know. He ordinarily operated through His laws, but He is not bound by them. When it pleases Him, He intervenes. Such Christians hold that the best possible world is one in which most of the time a just and loving God rules through laws. But occasionally, when He sees fit, He uses a higher law. Such Christians view healings in the name of Christ as demonstrations of the power of God.

Some would add that the healings are a mixture of God's acts and man acts, thus we see many incomplete healings, and failures of healings, due to lack of faith or sincerity.

Some hard-headed Christians, who would normally be highly sceptical about divine healing, have gradually come to accept healing campaigns upon seeing he great numbers who throw away crutches, plus those healed of deafness and blindness and cured of heart disease. They have seen large numbers of recent non-believers rejoicing at Christ's power, singing His praises, hearing His word, and praying to Him. The facts overwhelm the hard-headed.

Finally, some Christians believe that God has called them to actively engage in healing the sick, exorcising evil spirits, and multiplying churches. They deliberately use the vigorous expressed faith in Christ which abounds in a healing campaign to multiply sound churches of responsible Christians.

All Christians ought to think their way through this matter and realize that here is a power which a great many of us have not sufficiently used.

Healing campaigns have occurred in Buenos Aires with Tommy Hicks in 1954 and Guayaquil, Ecuador, in the mid 60's. The latter was a very interesting case. The Full Gospel Church had three mission fields with growing younger churches in Brazil, the Philippines, and Panama. In their other fields converts were not being won, congregations were not multiplying. In the late sixties in Guayquil healings took place in a small way. Immediately, a big tent was flown in from Los Angeles and pitched right where the crowd gathered. For the next six weeks every night in that tent faith healing followed the preaching of Christ. Twenty branch churches were planted in various parts of the city. Guayaquil became a mission field where churches multiply.

In South Africa there is an Indian community of about 800,000 that has been solidly opposed to the Christian faith. Very few Indians became Christians. About 20 or 25 years ago through a series of healing campaigns, two Pentecostal denominations began to grow among the Indians. One of those Pentecostal churches is now 25,000 and the other 15,000. They got their start in healing campaigns in South Africa. Healing campaigns are occurring today and they will occur tomorrow. They are a part of today's context. When one talks about contextualization, healing campaigns should be mentioned.

Christians, especially missionaries and missionary societies, must ask, "What is the biblical response to divine healing campaigns? What do Christians do when faced with the excitement and faith-heightening of a divine healing campaign?" Many for the first time become able to hear the Gospel with the inner ear.

What ought we to do after a campaign when many decide to become Christian? The following answer was formed in my mind when I was in the Christian Missionary Alliance field in Ivory Coast, at Yamoussoukro. A church growth workshop sponsored by the Evangelical Churches and missions was being held. This amazing story was told by the Ivory Coast pastors and American missionaries gathered there to study the growth of their churches and to find ways of proclaiming the Gospel more effectively. It illustrates very well the problems and opportunities which healing campaigns bring.

The Church in Ivory coast was typical of many countries in Asia, Africa and Latin America. Ivory Coast has about 4 million people with the Roman Catholic Church numbers about 30,000. The Methodist Church dates from 1924 and has 60,000. Seven small Protestant denominations, with a total baptized membership of about 11,000, have arisen because of the faithful work of American missionaries. They have a growing rate of 70% per decade, led by Ivory Coast ministers. About 100 dedicated American missionaries are helping these churches and are doing a multitude of good deed.

Pastor Jacques Giraud, a French missionary tot he West Indies, arrived in Ivory Coast in March, 1973, to dedicate and Assemblies church building in Abidjan. As the meetings progressed, people began to be healed. The crowds grew and the meetings were moved to the stadium. Truck loads of people came from all parts of Ivory Coast. The papers were full of the event. The radio broadcast daily concerning it.

Leading government officials and their wives flocked to the stadium. Pastor Giraud would tell of one of Christ's miracles and preach for an hour on God's mighty power to heal. Then he would say, "I don't' heal; God heals. I ask Him to release His power. Put your hand where it hurts and join me in prayer." He would pour out his heart in believing prayer to God for healing. After a half hour of prayer he would invite those who God had healed to come to the front; crutches were thrown away, bent and arthritic persons stood erect, blind men walked forward seeing, scores and sometimes hundreds came, some hobbled, some limped, some saw 'men like trees walking' but they believed. God had given them at least a measure of healing. Thousands were also not healed.

After several healing sessions, Pastor Giraud would begin preaching salvation, repentance, atonement, and sanctification—straight from Bible preaching. A blind pagan from 600km north promised his fetish a sacrifice if he was healed. He went by bus to the Giraud meeting. At the meeting he saw for an instant, but then darkness returned. He stayed on and heard the gospel. When he returned home, he burnt his fetish and declared himself a Christian, saying, "I was not healed, but I heard the gospel and I am sure that God is the real power."

This incident illustrates the truth that a healing campaign has dimensions far in excess of the healings. Groups of men and women seeing he power of Christ and hearing the message under favourable conditions declare their faith in Christ. Theirs in not an illumined faith but it is strong enough for them to burn their fetishes. They can be incorporated into existing congregations and formed into new ones.

After the Abidjan campaign in the very southern tip of the country, a high government official, who had been greatly blessed by the meeting, arranged for Pastor Giraud to hold a healing campaign in his home town of Toumoudi. He directed the leading government administrator there to arrange, at his expense, a place for meetings, and lodging and food for pastor Giraud and his party. A campaign similar to the Abidjan campaign was held. Radio and newspapers again broad- cast the huge nightly meetings. The next meeting, again on the initiative and expense of leading government officials, was held in the city of Bouake in late August of 1973. Then at Yamoussoukro, another campaign with Giraud was held. Pastor Giraud conducted healing campaigns in many towns and cities of the Ivory Coast.

Although he was a minister of the Assemblies of God, it is his practice to direct converts to the local churches and missions for shepherding. At Toumoudi he had the Alliance missionaries and ministers on the platform with him. He said to the people, "When you place you faith in Jesus Christ, call these men to baptize you and shepherd you."

Reverend Fred Pilding, a missionary of the Christian and Missionary Alliance working in Ivory Coast fills in some details in the *Alliance Witness*, Sept. 26, 1973.

The crusade began in Bouake June 18th and continued for three weeks. Morning attendance averaged about 4,000. From 6 to 15,00 turned out in the evenings with a high of 25,00 one Sunday. The sick were seated on the grass on the playing field and all the others occupied the grandstands. As the evangelist presented Jesus Christ, the same yesterday, today and forever, people became aware of His continuing power today, through a healing receptive place. It became easier for them to trust Him as Saviour. A hunchback came to the meeting, grovelling in the dirt, under the influence of demons. The demons were exorcised in the name of Jesus and he was instantly healed. The next day he attended the meetings nicely dressed, perfectly calm, and gave his testimony. Whenever those who were healed testified, witnesses were asked to verify each healing. Pastor Giraud again and again cited Mark 16:15-18 as every believer1s commission and emphasized that in Christ's name they were to cast out devils and lay hands on the sick and they shall recover. He refuted vigorously the title of healer. His ministry, he said, was to inspire faith in the gospel. "It is in the name of Jesus that people are healed."

After the Toumoudi meeting, groups of converts from 81 villages around Toumoudi sought out the Alliance missionaries and ministers, begging them to come and make them Christians. After the Bouake meeting, responses were received from over 100 villages. A hundred and forty cards were filled out from one small town alone. From one village near Bouake 10 cards had been received. The missionary went to visit this village. Seeing him, one of the men who had been healed rushed off to get some of the pagan village elders. While waiting, the missionary said to the children, "Do you know Pastor Giraudls song?" Immediately they broke into joyful singing, "Up, up with Jesus, down, down with Satan, Alleluia!" People carne pouring out and the missionary preached and then asked, "How many will follow God and leave their old ways?" More than half immediately said, "We will." In another village the Chief said, "Fetish is dead, we shall all become Christians." The pastors and missionaries were faced with great opportunities. The challenge was to take advantage of this enthusiasm, which could dissipate rapidly, and channel these people into ongoing responsible churches of Christians who know the Lord and obey His word. Nothing like this had happened in their experience in the Ivory Coast, and they were naturally fearful, lest the excitement prove transient as it very well might.

What are Christians to make of faith healings and exorcisms? Missionaries, other church leaders and evangelists all over the world face many different situations, populations, oppositions, and opportunities. In some places mission is very largely good works and proclamation of Christ which very seldom .is followed by open acceptance of Jim as Lord and Saviour. In other places multitudes are accepting Christ and becoming members of multiplying congregations. In places the entire work is carried on by national pastors and their comrades. In other places, the missionary is the chief agent. He recruits, trains, employs, and deploys the national pastor and their comrades. In other places, the missionary is the chief agent. He recruits, trains, employs, and deploys the national evangelists and pastors. each of these men -missionaries and pastors -face a unique situation.

In view of all the evidence, missionaries in training in the (rapidly multiplying Schools of Evangelism and Mission now found in many parts of the world must ask themselves:

What place ought we to give to faith healings and exorcisms?

It would be foolhardy to attempt a single answer which would be equally true for all pieces of the vast mosaic of mankind. But certain truths may be emphasized.

First, God does give a few Christians the gift of healing. This is the clear statement of Scripture, and the convincing witness of history. It would be both unbelieving and foolish to disregard the massive evidence. It would be unscientific, if you please, to close one's eyes to the facts of faith healing. It would be unChristian to deny those parts of the Bible which tell us clearly that on occasion, in response to faith, God does heal in miraculous ways. Biblical faith requires faith in miracles. If we cast them out, we cast out the whole Bible, or adopt a system of hermeneutics which destroys while it interprets.

Second, many healings in Christ's name are incomplete, temporary, or even contrived. The facts are clear. Some faith healers are charlatans, and do it for the fame or money they receive. But this fact must not destroy our ability to see that God does heal in response to faith and prayer.

Third, when healing in Christ's name has gone on and has attracted wide attention, multitudes can hear the gospel and many will obey it. This is the convincing witness of the New Testament and of modern history in many parts of the world, including the Western World. God wishes us to recognize white fields. When the disciples were saying, "No one will believe. The harvest you speak of is four months off. We are just sowing the seed or ploughing the field," it was exactly then that the Lord Jesus said, "You are wrong. Lift up your eyes and look on the fields which are white to harvest. Pray God to send labourers into the ripe fields." Pastors of congregations, missionaries at work in new populations, executive secretaries of mission boards, professors of missiology - all ought to practice and teach that healing campaigns are frequently accompanied by periods of great receptivity. *It is required of Christians that they recognize these periods and multiply congregations in receptive populations.*

Fourth, God's man is sometimes faced with highly secular company of Christians who do not believe in faith healings or any other miracles, and who would be put off by any advocacy of them. They would turn away from something which, to them, seemed impossible. Facing such an audience, what should God's man do?

He should do what thousands of ministers and missionaries have been doing during the past century. He should commend Christ in ways which that audience will accept as commendation. He should recognize that faith healing claims will turn some people away from Christ. When God sends him to minister or to evangelize to such people, he must present the gospel in terms which they understand and which raise up no insuperable obstacles before them.

I would hope, however, that even to this audience some of the facts of faith healing could be and would be presented at suitable times. As modern secular Christians give themselves utterly to Christ, and as they accept the full authority and infallibility of the Bible, they will come to the place in which they too will believe that with God nothing is impossible

Reproduced with permission from MC510: Healing Ministry and Church Growth class notes, Fuller Theological Seminary, 1983, a course taught by John Wimber.

Cleanse Me

J. Edwin Orr, 1912-

Maori Melody
Arr. by Norman Johnson, 1928-1983

1. Search me, O God, and know my heart to - day; Try me, O
2. I praise Thee, Lord, for cleans-ing me from sin; Ful - fill Thy
3. Lord, take my life and make it whol - ly Thine; Fill my poor
4. O Ho - ly Ghost, re - viv - al comes from Thee; Send a re -

Sav - ior, know my thoughts, I pray. See if there be some wick-ed
Word and make me pure with-in. Fill me with fire where once I
heart with Thy great love di - vine. Take all my will, my pas-sion,
viv - al - start the work in me. Thy Word de - clares Thou wilt sup -

way in me; Cleanse me from ev-'ry sin and set me free.
burned with shame; Grant my de-sire to mag-ni-fy Thy name.
self and pride; I now sur-ren-der, Lord-in me a-bide.
ply our need; For bless-ings now, O Lord, I hum-bly plead.

Revival hymn written by J Edwin Orr in New Zealand
at the Easter revival there in 1936. Tune: The Maori Farewell.

Based on Psalm 139:23-24

Search me, O God, and know my heart:

try me, and know my thoughts:

and see if there be any wicked way in me,

and lead me in the way everlasting.

7 Sounds of Revival

Sue Armstrong

Mrs Sue Armstrong travels and ministers wit her evangelist husband the Rev. Dan Armstrong. They direct Kairos Ministries in Australia and organized the Vineyard Conferences here with John Wimber and his teams. Sue reports on revival moves they have seen, including the Wimber Conferences in Brisbane and Perth in 1994. This article is expanded from the June and September 1994 'News Across Australia'.

Once you have been in a place that is experiencing revival you will never forget the sounds! I have heard these sounds in other countries and up in the North amongst our aboriginal people and I have longed for the time when I would hear them here in our churches.

The Islands

I will never forget a night in Papua New Guinea at Manngai High School, New Ireland, when the Holy Spirit fell on the young students gathered. They cried and wailed. They fell. They shook. Repentance was there. Salvation came to many and deliverance from demonic powers came to some. I remember driving back to our village late that night singing, 'Mine eyes have seen the glory of the coming of the Lord,' and truly knowing what that glory was!

I remember a night at Lelean High School in Fiji when the Holy Spirit fell on around 600 school children. It was pitch dark as there was a blackout with no power. Yet, we sure had Holy Spirit power! Bodies were lying everywhere, some pleading the mercy of God as their sin was revealed, some praising, some sobbing, some resting under the power of God. Suddenly people appeared from nearby houses. They saw flames coming from the buildings and they came to put out the fire, but there was no fire!

On another occasion in Fiji the Spirit fell during worship. We were singing to the Lord and suddenly weeping broke out. The Indian Fijian young folk and the Fijian kids began to run to each other and embrace. Racial hatred was dealt a severe blow as these kids repented and loved one another. We had no way of knowing that there would be a coup in a matter of weeks and that this touch from God was a moment of great importance.

In Indonesia we saw people flocking to the front of the large galvanised iron building. Some fell as they came and remained motionless. Some shouted as they had a common vision of Jesus. A group of Muslim school girls had a common vision of hell. People received healing and many were set free from demonic forces. The noise was ear splitting and the place was like a battle field – not at all the way I imagined revival would be. As people lay motionless on the floor some panic stricken people tried to administer smelling salts, but the 'sleeping people' remained on the floor with beatific smiles on their faces.

Africa

On a visit to Africa to the Transki, Dan was in a big gathering of blacks. He was listening to a massed choir singing in that amazing close harmony that only Africans can achieve when the Holy Spirit fell on the meeting. The whole choir fell to the floor. The pastors jumped to their feet exclaiming, 'The Holy Spirit is here!'

Dan describes the next event as 'like watching wind in a wheat field'. The Spirit moved among the people in waves and they swayed and fell as the Holy Spirit touched them. Many experienced miraculous healing and some who had come as spectators were saved.

Australia

The revival was different again in Arnhemland, Australia. It was much more gentle in its beginnings. The meetings were held at night in the open air, and people came out of the darkness to kneel on the ground and acknowledge Jesus as Lord. After that they jumped to their feet and joined with those praying for others. This was spontaneous. Immediately they began to experience the gifts of the Holy Spirit operating in their new lives.

There were special manifestations. One night we went with them at their request to cleanse the ceremonial grounds. Satan manifested in some of the people with bizarre happenings. One man bit a young woman. Another man tried to crucify himself on the cross the people had erected. Dogs went wild, barking, biting, fighting and howling all over the island. Then came the presence of the Lord over the place and a great release of joy and celebration.

I have read accounts of revival by J Edwin Orr, John Wesley, John Whitefield, and Jonathan Edwards. They describe the falling, shaking, wailing, laughing and even rolling and drunken behaviour. But that was then. It's surely not for our sophisticated society!

Over the past year reports have filtered through of churches experiencing some of the above phenomena, just here and there in regular services or home groups. Just the whisper that revival is on the way.

In Brisbane and Perth at the Wimber Conferences last April, right from the first meeting it became clear that God had his own agenda. During the initial worship time the Holy Spirit began to rest on individuals across the auditorium and ripples of laughter could be heard. Before John Wimber gave the opening message he called out young folk who had obvious signs of the Spirit resting on them – shaking, trembling, laughing and one just quiet and transfixed. He spoke of the way the Spirit moves on people's lives and that we must trust the Holy Spirit and not try to stop or control what God is doing.

Each meeting the Holy Spirit came and people were touched in all kinds of ways. Here are a few testimonies.

* Although just a young married man I had to resign from my job because of chronic fatigue syndrome. The first night at the conference I was released with amazing laughter and the fatigue completely left during the conference. Energy has returned.

* I stood up and was really praising God, in my tongues language, and beseeching him to heal my back (where a tumour had been removed) which seemed to have got worse in terms of niggling pain of late. One of the members from my church put her hand right where the operation had been. After a few moments there seemed to be a real heat, like a hot water bottle, beneath her hand. John Wimber said, to the effect, 'God is touching a man right now and putting his spine back together!' The heat stayed around my waist area for some time and then, like honey running out of a container quite slowly, the feeling of heat extended down my leg following the sciatic nerve – I know my sciatic nerve! This feeling of heat ran right down to my foot where it stayed for several minutes. I could literally feel the power of God around me. I met with God that night. (He has been free of pain and can move his leg at the hip and knee.)

* I have had severe scoliosis for 35 years. I sought healing on Wednesday night and when I arrived home my wife (a registered nurse) agreed that the hollow on the left side of my lower back had changed and become more like the right side. It would appear that a rotated vertebrae may have been realigned.

* I received prayer for hearing loss Wednesday night and today I have not had to wear a hearing aid and my hearing is much improved.

* I had been walking with two walking sticks for four years. I had a fall after my hip replacement surgery causing the bone not to knit. This caused pain when I walked. On Tuesday night John Wimber had a word for someone who had had hip problems for 63 years causing pain in the right leg. Members of the team prayed for me and I am now walking without my sticks and the pain gets less every day.

* I have had arthritis in both knees for three years. Two of the girls in the team prayed for me and the pain and discomfort has completely gone. I can now move quite freely without discomfort.

* I have received the most special healing of major pain from a broken heart. Two young kids from the American team prayed for me. This has opened my eyes and given me a new vision for youth ministry.

* No one can know what it is like for someone who has believed for 39 years that she cannot be loved or should even exist, to suddenly discover that she is loved by the living God.

God touched people powerfully, in many different ways.

But the sound was there! I heard the Spirit come. John Wimber spoke from Judges 13:3, speaking to the nation of Australia: 'You are sterile and childless but you are going to conceive and have a son.' Revival is being brought to birth in this nation. Listen for the sound. Revival has begun!

North America and England

We have received reports of similar moves of God this year.

Charisma magazine, June 1994, told of people from all denominations flocking to a small church in Toronto, the Airport Vineyard, where revival has been stirring this year. People tell of the manifest presence of God. Many rest in the Spirit. Many exhibit laughing and drunken behaviour. Many report healings and release from emotional problems. The meetings have been dubbed 'the laughing revival' in which ordinary people, not high profile leaders, have suddenly begun ministering powerfully in the Lord.

Terry Virgo reports in *New Frontiers* magazine, July 1994, on moves of God this year following his return from ministry in South Africa:

On my return to Columbia, Missouri, I found our church meetings were totally transformed and that a new release of the Holy Spirit had overtaken us. We have seen extraordinary sights in terms of people being filled with the spirit of joy and 'drunkenness'. We have seen lives totally transformed. People have a new hunger for God and a new zeal to see him glorified. I have seen lives changed so rapidly and the atmosphere of a church changed so swiftly.

He also describes moves of God this year in England:

I returned to England and found that wherever I went to report news of this outbreak, God accompanied us with more signs of his mercy and overwhelming love for his church.

First of all I met with a number of leading brothers in New Frontiers and we had two days of amazing experiences of God's presence and a release of prophesying such as I have never known. After that came an unforgettable evening in my home church in Brighton which continued till 11.30 p.m. Many were overwhelmed by the power of the Holy Spirit.

Following this, over two hundred full-time elders from New Frontiers gathered for fasting at Stoneleigh where once again the Spirit of God was poured out in phenomenal measure. I have never seen such spiritual drunkenness and joy in my life. And once again the release of prophecy was breathtaking.

God moves powerfully in revival. People repent. Many are healed and delivered. God pours out his Spirit. Christians minister as Jesus did, and as he taught his disciples to do.

The sounds of revival are stirring again. You'll hear cries of repentance, great joy and liberty, and awe and excitement at the amazing grace of God.

8 Revival Fire at Wuddina

Trevor Faggotter

The Rev Trevor Faggotter is a Uniting Church minister in South Australia. This article is adapted from a paper he wrote in his B.Th. studies.

The story is simple. The happening is unique.

It illustrates the way in which the Christian gospel can

profoundly penetrate and radically re-orient a country church.

Australian Christians have often thought that revival was 'just around the corner' (Wilson 1983:26). However, since the mid 1960s the prevailing trends in Church attendance in Australia have shown a steady decline, apart from the growth of the Pentecostal Churches (Chant 1984:219-224). Without doubt Pentecostals have had many new conversions but it can be argued that the new growth is also transitional – dissatisfied people coming from mainline denominations. But, have there been any signs of genuine revival in recent times?

Ian Murray (1988:333) writes, 'The Christian past of Australia has largely vanished out of sight. Not surprisingly, many have drawn the conclusion that the country has no Christian history of which it is worth speaking.' However, this paper outlines an episode of Australian Christian history which is well worth retelling.

The story is simple. The happening is unique. It illustrates the way in which the Christian gospel can profoundly penetrate and radically re-orient Australian people.

Ministry at Wudinna

Wudinna. This was the Rev. Deane Meatheringham's first appointment following his training at Wesley College. The town is somewhat isolated, being situated about 250 kilometres west of Port Augusta on the Eyre Peninsula in South Australia.

'What a depressing picture the Wudinna Circuit must have presented to the young, enthusiastic probationer, Rev. Deane Meatheringham and his new bride, Rosslyn, as they arrived in 1967 to live and labour there' (Curnow 1977:81).

The district was known to be one of the hardest Methodist circuits in the state, and hard for others also. At one time the residents in nearby Minnipa quite literally ran the Anglican minister out of town.

Deane Meatheringham began by preaching the basic doctrines of the Christian faith. He attempted to form small Bible study groups but this didn't arouse any interest (Meatheringham 1981:3). At best, the Wudinna congregation consisted of about 40 to 50 members. About 8 families were regulars. By October 1967, the numbers attending Sunday services were actually down to about 9 or 10 people, and most of those were reluctant even to speak of spiritual matters. The status quo prevailed.

Even so, Meatheringham persisted with his preaching and teaching. 'He pounded the gospel, the grace of God,' remembers Marj Holman. In November 1967 he preached a sermon at Minnipa entitled 'God has acted; we must react.' He invited a formal response and much to his surprise three women who only haphazardly attended church came forward. For the regular worshippers, this occasioned a slightly embarrassing end to the service, but it also marked the beginning of an outbreak of groups in which many people expressed an unprecedented desire to learn and grow in their faith.

The three women were eager to become involved in confirmation classes, and they invited some of their friends to join the class at Mount Damper. About 15-20 people had attended the first teaching group in which the preparation for confirmation took place. Then, early in 1968, another confirmation class began with others who had been affected by Meatheringham's preaching and teaching of the gospel. Studies were given on the meaning of baptism and also on justification by faith. A continual stream of people found their lives renewed as they happily put their trust in Jesus Christ.

The Leighton Ford Crusade came to Adelaide from 31 March to 7 April, 1968. Participation in and prayer for the Crusade was commended to all Methodists, 'in the strongest possible terms', by the President of the Methodist Conference, the Rev. Merv Trenorden. About 150 people attended the hall in Wudinna to listen to Leighton Ford via a land-line. An appeal was made and again people came forward. Soon after, when Merv Trenorden came to Wudinna to preach for the Confirmation Service, he was astonished by the activity which was taking place.

Twenty new converts were confirmed. People who had held nominal roll membership for years were experiencing Christian conversion – new birth. A group of teenagers had responded to the gospel. In October, 1967, the Wudinna Youth Group had joined with Glen Osmond Baptist youth for a Church camp at Crystal Brook. This had been a significant time for several of them. A vibrant Christian Endeavour group was formed and lead by Meatheringham. The Churches of Christ people were welcomed as associate members of the Methodist Church. People were starting to ask for Bible study groups and there was a growing hunger for Christian teaching and literature (Curnow 1977:81).

Wudinna has known many hard times and had experienced a severe drought in 1959, but interestingly enough locals recall how 1966, 1968 and 1969 were particularly good years. The country flourished, the economy was buoyant and it was a very busy time for farmers. At this time, the Jehovah's Witnesses had been quite active within the area and it is not insignificant that people were very aware of 'the law' and of morality. However, the people here were largely unaware of and unaffected by the charismatic movement which was making some impact within the Australian churches. In this sense, the message of unconditional grace was being sown in well-prepared and virgin soil.

Mission at Wudinna

Meatheringham was authorised by his local 1968 September quarterly meeting, to make enquiries concerning a mission. As a result, the former overseas missionary, Anglican minister and Principal of the Adelaide Bible Institute (now the Bible College of South Australia) the Rev. Geoffrey Bingham, was contacted and he agreed to come. Meatheringham sought Bingham's advice regarding preparation for the mission. It was recommended that prayer groups be formed. A total of 12 groups soon began meeting around the circuit.

The Wudinna folk also had a strong desire to be trained in some way. This happened through the Lay Institute For Evangelism (L.I.F.E). It was a wing of the Department of Evangelism in the Church of England Diocese of Sydney. Rev. Geoffrey Fletcher was the Director. The L.I.F.E. programme was designed to teach lay people 'how to present Jesus Christ, how to avoid religious jargon, how to overcome anxiety in sharing, how to answer questions, how to avoid arguing' and so on. Deane Meatheringham led the studies.

The enthusiastic desire to participate in these training courses was beyond anyone's expectation. Sixty people came along to listen to the hour long tapes and to take part in the drill. A telegram was hurriedly sent off to Sydney: 'Rush Twenty Extra LIFE Manuals to Wudinna S.A.' While some folk did become Christians or were renewed through these programmes, they were primarily times of preparation for the mission.

The mission was planned for 24-31 August, 1969, and was a joint venture of the five congregations in the Wudinna Methodist Circuit. The few Churches of Christ families in the district were also closely associated with the Methodist Church. The Anglican parishes of Elliston and Streaky Bay joined in encouraged by the Rev. Dennis Crisp, the Anglican Minister from Elliston. It also had the support of the Lutheran Church. The Catholic Priest at Minnipa, Father Wesley Heading indicated his personal enthusiasm and prayerful support by sending Meatheringham a telegram prior to the mission. A combined Methodist-Anglican committee consisting of 8 members was elected to promote and make arrangements for the programme.

The mission was entitled FREE INDEED. The theme was taken from John 8:36, 'If the Son therefore shall make you free, you shall be free indeed.' It was well advertised using posters, personal and printed invitations, and through the use of articles written for local papers. As it was intended to be a ministry of the body of Christ it was agreed that no offerings be taken up at meetings.

Geoffrey Bingham came to Wudinna with a team of 11 students from the A.B.I. They played an active and significant part in the worship services and shared their own personal testimonies with the locals. Bingham was no newcomer to missions, nor to revival. He brought wisdom and experience with him. At one time he was the minister of a strong, dynamic congregation which sometimes attracted up to 1000 people at Holy Trinity Church, Millers Point in Sydney. Historian Stuart Piggin described him as probably the most successful young minister in Sydney during the 1950s (Lecture, 1992).

In 1957 Bingham had gone to Pakistan as a missionary (Loane 1988:90). Then in 1961 he founded the Pakistan Bible Institute and during a nine year teaching career from 1957-1966, witnessed two great waves of revival in this predominantly Muslim Country (Bingham 1992:95-120).

Bingham came to Wudinna not give revival messages, but to simply preach from the Bible. The messages were solid teaching about bondage to sin and Satan and the powers of darkness and the flesh and the world and so on; and the true freedom which Christ gives from such powers. Bingham is a powerful preacher. He has a commanding presence and a winning sense of humour.

Startling response

The huge turnout for the first meeting at the Minnipa Anglican Church startled the organisers, impressed the visiting preacher and surprised the crowd of about 150 locals who came to hear him. 'No one gets West Coast people to come out if they don't want to,' observed John Kammermann.

But this was a phenomenon which continued throughout the week of the mission. The atmosphere was expectant, people listened intently and many who attended were people no one even expected to be interested in Christian things. One well known local businessman who was an avowed atheist and communist attended more than one of the meetings!

On the first Sunday morning in Wudinna, the Church was so packed with 200-300 people that the ministers had to tip toe through the sanctuary in order to get past the overflowing masses of people. Many folk were crammed into the porch and some were even forced to listen from the windows outside.

At the service at Koongawa on Sunday afternoon, Ruth Toy, the organist, who usually put out about 6 chairs for the congregation, added enough extra to allow for the mission team! By the time the meeting began, the entire hall was filled with about 100 people. Ruth Toy was stunned. Not surprisingly, she was one of those who was deeply affected by the mission. She experienced such an amazing conversion, that her husband approached Rev. Bingham and asked him what he had been doing with his wife. When Bingham asked what he meant, the husband replied 'Well she was a chain smoker and she stopped smoking and she was a pretty powerful swearer and she doesn't swear a word and she was a very angry woman and I don't see any anger.'

Things like that happened one after the other. All meetings were extremely well attended. Kyancutta Hall on the Monday night had 200-300 in attendance.

Wudinna local Marj Holman vividly remembers how she was completely renewed through the mission. Both young and old, those who had been pew sitters for many years, plus those who had been newly drawn into the church scene, repented, were brought to tears, brought to their knees, received forgiveness and were given new life and unimaginable joy in the Spirit. Some were amazed that even their headaches were healed immediately. Yet, there seemed to be no pattern at all to the way in which God was moving.

On the Monday night at Kyancutta as Bingham was preaching, he could hear strange noises going on during the meeting. He had been fighting to get his words out. He couldn't see anyone's mouth open and it struck him that it was a demonic phenomenon. He had previously witnessed meetings like that in Pakistan, and so he said, 'Satan, in Christ's name we rebuke you, and command you to leave this meeting.'

There was a loud bang. People sat there a little bit astonished at what had happened, but, the whole place was absolutely quiet.

People later remarked that up until that point they had felt their minds were very scrambled and they couldn't hear what the preacher was saying. It had not made sense, people couldn't hear rationally. But at once, everything changed and the preaching was full of power. Many people remained behind after this meeting and refused to go home until they had spoken with someone about becoming converted to Christ.

Impact of the Spirit

John Dunn, one of the students on the mission team, testified to being healed of a longstanding problem during the week of the mission. He also recalls some of the unusual events: A farmer who had not been coming to the meetings, although his wife did, was out on his tractor when great conviction came upon him and he got down in the dust and gave his life to the Lord. A woman believed she was healed of a kidney complaint in one of the meetings, and tests at the hospital the next day showed that there was no longer any problem with the kidney. Many were converted. There was also great opposition. Some shouted back or walked out as Geoff was preaching.

John Kammermann was another local Wudinna farmer who became a Christian at this time. He was a man who had previously listened thoughtfully to preachers, but had always known that he had insufficient resources within himself to sustain a commitment to Christ. However, this mission was different. He had a strong desire not to attend the meetings at all, yet somehow he was compelled to go.

'I remember that by the time we got to the Sunday service,' he recalled wryly, 'there were only seats right down the front under the preachers nose. However in the wisdom of God that's where you get a good look at the conviction of the messenger! I was convinced that he knew God. If he could know God like that then maybe I could as well.'

The reality of God's presence and the singing in the meetings was quite extraordinary. It was something John and others had never expected. He recalls how the truth and words of one particular song kept coming back to him: 'Surely goodness and mercy shall follow me all the days, all the days of my life. And I shall dwell in the house of the Lord for ever, and I shall feast at the table set for me.'

In many ways the situation and the events of those glorious days defies both explanation and description. God was at work graciously revealing himself, giving to each what they needed. It was remarkable, and somewhat unusual, to see the way in which children would happily go to sleep on the seats of motor vehicles or on the floor of the meeting halls. Bingham (1992:99) comments on this same phenomenon during revival in Pakistan.

Some folk surprised their own friends and relatives, as they deliberately broke normal patterns of behaviour and hurried off to be in time for the meetings. 'I think our parents thought we were a bit strange,' recalled Kay Kammermann.

The gift of the Spirit

On the Saturday night Bingham taught concerning the Holy Spirit. He made the point that the Father was pleased to give the gift of the Holy Spirit to those who asked. He said, 'What the cross cleansed, the Spirit comes to fill.' The assurance given was that God was true to his Word and that he delighted for the West Coast folk to receive his gift. Many did.

'God was in the place forgiving the sin of our past godlessness, and giving the gift of His Spirit,' John Kammerman remembered. 'Even now that memory still evokes emotion.'

The promise of a rich future from God's hand was something many could not contain. The atmosphere at the meetings could neither be explained or induced. People felt the presence of the Lord and had the expectation that all was well with them on account of that Presence.

At the end of the meetings crowds of people would just sit silently in wonderment for half an hour not moving.

One woman was so settled in her seat a member of the mission team invited Bingham to meet her. She spoke in a voice of wonderment saying 'I never knew he loved me like that!'

Deane Meatheringham reported, 'We couldn't get people to stand up and leave. This is the closest I have come to seeing things we read of in Acts or in John Wesley's Journal.'

There was a woman who had heard the Christian message many times before. For years she had experienced the agony of various shoulder aches and pains. Some time after the mission, she stood up in Church and told how as she was sitting down milking the cow one morning it dawned on her what the Word of God had been saying to her for years. And that was that she was free! All her aches and pains went and she was liberated.

Other occurrences were similar to those described in the New Testament such as Acts 2:13 where newly Spirit-filled believers were described as drunk. One man, Trevor Gerschwitz, was so excited and effervescent when he called in to speak with his Lutheran Pastor, Ron Wilsch, on the way home from one of the meetings, that the Pastor later commented that if he hadn't known him better, he'd have sworn he was drunk.

One burly farmer approached Bingham one night and said, 'My wife and I made decisions when we were teenagers, but I've never seen her like that. I want what she's got. You've got to give it to me.'

Bingham explained that what she had was freedom and that he could not give it to him; only Christ could do that. So one night the man stood in a prominent place at the back of the great mob at Minnipa while Bingham preached. All of a sudden he put his hand up and waved at Bingham as much as to say, 'It's happened you know; I've got it, this freedom'.

One night after the meeting, a local man, Ron Holman, 'fairly stoic by nature,' went and sat down beside Bingham. When asked what he thought of the meeting, Holman replied that he thought it was all right.

Bingham recognised that here was a man who generally didn't seek conversation, so he said to him 'Have you ever received the gift of forgiveness?'

Holman replied, 'No I haven't.'

Bingham then asked him if he wanted to.

The reply was blunt: 'Why do you think I'm sitting next to you?'

Within a few minutes he was absolutely liberated. Holman has since had quite a history of helping on mission teams, and regularly having witness and ministry.

The mission included a civic luncheon and visits to schools. Each day the mission team would meet for prayer. Throughout the week there were also numerous small informal gatherings for meals and discussions all across the 80 mile circuit, as well as a Saturday afternoon picnic, where people took the opportunity to talk more intimately with one another. Numerous folk sought out Bingham to ask him further questions concerning his messages.

Natural Christianity

Many beheld a previously unseen phenomenon – West Coast men actually had their Bibles out while they were cooking the BBQ – and were more interested in the message of the Bible than the food on the fire. But what was so strikingly unusual about all this, was that it seemed so natural.

Bingham notes that revival should be natural.

We need to understand God's purpose for history. We need to see why, and how, revival is essential as a phenomenon in the course of history. We need to understand its goal. When we do, then the whole subject of revival is removed from the theoretical area, from mere human theologising, or human attempts at manipulating God into action. It comes into the realm of necessary action. We discover, in fact, that the word 'revival' in one sense covers the whole of the action of God in history. The principle of giving life, sustaining it and renewing it – that is, revival – is the work which God is about continually' (1983:ix).

This was not religion but life. People were free indeed. Consistent with Bingham's style, the mission had been free of gimmicks and tricks aimed at manipulating people. From one point of view, there was no need for it, it was an evangelist's delight. 'People were getting converted hand over fist,' and this left a deep impression upon everyone.

The climate was such that in fact 'someone could have got up to skull duggery,' John Kammermann noted. The West Coast community had seen their fair share of entertainers, hypnotists and spiritualists. Bingham was aware of the pitfalls of such an atmosphere and was well acquainted with his own powers as a speaker. On the Wednesday night at the Wudinna Hall, in his concern that people not be manipulated, he gave a demonstration of the effects which could be induced by a speaker. He deliberately vocalised a hissing noise. The whole gathering reacted and a loud clunk was heard as everyone's feet hit the floor together. People have commented how thankful they were that the potential of the situation had been publicly exposed and recognised. A clean, clear atmosphere prevailed.

Like Pentecost

The last planned meeting on the Sunday afternoon was quite amazing. There were well over 400 at the meeting. People came from as far away as Ceduna and Cummins. Many have said it was like the first Pentecost but without tongues.

Of the final night Bingham said, 'Like a great rain of beauty and silence and joy, it just descended on the whole congregation. It was quite remarkable. I'd have called it a very gentle but a very powerful outpouring of the Holy Spirit. And I can remember the joy in the worship and praise that night.'

During the mission there had been no appeals for people to come forward. There had been no pressure applied. But there had been an astonishing response. Children and people right up to those in their seventies, and many from each age group, had been deeply moved.

At the close of the final meeting, people wanting to talk with someone about faith were invited to move about halfway down the hall and enter into the supper room, where the team and other local folk were waiting to help. Over 50 people were counselled by those who had been prepared for the task.

In the weeks, months and years that followed the mission, God continued to reveal his love to his people at Wudinna. The mission had been no seven day wonder, but folk continued to be converted to Christ (Curnow 1977:82-83).

During the week immediately after the mission, John Kammermann arrived home from work keen to share with his wife Kay the details of a marvellous encounter with God, which he had experienced while shearing a sheep. In it he had understood anew the dynamic truth of God's love. 'It was not that God is love AND sent his Son; but rather IN the sending of his Son, God is love.'

How might that be communicated to a farmer in a shearing shed? As he recounted the somewhat unusual, yet seemingly natural happening, Kay quickly replied, 'Guess what? The very same thing happened to me today while I was hanging out the washing.'

Many enriching conversations took place. Neighbours would sit down together somewhere out on the boundary fence of their large properties and go through the great events of salvation together, or read and ponder the words of Scripture while working on a tractor.

There had been something like 31 home groups in the week leading up to the mission. Some of these now combined and turned into Bible studies. The Ladies Guild virtually became a Bible Study Group (Curnow 1977:82).

Meatheringham was untiring in his efforts to nurture his people. This included writing a counselling booklet entitled 'Christianity is Christ.' As a Pastor he moved well among the community and encouraged people to continue in their faith. There were 61 confirmees during his 5 year term at Wudinna (Curnow 1977:83). Pastoral letters were written to teach, exhort and encourage people. The instruction given was clear and simple. People were enjoined to accept their salvation joyfully, live by faith in Christ, read the Bible diligently, pray earnestly and worship regularly.

Following the mission the Wudinna folk regularly sent teams of young preachers out to places like Haslam and Streaky Bay to help out. Families and groups would often get into cars with all their kids, and they would sing from chorus books all the way to and from their destination. Many people opened their lives and homes to one another. Spontaneous sharing of meals took place and people loved to gather together in homes after Church. There was a general air of excitement in the Church and people eagerly heard the Word from Deane and guest preachers.

One of the leaders, when praying during the mission 'saw' a large heap of leaves and a strong gust of wind scattering them all over what seemed a map of Australia. This was interpreted as indicating that lots of people touched by God would be moved on into many parts of this land; and it happened that way. Many people moved in later years to Western Australia, Victoria, Queensland and other parts of South Australia.

A consolidating mission entitled WE REIGN IN LIFE was organised in 1972 with the circuit now being pastored by the Rev. Ian Clarkson. Bingham and another team of students returned to lead the mission and the important question put to the Wudinna folk was taken from Galatians 3:3 'Having begun in the Spirit' where are you now?

There had in fact been some difficulties within the church community since the time of the first mission. Some had sought to place greater emphasis upon the role and work of the Holy Spirit, and this caused divisions. One group broke away and later became the Christian Revival Crusade (C.R.C). To this day, hurts are slowly being healed.

After the first mission, it was natural enough that reports of revival soon began to circulate. Fellow pastors were eager to discover what techniques were used. When faced with this question at the Annual Methodist Conference, Deane Meatheringham made the now famous reply: 'We organised a mission and God got out of hand.'

In a report on the happening, Meatheringham concluded: 'Some people might say that we have had a revival. But in such arid days as ours I think this is exaggeration. We have seen the sparks of revival, and possibly the beginnings of even greater things.'

Apart from the movement in Pakistan, Bingham describes this event as the second closest thing to revival he has seen. The closest being what began at the Garrison Church in Sydney and spread from there to other churches during the mid 1950s.

This was the episode of Christian life which took place at Wudinna in 1969. In manifold ways the story continues to unfold.

References

Bingham, G. C. (1983) *Dry Bones Dancing.* Adelaide: New Creation Publications.

— (1985) *The Day of the Spirit.* Adelaide: New Creation Publications.

— (1985) *Christ the Conquering King.* Adelaide: New Creation Publications.

— (1992) *Twice Conquering Love.* Adelaide: New Creation

Publications

Chant, B. (1984) *Heart of Fire.* Adelaide: The House of Tabor.

Curnow, E. A., ed. (1977) *Faith on the Western Front.* Aldis.

Loane, M. L. (1988) 'Geoffrey Cyril Bingham' in *These Happy Warriors.* Adelaide: New Creation Publications.

Meatheringham, D. (1981) *Gospel Incandescent.* Adelaide: New Creation Publications.

— (1969) Pastoral Letter: 'The Assurance of God's Word.'

— (1969) Pastoral Letter: How to Succeed as a Christian.'

— (1969) Report of Mission Held at Wudinna, August 21-31.

Murray, Ian. H. (1988) *Australian Christian Life from 1788.* The Banner of Truth Trust.

Piggin, Stuart (1992) Lecture: 'Piety and Politics in Australia in the 1950s,' given to 'Australian Religious History' class at Flinders University (S.A.), on 21 May.

Wilson, B. (1983) *Can God Survive in Australia?* Albatross Books.

© Trevor Faggotter

Reviews

Francis MacNutt. 1988. *Healing* **(Revised Edition)** Lake Mary: Creation House, 333 pages. (Originally 1975, Ave Maria Press, and Bantam).

Here is a classic, still being reprinted and read widely. Francis MacNutt writes from the background of a Ph.D. in Theology and many years in a powerful healing ministry among Catholics and others in the whole church, specially working in teams and in loving communities of praying people.

This book avoids the 'faith healing' jargon, is written with sensitivity, honesty, humility and compassion. Your faith grows as you read.

The 21 chapters are arranged in four parts.

Part 1 deals with the underlying meaning and importance of the healing ministry. Chapters cover our prejudices against healing, salvation and wholeness, miracles and God's love. It notes some of our resistances to God's healing grace.

Part 2 covers faith, hope and love as they touch upon the healing ministry. It acknowledges the mystery involved and emphasises the importance of love. This section recognises the importance of faith and also acknowledges that healing does not always occur, even when there is faith for healing.

Part 3 explores four basic kinds of healing and how to pray for each. These include spiritual conditions including forgiveness of sin, emotional conditions including inner healing, physical conditions including the importance of soaking prayer (not just a quick fix), and demonic conditions needing deliverance.

Part 4 looks at special considerations including discernment of root causes, eleven reasons why people are not healed, medicine and healing, the sacraments, and answers to questions most often asked.

The book is now available in a revised version more acceptable to people who may have had difficulty with some of the Catholic expressions in the first edition. Both versions build faith and compassion. It is excellent (G.W.).

Wimber, John with Springer, Kevin. 1986. *Power Healing.* London: Hodder and Stoughton.

This best seller is filled with faith building accounts of healing through the power of God. Thousands of people have learned to pray with compassion and sensitivity to the leading of God's Spirit from the teaching and examples in this book and in John Wimber's ministry.

Part 1: Why does Jesus heal? is autobiographical, dealing with John Wimber's long struggle to accept the healing ministry as valid and his conviction of God's compassion and mercy and its expression in healing, even through the prayers of an unlikely healer.

Part 2: What does Jesus heal? deals with the healing of the whole person, overcoming effects of past hurts, healing the demonised, physical healing, and why everyone is not healed. Like MacNutt, Wimber's refreshing honesty acknowledges the mystery and sovereignty of God in healing but also stresses that healing happens through prayer and faith.

Part 3: How does Jesus heal through us? gives practical guidance on how to learn to pray for the sick including an integrated model of healing involving 5 steps: Step 1 the interview, answers 'Where does it hurt?' Step 2 the diagnostic decision, answers 'Why does this person have this condition?' Step 3 the prayer selection, answers 'What kind of prayer is needed to help this person?' Step 4 the prayer engagement, answers 'How effective are our prayers?' Step 5 post-prayer direction, answers 'What should they do to keep their healing, and what should they do if they were not healed?

Horrobin, Peter. 1991. *Healing through Deliverance.* Sovereign World, 314 pages.

Deliverance from demonic influence or oppression is a controversial subject, but clearly described and demonstrated in Scripture. Peter Horrobin, writing from his team's extensive healing ministry in the north of England, has produced a well written and balanced approach to deliverance.

The book gives a comprehensive biblical assessment of the place of deliverance in the ministry of Jesus, in the early church, and applies this biblical basis to ministry in the church today. It discusses the supernatural realms of angels and demons and shows how these can affect our lives.

This book tackles the difficult questions raised by deliverance ministry including whether Christians can be affected by demons, and why. It gives many helpful examples, directly applying biblical accounts to ministry with people today.

Written with delightful English reserve and understatement by an Oxford graduate, the book argues for obedience to Jesus' teaching by ministering as he did: 'Jesus' ministry was totally balanced, which in practice meant that he taught with radical authority on the whole range of life's issues. For Jesus, balance did not mean middle of the road compromise, but decisive teaching and action which was sufficient to meet the needs of all who came to him' (p. 21).

Here is a biblically based description of healing through deliverance which can help you believe and obey Jesus more fully. (G.W.).

Hunter, Harold and Hocken, Peter. 1993. *All Together in One Place.* Sheffiled: Sheffield Academic Press, 280 pages.

This book is solid theological and academic reading from the papers and discussion at the Brighton Conference on World Evangelization in 1991. The Conference addressed Pentecostal and charismatic issues in a symposium of scholars drawn from six continents.

The editors note that ' Brighton '91 should lay to rest a number of misconceptions that still cloud academic and ecclesiastical circles, chief among them the notion that serious scholarly work is absent from the movement. This conference also illustrates why Pentecostalism is not correctly classified as a subcategory of Evangelicalism, and why not all charismatics are rightly described as Protestants. Another prejudice that dies hard is the assumption of endemic indifference on the part of Pentecostal and charismatic Christians towards social injustice. The contributions from South Africa with the presentation of The Relevant Pentecostal Witness, as well as the papers on liberation theology, tell a different and encouraging story.'

The Archbishop of Canterbury, George Carey, gives the Introduction on 'The Importance of Theology for the Charismatic Movement' noting that theology is the task of understanding the Christian faith with the tools of faith, experience, history and critical reason; that the task of theology is to mediate between a faith and a culture; and that experience needs to infuse the academic process as academic study informs and underpins experience.

Jurgen Moltmann, well known theologian, gives the leading paper in Part I on 'The Spirit gives Life: Spirituality and Vitality'. He comments on the charismatic vitality of the new life, speaking in tongues ('a strong inner grasp of the Spirit that its expression leaves the realm of understandable speech and expresses itself in an extraordinary manner'), the awakening of the charismatic experience ('Those who believe will become persons of possibilities. They will not limit themselves to prescribed social roles nor allow themselves to be defined by them. They believe themselves capable of more. And they do not tie other people down with prejudices. They do not define other people by their reality, but rather see them together with their future and hold their possibilities open for them'), healing of the sick ('occurs in the interaction between Jesus and the expectation, the faith and the will of the people. This means that these healings are contingent. They are not 'made', they occur where and when God want it. There is no method for such healings because they are not repeatable and replicability is the presupposition for all methods. The healing of all ill is prayed for. Hands are laid on ill ones for healing which is to be obtained by prayer'), the gift of the disabled life ('Communities without disabled persons are disabled communities. In the Christian sense, a charismatic community is always the serving community since gift implies service.'), each according to ability each according to need, and the Holy Spirit as the power of life and Space of Life. Two papers respond helpfully to Moltmann. Other major papers, with responses, cover 'Pentecostalism and Liberation Theology: Two Manifestations of the Work of the Holy Spirit for the Renewal of the Church', 'Charismatic Churches and Apartheid in South Africa', and 'African independent Church Pneumatology and the Salvation of all Creation.'

Part II deals with Pentecostal/charismatic issues including the work of the Holy Spirit in urban and multicultural society, poverty and persecution, women and Pentecostal spirituality, Pentecostal origins in global perspective, and progress in the light of the Eschatological Kingdom.

Part III covers evangelical topics including an evangelical charismatic perspective on other living faiths, evangelism and charismatic signs, miracles and martyrdom, evangelism and eschatology, and ecumenical issues in evangelising together.

This is a significant book of theological reflection which should be included in theological college libraries as well as in church libraries (G.W.).

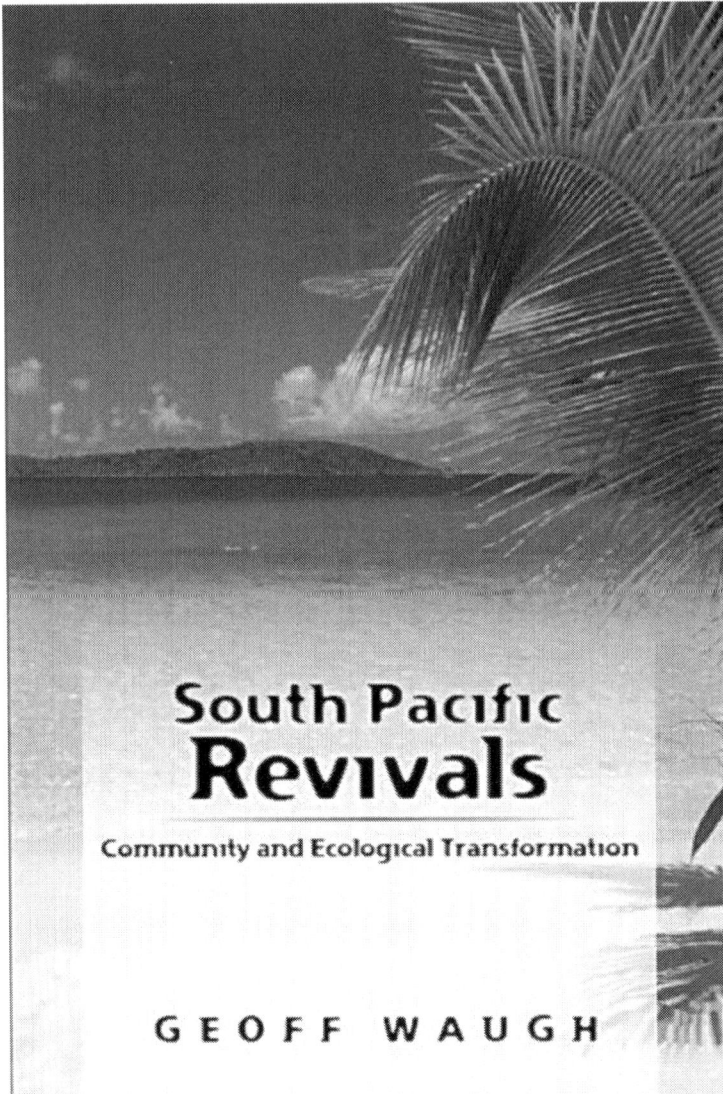

South Pacific Revivals

Community and Ecological Transformation

Renewal Journal
5 Signs and Wonders

Contents

Renewal Journal 5: Signs and Wonders

Cover photo: 5 Signs and Wonders
Pastors and leaders in Myanmar (Burma) pray together
and see signs and wonders amid persecution.

Editorial

Confirming the Word with Signs Following (Mark 16:20)

Signs and wonders are controversial. They were in Scripture. They are still.

The early church prayed earnestly for signs and wonders (Acts 4:29-31). It was extremely controversial. But the kingdom of God came in power and the church grew rapidly with thousands added to the faith, amid persecution. That now happens for millions of Christians today.

Some people argue that signs and wonders ceased with the passing of the apostles. However, Scripture and church history indicate the opposite (John 14:12; Matthew 28:20). The kingdom of God is not a matter of words but of power – the power of God. Signs of the kingdom and wonders declaring the reign of God break in upon us still.

We see this most powerfully in Jesus' life and ministry. He proclaimed and demonstrated the rule of God in everything – in people's lives, over demonic powers, in creation and history. It was true in the early church. It continues to be true.

The cross is the power of God for salvation to all who believe. We can have a diminished view of the cross of Christ and the incredible salvation wrought by Jesus on the cross. It involves far more than providing a personal entry to heaven for individual believers. Our concern with personal salvation can obscure for us the immense power and glory of God revealed in Jesus' total and awesome victory on the cross. In Jesus' death and resurrection the power of evil was defeated forever. The Lord reigns. All the powers are subject to Jesus Christ the Lord (Colossians 1:20; Philippians 2:11).

Signs of God's kingly rule testify to Jesus' triumph. God reigns. We don't initiate signs and wonders. We can't. But we can obey God. We can repent (especially of our unbelief) and believe. We can do what Jesus commanded all his followers to do in his name and authority. Then, as in the early church, the gospel is proclaimed with signs following.

We live in a time in history when millions of Christians are learning that again, especially as the Spirit of God renews life and faith in us. We have not always believed or obeyed God's word to us. We can rationalise our sin of unbelief and disobedience, calling it theological wisdom. Yet, Jesus, who alone is the truth, confronts and unnerves us with his awesome claims and authority. Those who found Jesus in Gethsemane fall backwards at his word. Soldiers at his resurrection shake in fear and collapse as dead. Saul is blinded by the glory of the Lord and falls to the ground overwhelmed. John falls at the feet of his Lord as though dead (Revelation 1:17).

No church tradition nor theological position can fully express the awesome reign of God. We still see and know only partially (1 Corinthians 13:12). For example, the Lord has one church – his. We often see the church mainly in cultural, doctrinal and denominational terms. These fall far short of the glory of God revealed in his people, the church. So we all need to walk humbly with our God as we proclaim God's reign and live in his kingdom.

Jesus' life demonstrated the reign of God fully. In our lives we merely glimpse it. However, as we allow the Spirit of God who anointed Jesus to also anoint us, we continue to glimpse even more of the signs and wonders of God's presence and power among us.

Controversial blessings

This issue of the *Renewal Journal* examines controversial blessings. Part of our difficulty is that God works in fallible people through fallible people – including you and me. Often our behaviour involves very human reactions to signs of God's reign and wonders of his power breaking in upon us.

Furthermore, our words and actions are affected by many influences – God's Spirit and other spirits, our personalities, our culture, our relationships. Normal expressions of joy and worship in Latin America may be regarded as wildly excessive in northern Europe. Our explanations are inadequate and incomplete. Who can express the inexpressible? God's thoughts and ways are far beyond ours (Isaiah

55:8).

Reactions to God's action are mixed. God moved powerfully in the Azusa Street Apostolic Faith Mission in 1906. That was controversial. Loud noise, tongues, fainting, and falling on the floor were common. Yet amid the varied reactions, it ignited Pentecostal fire around the world. Gamaliel suggests we leave the jury out for a while on such matters lest we fight against God (Acts 5:39).

Often visitations of God's Spirit stir up varied reactions. Then, later we learn to incorporate these new developments effectively and powerfully in our work and witness. Remember the youthful zeal of the Jesus People, the rediscovery of spiritual gifts, the fresh insights of inner healing, the new awareness of deliverance, the leaps of faith to release millions of dollars and thousands of people for mission in the power of the Spirit?

Fortunately we have Scripture as our guide – not just our interpretations of Scripture. Our interpretations often include unbiblical rationalising which may deny the powerful presence of God's Spirit among us. Many of the articles in this issue of the Journal examine our reaction to God's action.

Brian Hathaway emphasises the importance of words, signs and deeds in proclaiming and demonstrating the gospel. Derek Prince reflects on the overwhelming impact of God's Spirit. John Wimber gives guidelines for coping with various phenomena. People involved in recent events in England and Australia offer their perspective. Jerry Steingard presents observations from Scripture, church history and current ministries. Bart Doornweerd tells how he learned to proclaim God's word with signs following. Stephen Bryar addresses charismatic issues in his tradition.

Sandy Millar and Eleanor Mumford describe the beginnings of this renewal blessing in their churches in England and Anglicans John Davies Phil Ashton, Geoff Glass and Tony Stevens report on early expressions of this blessing in Australia.

May we repent of our unbelief, believe and proclaim God's word in the power of the Spirit with signs following, and see the kingdom of God break in upon us more fully. May God grant an impact of his Spirit with thousands converted, filled with the Spirit, and living for the glory of God as Jesus our Lord is honoured and glorified among us all.

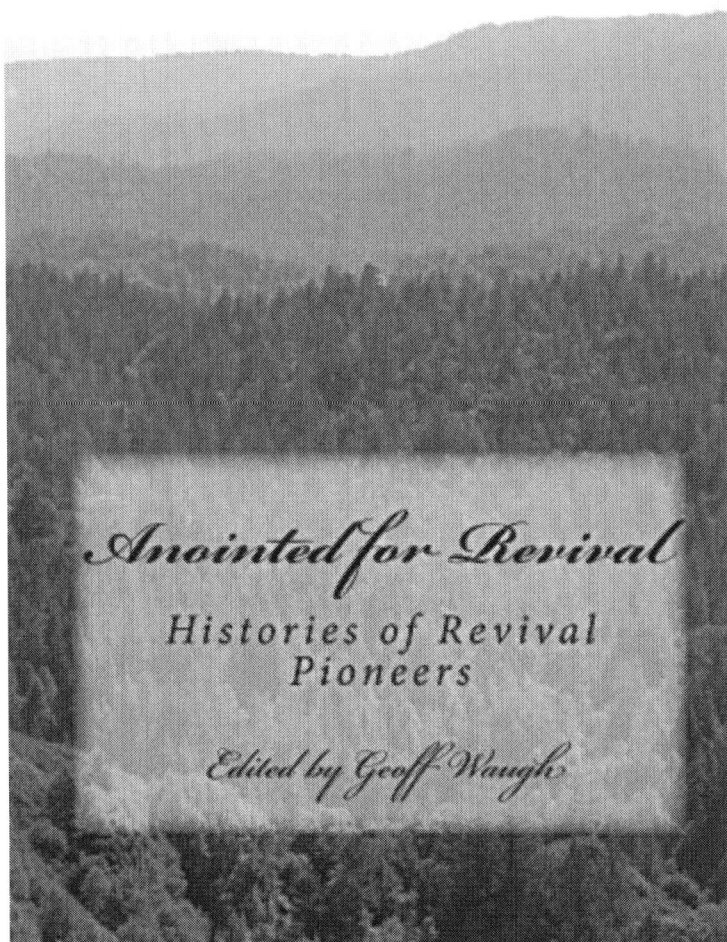

Anointed for Revival

Histories of Revival Pioneers

1 Words, Signs and Deeds

Brian Hathaway

Brian Hathaway, an elder in a Brethren church in Auckland, and national principal of the Bible College of New Zealand, wrote of the journey towards integration in ministry.

Words announce the truth of God

Signs demonstrate the power of God

Deeds express the love of God

The Beginnings

Our congregation in West Auckland was formed in 1965 as an offshoot of a Brethren church in Auckland. In its early days it was very much a youth outreach. In the 1970' s we were impacted by the Charismatic Renewal that was going on in New Zealand. People in our congregation attended services and conferences, read books, listened to tapes and of course came back and discussed this in the church and home groups. Not surprisingly, this created a degree of conflict and tension in the congregation.

However, previous to these events God had brought us to an understanding of the importance of relationships in the church: the need to be honest, open and transparent with each other so that we could handle tensions. I'm grateful to God that he brought that to our attention first. It enabled us to handle more easily the pressures that the renewal brought to us.

I need to say that at no time in our history did we ever sit down and devise some sort of master plan for what has happened in our congregation. All we sought to do as an eldership was take the steps that God led us into. In Mark 4:24 Jesus says, 'Consider carefully what you hear. With the measure you use, it will be measured to you and even more. Whoever has will be given more; whoever does not have, even what he has will be taken from him.' It is crucial to understand that we must use what God gives us.

If God teaches us something, use it. Apply it. The measure we use whatever you apply, whatever you use, whatever you appropriate that will be measured back to you again and even more. This principle is fundamental in leadership. It's about going forward individually and corporately; growing together personally and as a group; listening to God privately and collectively. We are on a pilgrimage. And that's a community activity, as the New Testament sees it. A 'walking with Jesus, and in the company of others' (Fung). Our history has been an expression of a desire to follow God through a series of doors he's opened to us.

With Charismatic Renewal occurring in many churches around our country, and people in the congregation becoming interested and involved, we clearly had to address the issue. In 1978 the elders decided to spend the year talking about Charismatic Renewal together. What was it? Could we embrace it? Were there things we could learn from it? We spent one night a month talking, praying, reading papers, looking into the Scriptures discussing the matter and by October we had come to the unanimous conclusion that we could embrace two main features of the movement.

1. We concluded that each Christian needed an empowering work of the Holy Spirit. We did not want to argue over what to call this or whether it came at or after conversion. What we were concerned about was that people knew the Holy Spirit experientially not just in their head, or as theology.

2. We decided that we would be open to all the gifts of the Holy Spirit and seek to operate these gifts along Biblical guidelines. To us it did

not seem consistent to believe that certain gifts ceased at the end of the first century.

Thus at the end of 1978 there was a change in the elders' attitude towards the work of the Spirit. A paper was presented to the Church outlining our conclusions, and then discussed thoroughly. The whole process evoked a very positive response from the congregation. People said that as last the elders knew where they were going. We didn't really! We had started on a pilgrimage and we are still on a pilgrimage, taking steps of faith. I hope we will always do this. Not to do so is to wither and die.

In a nutshell I guess what we said was, 'Lord, do anything you want to. With your help, from our Brethren foundation, we will seek to discover in practice what it means to follow your Spirit. We don't want to be a Pentecostal church; neither do we want to copy Charismatic churches. We may go to them to receive insight, but we want this to be unique for us.' Can't the God who makes unique snowflakes also make unique congregations?

At the beginning of 1979 the congregation started to grow very rapidly. Nothing had changed but our attitude towards the Holy Spirit. People became Christians in January. Unusual for New Zealand! God's in the Northern Hemisphere over January New Zealanders are at the beach! To see six adults converted in January was staggering; and it continued month after month.

Over the next ten years, as best as we can estimate, we saw about 1,000 people come to faith in Christ. As we look back on this, all we can say is that God saw our unity and change of attitude towards his Spirit and began to work in a new way among us.

New Directions

Within a year, God led us into penetrating the community. Normally when a church starts to grow, the first thing you think about is getting a fulltime pastor. God seemed to be saying to us, though, that we should think about our wider community first. So we approached a couple about this, and for eighteen months financially supported by the congregation they worked within the local community. Via newspapers, local groups and Government departments, they signalled availability to senior citizens, single parents and those who were sick. They cut hedges, mowed lawns, cleaned windows, provided transport.

Often after doing a job they would be invited in to have a cup of tea. The person helped would want to know how much they owed for the service provided. Hearing it was nothing would inevitably open up further discussion as to how and why this was possible. This would lead quite naturally to sharing about Christ. In eighteen months this couple led about 8 people into a totally new relationship with the Lord. We now realise that we had linked together social concern and evangelism.

From there a cluster of community ministries developed to begin to meet peoples' needs within the community. We were also involved in overseas mission and most recently we have been engaged in church planting. Currently we have three congregations that are seeking to work together. Our premise here is that it is a little short sighted to form a new congregation and lock up all the resources of that congregation within itself. Our aim is to have congregations with their own responsible elderships inter relating, with a free flow of resources, people and training across congregations.

A co-ordinating group facilitates combined arrangements and there is recognition of visionary people who can maintain the bigger view. You will probably realise that this is not a Brethren pattern. Nor has it been easy to implement. In the past, new Brethren congregations fairly quickly isolated themselves from others or the birthing body to go their own, totally autonomous, way. We do not feel that this is a Biblical model. There seems to be a degree of liaison between the churches of the New Testament.

Thus our aim is to get the best of both worlds local elders committed to the establishment of work in the local area, while at the same time maintaining relationships between elders in each congregation to enable a free flow of resources.

For us, combined areas involve overseas missions, youth, equipping, about six combined celebrations a year, and elders retreats. Currently we are responsible for somewhere over 1000 adults and children across the three congregations.

As we look back on the steps that we have taken, we recognise that we have been seeking to integrate three major emphases. Onto our heritage of a *conservative evangelical* church we have sought to build the strengths of the *Pentecostal/Charismatic* streams of the Church and then the strengths of the *social justice* stream of the Church.

In endeavouring to interweave the strengths of these three movements we have also come to recognise their weaknesses. Let me sketch these quickly for you. I am indebted to Roger Forster from the Ichthus Fellowship, London, for some of these insights.

The Conservative/Evangelical Position

The first weakness we see in this position is the rather emasculated gospel of 'souls'. Two things that were impressed on me in my younger days were the necessity of living a holy life and the need to save souls. I have discovered that these goals are not wrong but they are insufficient.

Another weakness of this position has been the tendency towards a bigoted, self righteous exclusiveness. I can remember in my Bible class days analysing the cults. We would discuss why the main world religions were wrong, why the Jehovah's Witnesses were wrong, the Methodists, the Presbyterians.....!

Let me, to be fair, say that I am talking about a conservative country assembly of 35 years ago. I also want to make it quite clear that I am very grateful for my Brethren heritage. I am not putting that down. I wouldn't dare to. Its innate strengths, prayerful parents and many Brethren friends make any rejection of my origins impossible. And it is part of God's good grace to me, anyway! I am just pointing out some of the weaknesses.

A further weakness for many conservative evangelicals has been the emphasis on personal piety at the expense of social concern or social issues. This has probably stemmed from, and been reinforced by, the idea of 'coming out from among them and being separate'. This was a strong element of teaching in my youth. In practice it often meant no dances; and no cinemas. When my Dad played cricket for a local Club he was criticised not for playing on Sunday but for playing on Saturday. 'You don't do that. You might get caught up in their sinful habits!' In Exclusive Brethren Assemblies such an attitude is taken to the extreme of not eating with people, not listening to radios, and blocking windows of churches so people cannot see into the buildings.

I do not want to criticise rather I would analyse. This is a far healthier approach as it invites us to work together on areas that create division and destabilise relationships.

The Pentecostal/Charismatic Position

A major weakness of this stream has been the lack of objectivity in assessing 'results' and an accompanying tendency towards extravagant claims. Objective assessment of healings may be seen as lack of faith and sometimes extravagant claims are made prematurely.

Another weakness here is what many would see as manipulation and guiltproducing techniques. Before an offering is taken up I have heard some preachers say, 'If you give $10 to God he will multiply it tenfold.' I have been in many Pentecostal services and I sometimes sense that the worship leader is trying to manipulate the congregation. Such activities are not what God requires. They worry me.

A further weakness is the personal indulgence, the selfinterest, the 'Ime' Christianity. This is not limited to Pentecostals and Charismatics, but is quite strongly reinforced in these groups, especially in Western nations. We see its extremes in Prosperity Teaching. 'What's in this for me?' is often the motivation. Such an attitude is fed by our selfcentred society and our highly individualistic culture. Very often we Christians do not realise that this is happening to us.

The Liberal/Social Justice Position

The first weakness here is the failure to recognise the spiritual base of evil. Jesus clearly identified two kingdoms in conflict and he came to destroy the works of darkness. We'll not overcome the kingdom of Satan or social injustice simply by using human force, ingenuity, education or organisation. I am not saying that such human activities are unnecessary or futile, but in themselves they are insufficient. Sin is at the root of social injustice and you can't overcome sin in human systems solely by human endeavour. This tendency leads to an involvement in social justice dealing with fruits rather than roots.

The result of this is often tired, worn out people, overwhelmed by the needs of society. We have to ask questions about that. I do not question such peoples' motivation. They are well meaning and very committed to relieving a hurting society. I am not saying that serving God is easy or that you won't get tired. Of course not. None of us would. However I do sense a stress level in some of my Liberal Church friends who are very passionate about social needs in the community. I also see them often having great difficulty peopling their ministries.

If I were to juxtapose the liberal position with the classical evangelical position I'd say that Liberals go for improvement of life but ignore sin, whereas Evangelicals go for forgiving of sin but ignore life. E. Stanley Jones, speaking of this tension, says 'the one preaches the Gospel of bodies without souls, while the other preaches the Gospel of souls without bodies. The first is a corpse and the second a ghost.'

Now let me now draw your attention to the great strengths in these three streams of the Church. It's here that we can really learn from each other.

Words: living by the truth of God

The major strength of the Evangelical position is clearly its strong biblical base and emphasis on the need for a personal encounter with God through Jesus Christ. The commitment to Scripture as the basis for our Christian faith and the commitment to faith in God through Christ for salvation. I am glad for the heritage of my Biblical base. I'd not trade it for anything. I'm glad my children have it. In such an uncertain world it is a great foundation on which to build.

Signs: living in the power of God

The major strength of the Pentecostal/Charismatic position seems to be the emphasis on the practical experience of the empowering, gifting and leading of the Holy Spirit. I choose the words 'practical experience' carefully. In most of my Brethren upbringing we never got practical in this area. If we talked about the leading of the Spirit we never learned how actually to experience it. I remember one of our early New Zealand evangelists telling about being led by God in the 1930's to visit a town not on his itinerary, to discover many people waiting to hear the Gospel. This same man later came out very strongly against Pentecostal and the charismatic movement in our country. Our denomination has closed off from this whole dimension for about 30 years.

The Holy Spirit to the average Pentecostal/Charismatic is more than a theology or set of ideas or verses. He is the dynamic source of their spiritual life and Christian activity. Most Pentecostals and Charismatics are so because of an identifiable encounter with the Holy Spirit often subsequent to their salvation experience/event. Many such encounters that I have observed are life changing and deeply motivating. Intoxication was the description used in Acts 2. For them, Christian faith moves away from a solely intellectual and rational appeal and touches the deepest regions of a person's being. Often expressed in vibrant life, it can be very attractive to the non-Christian.

Much of our Brethren expression of our Christian faith (in New Zealand anyway) has been legal, rational and intellectual in its approach. Scripture assures us that 'the letter kills; the Spirit gives life.' To put the two dimensions of mind and spirit together is one of the greatest challenges facing Christians worldwide. I am very glad that our four children have been brought up in a church which understands this. They have seen people healed, they have experienced miraculous things, they have sensed the vibrancy and the expectancy of faith. They have all had a deep experience of God. We are glad about that. It has brought great strength to them.

I acknowledge that in this area there is also a danger of 'froth and bubble'. Lack of depth or maturity which may lead to post-pentecostals and post-charismatics (See Barratt, *International Bulletin of Missionary Research*, Vol. 12, No.3, July 1988).

Let me add that the Maori people have taught me a lot about sensitivity to the Holy Spirit. They are often very sensitive spiritually; sensitive to God and sensitive to the presence of demonic forces. It is those of us from a Western world view and I identify myself here in particular, coming as I do from a rational scientific background and a conservative Brethren heritage who have had particular struggles with aspects of the work of the Holy Spirit. This has been a great part of our pilgrimage over the past decade, seeking to discover this dimension and outwork it within the framework and guidelines of Scripture.

Within this major strength in the Pentecostal/Charismatic stream of the Church I have observed three further highlights. Each seems to have inherent strengths and weaknesses.

i. The evidence of spiritual gifts

Strength: The expectancy (faith) that the God of heaven is not dead, but loves to manifest his grace gifts among his people, is a characteristic feature of this `stream' of the Christian church. I well remember a Saturday morning just over two years ago, when a group of about 40 young people from our congregation were waiting expectantly for a session to begin. We had invited a person with a prophetic gift to our congregations and I knew that he had never met any of these young people before. One by one he stood them before him and spoke what he sensed God was saying to him. The group laughed as he touched on personal character traits that they recognised. Some cried as he mentioned their deepest longings and encouraged them to follow closely as God led them on.

Time after time we were awed as he spoke of things that he could have had no previous knowledge of. To the young man in the process of closing a business and with very little else offering 'You are having financial struggles but God is going to open up something new to you.' And it happened within a few weeks. To a young woman who had just returned from working with drug addicts and prostitutes in New York 'You have the underprivileged on your heart.' To another whose family was going through deep waters 'You have been grieving for your family and God has seen your great concern.' To one of the 'characters' of the group 'Come here stirrer!' And so it went on. Clear insights that could only come from the Spirit of God. Those young people left the room that morning walking on air God had spoken to them directly.

That type of prophetic gifting operating in a church is very powerful. Over recent years we have sought to encourage people who have sensed God leading them in this way to use this gifting.

Weakness: People can get 'hooked' on the supernatural and may be unable to handle periods of struggle or suffering. Then there is also the problem of hyper-faith and presumption. When you get involved in praying for healing, make sure that you have a theology of nonhealing as well, because pastorally you will need it. I have no problem if people get healed; the problem is when they don't.

ii. A heightened awareness of spiritual warfare and the need for prayer

Strength: The awareness of the spiritual dimension of life and the nature of the spiritual battle that is occurring on this planet are taken very seriously by most Pentecostals and Charismatics. Intercession is a word more commonly used by people of this stream of the Christian Church than by most of those in our Brethren assemblies.

Weakness: The danger of attributing everything to the devil and not recognising that much evil still lurks within the human soul.

iii. Dynamic music, worship and praise

Strength: There is little doubt that much of the best Christian music has come out of this stream of the Church over the past 30 years, inspired, they would claim, by the Holy Spirit. It's very attractive especially to young people. Many of the melodies and words seem to touch people deeply, often producing an outpouring of genuine love and adoration to the Lord.

Weakness: Worship may degenerate into a form of mushy sentimentality which caters for the prevalent existential ethos of much of our current society.

While I am discussing the Pentecostal, Charismatic and Third Wave (those who embrace the gifts and miraculous dimensions of the ministry of the Holy Spirit without wanting to be identified as Pentecostals or Charismatics) stream of the Church, let me remind you of its incredible growth over this century. From about 1% of the Christian Church at the commencement of 20th century to an estimated 30% by the end of the century. That's somewhere in the vicinity of 600 million people. An incredibly significant increase by anybody's reckoning! It has been noted that both the first century and the 20th century have been centuries of the Holy Spirit. Recent research reveals a correlation between the evidence of the supernatural power of God and Church growth, particularly in the two-

Deeds: living out the love of God

Finally let me outline what I see as the great strength of the Liberal stream of the Church their passionate concern for social justice.

Frequently their perspective on Scripture has 'brought me up with a jolt', as I have seen something of the passion of God's own heart for justice and his desires for his people.

Put another way, its strength lies in the understanding that the gospel has implications beyond personal salvation. I have come to understand that God is committed to the salvation, the reconciliation and the redemption of the whole universe. The cross does not only address personal sin. Its implications are much bigger. Ultimately everything that sin has touched and spoiled, God wants back under his rule and authority. He has commissioned us to go down that track as far as we can.

Conclusion

One of the problems we human beings have is ignoring strengths when we find weaknesses in a position contrary to our beliefs. If I can find weaknesses, I will focus on them and use them to dismiss and undermine strengths in an alternative position that I should be examining. This happens in all areas of life. As a leadership we have tried to listen to and learn from the insights of other perspective of the Church . We have sought to integrate the strengths of our evangelical heritage with those of the Pentecostal/Charismatic stream and the Liberal stream of the Church. We still have a long way to go, with much to learn and embrace; but then I guess that's what it means to be on a pilgrimage.

For the Evangelical the Gospel is most powerfully proclaimed by *words*; for the Pentecostal/Charismatic the declaration is most clearly emphasised in *signs*; for the Liberal the good news is most meaningfully expressed in *deeds*.

Words announce the truth of God. *Signs* demonstrate the power of God. *Deeds* express the love of God.

If we only have *words*, we compete with all the philosophies and the theories that are circulating in society and we compete poorly because often churches are poor at communication. If we only have *deeds*, we find we are competing with philanthropic agencies in our society and what difference do people in the community see between these and the Church? If we only have *signs* we end up competing with the demonic.

I believe that the key for the Church today is to integrate make one these three dimensions. Not to lose evangelism, for example, but to link it to the power of the Spirit flowing through social concern and bringing them together in a biblically holistic Gospel.

This is what it means to follow Jesus. He is both the Head and Source of our faith. He is also our example. In Luke 4:18 he could say 'The Spirit of the Lord is upon me (pentecostal/charismatic emphasis). He has anointed me (again the pentecostal/charismatic emphasis) to preach good news (evangelical focus) to the poor (Liberal emphasis), he has sent me to proclaim freedom to the prisoners (double emphasis announce; justice), recovery of sight to the blind (double emphasis announce; miraculous sign), to release the oppressed (triple emphasis announce; deed; identify with), and to proclaim the year of the Lord's favour' (again surely the triple emphasis).

In his second book, Luke reports Peter as saying to Cornelius: 'You know the message that God sent the people of Israel telling the Good News of peace through Jesus Christ. How God anointed Jesus of Nazareth with the Holy Spirit and power. How he went around doing good deeds, healing all that were under the power of the devil, because God was with him' (Acts 10:37-38).

Thus in the life of Christ we see the integration of these three dimensions. A commitment to words and truth; a commitment to signs and power, a commitment to deeds and love.

I believe it is God's intention to raise up congregations all over Australia that embrace these three strands. Leaders are needed that seek to integrate them, struggle to maintain a healthy balance between them, and equip and release their people for them.

(c) *Grid* Autumn 1993, published by World Vision Australia, GPO Box 399C, Melbourne, Vic. 3001. Brian Hathaway has traced more fully the pilgrimage of the Te Atatu Bible Chapel in his book *Beyond Renewal: The Kingdom of God* (Word Publishing, 1990). Used with permission.

2 Uproar in the Church

Derek Prince

Dr Derek Prince (Ph.D. Cambridge) held a Fellowship in Philosophy at King's College, Cambridge. He produced many books and teaching videos/DVDs on renewal.

—————————————

that is how I was saved

more than 50 years ago

—————————————

Reports have been coming in from Christian groups in widely separated locations of what appears to be a strange new phenomenon. Believers of different ages and widely different social backgrounds are being overcome by prolonged outbursts of laughter which have no obvious cause. Sometimes they may also act as if they are drunk.

Often this laughter appears to be contagious. Those who have experienced it apparently 'transmit' it to others. Large groups may be seized by it simultaneously.

Both ministers and lay people from a wide range of denominations have been affected in this way. Some testify that it has had a stimulating effect on their faith and has brought them closer to the Lord. On the other hand, there are those who are sceptical and view this kind of experience as a deception of the enemy.

As a result of all this, I am frequently being asked whether I believe that the Holy Spirit at times produces in people prolonged, exuberant and apparently causeless laughter. 'I have to believe it,' I reply, 'because that is how I was saved more than 50 years ago.'

In the summer of 1941, I was part of a medical unit of the British Army billeted in a hotel on the North Bay of Scarborough in Yorkshire. The hotel had been gutted of all its furniture and fittings. Our 'beds' were simply straw mattresses on the floor.

While in Scarborough I had some brief contacts with Pentecostal Christians, who confronted me for the first time with my need to receive Christ as my personal Saviour. At that point in my life I was a nominal Anglican, who never voluntarily attended church. I had never before heard of Pentecostals, and I had no idea what they believed or what kind of people they were.

About nine months previously, however, I had started to read the Bible through from beginning to end. I had no religious motive. I regarded the Bible merely as a work of philosophy. As a professional philosopher, I felt it was my academic duty to find out what the Bible had to say. At that point I had come as far as the book of Job – but it had been a dreary task!

Confronted in this was with the claims of Christ, however, I decided about 11 o'clock one night to pray 'until something happened'. I had no idea what I might expect to happen. For about an hour I struggled in vain to form some kind of coherent prayer. Then about midnight I became aware of a presence and I found myself saying to some unknown person what Jacob had said when wrestling with the angel at Peniel: *'Unless you bless me, I will not let you go'* (Genesis 32:26).

I repeated these words several times with increasing emphasis: 'I will not let you go, I will not let you go ...' Then I began to say to the same unknown person, 'Make me love you more and more'. When I got to these last words, I began to repeat them: 'more and more and more ...'

At this point an invisible power came down over me and I found myself on my back on the floor, with my arms in the air, still saying, 'more and more and more ...'

After a while my words changed to deep sobbing which rose up from my belly through my lips, shaking my whole body convulsively. The sobs did not proceed out of anything in my conscious mind. I had no special sense of being sinful.

After about half an hour, without any act of my volition, the sobbing changed to laughter. I had no more conscious reason for laughing than I had had for sobbing. The laughter, like the sobbing, flowed from my belly. At first, it was quite gentle, but it gradually became louder and louder. I had the impression that I was being immersed in a sea of laughter that reverberated around the room.

At this point the soldier who shared the room with me woke up to find me on my back on the floor clothed only in my underwear, with my arms in the air, laughing uproariously. Rising from his mattress, he walked around me rather helplessly two or three times, keeping at a safe distance. Finally he said, 'I don't know what to do with you. I suppose it's no good pouring water over you.' An inaudible voice within me responded, 'Even water wouldn't put this out!'

However, I remembered dimly having heard years earlier in church that we should not blaspheme the Holy Spirit. Contrary to all my natural reasoning, I knew that what was in me was the Holy Spirit. In order not to offend my friend, I rolled over onto my face and laboriously crawled to my mattress. Pulling the blanket over my head, I eventually fell asleep, still laughing – quietly.

A totally different person

Next morning I awoke to an amazing, but objective fact: **I was a totally different person.** No longer did vile language flow out of my mouth. Prayer was no longer an effort, it was as natural as breathing. I could not even drink a glass of water without pausing to thank God for it.

At six o'clock, as was my usual custom, I went to the pub for a drink. But when I got to the door, my legs 'locked'. They would not carry me inside the pub. I stood there having an argument with my legs. Then, to my surprise, I realised I was no longer interested in what the pub had to offer. I turned round and walked back to my billet.

Back in my billet once again, I opened my Bible to continue reading. At this point, however, I discovered the most amazing change of all. Overnight the Bible had become a completely new book. It was as if there were only two persons in the universe – God and me. The Bible was God speaking directly and personally to me. This has never changed, and it is equally true of the Old Testament and the New.

I opened by chance at Psalm 126:1-2: *'When the Lord turned again the captivity of Zion, we were like them that dream. Then our mouth was filled with laughter...'*

At that point I paused. 'That's exactly what happened to me,' I thought. 'It wasn't I who was laughing. My mouth was being filled with laughter from some other source!' Upon further reflection, I saw that this strange, supernatural laughter was the way that God's people expressed their joy and excitement at being delivered from captivity.
...

One evening about ten days after my first encounter with the Lord, I was lying on my back on my mattress in the billet and I began to speak an unfamiliar language that sounded to me like Chinese. Once again, I dimly recalled something I had heard in church about 'speaking with other tongues'. I knew it was connected somehow with the day of Pentecost. At first I spoke timidly and hesitantly, but as I relaxed, the flow of words became free and forceful.

Once again, the initiative did not come from me. I was responding to a powerful inner force that came very specifically – like my previous laughter – from my belly.

The following evening I again found myself speaking an unknown language, but it was obviously different from the language I had been speaking the previous evening. This time I noticed that the words had a very marked poetic rhythm.

After a few moments of silence, I began to speak in English, but the words were not of my choosing, and their content was on a level far above that of my own understanding. Also, they seemed to have a rhythm similar to that of the words that I had previously spoken in an unknown language. I concluded that my words in English were an interpretative rendering of what I had previously said in the unknown language.

One brief section of what I said in English remains indelibly impressed upon my memory. In vivid imagery, it outlined God's plan for my life. Looking back over more than 50 years, I can see how God's plan has been – and is still being – progressively worked out in my life.

In retrospect, too, I have gained a new understanding of my initial experience of supernatural laughter. Unconventional as it was, it proved to be the divinely appointed door through which I entered a lifelong walk of faith. It also had the effect of liberating me from many preconceptions of my background and culture which could have been a barrier to my further spiritual progress.

In Matthew 12:33 Jesus states the most decisive test that must be applied to all forms of spiritual experience: *'a tree is known by its fruit.'* I have to ask myself therefore: What has been the fruit of my strange experience? Is it possible to give an objective answer?

Yes, the fruit of that experience has been a life converted from sin to righteousness, from agnostic dabbling in the occult to unshakeable faith in Jesus Christ as he is revealed in the Scriptures – life that has been bringing forth fruit in God's Kingdom for well over 50 years. Certainly that was no transient product of autosuggestion or of some mere emotional extravagance.

From time to time, in the succeeding years, I have received a renewed experience of supernatural laughter. I have also seen other believers touched by God in a similar way, but this has never been a main emphasis of my teaching. Almost invariably I have found this kind of laughter has a double effect: it is both cleansing and exhilarating. At times it has been accompanied by miracles of physical healing or of deliverance from emotional conditions such as depression. ...

The fruit we should look for

I have been emphasising the principle that 'a tree is known by its fruit.' Logically, therefore, in evaluating the current move in the church, we should ask: If this move is from God, what kind of fruit should we look for? In reply, I would suggest five main kinds of fruit that would authenticate the present move.

1. The fruit of repentance

All through the New Testament the first thing that God demanded was not faith, but repentance. John the Baptist prepared the way for Jesus by calling for repentance (Matthew 3:2). When the religious people came to him for baptism, he demanded that they first produce in their lives the fruits of repentance (Matthew 3:7-8).

The first word that Jesus preached was, *'Repent'* (Mark 1:15). He told the multitudes, *'Unless you repent, you will perish'* (Luke 13:3-5). After his resurrection he told his disciples that repentance, first, and then forgiveness of sins should be preached to all nations (Luke 24:17).

On the day of Pentecost the first demand that Peter made of the convicted but unconverted multitude was *'Repent* – then be baptised (Acts 2:38).

Speaking to the people of Athens, Paul said, *'God now commands everyone everywhere to repent'* (Acts 17:30). Throughout his ministry he required, first repentance toward God, then faith toward Christ (Acts 20:21).

True repentance is not an emotion, but a decision of the will – a decision to turn away from all sin and unrighteousness and to submit unreservedly to the Lordship of Jesus.

Repentance is the first of the six foundational doctrines listed in Hebrews 6:1-2. Those who have not truly repented can never have a solid foundation for their lives as Christians. Over the years I have counselled hundreds of Christians with various problems in their lives. As a result, I have concluded that at least 50 per cent of the problems in the lives of Christians are due to one simple fact: they have never truly repented.

I believe that a renewed emphasis on repentance is the most urgent need of the contemporary church in the West. To be effective, any move in the church must deal with this issue.

2. Respect for Scripture

A second decisive factor in our lives as Christians is our attitude to Scripture. Jesus called the Scripture *'the word of God'* and he set his personal seal upon it by five simple words: *'the Scripture cannot be broken'* (John 10:35). No amount of 'higher criticism' can set aside the plain meaning of these words. If we believe in Jesus then we believe in the Bible. If we do not believe in the Bible, then we do not believe in Jesus.

In Isaiah 66:2 the Lord says: *'This is the one I esteem: he who is humble and contrite in spirit, and trembles at my word'* (NIV). God here combines repentance – a humble and contrite spirit – with faith in his word.

440

Why should we tremble at God's word? First, because it is the way that God the Father and God the Son come to us and make their home with us (John 14:23). Second, because God's word will one day be our judge (John 12:48).

From creation onwards, God has worked through two main agents: his word and his Spirit. First, the Spirit of God moved; then God's word went forth (Genesis 1:2-3). The result was creation.

Ever since then the Spirit and the word have always worked together in harmony. Anything that the Spirit does harmonises with what the word says. Furthermore, all Scripture is inspired by his Holy Spirit and he never contradicts himself (2 Timothy 3:16).

This means that every kind of spiritual manifestation must be tested by this standard: Is it in harmony with Scripture? If so, we can receive it. If not, we must reject it.

3 Exaltation of Jesus

In John 16:13-14 Jesus promised his disciples, *'When he, the Spirit of truth has come, he will guide you into all truth... He will glorify me...'*

Jesus here reveals two important facts about the ministry of the Holy Spirit. First of all, his supreme function is to glorify Jesus. This provides an authoritative test of any spiritual manifestation. Does it focus our attention on Jesus? Does it exalt Jesus?

As soon as human personalities are allowed to take the centre of the stage, the Holy Spirit begins to withdraw. The exaltation of human personalities has many times quenched what was originally a genuine move of the Holy Spirit.

Then we need to notice that Jesus is careful to emphasise that the Holy Spirit is not an 'it' but a 'He'. When people begin to explain spiritual experience in terms of getting 'it', it can easily happen that they get the wrong 'it'.

Jesus is a person and the Holy Spirit is a person. The Holy Spirit, as a person, draws believers together around the person of Jesus. When we make a doctrine or an experience the focus of our gathering, we are spiritually 'off centre'.

4. Love for our fellow Christians

In John 13:35 Jesus told his followers, *'By this all will know that you are My disciples, if you have love for one another.'* In 1 Timothy 1:5 Paul said, *'The goal of our instruction is love from a pure heart and a good conscience and sincere faith'* (NASB). Any form of religious activity that does not produce this result, he dismissed as *'fruitless discussion'.*

In 1 Corinthians 13:2 Paul applied this test to himself: *If I have all the spiritual gifts of power and revelation, but have not love, I am nothing.*

Before we apply this test to others, we need to do the same as Paul and apply it to ourselves. We each need to ask: Has my faith made me a loving person?

Then – and only then – can we apply this test to the present move in the church. Is it producing Christians who sincerely love one another – regardless of denominational labels? Will it cause the unbelievers to say of these people what the world said of the early church: 'See how these Christens love one another?'

5. Loving concern for the unreached

In John 4:35 Jesus told his disciples, *'Lift up your eyes and look at the fields, for they are white already for harvest.'* If those words were true even in the time of Jesus, they are certainly more true today. I have been privileged to travel and minister in many nations and I have formed one firm conclusion: **We are living in the harvest hour!**

Yet, alas, many Christians, who could be working in the harvest fields of the world, are caught in a snare of materialistic self-centredness. I believe that any genuine move of the Holy Spirit will result in multitudes of new labourers being thrust forth into the world's harvest fields. Otherwise it does not truly reflect the heart of God.

If a significant number of Christians in the current move successfully pass all, or most, of the five tests outlined above, then it is safe to conclude that this is, essentially, a move of God. This does not mean that everyone or everything in it is faultless. God has no faultless people to work with.

It is amazing what he can do with weak and fallible people who are truly surrendered to Him.

3 A Season of New Beginnings

John Wimber

Pastor John Wimber, leader of the Vineyard Christian Fellowships, wrote this leadership letter in May 1994 about current moves of the Spirit of God in the Vineyard and in other churches around the world including Australia.

What many people in our churches

are experiencing is NOT revival.

But it is the only thing that becomes revival

In recent months the Holy Spirit has been falling in meetings throughout the Vineyard. This season of visitation began about the same time in Toronto, Canada at the Airport Vineyard and in Anaheim, California, then rippled out across America, Canada, United Kingdom, Australia, New Zealand, and to other parts of the world by now.

As the leader of the Vineyard, I am often asked, 'What is this?' and 'Is this revival?'

My answer is, in my opinion, not yet. But it is the only thing that becomes revival. We're seeing the early stages of an outpouring of the Spirit of God. Some have estimated that as many as 80,000 individuals have been significantly touched and revived to date [200,000 by February 1995]. It has not yet evolved into what most church historians define as revival: an outpouring of the Holy Spirit in the church and then in the aftermath, through the church into the community resulting in the conversion of thousands.

What is revival? I like John White's definition: 'an action of God whereby he pours out his Holy Spirit, initially upon the church, and it comes as an alternative to his judgment which is about to fall on the church and on the secular world' (John White, 'Prayer and Renewal' course, Canadian Theological Seminary, 1 July 1991).

True revival is marked by widespread repentance both within the church, and among unbelievers. Although as many as four thousand have been converted to date (in various Vineyard churches by May 1994) we've not yet seen the dynamic of thousands and thousands of people coming to Christ rapidly. Of course, that is our prayer and I thought that it would be helpful to review some basic things concerning revival to get us focused.

Vineyard history

During the last approximately 17 years God has poured out his Spirit, beginning in what is now called the Vineyard Christian Fellowship in Anaheim and extending through us to churches all over the United States, Canada and Europe, as well as to other places in the world.

Beginning some time in September of '76, Bob Fulton, Carol Wimber, Carl Tuttle, along with others, began assembling at the home of Carl Tuttle's sister. The agenda was simple: praying, worshipping and seeking the Lord. By the time I came several months later, the Spirit of God was already moving powerfully. There was a great brokenness and responsiveness in the hearts of many. This evolved into what became our church on Mother's Day in 1977.

Soon God began dealing with me about the work of the Spirit related to healing. I began teaching in this area. Over the next year and a half God began visiting in various and sundry ways. There were words of knowledge, healing, casting out of demons, and conversions.

Later we saw an intensification of this when Lonnie Frisbee came and ministered. Lonnie had been a Calvary Chapel pastor and evangelist, being used mightily in the Jesus People Movement. After our Sunday morning service on Mother's Day 1980 (i), I was walking out the door behind Lonnie, and the Lord told me, 'Ask that young man to give his testimony tonight.' I hadn't even met him, though I knew who he was and how the Lord had used him in the past. That night, after he gave his testimony, Lonnie asked the Holy Spirit to come and the repercussions were incredible. The Spirit of God literally knocked people to the floor and shook them silly. Many people spoke in tongues, prophesied or had visions.

Then over the next few months, hundreds and hundreds of people came to Christ as the result of the witness of the individuals who were touched that night, and in the aftermath. The church saw approximately 1,700 converted to Christ in a period of about three months.

This evolved into a series of opportunities, beginning in 1980, to minister around the world. Thus the Vineyard renewal ministry and the Vineyard movement were birthed.

Ebbs and flows

By July of 1993, VCF (Vineyard Christian Fellowship) Anaheim had an ongoing interaction with the Holy Spirit in which we'd had ebbs and flows. There were times when we had a great sense of nearness and times in which there seemed to be a withdrawal to some degree. But there was never a time in which God was not willing to bless, heal, deliver and touch people. It just wasn't with the same intensity that we'd had early on. Sometimes your family may have fillet mignon for dinner, and sometimes you have leftovers. But you still eat, and you're thankful for whatever it is you have to eat.

Most of you know about the discovery of my cancer in April of 1993 and the ensuing treatment. In July of 1993, right before the International Vineyard Pastor's Conference began, the Holy Spirit spoke to Carol, my wife. He told her I was to go to the nations. We understood then it meant going to the church in the nations, as over against going to evangelise the lost of the world. This in my mind meant a ministry of renewal and revival.

---

i Date of service cassette (not 1979 as in original article).

Carol responded, 'Lord, my husband is sleeping 20-22 hours a day. He has no voice. Tomorrow pastors from all over the world are going to be here and he won't even be able to participate. If this is indeed your will, touch him tonight. Please give him his voice back so that he may minister.'

That's exactly what he did the next morning. I woke up able to speak and with just barely enough energy to go and participate in the conference. It was a very blessed event for me as well as for those that love me in the Vineyard.

By October of 1993 God had spoken 27 times confirming that I should go to the nations. Seventeen times he spoke in the same context and said that this would be a 'season of new beginnings'. The Lord was saying, 'I'm going to start it all over again. I'm going to pour out my Spirit in your midst like I did in the beginning...

I felt like Abraham might have felt when he was waiting for the fulfilment of God's promises. The New Testament credits Abraham with not wavering in his faith. He had faith that God was going to do it, but I'm sure Abraham and Sarah had a few moments when they wondered *how* it was going to come together. (That's how Ishmael came about.) Anyway, I was looking at my age – 59, going on 90. I was coming through an incredibly tough year with the cancer. The church had endured the season of adversity coming through it with a new sturdiness and strength. I saw a new strength in our movement. I knew God was moving.

But I looked at myself, and thought, *I'm out of energy.* In my spirit I was just murmuring, 'Oh God, oh God'. And at that point (mid January) the Lord gave me a word. I heard myself say: *Shall I have this pleasure in my old age?* The very words that Sarah laughingly said to herself when she overheard the Lord say she was going to have a son from her 90-year-old womb by her 100-year-old husband (Gen. 18:10). This was a word of life from the Lord, and it touched me deeply.

I had brought this message of new beginnings to our AVC (Association of Vineyard Churches) National Board and Council meeting in November of 1993 at Palm Springs. Then the Lord confirmed this word in the hearts and minds of our national leadership. They laid hands on Bob Fulton and me and they blessed us to go, and stir up the church.

At the same meeting John Arnott (from Ontario, Canada) learned how the Holy Spirit had recently powerfully renewed and refreshed Randy Clark (VCF St. Louis) in a meeting conducted by Rodney Howard-Browne in Tulsa, Oklahoma. How the Lord got Randy to Tulsa for a meeting conducted by a South African Pentecostal is a story in itself. Nevertheless, Randy began seeing similar outpourings of the Spirit in his home church and elsewhere as he had occasion to minister. It was as if the 'times of refreshing' had begun.

So John Arnott, knowing that a season of new beginnings in the Vineyard was near at hand, and hearing about Randy Clark's transformed ministry, invited Randy to come to Toronto to minister in his church, as well as to those folks from the surrounding area that would like to attend.

This occurred on 20 January, 1994. Four days of meetings turned into five months [now over a year] of almost nightly meetings in numerous locations in Ontario. It has since poured out through those who have visited there into similar renewal meetings all over the United States, Canada, the United Kingdom, and even Europe.

Anaheim

Meanwhile at the Anaheim Vineyard beginning on Sunday, 5 December, 1993, the Holy Spirit told me to stir up the gifts of the Spirit that our people may have a greater hunger for the Giver, Jesus. Throughout the month of December and early January, we set aside nights for that with an ever increasing sense of the Lord's presence and willingness to bless.

On the afternoon of Sunday, 16 January, 1994, the Holy Spirit gave me the word 'Pentecost'. I spent the rest of the afternoon asking the Lord what he meant by it. No answer. At that evening's church service, the Lord gave me a vision of young people in a certain set and order. During the ministry time, from the pulpit I asked the young people to come forward. They did and the Lord came, consuming them in a beautiful and powerful way. It began a significant increase of the outflowing of power at Anaheim that has continued until this writing.

In interaction with leaders and workers across both the United States and Canada, I have encouraged the Arnotts, as well as Randy Clark and others that have been touched by the Spirit and are being used to share with others, to refer to this present visitation of the Spirit in our churches as a 'refreshing' or 'renewal' rather than a revival. I have no problem with the notion that people are being revived. I just have a problem with our using a term that most evangelicals at least reserve for that *phase* of revival that is an outpouring, not only *on* the church but *through* the church and *into* the community. The result is the salvation of thousands.

What about the phenomena?

Nearly everything we've seen (falling, weeping, laughing, shaking) has been seen before, not only in our own memory, but in revivals all over the world. One of my colleagues on the AVC staff, Steve Holt, has compiled an extremely helpful summary of Jonathan Edwards' thoughts on the place of physical manifestations and phenomena in the midst of revival.

During the first Great Awakening in America, Edwards was right in the middle of it all. Not only was he a thoughtful participant, and observer, but he applied his keen theological mind to the 'problem' of religious enthusiasms, which were the object of much scorn and criticism among the religious establishment. Edwards' perspective on revival can be very helpful to us as we evaluate some of the manifestations of the Spirit that we see in our meetings. Edwards saw them too, and he developed a very wise counsel regarding it.

Edwards attempted to answer the question, 'How do we judge whether these phenomena are from God or the Devil? Edwards' logic is lucid and spiritual, but after 250 years, some of his language is a challenge. The following are his main points in outline from. For further details on the writings of Jonathan Edwards, I refer you to his *Complete Works.*

1. *We do not judge by a part: the way it began, the instruments emphasised, the means used, the methods that have been taken.* We judge by the effects upon the people (Isa. 40:13, 14; Jn. 3:8; Isa. 2:17). Edwards reminds us that God often uses the most foolish things to confound the wise.

2. *We should judge by the whole of Scripture, not our own personal rules and measures, nor some portion of Scripture.* Furthermore, Edwards enjoins us not to judge phenomena negatively just because we have not personally had such an experience.

448

3. *We should distinguish the good from the bad, and not judge the whole by the parts.* Summation: We can become so paranoid of extremism that we actually sin by grieving the Holy Spirit and stopping his work. To accomplish his work, God seems more willing at times to tolerate extreme behaviour (that is not clearly sinful) than we are.

4. *We should judge by the fruit of the work in general.* Edwards could justify in his own mind the extravagance of some in the revival because of the revival's impact in New England. The Bible was more greatly esteemed; multitudes had been brought to conviction of truth and certainty of the gospel; and the Indians were more open to the gospel than ever before.

5. *We should judge by the fruit of the work in particular instances.* Edwards wrote of many examples of people who had been transported into the glories of the heavenlies for hours at a time. Great rejoicing, transports (visions and dreams), and trembling have produced an increase in humility, holiness, and purity. Answered prayers became the norm.

6. *We should judge by the glory of the work.* Edwards passionately called for the church to be seized by the rapture, glory, and enthusiasm of God. In his view, the Great Awakening (with all its various manifestations) was exceedingly glorious in the extraordinary degrees of light, love, and spiritual joy that God had bestowed on great multitudes.

Restoration and Revival

There's a time of restoration coming. There's a time of revival coming. There's an outpouring of the Spirit that's preparing the hearts and lives of men and women across our country, and around the world. We saw it recently in New Zealand, and in Australia.

The Lord poured out his Spirit mightily. We've seen it in the Anaheim Vineyard. We've seen it across the country. It's happening wherever there's receptivity.

Remember, as long as people keep hearing about this, and as long as people keep coming, the Spirit will be poured out. The laughter will bubble forth. So don't be afraid of it. It indicates the ongoing truth of God's word. It's another verification that God is among us.

It's another standard if you will, being lifted up and exalted unto the Lord. It's his work. It's not craziness. It's not people acting weird (Not that they don't look crazy and seem strange). But it's appropriate.

The Lord is being exalted by his own means. Remember, the Lord says, 'My thoughts are not your thoughts, neither are your ways my ways' (Isa. 55:8). And God just goes about doing things differently than you or I would.

What do the phenomena mean?

Our theology and experience of revival must be tempered by our understanding of sanctification. Sanctification is the necessary counterpart to justification, or the forgiveness of sins.

I view sanctification as that work of the Holy Spirit that takes place both as 'a one-time act, valid for all time, imputing and imparting holiness, and as an ongoing, progressive work' (*New Dictionary of Theology*, p. 615). In the sense that it's ongoing, we co-operate with the Holy Spirit.

All Christians need to be cleansed, and dedicated to the service of God (Rom. 12:1-2) and thereby make practical our prayer, 'Your kingdom come, your will be done on earth (and in my life) as it is in heaven.'

Let us not allow ourselves to equate the experience of various manifestations of the Spirit with sanctification. Such experiences may accompany, accent, or provide a milestone on the journey of sanctification, but they are not necessarily the agents of sanctification.

Summary

In summary I believe that this could readily become the revival we've all longed for and prayed for. I do not believe that it has reached its full stature yet, but I believe it may be around the corner. People have asked me what I think the next step may be. I've said that I know that at some point in time we must give a call to full scale repentance undergirded by deep and heart felt contrition. Changed lives and the fruit of true repentance will result.

(c) *Vineyard Reflections,* May/June 1994. Used with permission.

4 Preparing for Revival

Jerry Steingard

Jerry Steingard wrote as pastor of the Jubilee Vineyard in Stratford, Ontario, Canada. In January 1995, he wrote these revised reflections on the 'Toronto blessing'.

God's presence intensified (fullness)

God's purposes accelerated (fulfilment)

We have been enjoying a 'season of refreshment' from the presence of the Lord (Acts 3:19) in Ontario during the past twelve months. We are calling it renewal, a precursor to revival. It began when John Arnott, pastor of the Toronto Airport Vineyard invited Randy Clark, Pastor of a Vineyard church in St. Louis, to come and conduct four nights of meetings in Toronto, commencing on 20 January, 1994. (Randy Clark had been prayed for by Rodney Howard-Browne several months previously.) The Lord surprised everyone by coming in power! Toronto Airport continues to run nightly meetings, except Mondays.

Conservative estimates are that at least 75,000 different people have attended from around the world, of which 10,000 are pastors. Many of these leaders have been significantly touched, refreshed and are consequently seeing their churches renewed.

Randy Clark and John and Carol Arnott came to our church, Jubilee Vineyard Christian Fellowship, the first weekend in February, 1994, to lead meetings with us. Many of us had already been touched by the services in Toronto, but the presence and power of the Holy Spirit were dramatically manifested in our midst on this weekend. As pastor of this church of about 275 people, it was overwhelming for me to see the auditorium floor strewn with bodies like the slain upon a battlefield!

All the strange phenomena that have often accompanied revivals of the past were happening right before my eyes with adults, teens, and children alike – falling, shaking, jerking, visions, prophecies, healings, laughter and tears! On the one hand I was thrilled; I knew this was of God. Yet I was stressed out because a pastor likes to have a good handle on what is happening with those in his flock. I personally have been refreshed and touched by the Spirit of God time and time again in this fresh move of God and in ways never experienced before. The same goes for my wife and three children. In fact my kids often beg to go to the meetings! They love to see God move.

In February we ran nightly meetings for three weeks, then went to only Thursday nights. Christians from many other churches in the area have come and been touched and now good things are happening in their churches.

I am thrilled to see much good fruit in our people in all this. We have observed that God is presently refreshing his people as well as empowering them for service. For example, the shaking is often an impartation of prophetic and/or intercessory gifts. In the first few weeks we saw about a dozen converts, a couple of dozen prodigals return to the Lord, an increase in hunger for the reading of God's word, worship and passion for Jesus, more prayer activity, physical and emotional healings, demonic bondages broken, repentance, and reconciliation in relationships.

We are seeing God raising up an army of intercessors, worshippers, prophetic people and teams to go out and minister elsewhere. We are finding the principle true: 'freely receive, freely give'. We get to keep what we are willing to give away!

This move is not about us, not about the Vineyard. It is about God and his grace and sovereignty. And we are believing God for more waves of his Spirit to come – not just to refresh and renew the church but to powerfully touch our neighbourhoods, our cities, and the nations with full blown revival.

Let us continue to embrace the cross, submit to Scripture, and also 'keep in step with the Spirit'. 'The kingdom of God is not a matter of talk but of power' (1 Corinthians 4:20).

'Now is the time of God's favour, now is the day of salvation' (2 Corinthians 6:2).

Preparing for revival

Winkie Pratney (1994:8,9) suggests we try this little survey with Christians:

How many of you know we *need* a revival?

How many of you *want* a revival?

How many of you know what a revival is?

How many of you have ever experienced a true revival?

Most would raise their hands to the first two questions. In fact, according to George Gallup, Jr., in the eighties, 80% of U.S.A. wanted a revival – including the lost! But very few would have an idea as to what a genuine revival really is, let alone ever experienced one.

It is imperative at this time in history that we get a better handle on this thing called revival. Hopefully this paper (used as seminar notes on the subject) can be of some help in this need for understanding by responding to the following six questions:

1. What is revival?

2. Why is revival needed?

3. When has revival occurred before?

4. Should we expect to see revival again soon?

5. What hinders revival?

6. How can we promote revival?

1. What is revival?

The term *revival* is not technically found in the Bible. Neither is *Trinity* for that matter, yet both concepts are found throughout the Bible.

Various forms of the verb *revive* are frequently used as well as such words as *restore, renew, awaken,* and *refresh,* for example:

Psalm 85:6 – 'Will you not **revive** us again that your people may rejoice in you' (prayer request).

Isaiah 57:15 – 'I **revive** the spirit of the humble and **revive** the heart of the contrite' (promise of God).

The theme of revival is described at times in such terms as an outpouring of the Spirit (like rain or fire falling or wind blowing), the renewing of God's mighty deeds (Habakkuk 3:2), the glory of the Lord returning to his temple (Malachi 3:1), God healing the land (2 Chronicles 7:14) and the time of God's visitation with his manifest presence (Micah 7:4; Luke 19:44).

(a) Definitions and descriptions of revival

* To revive is 'to live again' (1 Kings 17:22; 2 Kings 13:21).

* 'When God comes down [Isaiah 64:1,2], God's Word comes home [Nehemiah 8-9; Acts 2:37], God's purity comes through, God's people come alive [Acts 2, overflow of joy and vitality], and outsiders come in' [Acts 2:41, 47; 1 Corinthians 14:25 'God is really among you'] (Packer 1984:244-245; Scriptures added).

* 'The inrush of the Spirit into a body that threatens to become a corpse' (D. M. Panton, cited in Wallis 1956:46).

* 'Revival is man retiring into the background because God has taken the field. It is the Lord making bare his holy arm and working in extraordinary power on saint and sinner' (Wallis 1956:20).

* 'Revival is divine military strategy; first to counteract spiritual decline, and then to create spiritual momentum' (Wallis 1956:45).

* 'Revival is like a rocket ship that gets us back up into the orbit of New Testament Christianity' (Charles Simpson, sermon 27 May 1994).

* God's presence intensified (fullness), God's purposes accelerated (fulfilment); (based on Bryant 1984:72-91, 169).

(b) Characteristics of revival

Revival is usually comprised of two stages: internal revival or 'renewal' (the church is set on fire and prodigals begin to come home) followed by external revival (conversion of those outside on a mass scale).

'True revival is marked by widespread repentance both within the church and among unbelievers' (Wimber 1994:4).

This repentance is the result of God coming in power, revealing his holiness and our sinfulness. One comes into the agonising grip of a holy God and is brought under awesome conviction. This manifested presence of God creates a divine 'radiation zone'.

Here are two examples:

During the 1859 revival, no town in Ulster was more deeply stirred than Coleraine. A schoolboy in class became so troubled about his soul that the schoolmaster sent him home. An older boy, a Christian, went with him and before they had gone far, led him to Christ. Returning at once to school, this new convert testified to his teacher: 'Oh, I am so happy! I have the Lord Jesus in my heart.' These artless words had an astonishing effect; boy after boy rose and silently left the room. Going outside the teacher found these boys all on their knees, ranged along the wall of the playground. Very soon their silent prayer became a bitter cry; it was heard by another class inside and pierced their hearts. They fell on their knees, and their cry for mercy was heard in turn by a girls' class above. In a few moments, the whole school was on their knees! Neighbours and passers-by came flocking in and all as they crossed the threshold came under the same convicting power. 'Every room was filled with men, women, and children seeking God' ...

During the same 1859 revival in America, ships entered a definite zone of heavenly influence as they drew near port. Ship after ship arrived with the same talk of sudden conviction and conversion. A captain and an entire crew of thirty men found Christ at sea and arrived at port rejoicing. This overwhelming sense of God bringing deep conviction of sin is perhaps the outstanding feature of true revival. Its manifestation is not always the same; to cleansed hearts it is heaven; to convicted hearts it is hell (Pratney 1994:24-25).

2. Why is revival needed?

Throughout biblical history and church history the hearts of God's people perpetually cool off and harden towards him, creating the need for revival. Nehemiah 9:25-28 describes this cycle or pattern of spiritual decline and renewal which involves six stages (Lovelace 1979:62-80):

1. God's people are alive and in love with him.
2. Spiritual decline – hearts are subtly cooling off.
3. Hearts of stone.
4. The Lord disciplines those he loves (for example, Israelites were taken into exile).
5. Cry for mercy – intercession and repentance.
6. God pours out his Spirit and revives his people.
Where in this cycle is the church in this country today?

3. When has revival occurred before?

The Bible records at least a dozen revivals within its history (Kaiser 1986:12-13) and many movements of renewal and revival took place prior to and including the Protestant Reformation of the 16th century and the Puritan and Pietist movements of the 17th century. Here I will focus upon the major revivals of Europe and North America of the last 250 years.

Note that the intensity of a revival may last only a few years, but the effects are felt in the church and society for decades to come.

The First Awakening (1727-80)

1727-80 (approximate dates) in Germany: Count Zinzendorf and the Moravians, with unity, prayer (their 24 hour prayer vigil lasted over 100 years!), and missions. Their motto was 'To win for the Lamb that was slain the reward of his suffering.'

1734-60 in North America's 13 colonies: Jonathan Edwards and George Whitefield, with prayer and preaching.

1740-80 in Great Britain: John and Charles Wesley and George Whitefield with outdoor preaching and class meetings (home cells).

Revival brought many social reforms including the abolition of slavery in Great Britain. Some historians believe this revival saved England from a bloody revolution like the one in France.

Then came a gradual spiritual slide. By 1794 moral conditions had reached their worst. For example, John Marshall, Chief Justice of the U. S. Supreme Court, a concerned believer, wrote his assessment to Methodist Bishop Madison of Virginia stating, 'The church is too far gone to ever be redeemed'. The famous agnostic Voltaire declared, 'Christianity will be forgotten in 30 years'. Later Voltaire's home became the headquarters for the Geneva Bible Society (Relfe 1988:26).

The Second Awakening (1792-1842)

1792 in England: William Carey, 'Father of the modern missionary movement' took as his motto, 'Expect great things from God, attempt great thing for God.'

By about 1800 revival fires were burning once again in the U. S. A. In the East, Timothy Dwight was used in the college setting. On the Western frontier, James McGready, Barton Stone and Peter Cartwright gave leadership.

In 1821 Charles Finney, a lawyer, was converted and became an evangelist and social reformer. This revival was characterised by evangelistic camp meetings, social reforms and missions. Finney's ministry overlapped the second and third awakenings.

The Third Awakening (1857-59)

1857 in North America: Called 'the Prayer Revival' it began when Dr Walter and Phoebe Palmer from New York City went to Hamilton, Ontario in early October. Revival broke out, then went south of the border.

Jeremiah Lanphier, a business man, began noon prayer meetings in New York City in September 1857. Within 6 months, up to 10,000 business men were praying daily for revival.

J. Edwin Orr states that 'revival went up the Hudson and down the Mohawk. The Baptists had so many people to baptise they could not get them in the churches. They went down to the river, cut a square hole in the ice and baptised them. When Baptists do that, they really are on fire!' (Relfe 1988:48). The revival spread from New York to Philadelphia and throughout the country. The emphasis was on prayer.

Revival spread to Wales, Scotland and Northern Ireland as well.

The fruit of this revival was 2 million converts (1 million within the church, 1 million from without) and in the following years slavery was abolished, and there were reforms in prisons, labour, education, and medical care.

Fourth Awakening (1904-7)

1904-5 in Wales: Youth and children featured in the Welsh revival. The key leader was Evan Roberts, aged 26 (and his brother Dan, aged 20, and his sister Mary, aged 16). Leaders came from around the world and were humbled to see how God used teens and children. Evan and others were not eloquent preachers but good followers of the Holy Spirit.

Their motto was 'Bend the church and save the world'. Evan Roberts' vision of seeing 100,000 converted in Wales was fulfilled in less than one year. People got converted just reading about the revival in the newspapers!

Crime dropped off to the point where many courtrooms and jails were empty and judges and police had very little to do. Horses in the coal mines were accustomed to obeying commands that involved yelling and cursing. Since the vast majority of miners were converted, the horses were confused with commands that were humane and wholesome, so the horses needed retraining!

Prior to the revival Wales was in a frenzy over their favourite sport, soccer. With the revival, the stadiums stood empty. No-one preached against soccer. The players and fans had simply become so captivated with the Lord that they were no longer interested in the game (Joyner 1993:51).

The fire spread throughout Great Britain, Scandinavia, Europe, Africa, India, Korea, as well as the U.S.A. The pastors of Atlantic City, New Jersey, reported only 50 adults not converted in a population of 50,000! The First Baptist Church in Paducoh, Kentucky, had 1,000 converts in two months and the elderly pastor, Dr J. J. Cheek, died of exhaustion (Krupp 1988:22).

In California, Bartleman, Seymore, and Smale were impacted by the reports and booklets on the revival in Wales in 1905 as well as from letters of encouragement from Evan Roberts. Shortly thereafter the Azusa Street Revival erupted into the great Pentecostal Revival that saw 5 million converts from 1905-7 and continues to impact millions of lives to this day.

Twentieth century

The twentieth century has been called by some 'The Century of the Holy Spirit'. Although we have not witnessed a major revival since the turn of the century, since 1947 God has been bringing smaller scaled revivals and renewal movements such as:

1947-53 – the Latter Rain movement in western Canada and the U.S.A.

1949 – Hebrides Islands, Scotland.

Here is a wonderful example of how a revival causes a geographical area to become a divine 'radiation zone' of conviction and repentance.

Duncan Campbell, en evangelist, came to the Island of Lewis in the Hebrides Islands. On the first night of his arrival, he preached in a church building. When he left the building at 11 p.m. he found 600 gathered outside, 100 from the nearby dance hall, the other 500 who had been awakened, got out of bed, and felt compelled to walk to this place. Campbell preached the gospel to them till 4 a.m., at which time he was requested to come to the police station where 400 people were gathered, baffled as to why they were there. On his way to the station he came across other people along the road who were crying out to God for mercy! Revival continued for 3 years with 75% of the converts coming to Jesus outside of church buildings (Krupp 1988:26-7).

The 1960s and 1970s saw the emergence of the charismatic renewal movement, including the Jesus Movement of the early 1970s.

The 1980s and 1990s saw the 'Third Wave' movement' or the 'signs and wonders' movement and the 'prophetic' movement. Peter Wagner describes three waves of the Holy Spirit in this century, each continuing to be used by God: the Pentecostal movement, the charismatic movement (largely in the Catholic Church and mainline Protestant churches), and the 'Third Wave' movement which is primarily impacting the evangelical churches.

4. Should we expect to see revival again soon?

YES! Many 'third world' countries in Africa, and Central and South America, as well as China and Korea, have been experiencing revival fires for a number of years.

Why should we expect to see revival again soon?

a. Biblical texts that create such expectation include:

Habakkuk 2:14 – 'for the earth will be filled with the knowledge of the glory of the Lord as the waters cover the sea.' (Reinhard Bonnke, evangelist in Africa, says, 'not one spot stays dry at the bottom of the sea.')

Joel 2:23 – 'He sends you abundant showers, both autumn (early) and spring (latter) rains.' Early rains soften the ground, making it suitable for ploughing and sowing. With the approach of harvest, heavy rain (latter) returns to swell and mature grain and fruit in preparation for the time of reaping. Pentecost marked the beginning of former rains. After the Reformation, outpourings became more distinct and significant. Latter rain is in preparation for the day of harvest.

Joel 2:28, 31 – 'I will pour out my Spirit on all people … before the coming of the great and dreadful day of the Lord.'

Acts 2 – Pentecost, a partial fulfilment of Joel.

Acts 3:19,20 – 'repent, turn to God, ...

John 14:12 – 'will do what I have been doing. He will do even greater things than these' (miracles). Not fulfilled yet!

John 17 – In his priestly prayer, Jesus prays for Christian unity. This prayer has not been fulfilled yet. Of all the prayers the Father answers, would not his Son's be answered? Rick Joyner says, ' Jesus is coming back for a bride, not a harem.'

Ephesians 5:26,27 – Jesus is preparing the bride to be presented to himself as pure, holy and radiant.

b. Based on previous patterns, revival usually occurs in a day of deep moral and spiritual bankruptcy. 'Before a great awakening, there must come a rude awakening' (Murillo 1985:11). The worst of times, in other words, precipitates the best of times. Who could deny the desperate need for a mighty revival in our day? Famine, poverty, pollution, war, crime, abortion, drug abuse, massive economic instability, and such like, stare us in the face. Nate Krupp (1988:34) argues that 'we are at a point in history where it is either world revival or world destruction.'

c. Church historians, theologians and church leaders are predicting it. Many leaders have discerned that God is up to something big! He's preparing new wineskins for the new wine, a fireplace for the fire, and barns for the harvest. Many even say that previous revivals are but a rehearsal for the big ones to come. 'Our study of awakening movements only turns up what appear to be rehearsals for some final revelation of the full splendour of God's kingdom... It is hard to believe that God will not grant the church some greater experience of wholeness and vitality than has yet appeared in the stumbling record of her history' (Lovelace 1979:425).

d. Many prophets of our day in unison are expecting it in the 1990s and beyond. These include Mike Bickle, Paul Cain, Rick Joyner, and John Paul Jackson.

e. The growing emphasis on prayer. Prayer mobilisation today is unprecedented in history. Examples include men's prayer movements, women's intercessory groups, youth in schools, Marches for Jesus, '10-40 Window' prayer project, city wide pastors' prayer fellowships, and so on. History demonstrates that revival is always preceded by a groundswell of prayer.

f. It's God's heart to bring revival. He longs to renew, restore, awaken us, and redeem humanity much more than we want him to. God is committed to renew his people and see the nations come to himself. 'Ask of me and I will make the nations your inheritance' (Psalm 2:8).

5. What hinders revival?

Don't be a 'fire-fighter' or a 'wet blanket'.

From a safe distance of several hundred years or several thousand miles, revival clearly looks invigorating. What could be more glamorous than a mighty work of God in our midst, renewing thousands and converting tens of thousands. ... But if we find ourselves in the midst of revival, rather than being invigorated, we may be filled with scepticism, disgust, anger, or even fear...

The irony of revivals is that they are so longed for in times of barrenness, but they are commonly opposed and feared when they arrive. ... The hostility in never to the idea of revival, which is ardently prayed for, but to God's answer to our prayers and the unexpected form it may take (White 1988:34, 39).

Why does revival produce all this opposition?

'We grow angry when we are scared. We fear what we cannot understand' (White 1988:41).

a. Fear of change and losing control

We are creatures of habit (as in nostalgia, traditionalism); changes unsettle us. We fear the unknown, the unfamiliar, and the unpredictable.

b. Fear of emotions

We should be scared of emotionalism, the artificial manipulation of emotion, but emotion itself comes from seeing, from understanding. When the Holy Spirit awakens people, he seems to cause them to perceive truth more vividly ... people see their sin as stinking cancer that will kill them and see the mercy of the Saviour with the eyes of those who have been snatched from a horrible death (White 1988:51).

Jonathan Edwards called emotions 'holy affections' and said they are essential for spiritual life. A hear heart (heart of stone) is an unaffected heart, a heart not moved by divine truth and revelation.

c. Fear of bizarre behaviour

Examples of unusual behaviour in revivals include shaking, jerking, falling, weeping, screaming, laughing, prophesying and being 'drunk in the spirit'.

Three questions must be asked about this:

i. Has it happened among the people of God before (the biblical and historical precedence)?

ii. What is the fruit of it?

iii. How do we explain these phenomena?

i. Has it happened before?

Yes, these phenomena of bizarre behaviour have happened among God's people during heightened spiritual activity. Martyn Lloyd-Jones points out that

it comes nearer to being the rule in revival that phenomena begin to manifest themselves – phenomena such as these ... people are in agony of soul and groaning ... sometimes people are so convicted and feel the power of the Spirit to such an extent that they faint and fall to the ground. Sometimes there are even convulsions, physical convulsions. And sometimes people seem to fall into a state of unconsciousness, into a kind of trance, and many remain like that for hours (1987:110-111).

There are also certain mental phenomena... You will find this phenomena of prophecy, this ability to foretell the future, frequently present (1987:135).

Martyn Lloyd-Jones goes onto say that 'these phenomena are not essential to revival ... yet it is true to say that, on the whole, they do tend to be present when there is a revival (1987:134). John White's research has brought him to the same conclusion.

Note these biblical examples:

1. 1 Samuel 10:11 – Saul was in a trance, prophesying when the Spirit came upon him (also 1 Samuel 19:23-24).

2. 2 Chronicles 5:13-14 – The glory of the Lord filled the temple so the priests were unable to stand to minister.

3. Ezekiel 1:28; 3:23; 43:4; 44:4 – Ezekiel fell face down before the glory of the Lord.

4. Daniel 8:17-18 – Daniel collapsed and sank into a deep sleep during a vision and an angelic visitation (also Daniel 10:7-11 – no strength left; on the ground trembling).

5. Matthew 17:6; Luke 9:32 – On the Mount of Transfiguration the disciples fell face down to the ground, but also became heavy with sleep.

6. John 18:6 – When the soldiers came to arrest Jesus they fell to the ground when Jesus said, "I am he".

7. Matthew 28:4 – On the morning of Jesus' resurrection the guards at the tomb 'shook and became like dead men'.

8. Acts 2 – At the Day of Pentecost the place shook, they spoke in strange tongues, and they behaved like being drunk. Peter responded (Acts 2:15) that 'they are not drunk as you suppose'. Paul makes a comparison between being drunk with wine and being filled with the Spirit (Ephesians 5:18).

9. Acts 9 – Saul on the road to Damascus fell to the ground, blinded by the glory. Later, in a trance-like condition he had a vision (2 Corinthians 12).

10. Revelation 1:17 – The apostle John said, 'When I saw him I fell at his feet as though dead.'

Not only in Scripture do we find that frail human bodies are affected by the manifest presence of God, but *most revivals in history* have had physical and emotional manifestations of the Holy Spirit. Some examples:

1. Jonathan Edwards, the great leader of the First Awakening of the 1730s and 1740s in New England wrote to a friend saying, 'many of the young people and children appeared to be overcome with a sense of the greatness and glory of divine things ... and many others at the same time were overcome with distress about their sinful and miserable state and condition; so that the whole room was full of nothing but outcries, faintings and such like. ... many were overpowered and continued there for some hours (Stacy 1842:546 in DeArteaga 1992:39-40).

2. John Wesley and George Whitefield spoke of the strange physical phenomena that took place in their meetings in England as well. Wesley describes in his Journal:

Monday, Jan. 1, 1739 – Mr Hall, Kinchin, Ingham, Whitfield, Lane, with about sixty of our brethren. About three in the morning, as we were continuing instant in prayer, the power of God came mightily upon us, insomuch that many cried out for exceeding joy, and many fell to the ground. As soon as we were recovered a little from that awe and amazement at the presence of his Majesty, we broke out with one voice, 'We praise Thee, O God; we acknowledge Thee to be the Lord' (MacNutt 1990:98).

Following the two events of John Wesley's Aldersgate experience, May 24, 1738, and this January 1, 1739 encounter, the supernatural element in his ministry became more pronounced. For fourteen years it was hardly there; for the next fifty it was (MacNutt 1990:98).

3. MacNutt (1990: 104) tells us that early in George Whitefield's career,

when he was working with Wesley in England and people started to fall, Whitefield decided to register a protest by letter: 'I cannot think it right in you to give so much encouragement to these convulsions which people have been thrown into in your ministry.' Ironically enough, when Whitefield came to confront Wesley in person he found himself reprimanded by reality, for when he, Whitefield, was preaching the next day, 'four persons sunk down close to him, almost in the same moment. One of them lay without sense or motion. A second trembled exceedingly. The third has strong convulsions all over his body, but made no noise, unless by groans. The fourth, equally convulsed, called upon God, with strong cries and tears. From this time,' Wesley writes, 'I trust we shall all suffer God to carry on his own work in the way that pleaseth him.'

'By the time he journeyed to America, Whitefield's preaching was ordinarily accompanied by people toppling over:

Some were struck pale as death, others were wringing their hands, others lying on the ground, other sinking into the arms of their friends' (Dallimore 1980:392-3, cited in MacNutt 1990:104).

4. Bishop Francis Ashbury, appointed by Wesley in 1771 as a missionary to the colonies, was a very disciplined man who insisted on meetings being conducted in a proper fashion, yet his meetings were characterised by shouting, falling, crying, and the 'jerks' (MacNutt 1990:107).

5. At the Cane Ridge camp meetings of 1801, which featured mostly Presbyterian preachers, one observer reported that

The vast sea of human beings seemed to be agitated as if by a storm... Some of the people were singing, others praying, some crying for mercy in the most piteous accents... While witnessing these scenes, a peculiarly-strange sensation, such as I had never felt before, came over me. My heart beat tumultuously, my knees trembled, my lip quivered, and I felt as though I must fall to the ground... Soon after, I left and went into the woods, and there I strove to rally and man up my courage...

After some time I returned... At one time I saw at least five hundred, swept down in a moment as if a battery of a thousand guns had been opened upon them, and then immediately followed shrieks and shouts that rent the very heavens (Johnson 1955:64-5; MacNutt 1990:109).

6. Peter Cartwright, one of the prominent camp meeting evangelists in the Kentucky area, spoke of the phenomena of the 'jerks': '... no matter whether they were saints or sinners, they would be taken under a warm song or sermon and seized with a convulsive jerking all over, which they could not by any possibility avoid, and the more they resisted the more they jerked... The first jerk or so, you would see their fine bonnets, caps and combs fly; and so sudden would be the jerking of the head that their loose hair would crack almost as loud as a wagoner's whip' (Cartwright 1956:17-18).

7. Charles Finney, at the village schoolhouse near Antwerp, New York, describes the phenomena of falling under the awesome power of God's presence and conviction: 'An awful solemnity seemed to settle upon the people; the congregation began to fall from their seats in every direction and cry for mercy. If I had a sword in each hand, I could not have cut them down as fast as they fell. I was obliged to stop preaching' (cited in Pratney 1994:24).

8. Note how the Quakers and Shakers got their nicknames!

Yes, cases of physical phenomena have been observed throughout the ages whenever there has been heightened spiritual activity.

ii. What is the fruit of all this?

Jonathan Edwards wrote a treatise in 1741 called *The Distinguishing Marks of a Work of the Spirit of God.* Edwards asked his readers to assess the awakening by looking past the enthusiastic behaviour and seeing the ultimate spiritual fruit. He argued that the authenticity of God's hand in the revival was demonstrated by five 'sure, distinguishing, Scripture evidences'. It

1. raises the esteem of Jesus in the community;

2. works against the kingdom of Satan;

3. stimulates a greater regard for the Holy Scriptures;

4. is marked by a spirit of truth;

5. manifests a renewed love for God and people (Edwards 1971, 1984:109-115).

In his concluding section, Edwards exhorted his readers not to oppose the Spirit of God in the revival for this is to commit the unpardonable sin of Matthew 12:22-32. Edwards' warning went unheeded by and large. By 1742 a majority of the New England clergy had come to the conclusion that the Great Awakening was merely an epidemic of emotionalism and what was needed was a return to sound theology. Rev. Charles Chauncey of Boston became the brilliant champion against the revival. He effectively articulated all the doubts, fears and criticisms of the revival. His books became best sellers and ensured the defeat of the Awakening. 'When Whitefield arrived in 1744 practically all the pulpits were closed to him, and the wind had gone out of the Awakening' (DeArteaga 1992:52).

It's worth noting the fruit at the end of the lives of these two prominent figures, Edwards and Chauncey. In 1757, Edwards became president of Princeton, but when he arrived in the area there was a threat of a smallpox outbreak. To set an example, he was quick to volunteer to take the experimental vaccine. He became ill and died. Chauncey became one of the founding theologians of Unitarianism which discarded the Trinity and advocated universal salvation. Chauncey is no longer considered a hero who saved the people from emotionalism. He is now 'seen as a religious bureaucrat who defended the status quo without comprehending the deeper issues of revival' (DeArteaga 1992:54).

iii. How do we explain these phenomena?

We must recognise the element of mystery in God's dealings with us. We should hold explanations tentatively and humbly.

Some explain it as the work of Satan. However, Martyn Lloyd-Jones questions, 'Why should the Devil suddenly start dong this kind of thing? Here is the Church in a period of dryness, and of drought, so why should the Devil suddenly do something which calls attention to religion and the Lord Jesus Christ? The very results of revival, I would have thought, completely exclude the possibility of this being the action of the Devil... [see Luke 11:14-18]. If this is the work of the Devil, well then the Devil is an unutterable fool. He is dividing his own kingdom; he is increasing the Kingdom of God... There is nothing which is so ridiculous as this suggestion that this is the work of the Devil' (Lloyd-Jones 1987:141-2).

What is the true explanation?

When God sovereignly visits an individual or group of human beings, his manifest presence and power often affects their bodies in some way.

John White (1988:23) states, 'God is, of course, present everywhere. But there seems to be times when he is, as it were, more present – or shall we say more intensely present. He seems to draw aside one or two layers of a curtain that protects us from Him, exposing our fragility to the awesome energies of his being.'

Martyn Lloyd-Jones (1987:145-6) tells us that 'we must never forget that the Holy Spirit affects the whole person... You see, man is body, soul, and spirit, and you cannot divide these... Man reacts as a whole. And it is just folly to expect that he can react in the realm of the spiritual without anything at all happening to the rest of him, to the soul, and to the body... these phenomena are indications of the fact that some very powerful stimulus is in operation. Something is happening which is so powerful that the very physical frame is involved.'

Lloyd-Jones also argues that such strange phenomena are a means that God uses to get our attention (1987:145). God is shaking us to wake us up (Ephesians 5:14).

God is also humbling us! Paul Cain says, 'God often offends the mind to reveal the heart.'

Both John White and Martyn Lloyd-Jones conclude that although a small portion of such strange behaviour would be of the flesh (the person's own need for acceptance and attention) or a demonic manifestation, the bulk of such activity in revival originates from the power and glory of God.

We should not be fixated on the manifestations, but on the person of the Lord Jesus Christ!

d. Fear of disorder

Charles Spurgeon, the great Baptist preacher, declared that 'revival is a season of glorious disorder' (Relfe 1988:8).

Martyn Lloyd Jones (1987:103) points out that 'always in a revival there is what somebody once called a divine disorder. Some are groaning and agonising under conviction, others praising God for the great salvation. And all this leads to crowded and prolonged meetings. Time seems to be forgotten. People seem to have entered into eternity. A meeting may start at six-thirty in the evening, and it may not end until daybreak the next morning with nobody aware of the passing of the hours.'

We don't like it when meetings get messy and unpredictable. It is embarrassing and offensive to most of us. But John White (1988:35) reminds us that 'revival is war, and war is never tidy. It is an intensifying of the age-old conflict between Christ and the powers of darkness.'

John Wimber (1985:31) offers this analogy: 'When warm and cold fronts collide, violence ensues: thunder and lightning, rain or snow – even tornadoes or hurricanes. There is conflict, and a resulting release of power. It is disorderly, messy – difficult to control.'

Understandably we prefer peace, decency, and order. We say, 'God is a God of order' but we must realise that to bring in order is sometimes a disorderly process... Chaos and darkness flee but they create a ruckus as they leave (White 1988:44).

Edwards was so convinced of this disorderly process as part of the work of God's Spirit that he cried, 'Would to God that all the public assemblies in the land were broken off from their public exercises with such confusion as this next Sabbath day' (1741, 1984:127).

Again, John White (1988:45) argues that 'if we insist that revival must be "decent and orderly" (as we define those terms) we automatically blind ourselves to most revivals.

Like the dwarfs in C. S. Lewis' children's story *The Last Battle*, we may spit out heavenly food, for to us it looks like, smells like, tastes like dung and straw.'

Question: Am I missing the burning bush for trying to keep the lawn cut?

e. Fear of controversy

We all shy away from controversy. However, the fact remains, 'renewal has always been controversial and will always be controversial. We must be ready for it (Mallone 1985:42).

Jonathan Edwards said, 'a work of God without stumbling blocks is never to be expected' (*Works* 2:273).

John Wesley prayed, 'Lord send us revival without its defects but if this is not possible, send revival, defects and all (Bartleman 1980:45).

If we find a revival that is not spoken against, we had better look again to ensure that it is a revival... No one would pretend to claim that every revival burns with a smokeless flame (Wallis 1956:26).

Remember, wherever Jesus or the apostle Paul went there was confrontation. Riots and controversy occurred. Luther, Wesley, Whitefield and Edwards were extremely controversial characters in their day – some kicked out of their churches! But once the dust settled centuries later, they have come to be highly revered and seen as fighters for orthodox Christianity.

Further objections and concerns that many may find themselves struggling with are included here. I am indebted to Bill Jackson of Champaign, Illinois Vineyard for his unpublished paper of April, 1994, called 'What in the world is happening to us?' for the following section extracted from this paper with his permission.

1. It's hard to understand

A. Our presupposition: If it were God, I would understand it. ...

B. All through the Bible, God revealed himself in ways that were hard to understand.

1. God's chosen people for the most part misunderstood Jesus. Pharisees said he was in league with Beelzebub, which was a term for the devil.

2. The disciples didn't understand the mission of Jesus until the Holy Spirit came (Acts 2).

3. The Jews as a whole never understood that God's heart was for all the nations. Even the disciples were shocked that God would offer the gospel to the Gentiles, law free. They muse in amazement in Acts 11:18, 'So then God has granted even the Gentiles repentance unto life!'

4. Historically, God has moved in ways that are hard to understand. The classic example of this is martyrdom. Martyrdom has always been an explosive key to church growth. One of the early church fathers, Tertullian, said, 'The blood of the martyrs is the seed of the church'.

2. It makes me afraid

A. Our presupposition: If it were God, I wouldn't be afraid.

B. Visitations produce fear throughout the Bible.

1. Lightning, thunder, and smoke on Mt. Sinai (Exodus 19).

2. Daniel in Chapter 10 had a great vision: 'I had no strength left, my face turned deathly pale, and I was helpless.' The angel, Gabriel, had to say, 'Don't be afraid,' because he was terrified.

3. Great fear seized the whole church in Acts 5 when Ananias and Sapphira dropped dead through a prophetic word when they lied to the Holy Spirit.

C. Note: This fear is not the same fear as that which comes from Satan. 2 Timothy 1:7 says that God has not given us a spirit of fear. The devil's fear robs us of faith and hope and renders us incapable of love. There is, however, a godly fear that the Bible says is the beginning of wisdom (Proverbs 9:10). It is this kind of fear that is produced by divine visitations. It results in a more godly life.

D. How could a visitation of a holy God on sinful people not produce fear?

1. How could our finite minds expect to understand the infinite ways of God? He is completely beyond us and holy.

2. Fear is caused by:

a) the holiness of God coming in contact with our sinfulness.

b) our anti-supernatural world view. Since we have no supernatural category in our western world view, when we encounter the supernatural we encounter the fear of the unknown. It causes the psychological state known as cognitive dissonance. We receive data that does not fit and it causes feelings of insecurity.

3. It causes division

A. Our presupposition: If it were God, there would be no division.

B. There are two kinds of division:

1. When the kingdom of light clashes with the kingdom of darkness, it causes godly division. Jesus said he had not come to bring peace but a sword. 'A man's enemies will be the members of his own household' (Matthew 10:36).

2. Backbiting, slander, and rebellion are ungodly because they cause the kingdom to be divided against itself.

C. Godly division is thoroughly biblical:

1. Korah was judged for his rebellion against Moses (Numbers 11).

2. Jesus caused division wherever he went.

3. The inclusion of Gentiles in the church caused division (Acts 15).

D. Godly division is thoroughly historical:

1. The Great Awakening broke out in New Jersey in 1725 and was violently opposed by more traditional churches.

2. G. Campbell Morgan called the Pentecostal Movement 'the last vomit of Satan'.

3. Leaders in the previous move of God often persecute the present one.

4. God over-rides my faculties

A. Our presupposition: God is always a gentleman and would never force anything upon us.

B. The Bible seems to say something else:

1. God is God and he does what he wants. In Isaiah, God says, 'I say my purpose will stand and I will do all that I please" (46:11).

2. God over-rode Balaam in Numbers 23 and caused Balaam to prophesy against his will.

3. God over-rode Saul and his men in 1 Samuel 19, and caused them to prophecy instead of killing David.

4. Jesus blinded Paul on the road to Damascus against his will.

5. God's killing of Ananias and Sapphira is the ultimate over-ride.

6. Far from treating us gently, God has promised his people persecution.

5. It causes me to be the centre of attention

A. Our presupposition: If it were God, he would not do it publicly.

B. Quite to the contrary, God often uses the person to be the message:

1. In Ezekiel 4-5, Ezekiel is told by God to lie on his side, naked, to shave his head and beard. God made him the centre of attention because he, himself, was the message.

2. Jeremiah was told to smash a jar in Jeremiah 18-19 to draw attention to his message.

3. Hosea was told to marry a prostitute as a message to the nation of Israel.

4. Ananias and Sapphira can be used as yet another example because their dead bodies were the message.

5. Stephen was 'glowing' when he was killed.

6. It doesn't happen to me

A. Our presupposition: When God moves, the same things happen to everyone.

B. Biblical perspective:

1. It's simply not true that some people seem to be 'favoured' while others are not. God's love is for the whole world. Under his sovereignty he treats everyone in a way that is beneficial for them. God ultimately determines what is best for us.

2. Jesus healed only one man at the pool of Bethesda despite the fact that there were many sick present (John 5).

This in no way meant that God loved the man who was healed more than the ones who weren't. Jesus said that he only did what he saw the Father doing and the Father was somehow loving all those at the pool that day.

7. A final caution

A. It's okay to have questions about what is happening but we must try to be honest about the motive behind our questions. What causes the questions?

1. If it's because of your personality, that's okay. But let's not let our personalities keep us from being touched by God during this season of divine visitation.

2. If it's because you are a 'noble Berean' (Acts 17:10-11), that's to be commended.

a) Search for the truth diligently.

b) When you find it, press in.

3. If it's because you are afraid:

a) Ask God why.

b) Don't run. If this is God, then you would be turning your back on him.

B. After the crucifixion, the disciples had questions too. The Jesus who walked with two of them on the road to Emmaus and opened their minds so they could understand the Scriptures is the same Jesus who walks in our midst by the person of the Holy Spirit (Luke 24:13-35). He will open our minds as well (Jackson 1994).

————-

My conclusion to this section:

Today we need the fire of God. Some are afraid of wildfire but there are always enough 'wet blankets' around to dampen it.

On the Day of Pentecost, the crowd responded to the supernatural manifestations of the spirit in three ways: some were amazed, some perplexed, and others mocked. Each generation has been no different.

Walter C. Kaiser, Jr. (1986:25) urges us to study past revivals because 'once we know how the Lord has acted in the past, we should be better prepared to accept the special working of God when it arrives... Every one of our preconceptions and built-in limitations concerning what God can or cannot do or what he is likely or not likely to do in exact detail must be jettisoned.'

In other words, don't put God in a box. Let God be God! He is the Great I Am, not the Great I Was! His thoughts are not our thoughts and his ways are not our ways (Isaiah 55). We should expect to have difficulty understanding and agreeing with the way God does things at times!

We are wise to take the advice of Martyn Lloyd-Jones: 'we must be careful in these matters... What do we know of the Spirit falling on people? What do we know about these great manifestations of the Holy Spirit? We need to be very careful lest we be found fighting against God, lest we be guilty of quenching the Spirit of God' (White 1988:13).

6. How can we promote revival?

Taking a survey on the street, a reporter asked a hurried pedestrian, 'Sir, do you know the two greatest problems in the world today?' The man responded, 'I don't know and I don't care.' Without missing a beat, the reporter declared, 'You got them both!' (ignorance and apathy).

We can overcome ignorance and apathy concerning revival. How can we promote revival?

1. We need to care

We need to care that God works in our nation. Note that Nehemiah had a cushy job as a cupbearer to the king but left to rebuild the walls.

2. We need to get informed

We need to get the big picture!

Read the Bible. Read biographies of leaders of past revivals. Go where the fire is, such as conferences and places where God is moving powerfully, and get first-hand exposure and experience. It is irresponsible to criticise that which you know nothing about. Slander is sin.

3. Cultivate daily intimacy with the Lord

This is what John Wimber calls 'developing a personal history with God'. Develop personal disciplines that cultivate a passion for Jesus such as prayer, fasting, Bible study, worship and obedience in the small things.

Jack Deere (1993:201) urges us to pray the following prayer on a daily basis: 'Father, grant me power from the Holy Spirit to love the Son of God like You love him (John 17:26).

Don't despise the day of small beginnings. Learn to hear God's voice and catch his heart. Get spiritually prepared so that when God's zero hour strikes, you're fit for action.

4. Intercessory prayer

Note these Scriptures and quotes, and many like them:

2 Chronicles 7:14 – 'If my people... will humble themselves and pray and seek my face and turn from their wicked ways, then I will hear from heaven, and will forgive their sin and will heal their land.'

Isaiah 62:6-7 – 'You who call on the Lord, give yourselves no rest, and give him no rest till...'

Isaiah 64:1 – 'Oh, that you would rend the heavens and come down.'

'God does nothing but in answer to prayer' (Wesley).

'Prayer is not overcoming God's reluctance; it is laying hold of his highest willingness' (Luther).

'Prayer is rebellion against the status quo' (David Wells).

'Prayer humbles us as needy and exalts God as worthy' (John Piper).

'Give me Scotland or I die' (John Knox).

'There has never been a spiritual awakening in any country or locality that did not begin in united prayer' (A. T. Pierson in Bryant 1984:40).

'When God has something very great to accomplish for his Church, it is his will that there should precede it, the extraordinary prayers of his people' (Edwards, *Works* 1:426).

Some argue that revival is sovereign and you can't do anything to make it happen, while others say you can pray and bring it about. I believe God initiates the prayer that precedes a revival; and in this hour he is stirring the church to be united, aggressive, and persistent in prayer for God to act and move again.

5. Be willing to pay the price

Are you willing to receive a divine 'baptism of desperation', a 'holy dissatisfaction' that puts your reputation, dignity and personal peace at risk?

We need to have the courage to be honest with God and say with Oswald Chambers, author of *My Utmost for His Highest,* 'If what I have is all the Christianity there is, then the things is a fraud' (Brown 1991:28).

We must force a crisis in our lives... when our very being aches with desire for his visitation, when we are consumed with hunger for his reality, when we radically cut back on other activities in order to seek his face, then we are ripe for transformation (Brown 1991:29).

We need to surrender our puny agendas, our need for security, safety and comfort zones. As Hebrews 11 tells us, we are not to shrink back and displease the Lord but to become risk-takers in this adventure of participating in the Kingdom of God.

Christians ought to be old friends with risk and when a church or an individual Christian builds a wall of safety, something very basic to the Christian faith has been violated... Christians ought to be the most gutsy people on the face of the earth (Brown 1983:113-114).

We must have more confidence in God's ability to lead us than in Satan's ability to deceive us (Deere 1993:215; see also Luke 11:11-13).

Arthur Wallis (1956:10) says, 'If you would make the greatest success of your life, try to discover what God is doing in your time and fling yourself into the accomplishment of his purpose and will.'

We, like Peter in the boat during a storm, need to hear Jesus' words, 'Do not be afraid,' and his invitation to 'come' and walk on water with him.

God's gracious disposition is always toward revival and he only looks to see if there is a people, a generation who dares enough and cares enough to pay the price. 'Now is the time to sanctify ourselves for tomorrow God will do wonders among us' (Joshua 3:5).

References

Scripture quotations from the *New International Version* of the Bible (1973, 1978, 1984).
Bartleman, Frank (1980) *Azusa Street.* Logos.
Brown, Michael (1991) *Whatever Happened to the Power of God?* Destiny Image.
Brown, Stephen (1983) *If God is in Charge.* Nelson.
Bryant, David (1984) *With Concerts of Prayer.* Regal.
Cartwright, Peter (1956) *Autobiography of Peter Cartwright.* Abingdon.
DeArteaga, William (1992) *Quenching the Spirit.* Creation House.
Deere, Jack (1993) *Surprised by the Power of the Spirit.* Zondervan.
Dallimore, Arnold (1980) *George Whitefield. Vol. 2.* Crossway.
Edwards, Jonathan (1974, 1992 reprinted) *Works of Jonathan Edwards,* Vols 1 & 2.
Banner of Truth.
Edwards, Jonathan (1741, 1984) *The Distinguishing Marks of a Work of the Spirit of God.*
Banner of Truth.
Jackson, Bill (1994) 'What in the World is Happening to Us?' Unpublished paper.
Johnson, Charles (1955) *The Frontier Camp Meeting.* Methodist University Press.
Joyner, Rick (1993) *The World Aflame.* Morningstar.
Kaiser Jr., Walter C. (1986) *Quest for Renewal (Revival in the Old Testament).* Moody.
Krupp, Nate (1984, 1988) *The Triumphant Church.* Destiny Image.
Lloyd-Jones, Martyn (1987) *Revival.* Crossway.
Lovelace, Richard (1979) *Dynamics of Spiritual Life.* InterVarsity.
MacNutt, Francis (1990) *Overcome by the Spirit.* Chosen.
Mallone, George (1985) *Canadian Revival: It's Our Turn.* Welch.
Murillo, Mario (1985) *Critical Mass.* Anthony Douglas.
Packer, J. I. (1984) *Keep in Step with the Spirit.* Revell.
Pratney, Winkie (1994) *Revival.* Huntingdon House.
Relfe, Mary Stewart (1988) *Cure of All Ills.* League of Prayer.
Wallis, Arthur (1956) *In the Day of Thy Power.* Cityhill.
Wallis, Arthur (1979) *Rain from Heaven.* Hodder & Stoughton.
White, John (1988) *When the Spirit Comes with Power.* InterVarsity.
Wimber, John (1985) *Power Evangelism.* Hodder & Stoughton.
Wimber, John (1994) *Equipping the Saints,* Fall Quarter.

---

5 How to Minister like Jesus

Bart Doornweed

Bart Dornweerd wrote as a Dutch missionary with Youth With A Mission, working in Holland.

───────────────────────────

openness to the promptings of the Spirit

led to some powerful times of ministry

───────────────────────────

In the summer of 1985 I was leading a four week Youth With A Mission (YWAM) training school for some fifty students in Holland. I had quit my job as a civil engineer and joined YWAM in 1977. A friend, and former YWAMer, Paul Piller from the Philippines, contacted me and offered to speak for a few days when he visited Holland.

I consented, although I wasn't thrilled about his subject: healing. I knew one had to watch out for people who only wanted to talk about healing, faith, miracles, and demons. I trusted Paul, but you never know what can happen to someone who has spent five years in the U.S. Paul had brought some others along: young fellows in T-shirts, blue jeans, and sneakers. I wondered why they had come. Were they going to sing or perform a drama?

As Paul began speaking, I relaxed. No screaming, no emotionalism. After the lecture, he and the young fellows moved around the group praying without saying much. One word stood out: 'more'.

'More of you Lord!' They seemed unperturbed as certain things I was unfamiliar with started happening. Someone started weeping, others collapsed on their chairs, someone else stood shaking. After three days the place was turned upside down. People were filled with joy, received healing, delivered from demons, released from grief. I had hundreds of questions! I had tasted the new wine and I wanted more.

Paul suggested I go to a conference in Sheffield, England, led by a man named John Wimber. Off we went, with a number of YWAMers. I was ready for anything. My 'holy frustration' had reached a point where I was willing to let God do whatever he wanted. I had been warned to get ready for change. God had spoken to me through the story in the second chapter of John's Gospel – the wedding in Cana – where Jesus performed his first miracle of changing water into wine. Interestingly, the servants at the wedding were allowed to participate, because they filled the jars and took the newly transformed wine to the leader of the feast. Somewhere between the jar and the lips of that man, the water changed into wine.

The application for me of that story is that God is looking for people who want to co-operate with him in bringing this about. I had run out of wine, and now I wanted to see the Lord bring out his best vintage. I wanted God to restore my joy, and fill me with the Holy Spirit. The conference was life-changing, even though I didn't have any spine-tingling personal experiences or visions of ecstasy. Nevertheless God gave me a deep inner peace and an affirmation that the teaching I heard, and the ministry I was observing was from his hand.

Giving the Holy Spirit room

My wife and I and others returned home with a clear sense of purpose. Like the servants at the wedding in Cana, our part was to obediently draw out the water and faithfully carry it to others. God would change it into wine.

During the following months, I discovered how exciting life becomes when we give more room to the Holy Spirit! I tried to cultivate a greater sensitivity to God's voice. My goal was to listen better to what he was saying, and act upon that in faith. As John Wimber likes to point out, another way to spell faith is R-I-S-K. This new openness to the promptings of the Spirit led to some powerful times of ministry. My emphasis during individual counselling changed to less talk and more prayer. We also learned that demons are for real, but we have been given authority to drive them out (Matthew 10:8).

Though this new realm of ministry was exhilarating, we needed people from outside to help, advise, and direct us further. We invited people like Barry Kissel from the Anglican church in Chorleywood, England. He imparted to us much in the way of ministry skills.

At a certain stage in this new development I sensed the Lord said: 'It's time for you to begin modelling the ministry, like I did.' After much hesitation, I announced we were going to start a training class with worship, teaching, and practical application. For the first lecture I had John Wimber on video. I led the practicum. The Holy Spirit ministered in a lovely way to a great many of the sixty who showed up. Some received comfort; others were healed. We decided to have a whole Saturday every month with those ingredients: worship, teaching, and ministry.

By word of mouth alone the group grew to about 350 after eight months. The team working with me had grown to about 30 persons. After each training day we evaluated, prayed, and discussed. I had learned the importance of multiplication. Your team can't be big enough!

Passage to India

For the first two years of our marriage, my wife Marianne and I had worked with YWAM in Nepal, a country located between China and India, astride the Himalaya Mountains. For some time we had felt God was leading us back to that part of the world. In early 1989 we left for India with our three children. We ended up living in Bombay for almost four years. From the start I knew I was to invest myself in people. I constantly asked myself, 'How can I give away what God has given me?'

I itinerated as a teacher in the discipleship training schools (DTS) which YWAM runs in different parts of the country. The theme that developed in my teaching was: 'How to minister like Jesus.' The teaching was simple, with lots of examples of how we should pray. After the lecture phase of the DTS, the students would go out for three months of outreach, usually involving evangelism and church planting. They came back with some amazing stories. For example:

The students were sent ... to five different villages. At the end of two months they had established three fellowships in three different villages. Half the village where they stayed is ready to follow Jesus as Lord. Within the next three weeks 68 believers will be baptised. Despite all religious strongholds, barriers, Hindu militants and oppositions, God showed his mighty power through healings, and signs and wonders. Some people saw visions of Jesus hanging on the cross and showing them how much he loves them.

In that area the crops suffered from a disease. The farmers came and asked the team to pray to Jesus. The very next morning the people went to the field and discovered the disease had been totally wiped out. They came with great joy to confess their belief in Jesus since he had heard their prayers.

Once, while I was leading a small seminar, a local pastor named Garry walked in while I was praying for someone in front of the class. He left thinking, 'I can do that.'

The first person he prayed for when he got home was his Hindu brother-in-law. For many years severe back pain had cost him many sleepless nights. The next day the brother-in-law returned, declaring the Lord Jesus had healed his back. He had slept through the night without waking up once.

Garry, who later became a good friend, had been having discussions with a strong Muslim about the Bible and the Koran. The argument always stopped where one would say 'The Bible is the word of God' and the other 'The Koran is the word of God'. This time Garry took a different approach.

'Can I pray for you?' he asked, when he met the man again. Because Indians are among the most religious people on earth, this man, like almost everyone in India, was glad to receive prayer. As Garry put his hand on the man's head and started praying the Muslim fell down and stayed on the floor for quite a while. Garry was puzzled! What next?

When the man got back on his feet, he shared what happened. While he was lying on the floor, he clearly heard a voice saying, 'The Bible is the word of God!' He went home with a Bible in his pocket.

Garry was on a roll. Wherever he went he prayed for people: in church, in the home groups, and especially in the streets while evangelising. In the time we worked together, several churches took root in the slums. People came mainly because they saw Jesus was more powerful than their own gods. Now Garry is going around equipping others to 'minister like Jesus'.

'Will this work?'

More and more I began to see the power of multiplication: invest yourself in a few people next to you and then let them go and do the same thing to others. You may never know the result until heaven, but it could be more powerful than the biggest healing crusade!

After a three week course, 25 YWAMers went back to their bases in different parts of the country. God had meet with us in special ways during those weeks, as we met together or as we went out to visit people and pray for them.

As two brothers went back to Varanasi, the holy city of the Hindus, they wondered, 'Will this work back home?' The first time they went into a Hindu village after their return, they started to worship Jesus. They intended to start a church there. Immediately the Holy Spirit started to come on people; demons manifested and were driven out. People *saw* the power of God and wanted to know more, providing an excellent opening to preach the Word of God.

While walking along the bank of the Ganges River, one of the brothers began talking to a Hindu priest. After a while, the Brahman complained about his headaches. Again, being highly religious, he was willing to receive prayer, even if it was offered in the name of Jesus. Under the power of God he fell down and after he got back up, his headache was completely gone. He sure wanted to know more about this powerful God!

Respect for God

India is more a continent than a country, with almost 900 million people who speak 1,600 different languages. Patrick Johnstone, in *Operation World*, estimates evangelical Christians comprise one per cent of the population, but the number is growing. Two thousand people groups have not been reached with the gospel yet. India must be reached by the spiritually equipped Indian church, but for a while non-Indian partners can help train and support Indian workers.

In YWAM, we have mixed teams of Indians and foreigners who plant churches, evangelise, and minister to the poor in various ways. Hindus and Muslims have great respect for God. The Hindus have millions of gods. Most Indians, especially the poor, are open to spiritual reality, and exercise great faith, upon hearing about a loving God who sent his Son to this world. In evangelism, miracles happen quickly and open many doors to preach the gospel.

I first experienced this in Bhopal, a city where some eight years ago a gas leak at the chemical plant killed at least 2,000 people. Today many still suffer the effects: eye problems, mouth sores and breathing difficulties. With a small team we visited the site where the calamity took place.

As some people gathered, one of us shared briefly who we were and our purpose for coming. One person was prayed for and got healed. More people came who wanted prayer. Some invited us to enter their huts to see those too sick to come out. We were busy for the next *two hours* to bless, comfort, and encourage. Many people received physical healing, saw visions of Jesus, were blessed with peace. We left many friends in this mainly Muslim community.

Of course, the nature of kingdom warfare is 'attack – counter-attack'. The gospel does meet with opposition. Militant Hinduism is experiencing a revival. The north of India is hostile toward the gospel and to Western influence. To make one convert there is like making a hundred in the south.

An Indian friend of mine desired to work in Bihar, a state in the north, also known as 'the graveyard of missionaries'. He had worked with me for sometime and learned more about how to minister in power evangelism. In Bihar, near the border of Nepal, he rented a home where he invited people. He shared with them, prayed for them and taught them how to pray for others. Many were blessed, healed, delivered, and came to salvation. A small church was established.

Across the border in Nepal, the spiritual atmosphere was different. Tremendous openings existed. Within a year almost a hundred people attended the newly started church! Approximately 50 churches have been planted in India by YWAM-trained workers through power evangelism.

More than eight years have passed since the visit of Paul Piller and since the conference with John Wimber in Sheffield. I have seen thousands of people who ran out of wine partake of 'the best wine' as I willingly brought them what I have: just plain water.

© *Equipping the Saints*, First Quarter 1994, pages 11-14. Used with permission.

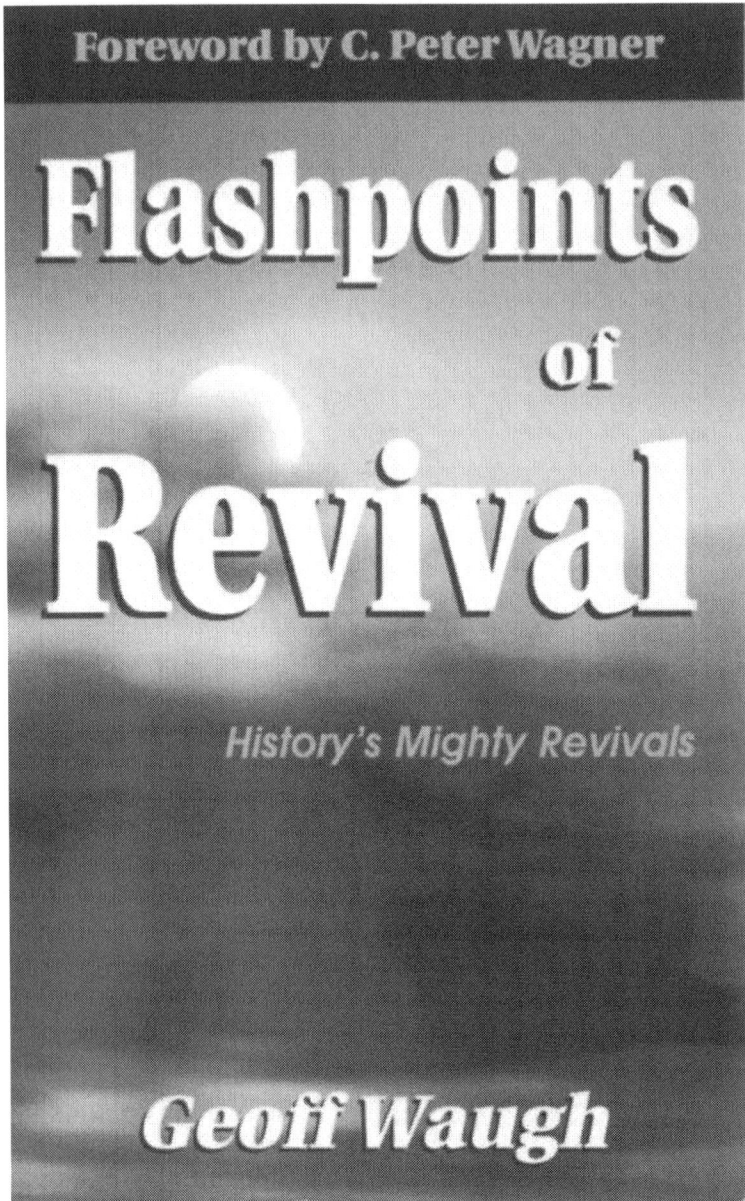

Flashpoints of Revival
History's Mighty Revivals

6 Reflections from England

Sandy Millar and Eleanor Mumford

Rev. Sandy Millar and Mrs Eleanor Mumford of London comment on refreshing from the Lord experienced in England.

Reminiscent of Revivals

Rev. Sandy Millar (now Bishop), then Vicar of the prestigious inner city Anglican church, Holy Trinity Brompton (HTB),describes renewal and refreshing which commenced in May 1994 in their church.

————————————————————

The manifestations themselves are not as significant as the working of the Spirit of God in the individual and the church

————————————————————

This is what was spoken by the prophet Joel! (Acts 2:16) Or, as the old version puts it: 'This is that which was spoken by the prophet Joel.'

This ... is ... that!

The immediate responses to the pouring out of the Holy Spirit at Pentecost included amazement and amusement. Some, Luke tells us, made fun of them and said, 'They've had too much wine' (v. 13). Why would anyone who wanted to be taken seriously suggest they'd drunk too much? Presumably because they looked drunk, sounded drunk and generally behaved as though they *were* drunk!

It is interesting that St Paul too in his letter to the Christians at Ephesus links and contrasts the effects on the body of alcohol ('Do not get drunk with wine which leads to debauchery...') with the effects of being immersed with the Spirit of God ('... but be filled with the Spirit') which leads to 'speaking to one another with psalms, hymns and spiritual songs, singing and making music in your heart to the Lord, always giving thanks to God the Father for everything in the name of our Lord Jesus Christ' (Ephesians 5:18-20).

Paul wasn't at Pentecost but many times he'd seen people genuinely filled with the Spirit. Indeed he seems to have been able to tell pretty quickly whether disciples were or were not filled with the Spirit!

He may have been thinking of his visit to Ephesus described in Acts 19 when he asked what we would think of as a rather direct question: 'Did you receive the Holy Spirit when you believed?' To which he got back an equally direct and honest answer, 'No we have not even heard that there is a Holy Spirit. And, as we all know, 'on hearing this, they were baptised into the name of the Lord Jesus and, when Paul placed his hands on them, the Holy Spirit came on them, and they spoke in tongues and prophesied'. Luke adds that there were about twelve men in all.

Astonishing outpouring

Since about Tuesday of two weeks ago we have begun to see an astonishing outpouring of the Spirit of God upon our own church and congregation. It seems to be a spontaneous work of the Holy Spirit and there are certainly some very surprising manifestations of the Spirit very excitingly reminiscent of accounts of early revivals and movements of God's Spirit.

Some of the manifestations include prolonged laughter, totally unselfconscious for the most part, and an inexpressible and glorious joy (1 Peter 1:8). For some it is prolonged weeping and crying with a sense of conviction and desire for forgiveness, purity and peace with God. For others it seems to be a silent reception of the Spirit of God sometimes leading to falling down and sometimes standing up, sometime kneeling, sometimes sitting.

There are great varieties of the manifestations of the Spirit. They are breaking out both during services and outside them in homes and offices. At times they are easy to explain and handle, and other times they are much harder and more complicated!

We had been hearing for several days of the movement of God's Spirit in the Vineyard Church in Toronto, Canada, and a number of people have come to us from there telling us about what was going on and of what they thought it all meant.

For that reason Jeremy Jennings and I decided to go to Toronto at the beginning of this month just for two and a half days to see what we could learn and what conclusions, if any, at this stage it was possible to draw. The manifestations are quite extraordinary and would undoubtedly be alarming if we hadn't read about them previously in history.

That's really why I started where I started in this article. You don't get accused of being drunk just because you speak in tongues. And many of the manifestations of this modern movement of the Spirit of God carry with them many of the symptoms of drunkenness. Laughter, swaying about, slurred speech, movements which are difficult to control ... all sometimes continuing for long periods of time.

The manifestations themselves of course are not as significant as the working of the Spirit of God in the individual and the church. The manifestations are the symptom and therefore of course it is to the fruit that we look rather than the signs.

Times of refreshing

The church in Toronto first experienced these symptoms on January 20th (1994) and since then they have been ministering to an increasing number of outside people: ministers and church members from all over America, Canada, now Europe and even further afield.

Meetings go on night after night (every night except Monday) and include a pastors' meeting on a Wednesday from 12 to roughly half past three in the afternoon. Their understanding is that God seems to be pouring out his Spirit, refreshing his people and drawing them closer to himself, revealing his love to them and a deep sense of preciousness in away that kindles their own sense of the love of God, their love for Scripture, and their desire to be involved in the activities of the Spirit of God today.

So this is primarily a movement toward God's people. Naturally we expect it to flow out and over into a movement that will affect the rest of the world but for the moment it's God's deep desire to minister to his church – to refresh, empower, and prepare them fora wider work of his Spirit that will affect the world to which the church is sent.

Charles Finney (1792-1875) – one of history's greatest evangelists – records his experience of the Holy Spirit immediately following his conversion:

The Holy Spirit descended upon me in a manner that seemed to go through me body and soul. I could feel the impression like a wave of electricity, going through and through me. Indeed it seemed to come in waves and waves of liquid love... And no words can express the wonderful love that was shed abroad in my heart. I wept aloud with joy and love; and I do not know but I should say, I literally bellowed out the unutterable gushings of my heart. These waves came over me, and over me, and over me, one after another until I recollect I cried out 'I shall die if these effects continue to pass over me'.

During the ministry of Jonathan Edwards in the 1735 revival in New Hampshire, he described some of the effects of the spontaneous work of the Spirit of God. 'The town seemed to be full of the presence of God,' he wrote. 'It was never so full of love, nor of joy, and yet so full of distress, as it was then.'

He describes something which happened during one of his sermons in New Jersey on March 1st 1746: 'Toward the close of my talk, divine truths made considerable impressions upon the audience, and produced tears and sobs in some under concern and more especially a sweet and humble melting in sundry that, I have reason to hope, were truly gracious.'

During the Cambusland revival in Scotland in 1742, Doctor Alexander Webster described some of the effects of the preaching there: 'There were two kinds – the outcrying and trembling among the unconverted and the ecstatic joy among believers... indeed such joy was more a part of this work than the sorrow over sin. It appears that many believers found themselves so moved by a sense of the Saviour's love to them and, in turn, by their new love to him, as to be lifted almost into a state of rapture.'

I could go on and on – and probably you could add your own accounts that you've read about in history. There are more than one in the Acts of the Apostles.

I think it's important that we should stay close to the Lord and be grateful for every sign of his grace upon us. Don't let's get too caught up with the symptoms of his Spirit, but more with him and his love for us.

Let's encourage those who think they have experienced nothing (it may or may not be true) – and let's above all continue to pray that through this outpouring of God's Spirit he will build a church worthy of him: holy, equipped, and full of love and grace towards him and the outside world.

Meanwhile let's pray that it may continue. And continue to pray for one another.

———

The current move of the Spirit

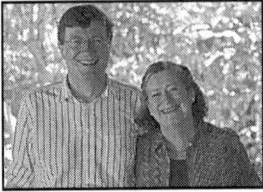

Mrs Eleanor Mumford, wife of the pastor of the South West London Vineyard church, comments on her visit to Toronto in this edited version of her message at Holy Trinity Brompton on Sunday morning 29 May 1994.

This whole move of the Lord
is all about Jesus

I have just been to a church in Toronto in Canada. I heard that there were things going on. I wanted to go and get into the middle. I went because I knew I was bankrupt and that I was longing. And I went with a spirit of tremendous expectancy.

So the first night I went forward and this delightful pastor said to me, 'Do tell me who you are and what you've come for.'

I said, 'I've come for all that you've got. I have two days and I've come from London.'

So he looked at me with a glint in his eye and then proceeded to pray for me on and off for the next two days.

At the same time there was a young Chinese pastor who arrived at Toronto from Vancouver where he was pastoring and he came fasting. The darling man looked as if he's spent his whole life fasting and he was the most wonderful and godly man. As he arrived at the church the Lord spoke to him clearly and said, 'You can forget about your fasting. This is a time for celebration.'

Indeed it was.

An ordinary little church

The Airport Vineyard church in Toronto is a funny little place. It's just a very ordinary little church set in an office block on the end of the runway of the airport.

Even that in itself, I thought, was gracious of the Lord because so many of us can get there so easily. It takes 10 minutes from the check-out to the church!

It was a very ordinary place. I was reminded when I went in there of how the people in the crowd said at Pentecost: 'Are not these Galileans? Are these not just terribly ordinary people?'

I went in and I thought, 'Well, God bless them, these are just ordinary people like me.'

It's just to do with Jesus, and yet the attitude and the sense of expectancy was enormous. As the worship leader strummed his rather tuneless guitar, he stood up and said, 'What have you come for?'

We all said, 'We've come for the Lord. We've come for more of God.'

And he said, 'Well, if you've come for God you'll not be disappointed.'

From that moment on that was the truth.

There was just a beauty on those who were ministering there – the leaders and the pastors and the worship leaders – the sort of beauty that I guess the people saw in Acts when they looked at the disciples and they said, 'These people have been with Jesus.'

These Canadians were just men and women who had spent 130 days in the company of Jesus who was pouring out his Spirit on them.

They shone with faces like Stephen.

It was beautiful to see.

I saw the power of God poured out in incredible measure and it was all accompanied by phenomena.

Great Awakening

Jonathan Edwards, a great man of God during the eighteenth century who was part of the Great Awakening in America, wrote this in his journal of a similar outpouring of the Spirit of God at that time: 'The apostolic times seem to have returned upon us, such a display has there been of the power and grace of the Spirit.'

He wrote of fear, sorrow, desire, love, joy, tears, and trembling, of 'groans and cries, agonies of the body and the failing of bodily strength.'

So I thought, 'Well, none of this is new. It may be unusual but none of it is new.'

Edwards also wrote, 'We are all ready to own that no man can see God and live. If we see even a small part of the love and the glory of Christ, a foretaste of heaven, is it any wonder that our bodily strength is diminished.'

That is indeed what happened to many of us despite ourselves.

The truth is that this whole move of the Lord is all about Jesus. I was there for only 48 hours. I never heard anybody talk about the devil. I never heard anybody talk about spiritual warfare. I never heard a principality or a power mentioned. We were so preoccupied with the person of Jesus that there was really no time. There was no space for talk of the opposition because there was just a growing passion for the name of Jesus and for the beauty of his presence among his people.

So I went scurrying back to the Scriptures and scurrying back to church history and it's all happened before. It's all in the book and there's nothing that I saw – however strange or unusual – that I haven't since been able to read about in the Bible.

Jonathan Edwards' wife had an intimate acquaintance with her carpet for 17 days during the time of the Great Awakening. For 17 days she was unable to make their meals or take care of the family or look after the visitors.

She said after 17 days that she had a delightful sense of the immediate presence of God – of 'his nearness to me and of my dearness to him.'

I thought to myself when I came home, that's what this is about. It's about his nearness to me and my dearness to him.' Wonderful, wonderful things are going on.

Pastors renewed

During the time I was there I saw all sorts of people coming and going. There were many very weary pastors who turned up with their even more weary wives, and they were so anointed by the Lord.

There was one very sensible middle-aged man who'd been in pastoral ministry for years and when he spoke to us after having been there for several days he was just behaving like an old drunk. It was funny. Once he stood up and talked about the intimacy that he'd gained with Jesus. Then the leading pastor said to him, 'Well thank you, Wayne, for telling us about this. May we pray for you?'

He said, 'I'd be glad for you to pray for me.'

They prayed for him and down he went and he rolled on the floor for the next two hours and no-one took any notice. He just continued to commune with his God.

I saw another young pastor who talked at the pastors' seminar that I went to. He was a very all-together young man – quite serious minded and godly and thrilled with everything but very much in control and very anxious when he came and not at all sure of what he'd come to.

For a day or two he just watched and he just basked in the presence of the Lord. After a day or two he started to twitch and he was a little embarrassed. Then he started to shake and he was very embarrassed. Then after a while of shaking and laughing in the presence of the Lord he decided, 'Who gives a rip? Who cares what people say?'

A verse in Psalms says, 'gladness and joy shall overtake me.' This young man had been overtaken by the gladness of the Lord. But he had a sense of responsibility and felt, 'I've got to keep my church on the road.'

So he decided that the obvious thing to do was to go into the office and to type out the church bulletin, the news sheet.

'Someone's got to keep a grip round here,' he said to himself.

So he went to type out the bulletin and as he got to announcing the seminar. The title of it was 'Come Holy Spirit'.

He typed, 'Come Holy Spirit' and fell under the power of God.

There was another young man who was a youth worker who arrived and he was worn down with ministry. His wife had said to him, 'Why don't you go to Toronto?' She thought he was getting far too straight and serious.

So he came to Toronto and arrived the night that I did. That night he fell on the ground and he laughed and laughed. I thought he would have died. The next day he spoke about what God had done for him and the refreshment that had come to his soul. Then they said to him, 'Would you like us to pray for you again?'

He said, 'I think so.'

So we prayed and down he went and just laughed his way through hour after hour of the pastors' seminar.

And you think to yourself, 'What is this?'

But this is just the refreshing of the Spirit of God. It talks in the book of Acts about times of refreshing from the Spirit of the Lord, and that's what God is doing.

He's pouring his Spirit out upon us. He's sending his joy and he's refreshing our spirits just because he loves us.

I'm not even sure that he's equipping us. I'm not even sure it's all about being better this, better that, better ministers. It think it's just his love for us. It's about his nearness to me and my dearness to him.

Joy and refreshing

I could tell you heaps of stories. There are stories about people who are ringing one another up and getting led to Christ over the phone.

There was a story about a young woman who'd lain on the floor and laughed for two hours. Then she got up and decided she was peckish and went off to a little fast food restaurant. She sat down. Opposite, she saw a whole family sitting at a table and, completely out of character, she went to them and said, 'Would you like to be saved?' And they all said yes! The whole family was led to Christ.

I went to the Dolphin school [a Christian school in Clapham] the other day and talked to them about what the Lord had been doing and I prayed for them. The Lord fell on those children aged five years old and they were laughing and weeping for the lost and crying out to the Lord. The teachers were affected and the parent were rolling around.

I thought, 'God, this is a glorious thing you're doing. This is fantastic.'

Jesus is breaking down the barriers of his church because he's coming for a bride, and he wants his bride to be one.

We've been meeting with Baptist pastors this week. We've been meeting with New Frontiers pastors. We've been meeting with the Anglicans. And God is pouring his Spirit out on us all and it's a glorious thing.

I was reminded of that verse in the Psalms (133:1,3), 'How blessed it is when brothers dwell together in unity ... for there the Lord commands the blessing.'

He doesn't just invite it, or suggest it. He commands a blessing on us when we dwell together in unity – when we love one another and we love one another's churches and we bless one another's people.

So God is moving, not just on this funny little church at the end of the runway. He's moving across the denominations. He's moving across the land. He's moving across London and England in a fantastic way. And he's moving across the world.

Greater love for Jesus

What are the perceived results so far?

For myself, there is a greater love for Jesus than I've ever known, a grater excitement about the Kingdom than I ever thought possible, a greater sense that these are glorious, glorious days in which to be alive. I'm thrilled about the Scriptures and I'm going back to the Word and finding that it's all been there from the very beginning.

I'm excited about church history. I have a heightened sense of what's been going on up to this point.

I have an ever stronger sense of the whole church than ever before. The Lord said to them in Toronto right at the beginning, 'This is not about the Vineyard; this is about the Kingdom.' This is not about any one church. This is about the Kingdom, and about the Bride of Christ. Right across the church Jesus' passion for his Bride is beginning to be understood.

I've also discovered that I'm desperate to give this away. I haven't had this appetite for ministry for years. I mean, I've always been enthusiastic but I've not had this passion before. I've just found that there's a greater recklessness in me than there's ever been before because God is coming upon us, and the joy of the Lord is coming on the church and Jesus is restoring his joy. And his laughter is like medicine to the soul.

In our church the people are getting freed and the people are getting healed. We've got people who have gone down on the floor and got up healed. Nobody ever knew they were sick and they got better without us even naming the words.

The Lord is coming with mercy and kindness.

The prodigal son went to look for parties but he discovered that the best party was in his father's house. Isn't that the truth?

© *HTB in Focus*, 12 June 1994, the monthly paper of Holy Trinity Brompton Anglican Church in London. *Renewal Journal* #5 (1995:1), pp. 24-31.

7 Reflections from Australia

John Davies, Phil Ashton, Geoff Glass, Tony Stevens

Anglican renewal leaders, Rev John Davies in Sydney, Revs Phil Ashton, Geoff Glass and Mr Tony Stevens in Melbourne comment on renewal blessings in Australia.

'Toronto Blessing' reaches Australia

Comment by Rev. John Davies, the Minister at the Anglican Church in Northbridge, Sydney and editor of the Anglican Renewal Ministries of Australia Sydney Newsletter (November 1994):

—————————————————————

A deepened sense of the presence of Jesus,
a heightened expectancy for the power of the Spirit
to work through me, and a refreshment in my spirit

—————————————————————

Earlier this year rumours began to reach our shores that some strange things were happening in one of the Vineyard churches in Toronto, Canada. It was reported that God was moving with new power and blessing. A particular feature was the outbreak of 'holy laughter' in their services.

Those who attended the Wimber conference in Brisbane in April reported something of this phenomenon happening there, where many were blessed. There seemed to be a new level of spiritual power.

Tri Robinson, from the Vineyard church in Boise, Idaho, who spoke at the Melbourne Pentecost Rally, and the Port Macquarie Conference in June, mentioned that he had been to the Toronto church. He told how he had been rather sceptical of the reported happenings, but had been convinced that it was God when he found himself on his face on the floor, unable to move for an hour.

At the end of May the phenomenon spread to several churches in London, UK, including the rather prestigious Anglican church, Holy Trinity, Brompton, just down the road from Harrods. Within weeks the London newspapers were beginning to take notice, and headlines in the daily papers proclaimed outbreaks of 'Holy Laughter'.

The religious press in England was also quick to comment. The *Church of England Newspaper* of June 17 had the headline 'Revival breaks out in London churches' and reported that 'Church leaders admit bewilderment as manifestations affect business and staff meetings as well as church services'. The *Church Times* of June 24 spoke of 'a mighty wind from Toronto which blew through Holy Trinity Brompton (HTB), laid flat a staff meeting, and then set a whole congregation laughing hysterically, crying and falling repeatedly on the floor'. There was a brief note of this report in the Australian *Church Scene* of July 1, but not much other mention in Australia...

The English *Renewal* magazine for July had a brief report under the heading 'Spreading Like Wildfire'. This was essentially a summary of the report to HTB by Eleanor Mumford, the wife of the pastor of the Southwest London Vineyard, on her visit to Toronto. She told how she saw the 'power of God poured out in incredible measure'. She said: 'I saw many very weary pastors who turned up with their even wearier wives, and they were so anointed by the Lord.'

Mrs Mumford also spoke of the personal effect on her: 'For myself, there is a greater love for Jesus than I've ever known, a greater excitement about the Kingdom than I ever thought possible. I haven't had such an appetite for ministry for years. **Jesus is restoring his joy, and his laughter is like medicine to my soul.**'

Further reports of what was happening at HTB, and at other churches in England, appeared in the August and September issues of *Renewal*. There was even an article in *Time Magazine* for August 10.

Rosemary and I managed to hear about this just before we left on 3 months Long Service Leave in July. And, by a series of small miracles, we were able to change our itinerary to include six days in Toronto, and visits to HTB and Chorleywood in England. What we saw, and what we received, has had a dramatic effect on our lives. And, since our return, has begun to affect members of our church.

Overall assessment

From what we have seen and experienced we have no doubt that at the heart of what is happening there is a genuine movement of the Spirit of God. Although some of the outward manifestations are unusual, and sometimes bizarre, the fruit that is being produced bears all the marks of true godliness.

There is, especially in Toronto, a strong emphasis on the centrality of Jesus, and the need for true repentance and faith. Many have shared of the deepening of their love for Jesus, and their increased desire to serve him. There has been a greater enthusiasm for sharing the gospel, and a steady stream of new converts. Numbers have been physically healed, including a girl with chronic ME and a ten year old boy, whom we saw, with severe asthma.

My own experience has been a deepened sense of the presence of Jesus, a heightened expectancy for the power of the Spirit to work through me, and a refreshment in my spirit.

Before Toronto

The so-called 'Toronto Blessing' did not, in fact, originate in Toronto. It began with a South African evangelist ministering in the USA by the name of Rodney Howard-Browne. During the early part of 1993 the Spirit of God began to move powerfully in his meetings and many were blessed.

A Vineyard pastor from St Louis, Missouri, Randy Clarke, was feeling very dry and weary after 10 years in the ministry and determined to get to a Howard-Browne meeting. As a result of the blessing he received, his whole church came alive. In September of '93 he shared what was happening in a Vineyard leaders' meeting and, as a result, John Arnott, from the Airport Vineyard in Toronto invited him to come for a series of meetings.

The Toronto 'fountain'

Randy Clarke came to Toronto for a 4-day mission on 20th January 1994. The Spirit of God moved so powerfully that the meetings were extended again and again for forty days.

Originally the church met every night of the week, with meetings going often until 2 a.m.! Eventually they decided to have Mondays off. They have continued to meet six nights per week, plus Sunday mornings, until the present time, and meetings still continue until 2 a.m.

The church is situated in a small office/industrial block beside the runway of Toronto airport. Although it only seats 400, with an overflow of 200, it regularly has congregations of over 700 as visitors flood in from all over the world. Just recently they have decided to ban visitors from their Sunday Morning Service so that they can care for their own congregation.

From the beginning the Toronto leadership realised that God was calling them to give away what they had received. A number of local Baptist, Presbyterian and other pastors were invited to come together for lunch on a Wednesday. Not only were the pastors blessed, but they took the blessing back to their churches.

Word soon began to spread, and pastors from further afield expressed an interest. The Wednesday pastors' meetings became a regular feature. When we were there, there were pastors from many parts of the USA and Canada, from Great Britain, Europe, South Africa, Cambodia, and South America.

It is as though the church in Toronto is a fountain to which the weary and thirsty from around the world might come and be refreshed. Those who come are encouraged to keep seeking after God for **all** that he has to give. The most common expression is 'More, Lord!' (The other is: 'It's a party!') While some have been overwhelmed by God's blessing on the first contact, the more common experience is that there is a progressive deepening of the blessing as people keep coming back for more.

Revival or refreshment?

The phrase 'Revival' was often used in the early stages, but more mature reflection has led to the conclusion that it is not fully 'Revival' yet. Wimber and others believe that this is, at present, essentially a refreshment for Christians. It may well be the preparation for the revival that many believe is coming soon. Or, it may be a preparation for coming persecution, or both! However, for the present, the streams of refreshment are flowing, and the invitation stands: *'Come all you who are thirsty, come to the waters'.*

Strange manifestations

While many of the physical manifestations associated with this phenomenon have been seen before in previous movements of the Holy Spirit, the widespread distribution of phenomena such as laughter that has occurred this time has led some Charismatic and Pentecostal leaders to confess to some scepticism. However, most have come away convinced that this is truly a work of God.

As in previous moves of the Hoy Spirit, there are some 'fleshly' excesses, but the leadership maintains a careful oversight. Their attitude is that even if there is 70% flesh, they do not want to crush the 30% Spirit.

While laughter was the chief characteristic in the early days, more recently there have been instances of people roaring like lions (e.g. David Pytches) ... Probably the most widespread manifestation is some kind of shaking or jerking.

It is quite common, though not universal, for people to fall to the floor under the power of the Spirit. 'Spending carpet time' is a common Toronto expression. In my observation, God often does a much deeper work once people are on the ground. It may be that in the surrender to his power there is an opening up of one's life to new levels of his ministry. The ministry team are encouraged to keep praying for those who are on the ground.

While falling down, jerking, laughing, etc., may not be normal Christian experience, especially in Anglican churches, they are not unknown in the Bible. Certainly, the history of revivals such as that in New England in the 18th Century, recorded by Jonathan Edwards, showed similar phenomena.

Spread of the blessing

The blessing has spread like wildfire in many places. When we were in Toronto in August it was reported that 800 English churches had been affected. Many more have been touched since then. At the evening service at HTB there was a queue of 200 outside the doors an hour before the service. A recent report said that it is now necessary to get a ticket to get into the church which seats 1200! 700 clergy and leaders turned up to a special day at St Andrew's, Chorleywood in August to hear an assistant pastor from Toronto.

Many have wondered why it is necessary to travel across the world to catch the blessing. All I can say is, that is how it is so often with the gospel. Only very few are converted without personal contact with someone who knows Jesus. God has chosen to work through personal contact to spread the blessing and it is not for us to argue.

Certainly, it is those who make the commitment of time and money to seek from God who generally go away filled (Jeremiah 29:13).

Australian outbreak

Spirit Life, the Anglican Renewal Ministries of Australia (ARMA) Victoria Newsletter, reported in its October issue: 'Two Anglican Clergy from Melbourne have just returned from Toronto ... I am led to believe that the blessing has now flowed to a number of other churches in Melbourne.'

There is news in the past few weeks of the 'blessing' having broken out in a number of churches in Sydney. Hills CLC, Sutherland Growth Centre, North Shore CLC and Randwick Baptist all report powerful moves of the Holy Spirit, particularly in their evening services.

In our own small church in Northbridge, God has powerfully touched a number of people. Some have been refreshed, others have been changed, and there is a new sense of expectancy in our meetings.

While we are learning afresh what it means to keep coming back to our Father for more and more of his unlimited grace, we are also seeking to give away everything he has given us.

No one knows just how long this blessing will last, or whether it will lead to widespread revival. Certainly it fits with a number of prophetic words, some going back to 1984, that 1993/'94 would see a great outpouring of blessing. In the end we can only tap into what God is doing in the present, and be very careful that we do not miss out because it does not fit our preconceptions.

———

The Blessing is spreading

Comment by Rev. Phil Ashton, the Associate Minister at Christ Church Anglican, Dingley in Melbourne (December 1994):

————————————————

people in quiet and in dramatic ways
were touched by God's Spirit

————————————————

The October edition of *Spirit Life* (the Victoria and Tasmania Newsletter of Anglican Renewal Ministries of Australia) noted that the 'Tronoto blessing' was being spread as the result of the Holy Spirit and a couple of Anglican clergy from Melbourne having visited Tronoto. I have to confess to being one of them!

The trip to Toronto for my wife Maryann and I was a miracle in itself. What with church commitments here at Dingley, four children to be looked after in our absence, a dog and a recently acquired mortgage, there was no way we could afford to go to Toronto, either commitment-wise or financially. Yet within ten days of seeking God's will in all this, every problem had been blown away. Three people offered to have the children, someone paid the airfare, – even the dog was looked after! There was no longer any reason why we could not go!

After the trip

Our time at the Airport Vineyard was challenging, refreshing, faith stretching and a real party! But the fun didn't stop there. Upon our return, in response to the question, 'What happened?', we decided to hold a testimony evening to share our story. At the end of the evening, being a safe, conservative sort of person, it would have been easier for me simply to pronounce the final blessing and send everyone home.

However, I felt God was calling us to move in faith; to stand on the edge of the cliff with him – and jump! We offered prayer to folk, and God's Spirit came in power. There were those who laughed, those who cried, those who rested in the Spirit. Talking to people in the days that followed, we realised however, that God was changing people's hearts. There was a desire for a second meeting following the Monday, to which about 60 people came, with similar results. A few visitors had come this time as well.

It was then decided to take, what for us was a huge leap of faith – to hold meetings on Mondays and Tuesdays for the whole month of October. We did not advertise in any formal sense, and our intention was that these meetings were for our own church folk as together we explored what God was doing in our midst.

The results, however, took us by surprise! The agenda for the meetings was kept very simple: some worship, a short teaching or encouraging word, some testimony from folk who had been touched by God previously, some practical issues were addressed (such as falling and not falling, and that people would not be pushed by the pray-ers, etc.), and then we went into a time of prayer with individuals.

The number of visitors increased as word got around, as people in quiet and in dramatic ways were touched by God's lovely Spirit. One boy who had lost his brother in a traffic accident and had not cried since then, sobbed for a long time, before the crying turned to a gentle laugh or giggle. The change in him has been dramatic. Others have had their love for Jesus renewed and restored, and have captured again that first love that John speaks of in Revelation chapter 2.

Where are we now?

At this point in time we have moved into the larger hall; last week there were 240 people at the Monday meeting and 200 on Tuesday. A recent development from some parishioners has meant that the ministry will continue. Cumulatively over 2,000 people have been to the meetings from more than 110 churches of many different denominations. We praise God for the breaking down of denominational barriers.

Leaders and people together are coming to God for a fresh touch, a renewing and refreshing touch of his Holy Spirit. The testimonies are often simple and real:

* *'Laid on the floor for one hour. Felt God's love and peace, smelt the fragrance of the Spirit. Next day had amazing breakthroughs in marriage relationship and real healing.'*

* *'God released me from anger and a feeling of unworthiness.'*

* *'Last night Jesus healed me from past memories of three people on different occasions molesting me. Praise Jesus.'*

Some people 'rest in the Spirit' on the floor for a while, and God meets them there. One or two have spoken of being held down on the floor, as if God has put a great weight on their limbs and they are unable to get up until he has finished with them. Not everyone goes down. One man stood for quite a long time as the power of God came upon him. Those around sensed what almost seemed like a strong electrical current flowing into him. Sometimes the pray-ers and the catcher are touched as the Spirit manifests himself.

God is certainly at work. Whether people stand of fall is not the point. As John White has written in his book *When the spirit comes with power*,

manifestations, while they may be a blessing, are no guarantee of anything. Their outcome depends on the mysterious traffic between God and our spirits. Your fall and your shaking may be a genuine expression of the power of the Spirit resting on you. But the Spirit may not benefit you in the least if God does not have his way with you, while someone who neither trembles nor falls may profit greatly.

Of one thing we are sure. This is no new work of the Holy Spirit. As we read church history we note that the same things were seen and experienced by George Fox (1624-1691), by Jonathan Edwards during the Great Awakening (1740-1742), and by Charles Finney (1792-1875), as people came under the conviction of the Holy Spirit and were drawn by God's love for them.

Our cry to God today is: **'Lord, do it again'.**

———————

Toronto in Melbourne? Really?

The Rev. Geoff Glass, Anglican Minister at Beaumaris in Melbourne comments (December 1994):

———————————————————

all have found a real spiritual refreshment,

a deepened awareness of God,

a bubbling joy and a deep peace

———————————————————

Some of us have heard stories of some remarkable happenings in a Vineyard Church in Toronto, Canada, and at Holy Trinity, Brompton, in England. Some of us have thought how good it would be to receive the blessings that are being poured out on people there.

On October 4 my wife Jan and I went to a clergy meeting over at Christ Church, Dingley, and found that their Vicar, Rob Isaachsen, and also his curate, Phil Ashton, had just returned from Toronto and Rob shared with us what had happened. It was obvious he had been profoundly touched by God and when he offered to pray for us I was first in. It wasn't long before I found myself on the floor for the first time in the 21 years I have been in renewal. I lay there for some time as the Holy Spirit continued to minister to me. When I got up I felt remarkably alive and peaceful and had a new sense of freedom. Jan was prayed for soon after and she too ended up on the floor for the first time ever. When she got up she too felt the same as I did.

Later that day I was speaking to one of my church wardens on the phone and mentioned what had happened to us. He asked if he and his wife could come and see us that evening. They did, and as we prayed for them they too ended up on the floor and were profoundly blessed. Both Jan and I had a sense of the Holy Spirit releasing enormous power as we prayed for them.

As I reflected on this the next morning the Lord kept bringing to mind the phrase 'times of refreshing'. It seemed familiar and I found a Bible reference using this phrase in Acts 3:19 that seemed to make sense of what had happened.

As we have shared this experience of the Holy Spirit with our congregations a number of people have asked for prayer. Nearly all ended up on the floor, but all have found a real spiritual refreshment, a deepened awareness of God, a bubbling joy and a deep peace. We are praying for the Holy Spirit to extend his blessing of refreshment to all of our congregation.

———

The Blessing reaches Mulgrave

Mr Tony Stevens, editor of 'Spirit Life' the Victoria and Tasmania Newsletter of the Anglican Renewal Ministries of Australia, comments (December 1994):

—————————————

Let us all pray that the Lord will keep his blessing flowing to the churches and people

—————————————

St Matthew's, Mulgrave, has been experiencing a mighty move of the Spirit this year. This all started around the time of Pentecost and has been heightened by the ministry of Tri Robinson and Lamar Junkins from the Vineyard.

Many people have been blessed by the ministry of the Rev. Brian Thewlis (whose home base is Christ Church, Dingley) who has been ministering here over the last couple of months. Many people from the 10.30 a.m. congregation have been freed, blessed and healed. Many of the congregation have also been to Dingley and received a blessing from the Lord there.

The church is praying for mighty things to happen next year. Praise the Lord for what is happening now! Let us all pray that the Lord will keep his blessing flowing to the churches and people during 1995. Let us all have open minds to what he is doing at this time in history.

———

Edited from the November 1994 *ARMA Sydney Newsletter* and *Spirit Life* the December 1994 Victoria and Tasmania ARMA Newsletter

8 The Legacy of Hau Lian Kham
(1944-1995)

A Revivalist, Equipper, and Transformer for the Zomi-Chin People of Myanmar (Burma)

By Chin Khua Khai

Reproduced from the Asian Journal of Pentecostal Studies No. 4, 2001, pages 99-107, from Dr Chin Khua Khai's research for his Ph.D. degree.

Although small and often unnoticed, Myanma (Burma) has had its share of great leaders. The late Reverend Hau Lian Kham, often referred to as the "John Wesley" of Zomi (Chin) because of the similar characters and patterns seen in his leadership, is a noted pastor-evangelist and teacher among the evangelical Pentecostal believers in Myanmar. From the early 1970s until his death in 1995, he was the key figure and leader of a renewal movement among the Zomis. The renewal began on a small scale in the early 1970s and has spread throughout the region to many parts of the country through evangelism and cross-cultural mission efforts (1). It has resulted in the planting of new churches in both rural and urban regions and to the establishment of leadership training schools. Kham has left his legacy as a revivalist, equipper, and transformer.

1. A Brief Story of His Life

Kham's legacy in Zomiss began against the backdrop of a predominantly nominal Christian atmosphere (2). The Zomi is a major ethnic group in Myanmar occupying the north-western region. They were 2.2% of countries estimated population of 49 million in the year 2000 (3). Christianity has been a dominant religious practice among the Zomis for half a century.

The Zomis received Christian faith through the efforts of missionaries. American Baptist missionaries first introduced the Christian faith to them early in the 1900s (4). Other missions such as the Methodists (1925), Catholics (1934), Anglicans (1934), Seventh-Day Adventists (1954), Presbyterians (1956), and Pentecostals (that is, Assemblies of God, 1960s) arrived as well. When missionaries were expelled from the country in the 1960s, more than half of the Zomi population had become professed Christians. At this stage, there existed among the Zomis Christians a moral laxity and a lack of salvation knowledge (5).

Out of this background, Kham arose as a giant of faith who launched the renewal movement in 1973. On November 24, 1944, he was the sixth of eight children born to devout Christian parents in Ngennung-Tedim, Chin State, Myamnar. Upon graduating from high school, he began serving as the headmaster of Zomi Baptist Academy, a primary school, in his native town of Tedim from 1963 to 1965.

Though poverty has always been a roadblock to education for the Zomis, Kham found a way to pursue his secular education as well as theological education. He attended night classes at Workers College on a work-study program, receiving a Bachelor of Arts (B.A.) degree in 1968. He then enrolled in Myanmar Institute of Theology, Insein, Yangon, and received a Bachelor of Religious Education (B.R.E.) degree in 1971.

Upon completion of his studies, he decided to return to Tedim to engage in full time ministry. Indeed, temptations prevailed when relatives asserted he was making an undesirable career choice due to the poor income ministers receive. After a strong prayer, he made a lasting decision to serve the Lord alone.

Kham's ministry went through enormous changes, which better equipped him for kingdom service. He was first installed as the senior pastor of Cope Memorial Baptist Church (April 1971 to 1974) in Tedim receiving his ordination credentials on February 25, 1973. He went on to become a leader of the Evangelical Baptist Conference (EBC) and the senior pastor of Tedim's Evangelical Baptist Church (1975-1976) when Cope Memorial Baptist Church dismissed him from membership because of his promotion of the renewal movement.

Eventually, he became a Pentecostal minister (1977-1996) because of his new experience with the empowerment of the Holy Spirit and a larger vision of the kingdom's mission. Regarding his joining the Assemblies of God of Myanmar, he once stated, "We must keep a large vision of the whole country, even the whole world, for the evangelization, while starting the work at the local area" (6). In 1979 Khain became the founding principal of Evangel Bible College in Yangon, the capital city of Myanmar, serving in this capacity as well as teaching until his death on December 29, 1995. During this time, he also held the position of the senior pastor of Grace Assembly of God Church. Kham was the general secretary of the Assemblies of God of Myanmar for a period. This position was relinquished when he was sent to the Philippines for graduate studies in 1987.

Kham received a Master of Divinity (M.Div.) degree from Asia Pacific Theological Seminary (APTS), Baquio, Philippines in 1991, a Master of Theology (Th.M.) degree from Asia Graduate Theological Seminary (AGTS), Manila, Philippines in 1994, and was a candidate for the Doctor of Ministry (D. Min.) degree at AGTS.

Kham's premature death was a great loss not only to his family, friends and relatives, but also to the body of Christ in Myanmar. He was the prospective leader of the whole evangelical-Pentecostal body in Myanmar. His remaining family members include his wife Mary Hau Lun Cing who also had reached candidate of D.Min. status at AGTS, and three daughters, Cing Lam Dim, Man San Lun, and Cing Lian Ciin. At the writing of tiiis article, with the help of her daughters, Mary carries on the Kham's ministries as the acting principal of Evangel Bible College and as by serving as the senior pastor of Grace Assembly of God Church.

2. Early Theological Paradigm Changes

Being raised in a pious family, Kham was a committed Christian since childhood. God-fearing in attitude, obedience, sincerity, friendliness, and humility were revealing marks in his life. He was a Bible lover, active churchgoer, and even a choirmaster. He was a genius in widespread reading, especially of Christian books. More than anything, he had a strong desire to serve the Lord as a full-time minister from his youth.

Two prominent experiences proved revolutionary in Kham's faith journey. He, like Timothy in the Bible, had a strong faith in Christ though he did not know the exact time of his rebirth. However, a paradigm shift of faith took place in him sometime in 1970 when he accepted the Bible as the infallible word of God. This conviction came by his reading of an article in a *Decision* magazine in which Billy Graham stated his acceptance by faith of the whole Bible as the word of God. This, in fact, was opposite to the teachings at the theological institute that Kham was attending at the time (7). The theology he had received at the institute led him to confusion, as it questioned the authority and inspiration of the scripture. He attributed his overcoming the theological dilemma to the work of the Holy Spirit (8). As a result, he asserted the authority and sufficiency of the Bible for faith and practice.

Another experience had caused him to pursue renewal. Being a newly ordained minister, he paid home visits to church members once a week. He soon discovered the church members were nominal and weak in their faith, having little knowledge about the salvation of Christ, lacking real commitment. This discovery led to a turning point in his ministry, for he felt compelled to preach and teach the people about the gospel of the salvation of Jesus Christ in order to help bring renewal to the church. This was his prayer, "These people must hear the gospel and repent and come to the cross of Christ. God, help me and use me" (9).

3. Serving with Multiple Gifts

Kham was a gifted preacher. His preaching was persuasive, forceful, and biblical. When preaching, he always referred to the authority of the word of God, often stating, "The Bible says...." His frequent use of body movement gave him the title, "The Action Preacher." With all of these qualities, his method was a breakthrough for contemporary preaching.

Kham was gifted in teaching. From the very beginning of his pastoral ministry, he taught the Bible and Bible doctrine from the evangelical perspective which was contrary to contemporary teaching in the vicinity. The people were amazed at his new teachings. Consequently, church attendance doubled for the first time since the death of the former pastor of his church in 1965. News about his ministry spread so quickly that the unchurched in the town and visitors from rural villages were persuaded to attend the worship services and his Bible classes.

Moreover, Kham was gifted in music, art, and literature. He conducted the church choir every Sunday, performed in and directed dramas on special occasions such as Christmas. The "Life of Jesus" attracted not only the town dwellers, but also people from the villages nearby. His first publication was a small handbook, *Khasiangtho Ngeina Nam Lite* [The Four Spiritual Laws], published and distributed in March 1973. He translated the books of Jeremiah and Jonah into the Tedim language for the Tediin Bible. Another work of his was the book *Upna Laigil* [The Essence of Faith] which was an evangelical position on Bible doctrine (10). Besides these publications, he wrote several articles and helped revise a local hymnal.

4. Revivalist

Kham was the pioneer leader of the renewal movement among the Zomis. A "burden for souls' was his motivating factor. He was convinced that soul winning was the most important task under heaven. Referring to the scripture in Luke 16:25, he asserted that a soul is more precious than the whole universe; to win a soul is more important than to gain the whole universe, and to help a soul being saved is the most precious task in the sight of God (11). Thus, to promote and bring renewal (12) within the church and to seek souls outside the church was the most urgent call of his pastoral ministry. Kham believed that prayer is a key to renewal (13). He said his supporters learned from historical evidences and personal witnesses that renewal often takes place when the people of God pray and seek him. They soon promoted individual and group prayer meetings for renewal.

Believing an open-air crusade would be the most appropriate strategy to reach the common people, the revivalist and his supporters launched a week-long crusade on April 30, 1973. They raised a bamboo pulpit on a football field where he preached seven nights about the salvation of Christ. This pioneer crusade was characterized by breakthroughs, a charismatic-style singing of revival choruses, a style in preaching the message that had direct implication upon the hearers, the altar call for repentance and acceptance of Christ, and face-to-face discussion of the personal assurance of salvation. These types of events marked a new breakthrough in ministry.

Furthermore, the revivalist learned to trust in the Holy Spirit. He acknowledged the dimension and crucial work of the Holy Spirit in bringing renewal. This factor prevailed as he surrendered himself by kneeling and crying to the Lord for the conversion of sinners, praying all night on the second day of the crusade (14). Preaching aggressively and persuasively for the first two nights did not draw a single sinner to the Lord. However, surrendering and trusting in the Holy Spirit made the difference.

A young man by the name Kham Lian Khup turned and stepped forward in the altar call and accepted Christ as his Saviour and Lord on the third night (15). The bold decision of this young man was a breakthrough that encouraged many to do the same in the days that followed. Converts were added every day.

Eventually, the pioneer crusade was the recognized launching pad of the renewal movement. The word "born again' became a catchword throughout the renewal movement. The born-again believers spread the gospel by preaching, teaching, and counselling. Repentance for sin confession of Christ as Saviour and Lord, baptism in water as a witness of discipleship, studying the Bible, praying, and sharing the word of God were phenomenon indicative of this renewal.

Kham, along with his itinerant gospel team, continued to make gospel tours throughout the countryside during the years of 1973 to 1979. His motto became, "To bring as many people as possible to Christ in the shortest possible time" (16). He conducted gospel crusades from town to town and from village to village.

Like revivalist John Wesley of England in the eighteenth century (17) he travelled hundreds and thousands of miles on foot to spread the good news of Jesus Christ. His brother Gin Za Lian like Charles Wesley, was a gifted musician throughout this renewal period. The two brothers worked hand in hand preaching and singing. During the next ten years, Kham would also preach the gospel to several other people groups throughout the country.

5. Leadership Equipper

Not a lone star, Kham trained up other effective leaders for servicing in the Kingdom of God. Teaching Sunday School was a regular ministry. His gospel crusades were two pronged: preaching and teaching the word of God. He also conducted Bible seminars every year, attended by believers from all the countryside.

Kham renovated the pattern of leadership by emphasizing lay witnessing. Like John Wesley, he motivated, challenged, equipped, and mobilized believers to carry out the work of the ministry. Prioritizing the evangelistic mandate, he emphasized witnessing and winning souls as the greatest call of believers. Their greatest accomplishment would come by fulfilling that call.

He often elaborated the urgency of the call, the doom of people who never hear the gospel, the reward of obeying the call, and the consequences of disobedience. He explained *agape* as God's kind of love, which meant loving others in the way God loves sinners who are doomed to eternal judgment. He also taught about how to witness, live a righteous and Spirit-filled life, and how to build the body of Christ.

As a result of his efforts, lay witnessing became the most dynamic factor of spreading the renewal throughout the country during the last three decades of his life (1970s-1990s) (18).

As stated earlier, Kham began teaching at the Evangel Bible College, serving as the founding principal as well. In fact this call was not a new challenge for him. He had long acknowledged the need to build armies for the Lord with deeper biblical knowledge.

Sensing the need to multiply himself by training leaders, he decided to take over the teaching role at the Bible school. Today, the school's graduates are ministering the mission of the kingdom of God in different capacities all over the country.

6. Transformer

One final legacy to be noted here is that of the transformational changes within the church and in the culture that resulted from the renewal. Kham's own rediscovery and subsequent preaching on key issues such as the Bible as the inspired word of God, the lukewarm nature of the church, the dispensation of law and grace, the atoning work of Christ, justification by faith alone, and other teachings laid the foundation of evangelical Pentecostal beliefs and practices. As a result, Evangelicalism (Fundamentalism and Neo-evangelicalism) and Pentecostalism emerged like a strong river among the born-again Zomi Christians. Half the Christian population label themselves Evangelical/Pentecostals today (19). The following figure shows the percentage of their attachments in 2000:

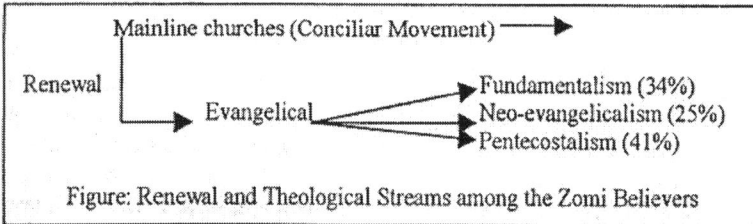

Figure: Renewal and Theological Streams among the Zomi Believers

Kham's pattern of preaching became a favourite model for young preachers. His messages were grounded not in mere knowledge but in sound biblical and theological teaching built upon solid theological terms in which Christ is the subject. He interpreted scripture passages from the root meaning and then adapted it to the local situation. He also drew examples from local contexts and biographical stories to support the message. He was an expert in coining and applying popular words and phrases in his preaching. Most often, he contextualized the husk and kept the kernel of the gospel unchanged. His method is a combination of the "translation model" and "adaptation model" of contextualization (20).

Moreover, the messages have facilitated a Christ-centred worldview among believers. They saw God not only as sovereign and transcendent but also as immanent. They recognized secular things as temporary and spiritual things as eternal. They accepted Christ as Saviour, Lord and King. Therefore, many believers chose to serve Christ rather than the world. Believers also gained positive self-images, liberating them from the low self-images of an inferiority complex.

Furthermore, the renewal has had a great social impact among the Zomis such that transformational changes occurred in the cultural subsystems (21). God was seen as the reservoir of blessings. Therefore thanksgiving celebrations toward God for blessings and success were and still are common phenomena in the communities today. Families give their children Christian names in order to express appreciation and acknowledgment of what He has done in a person's life. Yet another outcome of the renewal is that the need to take the cultural mandate is more recognized among evangelical Pentecostal believers today than ever before. Churches and individual believers continue to establish orphanages, open private clinics, donate relief funds and take on social responsibilities in their communities.

With all these patterns and characters of the renewal, many believers in Myanmar have regarded Kham as a great revivalist, a great leadership equipper, and a great transformer whose legacy will speak to many generations to come. He could say as Paul did, "I have fought a good fight I have finished the race, I have kept the faith" (2 Tim 4:6 NIV).

References

(1) Chin Khua Khai, "Myamnar Mission Boards and Agencies," in *Evangelical Dictionary of World Missions*, ed. A. Scott Moreau (Grand Rapids: Baker, 2000), pp. 667-69.

(2) The Lausanne Committee for World Evangelization describes a nominal Christian as one who would call him/herself a Christian but has no authentic commitment to Christ based on personal faith. See Lausanne Committee for World Evangelization, *The Thailand Report on Christian Witness to Nominal Christians Among Protestants*, Lausanne Occasional Paper No. 23 (Wheaton, IL: Lausanne Committee for World Evangelization, 1980), p. 5.

(3) Sein Tin, Central Statistical Year Book of Myanmar 1995 (Yangon, Myanmar: Central Statistical Organization, 1995), pp. 26-7. These statistics do not include the Asho-Chin (plain Chin), Mizos and Zomis in India and Bangladesh.

(4) Robert G. Johnson has documented in detail the work of the American Baptist missions among the Zomis. Robed G. Johnson, History of American Baptist Chin Mission, 2 vols. (Valley Forge, PA: Robert G. Johnson, 1988).

(5) I briefly discussed in my dissertation mission works among the Zomis and argued why the churches fall into a nominal state. Chin Khua Khai, "Dynamics of Renewal: A Historical Movement among the Zomi (Chin) in Myanmar' (Ph.D. dissertation, Fuller Theological Seminary, 1999), pp. 128-165.

(6) Chin Khua Khai, *The Cross Amidst Pagodas* (Baguio, Philippines: APTS Press).

(7) Myanmar Institute of Theology (formerly known as Burma Institute of Theology), Insein, Yangon, is the largest theological school in Myanmar. It has been largely influenced by the teachings of theological liberalism since the 1960's. "The Church in Myanmar," in *Church in Asia Today: Challenges and Opportunities Today*, ed. Saphir Arthyal (Singapore: Asia Lausanne Committee for World Evangelization, 1996), pp. 349-60.

(8) Hau L. Kham, 'My Testimony" (unpublished manuscript, 1994), p. 7.

(9) Hau L. Kham, Personal Diary, June 25, 1971.

(10) Khai, "Dynamics of Renewal" pp. 178, 205.

(11) Chin K. Khai, Personal Sermon Note, 1973.

(12) The term "renewal" has been defined in several ways. What I mean by "renewal" and "renewal movement" here is an inward experience of a spiritual dynamic that involves a new, deeper experience of God's transcendence and holiness, of grace and forgiveness, coupled with a new dimension in worship and a reaching out in mission (Khai, "Dynamics of Renewal," p. 4).

(13) Kham, Personal Diary, January 27, 1973. Referred to in Khai, "Dynamics of Renewal," pp. 180-181.

(14) KhaM, Personal Diary, May 2, 1973.

(15) Publication Committee, *EBC Taangthu.. History of the Evangelical Baptist Conference* (in Tedim-Chin) (Tedin Myanmar: EBC Church, 1990), p. 29.

(16) Kham, Personal Diary, January 18, 1995.

(17) W H Fitchett, *Wesley and His Century: A Study in Spiritual Forces* (London, Smith, Elder & Co., 1906), p. 16.

(18) Khai, "Dynamics of Renewal," pp. 245-46.

(19) Khai, "Dynamics of Renewal," pp. 92,298.

(20) Dean S. Gilliland, "Contextualization Models," in *The Word Among Us: Contextualizing Theology for Mission Today*, ed. Dean S. Gilliland (Dallas, TX Word, 1989), pp. 313-17.

(21) Khai, "Dynamics of Renewal," pp. 354-62.

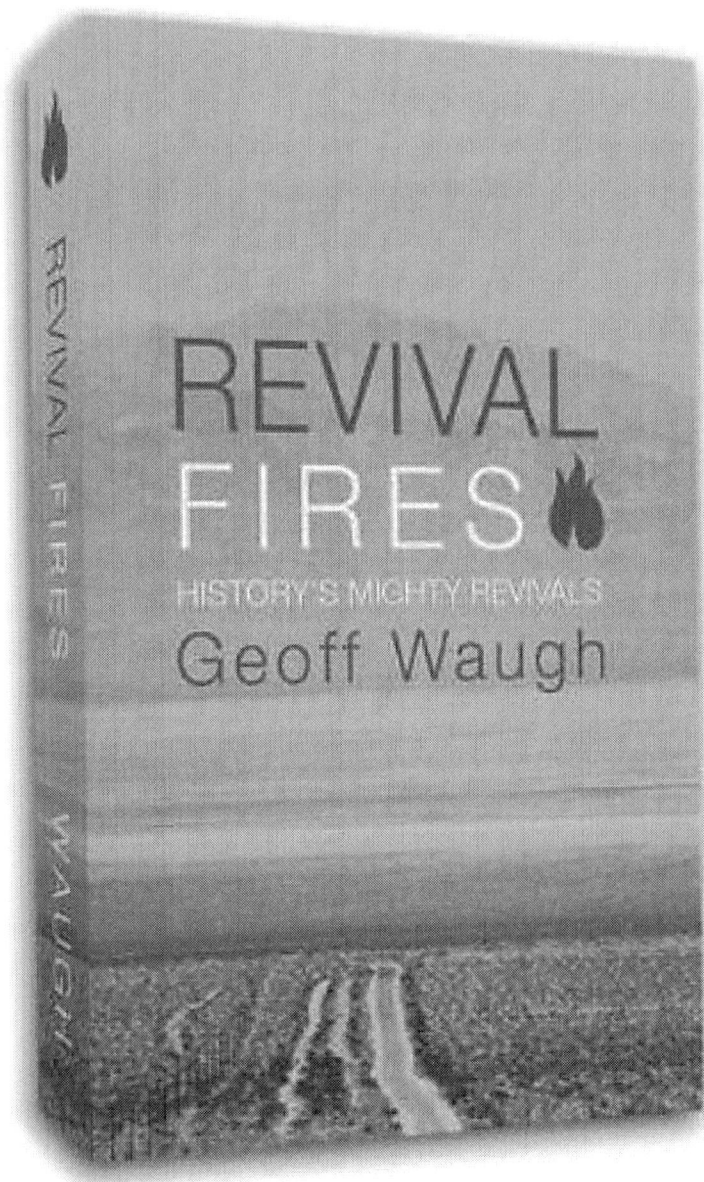

Revival Fires

History's Mighty Revivals

Reviews

Many books examine the place of Signs and Wonders in the church today.

John White's *When the Spirit Comes with Power: Signs and Wonders among God's People,* Hodder & Stoughton, revised 1992, gives many current accounts and helpful comments.

John Wimber's classics written with Kevin Springer, *Power Evangelism* (revised 1993) and *Power Healing* (1986), both Hodder & Stoughton, are now well known and give detailed examples and principles.

Charles Kraft's *Christianity with Power: Experiencing the Supernatural,* Marshall Pickering, 1990, examines cultural concerns such as worldview as it affects our understanding of the Bible, and offers helpful ministry guidelines.

Video/DVD Review: Biblical Holism

Biblical holism: where God, People and Deeds Connect is a Christian Interactive Video Workshop – a Journey Towards Understanding – prepared by John Steward, the Development Services Manager of World Vision in Australia. World Vision has a brochure that introduces this resource. The workshop is for small groups who work through, with the help of a 3 hour video, a study on the Lordship of Christ over every area of life. This foundation leads to studies on the application of the biblical material to Christian life and service.

Of particular interest to the theme of Signs and Wonders, one section of the study shows how these are part of the divine activity in the world that often leads to questions which open the way for the word of witness. Brian Hathaway shares how God led the Te Atatu Church in New Zealand into this awareness. A case study shows the critical importance of Signs and Wonders among Folk religions.

For a free introductory video/DVD about the workshop, write to World Vision Australia Book Shop, GPO Box 399C, Melbourne, Victoria 3001. Ph. (03) 287 2297; Fax (03) 287 2427. (G.W.)

Resources

Renewal Journals

Renewal Journal articles, available now on
www.renewaljournal.com and **Blog**

Contents – 2nd edition 2011

No. 1: Revival
Praying the Price, by Stuart Robinson
Prayer and Revival, by J Edwin Orr
Pentecost in Arnhem Land, by Djiniyini Gondarra
Power from on High: The Moravian Revival, by John Greenfield
Revival Fire, by Geoff Waugh

No. 2: Church Growth
Church Growth through Prayer, by Andrew Evans
Growing a Church in the Spirit's Power, by Jack Frewen-Lord
Evangelism brings Renewal, by Cindy Pattishall-Baker
New Life for an Older Church, by Dean Brookes
Renewal Leadership in the 1990's by John McElroy
Reflections on Renewal, by Ralph Wicks
Local Revivals in Australia, by Stuart Piggin
Asia's Maturing Church, by David Wang
Astounding Church Growth, by Geoff Waugh

No. 3: Community
Lower the Drawbridge, by Charles Ringma
Called to Community, by Dorothy Mathieson and Tim McCowan
Covenant Community, by Shayne Bennett
The Spirit in the Church, by Adrian Commadeur
House Churches, by Ian Freestone
Church in the Home, by Spencer Colliver
The Home Church, by Colin Warren
China's House Churches, by Barbara Nield
 Renewal in a College Community, by Brian Edgar
Spirit Wave, by Darren Trinder

No. 4: Healing
Missionary Translator and Doctor, by David Lithgow
My Learning Curve on Healing, by Jim Holbeck
Spiritual Healing, by John Blacker
Deliverance and Freedom, by Colin Warren
Christian Wholeness Counselling, by John Warlow
A Healing Community, by Spencer Colliver
Divine Healing and Church Growth, by Donald McGavran
Sounds of Revival, by Sue Armstrong
Revival Fire at Wuddina, by Trevor Faggotter

No. 5: Signs and Wonders
Words, Signs and Deeds, by Brian Hathaway
Uproar in the Church, by Derek Prince
Season of New Beginnings, by John Wimber
Preparing for Revival Fire, by Jerry Steingard
How to Minister Like Jesus, by Bart Doornweerd
The Legacy of Hau Lian Kham of Myanmar/Burma

No. 6: Worship
Worship: Intimacy with God, by John & Carol Wimber
Beyond Self-Centred Worship, by Geoff Bullock
Worship: to Soothe or Disturb? by Dorothy Mathieson
Worship: Touching Body and Soul, by Robert Tann
Healing through Worship, by Robert Colman
Charismatic Worship and Ministry, by Stephen Bryar
Renewal in the Church, by Stan Everitt
Worship God in Dance, by Lucinda Coleman
Revival Worship, by Geoff Waugh

No. 7: Blessing
What on earth is God doing? by Owen Salter
Times of Refreshing, by Greg Beech
Renewal Blessing, by Ron French
Catch the Fire, by Dennis Plant
Reflections, by Alan Small
A Fresh Wave, by Andrew Evans
Waves of Glory, by David Cartledge
Balance, by Charles Taylor
Discernment, by John Court
Renewal Ministry, by Geoff Waugh

No. 8: Awakening

Speaking God's Word, by David Yonggi Cho
The Power to Heal the Past, by C. Peter Wagner
Worldwide Awakening, by Richard Riss
The 'No Name' Revival, by Brian Medway

No. 9: Mission

The River of God, by David Hogan
The New Song, by C. Peter Wagner
God's Visitation, by Dick Eastman
Revival in China, by Dennis Balcombe
Mission in India, by Paul Pilai
Pensacola Revival, by Michael Brown, and Becky Powers

No. 10: Evangelism

Power Evangelism, by John Wimber
Supernatural Ministry, by John White interviewed by Julia Loren
Power Evangelism in Short Term Missions, by Randy Clark
God's Awesome Presence, by Richard Heard
Pensacola Evangelist Steve Hill, by Sharon Wissemann
Reaching the Core of the Core, by Luis Bush
Evangelism on the Internet, by Rowland Croucher
Gospel Essentials, by Charles Taylor
Pentecostal/Charismatic Pioneers, by Daryl Brenton
Characteristics of Revivals, by Richard Riss

No. 11: Discipleship

Transforming Revivals, by Geoff Waugh
Standing in the Rain, by Brian Medway
Amazed by Miracles, by Rodney Howard-Brown
A Touch of Glory, by Lindell Cooley
The 'Diana Prophecy', by Robert McQuillan
Mentoring, by Peter Earle
Can the Leopard Change his Spots? by Charles Taylor
The Gathering of the Nations, by Paula Sandford

No. 12: Harvest
The Spirit told us what to do, by Cari Lawrence
Argentine Revival, by Guido Kuwas
Baltimore Revival, by Elizabeth Moll Stalcup
Mobile Revival, by Joel Kilpatrick

No. 13: Ministry
School of Ministries, by Pastor Peter Earle
Pentecostalism's Global Language, by Walter Hollenweger
Revival in Nepal, by Raju Sundras
Revival in Mexico City, by Kevin Pate
Interview with Steven Hill, by Steve Beard
Beyond Prophesying, by Mike Bickle
The Rise and Rise of the Apostles, by Phil Marshall
Evangelical Heroes Speak, by Richard Riss
Spirit Impacts in Revivals, by Geoff Waugh
Primacy of Love, by Heidi Baker

No. 14: Anointing
A Greater Anointing, by Benny Hinn
Myths about Jonathan Edwards, by Barry Chant
Revivals into 2000, by Geoff Waugh

No. 15: Wineskins
The New Apostolic Reformation, by C. Peter Wagner
The New Believers, by Dianna Bagnall (Bulletin/Newsweek journalist)
Vision and Strategy for Church Growth, by Lawrence Khong
New Wineskins for Pentecostal Studies, by Sam Hey
New Wineskins to Develop Ministry, by Geoff Waugh
The God Chasers, by Tommy Tenny

No. 16: Vision
Vision for Church Growth by Daryl & Cecily Brenton
Almolonga, the Miracle City, by Mell Winger
Cali Transformation, by George Otis Jr.
Revival in Bogotá, by Guido Kuwas
Prison Revival in Argentina, by Ed Silvoso
Missions at the Margins, by Bob Eklad
Vision for Church Growth, by Daryl & Cecily Brenton
Vision for Ministry, by Geoff Waugh

No. 17: Unity
Snapshots of Glory, by George Otis Jr.
Lessons from Revivals, by Richard Riss
Spiritual Warfare, by Cecilia Estillore

No. 18: Servant Leadership
The Kingdom Within, by Irene Brown
Church Models: Integration or Assimilation? by Jeannie Mok
Women in Ministry, by Sue Fairley
Women and Religions, by Susan Hyatt
Disciple-Makers, by Mark Setch
Ministry Confronts Secularisation, by Sam Hey

No. 19: Church
The Voice of the Church in the 21st Century, by Ray Overend
Redeeming the Arts: visionaries of the future, by Sandra Godde
Counselling Christianly, by Ann Crawford
Redeeming a Positive Biblical View of Sexuality, by John Meteyard
and Irene Alexander
The Mystics and Contemporary Psychology, by Irene Alexander
Problems Associated with the Institutionalisation of Ministry, by
Warren Holyoak

No. 20: Life
Life, death and choice, by Ann Crawford
The God who dies: Exploring themes of life and death, by Irene
Alexander
Primordial events in theology and science support a life/death ethic,
by Martin Rice
Community Transformation, by Geoff Waugh

Bound Volumes
Nos. 1-5: Revival, Church Growth, Community, Signs & Wonders
Nos. 6-10: Worship, Blessing, Awakening, Mission, Evangelism
Nos. 11-15: Discipleship, Harvest, Ministry, Anointing, Wineskins
Nos. 16-20: Vision, Unity, Servant Leadership, Church, Life

Books by Geoff Waugh – summary
Details on 'Geoff Waugh' at www.amazon.com
Free shipping at 'Geoff Waugh' on www.bookdepository.com
Discounted on www.renewljournal.com

Looking to Jesus: Journey into Renewal and Revival (2009)
Light on the Mountains: Pioneer Mission in PNG (2009)
Flashpoints of Revival (2nd ed., 2009)
Revivals Awaken Generations (Korean, 2006)
Revival Fires: History's Mighty Revivals (2011)
South Pacific Revivals (2nd ed., 2010)
Anointed for Revival: Histories of Revival Pioneers (2011)
Great Revival Stories (2012), compiled from 2 books:
  Best Revival Stories, and *Transforming Revivals* (2011)
Renewal and Revival (2012), compiled from 2 books:
  Renewal and *Revival* (2011)
Body Ministry: The Body of Christ Alive in His Spirit (2012)
  Compiled from *The Body of Christ, Parts 1& 2*(2010)
Church on Fire (1991, 2009).
Living in the Spirit (2nd ed., 2009)
Your Spiritual Gifts (2011)
Fruit and Gifts of the Spirit (1992, 2009)
The Leader's Goldmine (1990, 2009)
Love One Another (2012)
Kingdom Life in Matthew (1992, 2009)
Kingdom Life in Mark (1990, 2009)
Kingdom Life in Luke (1991, 2009)
Kingdom Life in John (2011)
A Preface to The Acts of the Apostles (2011)
Keeping Faith Alive Today (1977, 2010)
Exploring Israel (2011)
Inspiration (2011)
Discovering Aslan: High King above all Kings in Narnia (2012)

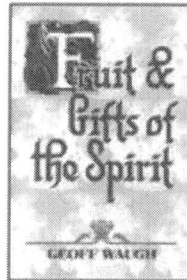

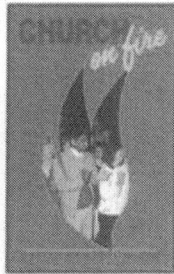

Books and Renewal Journals at Blog on www.renewaljournal.com
Free postage at 'Geoff Waugh' on www.bookdepository.com
Book details at 'Geoff Waugh' on www.amazon.com

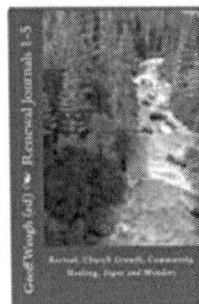  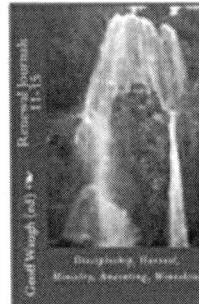 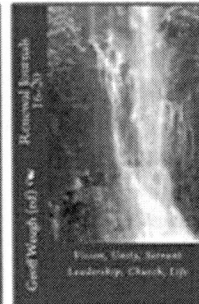

19187070R00292

Printed in Great Britain
by Amazon